Product
Plus

Product
Plus

How Product + Service = Competitive Advantage

Christopher Lovelock

McGraw-Hill, Inc.

New York   San Francisco   Washington, D.C.   Auckland   Bogotá
Caracas   Lisbon   London   Madrid   Mexico City   Milan
Montreal   New Delhi   San Juan   Singapore
Sydney   Tokyo   Toronto

Library of Congress Cataloging-in-Publication Data

Lovelock, Christopher H.
     Product plus : how product + service = competitive advantage /
Christopher Lovelock.
          p.   cm.
     Includes index.
     ISBN 0-07-038798-2
     1. Customer service. 2. Competition. I. Title.
HF5415.5.L68   1994
658.8'12—dc20   93-28217
                                                      CIP

1 2 3 4 5 6 7 8 9 0   DOC/DOC   9 9 8 7 6 5 4 3

ISBN 0-07-038798-2

*The sponsoring editor for this book was Betsy N. Brown, the editing
supervisor was Jane Palmieri, the designer was Susan Maksuta, and the
production supervisor was Suzanne Babeuf. It was set in Century
Expanded by McGraw-Hill's Professional Book Group composition unit.*

Printed and bound by R. R. Donnelley & Sons Company.

The cartoon illustrations in this book were created by C. H. Lovelock and
prepared by "Berger" (Philippe Gallaz) and are used with permission.

This book is printed on recycled, acid-free paper containing
a minimum of 50% recycled, de-inked fiber.

To the memory of my father

COLIN LOVELOCK

a pilot and navigator of exceptional skill
whose four-part career in
the Merchant Navy, Royal Air Force,
civil aviation, and public education
first inspired my interest in services

1. The Little Airline That Could 1

Customer dissatisfaction with two existing carriers gave the creators of Southwest Airlines a chance to launch an airline that loves its passengers and has grown to become America's seventh largest.

If a business can't perform well on its core product, its chances of survival are bleak. But innovations on the core are often quickly copied. For customers, the product plus of differentiation and added value comes from a whole bundle of supplementary services that enhance the appeal of the core product.

2. What Type of Service Are You Offering? 9

Some managers tend to overlook innovations and strategies that arise outside their own industry. Yet seemingly different services may share common operational and marketing characteristics, depending on whether they are processing people, physical objects, or information.

4. User-Friendly versus User-Hostile 32

An operations-driven business risks presenting a hostile face to customers. Yet efficiency, cost control, and employee well-being are important. Can there be a happy meeting of minds between operations and marketing?

5. Product Plus Management: In Pursuit of Compatible Goals   50

Organizations succeed in the long term by offering customers better value than do competitors; by employing people and suppliers who see value in their relationship with the organization; and by creating value for their owners. Reducing costs may be as important as adding benefits.

6. The Search for Synergy in Service Management   67

Successful service businesses create operations and delivery systems that simultaneously appeal to their target customers, are well matched to the capabilities of a willing work force,

and allow the firm to operate efficiently. We contrast approaches at Firstdirect, the all-telephone bank, which has reengineered traditional banking procedures, and Southwest Airlines, which takes a contrarian approach to airline operations.

7. Service as an Art Form   86

The theater provides a good analogy for service delivery, with actors, stage sets, scripts, costumes, and even music. Backstage activities (which the customer doesn't see) exist only to create and support good performances front stage, where service is delivered.

8. Who Defines Quality: You or the Customer?   97

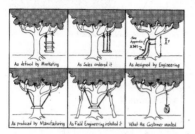

As defined by Marketing | As Sales ordered it | As designed by Engineering
As produced by Manufacturing | As Field Engineering installed it | What the Customer wanted

Historically, quality was defined by operations managers. Only recently has quality come to be defined with reference to customer needs and expectations. Many quality improvement programs have disappointed; we consider some of the reasons why.

9. Absolutely, Positively: Systemic Quality at Federal Express   119

Few service firms have made such concerted efforts to improve quality on a companywide basis as Federal Express. We look at how FedEx's highly systemic operation works, see how information parallels physical movements, and review lessons from its award-winning quality program.

10. Process and Progress: Understanding the Customer Experience   142

To obtain the benefits they want from a particular service, customers move through a series of steps. By flowcharting the process from start to finish, managers can understand how a particular type of customer experiences the service drama. We see how Boston's Beth Israel Hospital has used this approach to redesign the hospital's emergency unit and improve the service that staff provide to patients.

11. From Turn-Offs to Turn-Ons   160

At each step in the unfolding of the service drama, any firm has numerous opportunities to turn off its customers. But those same customers also have an ideal scenario in mind of what they would like the process and output to be. Restaurants provide a fertile example. We follow two diners to see what can go wrong—and how to do it right.

12. Product Plus Service: Like Petals on a Flower 177

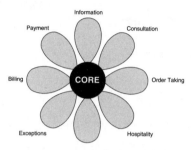

Core products vary widely from one type of business to another, but supplementary services are often common to a great many different industries. These supplementary services can be clustered into eight groups.

13. Cultivating the Flower of Service 191

In today's economy, manufacturing firms are hybrids. Not only must they excel at the physical aspects of production, they also have to be skilled service providers. Some firms subcontract key service tasks, but outsourcing is not for everyone, especially if, like White Flower Farm, you want to control the complete package presented to customers.

14. Problem Solving and Service Recovery 206

Losing customers hurts profits. The art of service recovery focuses on fixing problems in ways that retain customer loyalty. Managers also need to make sure that problems don't recur. This means getting to the root cause, not just treating the symptoms.

15. Sometimes the Customer Is Wrong 223

Nobody really believes that the customer is always right—and they shouldn't. One type of wrong customer simply doesn't fit the firm's capabilities; another meets the target market profile but behaves badly toward the business, its personnel and facilities, and even other customers.

16. Getting the Most Out of Your Productive Capacity   239

Most service operations have upper limits to their productive capacity. Under conditions of fluctuating demand, management needs to balance supply and demand in ways that ensure that the firm's human and physical assets are being utilized in the most profitable way.

17. Technology: Servant or Master?   262

Product plus performance today depends on intelligent use of technology—especially information technology. New developments often generate the most interest, but service firms should focus their attention on how to integrate technology's capabilities with customer needs and corporate goals.

18. 24-365-Global: Service Anywhere, Anytime   283

As companies expand their marketing horizons from local to regional to continental to global, customers increasingly expect to be able to obtain information, place orders, and resolve problems 24 hours a day, 365 days a year, wherever they may be. We see how Hewlett-Packard obliges.

19. Parlez-Vous Français?
日本語を話しますか。 295

Doing business only in English may become a product minus as societies become more multicultural, as people travel more, and as markets become more international. Fortunately, many solutions are available to help firms solve the language problem.

20. Sustaining the Human Side of the Enterprise 315

Despite advances in technology and self-service, many businesses still depend heavily on employees to serve customers directly or to work backstage in support of front-stage activities. Current thinking from both academic research and innovative companies offers insights.

21. The Strategic Route to Product Plus Management 340

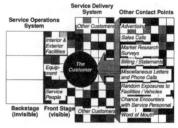

Becoming and remaining a product plus organization can't be accomplished through a series of tactical moves. There has to be an overarching strategy that reflects holistic thinking and involves integration of the marketing, operations, and human resource functions.

Preface

Perhaps the most memorable character that Agatha Christie created is her Belgian detective, Hercule Poirot. The cerebral Poirot loves to tap his forehead and draw attention to the importance of using "these little gray cells." Managers need to use theirs, too—less to solve murder mysteries than to prevent their businesses from being murdered by the competition.

Product Plus is addressed not to mystery fans, but to managers in manufacturing companies, service firms, and not-for-profit organizations. It's designed to stimulate your little gray cells as you ponder the role that service plays in helping your business gain competitive advantage. In the few years that remain between now and the twenty-first century, businesses that fail to meet customer performance standards on their core products—whether these be cars, computers, bank accounts, hotel rooms, or whatever—will simply flounder or be merged out of existence.

The terms of competition are shifting in nearly all industries, as value-seeking customers come to place greater emphasis on supplementary service elements. These "product pluses" are the activities that help customers make the right choice of core product, simplify purchase, add value to usage, and generally make the supplier a good organization with which to do business. Much of the innovation taking place in such activities is driven by new developments in information technology. But talented employees also add a competitive advantage to service delivery—and it's one that's harder to match.

Even as manufacturers and service businesses strive to compete on service, they still have to watch the bottom line as well as making sure that they can attract and retain the best employees for their needs. So, to survive and prosper through the year 2000 and beyond, firms will have to create a synergy among customer satisfaction, operational productivity, and employee performance. This is the broader essence of what I call product plus management.

I don't know who coined the term product plus, which I've borrowed for the title of this book. It probably came from advertising, since the term is sometimes used in a marketing context to describe some product feature—in either a manufactured good or a service—that offers customers something extra. Certainly, a customer perspective drives the book, offering a holistic view of the processes by which services are created and delivered, as well as detailing the full experience of customers in purchasing and using specific goods and services. However, my own definition of product plus goes further, extending to service-driven ways of adding value for all stakeholders: not just for customers, but also for employees, suppliers, owners, and even the broader community.

Managers of product plus organizations are interested in building employee loyalty at the same time that they build customer loyalty, because they see a clear connection between the two. And since they recognize that value for the owners of a business comes at least as much from enhancement of revenues as from curtailment of costs, they are especially interested in product and process improvements that simultaneously attract customers and improve productivity. Innovation in services often requires rethinking the ways in which a firm and its customers interact—and in which employees interact with each other—and then reengineering traditional processes.

The underlying imperative thus becomes one of creating synergy among the marketing, operations, and human resource functions, rather than elevating one function (usually operations in a service context) to lord it over the other two. If you, as a manager, can find ways to do business that not only convey marketing advantages but also lead to more efficient operations and more job satisfaction for employees, your firm will be better poised in the long run to improve profits and serve the community at large.

I'm a strong believer in the power of simple concepts to structure ways of looking at real-world problems. In writing this book, I've tried to strike a balance between conceptual frameworks and descriptions of actual practice. The models, frameworks, and metaphors that I present are ones that participants in executive programs tell me they have found especially helpful in coming to grips with service issues. I hope they will also stimulate your "little gray cells."

Important insights come from studying how different companies have approached specific challenges. Some of the frameworks that I use are designed to help you look for useful parallels and analogies across companies from seemingly different industries. When faced with a choice between offering numerous quick illustrations and presenting a smaller number of examples in greater depth, I've more often chosen the latter route. The result is that fewer firms and industries are depicted; but, as I take you behind the scenes at specific organizations, I hope that you'll gain a richer understanding as a result.

Several of the organizations thus described are ones that I've been following for many years, enabling me to watch them evolve, innovate, sometimes make mistakes (and learn from them), grow, and improve. I'm confident that you can learn from them, too.

Christopher Lovelock

Acknowledgments

Product Plus has its roots in both academic research and in work for professional clients across a broad array of industries. In the academic arena, I'm particularly indebted to former colleagues at the Harvard Business School—including Theodore Levitt, James Heskett, Earl Sasser, Leonard Schlesinger, and the late Daryl Wyckoff—all of whose work has influenced my own. Subsequent visiting appointments on the faculties of MIT's Sloan School of Management, the International Institute for Management Development (IMD) in Lausanne, Switzerland, and the Theseus Institute in Sophia Antipolis, France, have since stretched me in new directions.

At IMD, as a visiting professor from 1990 to 1992, I was able to undertake field research in Europe and Singapore as well as to interact with colleagues and participants in IMD programs and seminars; I was particularly glad to have the opportunity to work with Sandra Vandermerwe. In addition, I'm grateful for the support provided by the institute and especially for the encouragement provided by IMD's director of research, Derek Abell.

Numerous other people have contributed to my thinking, providing valued insights, suggestions, and criticism. They include not only executives who were kind enough to let me study their organizations at first hand, and to talk about their own experiences and insights, but also authors, conference presenters, and participants in courses and seminars. Many of these individuals are mentioned by name in the text or cited in the references. Warm thanks are due especially to Michael Epelman, David Garvin, David Maister, Dick Munn, Chuck Weinberg, and my wife, Molly, for sharing their expertise with me and letting me use them as sounding boards on specific topics. I'm also grateful to Jill Kneerim and Ike Williams for their professional advice and support.

This book has quite a lot to say about the impact of technology on services. Similarly, technology has had quite an impact on this book—it's the first manuscript that I have word-processed on a computer for electronic production. The handsome graphics, were developed electronically by Michele Mayer and Brigitte Beuchat at IMD and by my son, Timothy, who prepared several of the tables as well. I'm very appreciative of their fine efforts. The cartoons that enliven the beginning of each chapter were drawn for me by Philippe Gallaz, employing the more traditional medium of pen and ink under his artistic pseudonym, Berger. *Merci infiniment!*

A final word of thanks goes to my McGraw-Hill editor, Betsy Brown, and the McGraw-Hill editorial, design, and production staff, especially Jane Palmieri, Sue Maksuta, Suzanne Babeuf, Terry Leaden, Jim Halston, Dave Fogarty, and Michele Byrd.

Southwest Airlines: A 500-pound cockroach too big to stamp out.

1 The Little Airline That Could

Customer dissatisfaction with two existing carriers gave the creators of Southwest Airlines a chance to launch an airline that loves its passengers and has grown to become America's seventh largest and its most profitable. Winning and keeping customers is the key to growth and profits, but it takes dedicated employees and a well-designed operation to create valued service that customers will keep on buying. Product plus organizations create value for customers, employees, suppliers, shareholders, and the communities they serve.

The Creation of Southwest Airlines

Almost 20 years ago, as a young assistant professor at the Harvard Business School, I went to Texas to develop a case study on a new airline. With just three Boeing 737s and a triangular route structure serving Dallas, Houston, and San Antonio, Southwest Airlines had quickly acquired a reputation as a feisty little underdog in the highly competitive Texas air market. And it was making life very difficult for its two, much larger, competitors.

In the course of my research, I learned how Southwest had come to be founded a few years earlier by Rollin King, an entrepreneur, working with attorney Herbert Kelleher, and a group of Texas businesspeople who saw an opportunity to exploit the strong dissatisfaction with existing air services within the State of Texas.

Unhappy Texans Get Their Own Back

Around 1970, if you wanted to fly a commercial airline between Dallas, Houston, and San Antonio—which are between 190 and 250 miles apart— you had two choices.

One was to fly Braniff International Airways, which was based in Dallas and was at that time one of the larger U.S. airlines. Its route structure extended north and east to Chicago and New York, and south down into Latin America. But Braniff had such a poor reputation for punctuality that it was popularly called "Braniff Intermittent" by Texans, who also referred to it as "the world's largest unscheduled airline." Passengers wishing to travel between Dallas and Houston often found themselves boarding a flight arriving late from New York and full of yawning passengers and tired flight attendants.

Competing against Braniff in rather desultory fashion was a smaller, regional carrier called Trans Texas Airways, usually referred to as TTA for short. TTA was perceived by air travelers as being a rather flaky operation, and it was claimed by some that its aircraft had been seen wobbling in to land with bits of greenery dangling from the landing gear. Wags used to say unkindly that the initials TTA stood for "tree-top airlines" or for "take the train, always!"

The story was told of an air traffic controller at Dallas who got a call over the radio from an aircraft in the vicinity of the airport.

"Hi, Dallas Tower!" said the pilot, "Can you give me a check on the time, please?"

"Would you please identify yourself, sir?" responded the air traffic controller, correctly following established procedure.

"Sure," replied the pilot. "The name's Mike."

The controller sighed. He needed to know the airline and flight number. "Would you please identify yourself, correctly, Mike!"

"For crying out loud, Dallas Tower!" Mike retorted (he was obviously in a snappy mood). "What difference does it make who I am? I'm not asking permission to land. All I need is a check on the time!"

The controller sighed again. It was a deep, sad sigh. "Mike, my friend," he said. "It makes all the difference in the world who you are. If you're Air Force, it's 1800 hours. If you're United Airlines, it's 6 p.m. If you're Trans Texas, the big hand is on 12 and the little hand is on 6. And if you're Braniff, Mike, if you're Braniff, it's Thursday."

This wicked story was repeated the length and breadth of Texas. It was told on television. It was told on the radio. People told it to each other in bars. They repeated it gleefully to their colleagues in the office and to their families at home. Whether it was true or—more likely—apocryphal didn't matter: The story captured how they felt about their local suppliers of airline service.

Faced with such a story making the rounds, how would you like to have been the vice president for marketing or public relations at either Braniff or Trans Texas? Braniff soldiered gamely on, promoting the exotic uniforms designed for its stewardesses by a famous French couturier. TTA faced up to the fact that it had a bad reputation and chose a solution adopted by many people or organizations that have become notorious: It simply changed its name and relaunched the airline as Texas International.

Let's Start an Airline!

It was in this context that Rollin King was able to attract some "walking around" money from a group of wealthy Texans to prepare a feasibility study on starting a new airline. The study found that there was, indeed, a large, latent market of potential air travelers in Texas who either preferred to drive or who avoided traveling altogether because the existing services were seen as being so unreliable and so unpleasant. "Let's do it!" King and his associates agreed at lunch one day, as one of them sketched out a route structure on a paper table napkin. Soon the ideas were flowing for the "product pluses" that would enhance their service and differentiate it from the competition.

As King, the airline's first CEO, later recalled, "The more we talked to people, the more we looked at figures of how big the market was, and the more we realized the degree of customer dissatisfaction with the services of existing carriers, the more apparent the opportunities became for us."

And so Southwest Airlines was born. But problems began long before its first flight. Braniff and Texas International (TI) did not take kindly to the prospect of new competition. When Southwest received a certificate from the Texas Aeronautics Commission permitting it to offer air service within Texas, the other two tried to block the start-up with a lawsuit claiming that the market was too small to support a third airline. Litigation to block or restrain new competition is often the first response of entrenched suppliers—a form of preemptive strike that might be described as the neutron bomb of competitive strategy.

> *Litigation to block or restrain new competition is often the first response of entrenched suppliers—the neutron bomb of competitive strategy.*

For a while, the ploy succeeded. Southwest was not allowed to begin operations until the suit had ground its way through the courts, eventually reaching the U.S. Supreme Court, which refused to overturn a unanimous ruling in Southwest's favor by the Texas Supreme Court. Finally, in June 1971, the new airline launched its first flights in a blaze of clever publicity, featuring numerous service innovations, a little fleet of spanking new aircraft, frequent and punctual service, easy check-in, highly motivated staff, and lower fares. Its cheeky slogan? "The somebody else up there who loves you."

A Competitive Dogfight and Its Aftermath

When their legal blocking tactics failed, Braniff and TI realized that they would have to compete on Southwest's terms. Service quickly improved at the two competitors. Braniff and TI greatly expanded their schedules, and tried to match Southwest's punctuality, high passenger service standards, and lower fares as they strove to drive the impertinent new upstart into the ground. They even resorted to an illegal conspiracy to keep passengers from their little competitor and were indicted for it. But Southwest persevered, and traffic grew and grew—there was a large market there after all. And there was a large group of loyal customers who flew Southwest again and again—in some cases, several times a week. The airline's new slogan became "Remember what it was like before Southwest Airlines?" as it fought to counter a half-price fare war initiated by Braniff in 1973 in a last-ditch effort to bankrupt the newcomer.

By the time I went to Dallas in 1974, however, it was clear that Southwest had emerged the winner in what the media had christened "The Great Texas Air War." The profits started to flow at Southwest, and the company has never looked back.

From that small beginning, Southwest has grown to become the seventh largest American airline, with over 150 aircraft in mid-1993 and services extending across the United States from Michigan, Maryland, and Alabama to Nevada and California. Sticking closely to its operating philosophy and market niche, Southwest has expanded relentlessly into one new market after another, winning and keeping new customers; in most instances it has gained a significant share of all short-haul passengers on the routes that it serves.

In the process, Southwest has greatly expanded the market for air travel, bringing frequent, inexpensive airline service to communities and people for whom air travel was previously inaccessible. It has also given meaningful and satisfying employment to thousands of people; it has created new business for the many suppliers who provide it with needed goods and services, from aircraft to peanuts, office stationery to jet fuel; and it has brought profits to its owners, both large and small shareholders. Attempts by competitors to crush the upstart have failed conspicuously. Indeed, one industry observer recently described Southwest as "a 500-pound cockroach too big to stamp out!" He meant it as a compliment.

One industry observer recently described Southwest as "a 500-pound cockroach too big to stamp out." He meant it as a compliment.

But what of the two competitors? Braniff shrugged off the beating it took from Southwest in Texas, eventually choosing to cut back its money-losing local services and to focus on interstate and overseas expansion after the American airline industry was deregulated in the late 1970s. Unfortunately, Braniff overdid its expansion and went bankrupt. The name was resurrected by new investors, and the company was relaunched as a regional domestic airline. But bankruptcy eventually overtook that venture, too. In 1991, another set of investors established a third and very small Braniff operation, based in New York State. That, too, has gone under. The name has lost its magic.

Texas International survived to undergo another name change when it was merged into Continental Airlines, an airline that is still operating as I write, but has been in and out of bankruptcy twice.

Drawing Morals from the Story

What can we learn from the start-up of Southwest Airlines? There seem to be two morals.

The first moral concerns what is sometimes termed word-of-mouth advertising. This is not the advertising the company does to promote its services, but what customers and other people say about the organization and its service characteristics. The joke about TTA and Braniff that swept Texas was an extreme example of negative word-of-mouth advertising.

Word-of-mouth recommendations to use or not use a service can be very influential, since customers and prospects are often highly skeptical of paid advertising messages. People are more likely to believe what friends and colleagues tell them. Word of mouth can be of great value to a company when it's positive. Sad to say, however, when it's based on reports of personal experience, the content is more likely than not to be negative. Research has shown that people who have had a really good experience with a product or service will, on average, tell four others about that experience. But those who have had a really bad experience will tell their story to between 10 and 11 other people. In short, word-of-mouth comments about suppliers are two-and-a-half times more likely to be reporting bad news than good news.

> *Word-of-mouth comments about suppliers are two-and-a-half times more likely to be reporting bad news than good news.*

I have a theory (which I must confess I have never tested scientifically) that folks enjoy getting their revenge on a supplier who has let them down by telling as many other people as possible about their misfortune.

Monitoring word of mouth is important, since managers need to know what is being said about their company and its services in the marketplace. Do you know what customers (or perhaps ex-customers) are saying about your organization? Market research can ferret out this information through surveys. A related approach involves content analysis of magazines, newspapers, and broadcast media to identify positive or negative coverage in the mass media that may be influential in shaping opinions and stimulating word-of-mouth comments at an individual level. This task is usually delegated to specialist research firms.

A second—and even more important—moral to the story is that if a firm falls down on the job (or is even perceived as slipping), it may open the door to new competitors. Braniff and TI effectively tilled the soil for new competition in Texas by failing so dismally to satisfy their existing customers. People saw TTA/TI and Braniff as offering poor service, so they avoided them if possible—even to the extent of not traveling by air at all.

Today, Southwest Airlines is a more than billion-dollar business with an enviable record of profitability in an industry where most players have been losing money heavily in recent years. But it might never have been founded if two existing airlines had not disappointed their customers so badly.

> *If a firm falls down on the job, it may open the door to new competitors.*

Keeping the Flame Alight

There is, of course, more to Southwest's long-term success than just a well-conceived start-up strategy. Many promising start-ups burn brightly, but only briefly, and then flicker and die. In fact, premature disappearance from the scene has been the norm rather than the exception for new airline start-ups during the past 20 years, from People Express to Air Europe. Three characteristics that underlie Southwest's continuing success will serve as themes that we shall revisit at various points in this book. You should be thinking about how they relate to your own business.

Repeat Customers. On any given day, about 80 percent of Southwest's passengers have ridden the airline previously. The most frequent users of Southwest's service are the roughly 20 percent of all passengers who belong to The Company Club (the airline's frequent flyer program). The key to success in most services—including, I suspect, your own—is repeat business. This means that marketing's task must be defined not just as winning new customers but, even more important, as keeping existing customers loyal, so that they will continue to patronize your firm for years to come. That, in turn, requires meeting their needs consistently with goods and services that offer good value. Southwest clearly does this very well.

A Simple, Coherent Operational Philosophy. Perhaps the most striking aspect of this company is the consistency with which it has maintained a contrary approach to providing passenger airline service. Quite simply, Southwest designs its operations in a different way from its competitors, who now include all the remaining major American airlines. At the heart of

Southwest's approach to operations is a search for simplicity that minimizes wasted time, keeps down expenses, and creates the inexpensive, reliable service that its passengers desire.

Employee Loyalty and Commitment.   The flip side of loyal customers who keep coming back for more is loyal, dedicated employees who remain with the company, not because they lack other choices but because they like their jobs and enjoy the working environment. There is growing evidence that high employee turnover pushes up costs and hurts service quality. When talented employees remain with the firm—and remain motivated—they develop a sense of ownership and pride that helps the company to improve quality and productivity, keep down costs, and act as role models for more recent hires. But employee loyalty is not a matter of luck, any more than is customer loyalty. Southwest's appreciation of its employees and concern for their well-being has gained it wide recognition as a wonderful place to work. It's not hard to recruit the best people for jobs at a company that has a reputation like that!

In Pursuit of Product Plus Management

We'll be looking at Southwest Airlines again later in the book to see what can be learned from the remarkable synergy between its operational, human resource, and marketing strategies—a synergy that lies at the heart of its ability to create a "product plus" not only for its customers, but also for its employees and shareholders.

As you will see from subsequent chapters, I define the term product plus to mean more than just something extra for customers. In my vocabulary, a product plus organization is one that in serving its customers well also offers better value to employees, suppliers, and the owners of the business—and creates a positive impact on the broader community. Product plus management looks to competitive advantage, but it's concerned with sustainable strategies, not short-term gain.

I started with the Southwest Airlines story because it deals with an industry to which you (and any other reader) can easily relate. Turning your own company into a product plus organization often starts with the realization that you can learn from another service provider that appears to be in a totally different line of business from your own. This theme will be established in the following chapter, which presents a simple framework that will help you look for points of similarity across "different" service businesses.

2 What Type of Service Are You Offering?

Many businesses are afflicted with a form of tunnel vision that leads managers to overlook service-based innovations and strategies that arise in firms outside their own industry. Four broad categories of services exist, each of which faces distinctive operational challenges and different types of customer involvement. Some services require direct physical contact with customers (e.g., health care or passenger transport); others center on contact with people's minds (education or broadcasting). Some involve processing of physical objects (repair or freight transport); others process information (accounting or insurance). Studying other services that face common problems is a hallmark of innovative firms.

Service as a Process

It's surprising how many managers in service businesses consider their industries to be unique—or at least distinctively different. Certainly, there are distinctions to be drawn, but I would argue that there's more insight to be gained from looking for similarities between "different" service industries than from making the most of various shades of gray. After all, the more you can identify meaningful parallels to your own situation, the better are your chances of beating the competition by taking a good idea from another industry and applying it to your own. In the search for new solutions, creativity is often stifled by digging deeper and deeper in the same location.

But it would also be a mistake to assume, as some commentators seem to, that there is an amorphous thing called "the service sector" (or "the service industries"), within which all organizations face more or less the same managerial problems.

The traditional way of grouping services has been by industry. "We're in the transportation business," managers will say. Or in lodging, or banking, or telecommunications, or repair and maintenance. Such groupings are helpful in terms of understanding customer needs and competition, but we must also try to find commonalities in operational processes, since managing the operation is at the heart of creating the benefits that customers desire. Let's try a different tack. What does your service operation actually *do?* What sorts of processes are involved in creating the service that you offer to customers? And speaking of customers, where do *they* fit into your operation?

What does your service operation actually do? What processes are involved in creating the service? And where do customers fit into your operation?

Service is sometimes described as a process rather than a product. A process implies taking an input and transforming it into output. But if that's the case, then *what* is it that you're processing, and *how* are you doing it? Two broad categories of things are processed by services: people and objects. In many cases, ranging from passenger transportation to education, customers themselves are the principal input to the service process; in other instances, the key input is an object, such as a computer in need of repair, or a piece of financial data.

Table 2-1. Understanding the Nature of the Service Act

What is the nature of the service act?	Who or what is the direct recipient of the service?	
	People	Possessions
Tangible actions	*Services directed at people's bodies:* Passenger transportation Health care Lodging Beauty salons Physical therapy Fitness centers Restaurants/bars Haircutting Funeral services	*Services directed at physical possessions:* Freight transportation Repair and maintenance Warehousing/storage Janitorial services Retail distribution Laundry and dry cleaning Refueling Landscaping/lawn care Disposal/recycling
Intangible actions	*Services directed at people's minds:* Advertising/PR Arts and entertainment Broadcasting/cable Management consulting Education Information services Music concerts Psychotherapy Religion Voice telephone	*Services directed at intangible assets:* Accounting Banking Data processing Data transmission Insurance Legal services Programming Research Securities investment Software consulting

And what about the nature of the process? In some services, as in all manufacturing, the process is physical: Something tangible takes place. In information-based services, the process can be intangible. By looking at services in this way, from a purely operational perspective, we see that they can be categorized into four broad groups (Table 2-1).

The first group involves tangible actions to customers in person; we'll call it *people processing*. Airline travel, hotels, fitness clubs, and health care are examples. Second come services, such as car repair, laundry, disposal, or freight transportation, that involve tangible actions to physical objects to improve their value to customers; we can call this group *possession processing*.

The third category of services is concerned with activities, such as education, broadcasting, or voice telephone, that are directed at people's minds rather than their bodies and so affect customers in intangible ways; for want of a better term, let's call this *mental stimulus processing* (I know it sounds awful, but it captures the meaning). Finally, we're left with intangible processing of inanimate objects, which lies at the heart of all *informa-*

tion processing; accounting, legal services, research, insurance, and banking are all based on creating value by collecting, combining, analyzing, rearranging, and interpreting information in useful ways. Let's take a brief look at each of the four categories.

People Processing

From ancient times, people have sought out services directed at themselves, such as being transported, fed, lodged, barbered, or made more healthy, To receive such a service, customers must physically enter the service system: They cannot deal at arm's length with the service supplier. Consider how many times you find yourself going inside a service factory. It's not called a factory, of course—at least not by the provider. Instead you know it as a hotel, a restaurant, a haircutting salon, a bus, or a hospital. Occasionally, the service provider may be willing to come to you with the necessary tools of the trade, as when you find a doctor who is willing to make house calls (lucky you!), or a haircutter who cuts clients' hair at their home.

If a customer wants the benefits that a people-processing service has to offer, he or she must be prepared to spend time cooperating with the service operation. The level of involvement may entail anything from boarding a city bus for a 5-minute ride to lying flat on one's back in a hospital and undergoing a lengthy course of unpleasant treatment. In between these extremes come activities such as ordering and eating a meal in a restaurant, having one's hair washed, cut, and styled, and spending a couple of nights in a hotel. The output (after a period of time that can vary from minutes to months) may be a customer who has reached her destination, or satisfied his hunger, or is sporting clean and stylishly cut hair, or has had a couple of good nights sleep away from home, or is now in physically better health.

It's important to think about process and output in terms of what happens to the customer (or other object being processed), because it helps us to identify what benefits are being created. And thinking about the service process itself clarifies some of the nonfinancial costs—time, mental and physical effort, even fear and pain—that are involved in obtaining these benefits.

It's important to think about process and output in terms of what happens to the customer (or other object being processed) because it helps to identify benefits and nonfinancial costs.

Possession Processing

Often, customers ask a service organization to provide treatment not to themselves but rather to some physical possession, which could be anything from a house to a hedge, from a car to a computer, or from a dress to a dog. Many such services are quasi-manufacturing operations working to tight deadlines to restore customers' possessions to good working order. Such activities may involve cleaning, maintaining, storing, improving, repairing, or otherwise taking care of physical objects, both live and inanimate, that belong to the customer in order to extend their usefulness. Additional possession-processing services include transport, storage, wholesale and retail distribution, installation, removal, and disposal—in short, the entire chain of activities that happens during the object's lifetime. Manufacturing firms often delegate such services to specialist intermediaries.

Customers tend to be less physically involved with this type of service than with people-processing services, since there's usually no real need for them to enter the service factory and accompany their possession while it's being processed. In fact, the customer's involvement can often be limited to requesting the service, explaining the problem, and paying the bill. If the object in question is portable, customers may have a choice between dropping it off at the service factory or (perhaps for an extra fee) having it picked up from their home or workplace. Alternatively, if the object to be processed is something that would be inappropriate or impossible to move, such as landscaping, vital equipment, or part of a building, then the factory must move to the customer, with service personnel bringing the tools and materials necessary to complete the job on-site.

The actual service process might involve treating a house to get rid of termites, trimming a hedge at an office park, repairing a car, installing software on a computer, cleaning a dress, or giving shots to the family dog. The output in each instance (if the work has been done properly) should be a satisfactory solution to a stated problem or some physical enhancement of the item in question.

Mental Stimulus Processing

Services that interact with people's minds include education, news and information, professional advice, psychotherapy, entertainment, and certain religious activities. Anything that touches people's minds has the power to shape attitudes and influence behavior. So when customers are in a position of dependency or there is potential for manipulation, careful oversight is required.

Receiving such services requires an investment of time on the customer's part. However, recipients don't necessarily have to be physically present in a service factory—just mentally in communication with the information being presented. There's an interesting contrast here with people-processing services. Although passengers can sleep through a flight and still obtain the benefit of arriving at their desired destination, sleeping in class or during an educational TV broadcast will not normally leave students much wiser at the end than they were at the beginning.

Entertainment, teaching sessions, and religious services are often delivered face to face, with many customers physically present together in the same facility. In such instances, managers find themselves sharing some of the same challenges as their colleagues in people-processing services. But these services can also be transmitted to customers in distant locations through telecommunication channels. Finally, since the core content is data-based (whether it's music, voice, or visual images), this type of service can easily be recorded for posterity and transformed into a manufactured product, such as a book, compact disk, videotape, or audiocassette, which may then be packaged and marketed much like any other physical good.

Information Processing

Information processing, one of the buzzwords of our age, has been revolutionized by computers. But not all information is processed by machines: Professionals in a wide variety of fields use their brains, too. Information is the most intangible form of service output, but it is often transformed into physical form as letters, reports, books, tapes, or diskettes to create a more enduring record. Among the services that are highly dependent on effective collection and processing of information are financial services, accounting, law, marketing research, management consulting, weather forecasting, medical diagnosis, and a variety of other professional services.

The extent of customer involvement in such services is often determined more by tradition and a personal desire to meet the supplier face to face than by the needs of the operational process. Strictly speaking, personal contact is quite unnecessary in fields such as banking or insurance. Why subject your firm to all the complexities of managing a people-processing service when you could deliver the same core service at arm's length? As a customer, why go to the service factory when there's no compelling need to do so?

> *Why subject your firm to all the complexities of managing a people-processing service when you could deliver the same core service at arm's length?*

Habit and tradition often lie at the root of existing service delivery systems and service usage patterns. Professionals and their clients often say that they prefer to meet face to face, since they feel they learn more about each other's needs, capabilities, and personalities that way. But there's ample evidence that successful personal relationships, built on trust, can be created and maintained purely through telephone contact.

Distinctive Problems Faced by Different Service Categories

Many firms bundle together lots of different activities as part of their effort to provide good service. But innovation in service delivery requires that a spotlight be focused constantly on the core activity. The nature of the tasks faced by managers working in the four different service categories that I have just described varies to some extent, so I'd like to highlight several broad problem areas that are particularly germane to certain types of services.

Help! There's a Customer in the Factory!

Every service has customers (or hopes to find some), but not all interact with them in the same way. Customer involvement in the core activity may vary sharply for each of the four categories that I have outlined.

Nothing can alter the fact that people-processing services require the customer to be physically present within the service factory. If you're currently in Washington and want to be in London tomorrow, you simply can't avoid boarding an international flight and spending time in a jet high above the Atlantic. If you want your hair cut, you can't delegate this activity to somebody else's head—you have to sit in the haircutter's chair yourself. If you have the misfortune to take people literally when they cheerfully say "break a leg," you will personally have to submit to the unpleasantness of having the bone X-rayed, reset by an orthopedic surgeon, and then encased in a cast for several weeks.

When customers are required to be physically involved in the service operation system, the process must be designed around them. Not only may they need parking (or other assistance in getting to and from the service facility), but the longer customers remain there, the more they are likely to need other services (including such hospitality basics as food, beverages, and toilets).

The factory itself must be designed with customers in mind. If it's noisy, smelly, confusingly laid out, and sited in an inconvenient location, then customers are likely to be turned off. If service delivery requires them to interact with employees, then both parties may need some basic training or guidance on how to work together cooperatively to achieve the best results. If customers are expected to do some of the work themselves—as in self-service—then facilities and equipment must be user-friendly.

Managers in each of the other three categories of services, by contrast, have rather more latitude (and so do their customers). Possibilities range from letting customers come to a user-friendly factory, limiting contact to a small front office, or keeping customers at arm's length— by relying on mail and telecommunication linkages—and never meeting face to face. Some firms like to offer an array of alternatives and let the customer choose.

Raising the Valleys and Lowering the Mountains

Sharp fluctuations in demand are a bane in the lives of many managers. Manufacturing firms can inventory supplies of their product as a hedge against fluctuations in demand. This enables them to enjoy the economies derived from operating plants at a steady production level. Service businesses can't do this, because it's not normally possible to inventory services. So the potential income from an empty seat on an airliner is lost forever once that flight takes off. Hotel room-nights are equally "perishable." Likewise, the productive capacity of an auto repair shop is wasted if no cars come in for servicing on a day when the shop is open. Conversely, when demand for service exceeds supply, the excess business may be lost. If someone can't get a seat on one flight, another carrier gets the business, or the trip is canceled.

In general, services that process people and physical objects are more likely to face capacity limitations than those that are information-based. Radio and television transmissions, for instance, can reach any number of homes within their receiving area or cable distribution network. In recent years, information processing and transmission capacity has been vastly increased by greater computer power, digital switching, and the replacement of conventional cables with fiber optic ones.

Yet technology has not found similar ways to increase the capacity of ser-

> *Services that process people and physical objects are more likely to face capacity limitations than those that are information-based.*

vice operations that process people and their physical possessions without big jumps in costs. So managing demand becomes essential to improving productivity in these types of services. Either customers must be given incentives to use the service outside peak periods, or capacity must be allocated through advance reservations.

The problem in people-processing services is that there are limits as to how long customers will wait in line: They have other things to do, and they become bored, tired, and hungry; hence strategies designed to inventory or ration demand should focus on adoption of reservation systems. Most physical possessions, by contrast, will not suffer if made to wait for an extended period; more relevant are the costs and inconveniences for owners caused by their absence. The issue of demand and capacity management is so central to productive use of assets (and thus profitability) that I devote significant coverage to the topic in Chap. 16.

People as Part of the Product

The more involved customers become in the service delivery process, the more they see of service personnel. In many people-processing services, customers meet lots of employees, often being served by them for extended periods of time. They are also more likely to run into other customers, too—after all, many service facilities achieve their operating economies by serving large numbers of customers simultaneously. As a result, other people become an important part of any customer's service experience.

The people factor in service production complicates management's task, since it means that customers are evaluating the quality of employees' appearance and social skills as well as their technical skills. So recruitment, training, and motivation of employees must cover a broad array of criteria.

Customers are also making judgments about other customers. So managers find themselves trying to manage customer behavior, too. Service businesses of this type tend to be harder to manage because of the human element. And consistent execution becomes that much harder to achieve.

Making the Most of Information Technology

Naturally, *information-based services* (a term I use to cover both mental stimulus-processing and information-processing services) have the most to gain from advances in information technology that allow their operations to be physically separated from customers.

Many examples of using technology to transform the nature of the core product and its delivery system owe their genesis to radio and television. From studio symphony performances to electronic churches to call-in gardening-advice programs, broadcasting (and now interactive cable) have created new ways to bring advice, entertainment, culture, and spiritual uplift to widely scattered audiences. One of the largest efforts of this nature is The Open University (OU) in Great Britain. The OU has been offering degree programs to students nationwide through the electronic campus of BBC television and radio for almost a quarter-century. Anyone can watch or hear the programs, of course, but students also receive printed course material through the mail and communicate with tutors by mail or telephone.

Modern telecommunications and computer technology are having a major impact on information-based services. These two forces are at their most powerful in influencing service design when they are linked together, so that customers can connect their own computers (or other input–output devices) with the service provider's system in another location. Sitting at home (or in the office), customers of a discount brokerage can manage their own investment portfolios, buying and selling stocks by keying in orders on their computers.

At a minimum, old-fashioned service concepts need to be reexamined in the light of new technological developments. Some firms are reengineering traditional operations, radically restructuring them to get customers out of the factory altogether. In Chap. 6, we'll look at the operations of Firstdirect, the 24-hour bank without branches that never closes and yet never sees its customers at all.

Old-fashioned service concepts need to be reexamined in the light of new technological developments. Some firms are reengineering traditional operations to get customers out of the factory altogether.

Value-Added Services for Physical Products

Developments in manufacturing also affect services. Any new physical product, especially if it's a high-value durable, may create a need for related services. These may range from transport, installation, refueling, maintenance, and cleaning to consulting advice, upgrading, repair, and ultimate disposal. Historically, such after-sales services have generated important revenue streams for many years after the initial sale for manufacturers or distributors of products such as cars, factory machinery, locomotives, and computers.

In the case of high-technology equipment, however, vendors are finding that revenues from traditional services such as repair and maintenance are shrinking. Ironically, a combination of higher quality and greater reliability often means that machines become technically obsolescent before they start to need major repairs. And thanks to more serviceable designs (including plug-in modules), the remaining maintenance work is open to more competition than formerly. Small, independent suppliers may offer to service equipment for less than the original vendor, and many customers have learned how to do their own maintenance. These developments are cutting into traditional sources of after-sales service revenues.

On the other hand, Dick Munn, a pioneering researcher into the factors leading to service business success for information technology vendors, points out that there are new opportunities for growth in developing and selling high-value-added professional services. "For instance," he says, "customers who have purchased hi-tech equipment from many different vendors may want to hire a single contractor to take responsibility for integrating and managing their networks on an ongoing basis." Other services requiring significant professional expertise (and therefore offering the potential for higher margins) include specialized education and training, software support, data center design and construction, advice on creating enterprise-wide networks, relocation of offices and their associated systems, safe storage of vital records ("vaulting"), and disaster recovery.

All manufacturers would do well to consider how they might help customers make more effective use of their products. Although some advice and information will have to be offered free, there may be many opportunities to sell specialized information and site-management services, too. And there's one other benefit in addition to the revenues: Think how much more you learn about your customers in the process!

Another type of high-value-added service—which can be applied to any type of manufactured product—is supply-chain management. Firms that specialize in business logistics take over responsibility for transport and warehousing of material inputs, finished goods, and spare parts on a national or even global basis. The linkages may extend from suppliers' plants to customers' manufacturing or assembly facilities, and from there to wholesalers, end users, or retail stores. The efficiencies obtained through supply-chain management are highly dependent on information systems that can track the presence of any item throughout the system.

The Core Product as Foundation

So far, we've focused on the core activity that defines the fundamental nature of the business. And we've seen that there are four broad categories of service, each of which presents its own special challenges from a managerial perspective. Many businesses are hybrids, still behaving like people-processing organizations when modern technology would allow them to reengineer themselves in new and simpler ways. Where does your business stand?

But there's more to constructing a service than just the foundation. In the following chapter, describe a whole host of supplementary elements that are either necessary adjuncts to use of the core product, or else designed to add value and differentiate it from competition.

At 11:33 p.m., Greg suffered a core product failure in his hotel room. He resolved not to stay at the Royal Imperial Plaza again.

3 Every Business Competes on Service

Regardless of industry—manufacturing, services, or natural resources—if a business can't perform well on its core product, its chances of survival are bleak. Innovations on the core are often quickly copied. For customers, the product plus of differentiation and added value comes from a whole bundle of supplementary services that enhance (or detract from) the appeal of the core product. Wise managers recognize that customer expectations drive the provision of supplementary services. In fact, one universally applicable definition of service is "all actions and reactions that customers perceive they have purchased."

One of the best definitions of service that I know comes from Federal Express (FedEx), which created the concept of overnight express package delivery as we know it today. For its first five years, the company had a near monopoly on nationwide overnight service in the United States, since competing organizations (mostly passenger airlines and air freight forwarders) could only guarantee next day delivery on a limited number of routes. During the 1970s, air freight services operated under tight government regulation, making it extremely difficult for new competitors to enter the market. FedEx itself was chartered as an air taxi operation, restricted to loads of a little more than 3 tons, which it transported in converted executive jets.

Seeking to fly larger, more economical aircraft such as Boeing 727s, FedEx lobbied vigorously in Washington for deregulation. The company won its goal, but correctly foresaw that deregulation of the air freight industry would lead to greatly increased competition as other companies entered the business or expanded existing services.

Many of these competitors were expected to perform well on the basic service of overnight transportation and delivery of packages, and some of them were likely to be cheaper. Federal Express's management decided that they would have to rethink their definition of service if the company was to continue as the market leader and charge a premium price. After some thought, senior managers decided to define service very simply as "all actions and reactions that customers perceive they have purchased."

Federal Express has defined service as "all actions and reactions that customers perceive they have purchased."

This statement can be applied to any business and clarifies what customers have known all along, namely, that "service" is a bundle consisting of the core product—which in FedEx's case consists of picking up a package, transporting it overnight, and delivering it by the promised time—plus a cluster of supplementary services (see Fig. 3-1), which for FedEx includes:

- Advice and information
- Taking orders over the telephone
- Providing labels and certain types of packaging
- Documenting pickups and deliveries
- Accurate, intelligible billing statements

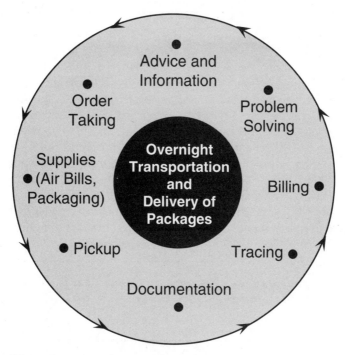

Figure 3-1. Core and supplementary services for express package delivery.

- Problem solving
- Tracing the occasional missing package

Pursuing its efforts to improve customer service, Federal Express invested heavily in information technology. Its COSMOS system, which has been regularly upgraded over the years, enhances the company's ability to respond to telephone requests for pickups, track packages through its system, trace missing packages, and provide accurate billing. The company has also invested heavily in recruiting employees with a service orientation and in teaching them how to deliver quality service.

Whatever your business, you have to think in terms of performing well on all actions and reactions that customers perceive they are purchasing. And you need to be clear about which of these various interactions constitutes the core product and which represent supplementary elements. The latter either facilitate use of the core product (such as a reservations system), or are integral aspects of doing business (such as sending bills and accepting payments), or are "extras" designed to add value or increase product appeal.

Core and Supplementary Services

If you look at most businesses—both service and manufacturing—you'll find that the core product tends to become a commodity as competition increases and the industry matures. In natural resources, such as oil, minerals, or agricultural produce, the product begins life as a commodity. It's very difficult to protect innovative products from imitation by competitors (brand names and proprietary software are among the few aspects of service design that can be legally protected). Even in manufacturing, where inventions can be patented, it's becoming increasingly difficult to sustain product leadership. Just look at how quickly innovative new high-technology products are cloned and their protective patents circumvented!

> *In most businesses, the core product tends to become a commodity as competition increases and the industry matures.*

Every business that aspires to market leadership should be working to enhance existing products and to develop new ones. But achieving significant innovation in the core product is nearly always time-consuming and expensive, sometimes requiring enormous research investments. In mature product categories, such innovation occurs only infrequently. Think for a moment: What was the most recent successful *major* innovation in airline travel, cars, hotels, or retail financial services? And when did each take place?

I'll give you my nominations. In airlines, it's supersonic travel on the Concorde (a financial disaster for the British and French governments that sponsored its development, but certainly a distinctive marketing tool today for British Airways and Air France). The first commercial supersonic flight took place back in 1982. That's not exactly recent.

What about cars? Many of the changes that have taken place in car design in recent years have been evolutionary enhancements in engine efficiency, emission controls, styling, and addition of new luxury extras such as cellular telephones. In my view, perhaps the most significant recent innovation affecting the basic vehicle has been antilock braking systems (ABS), designed to prevent the skids that result when brakes lock up. ABS brakes first became commercially available in the mid-1980s; today, they're no longer just a luxury option, but are being offered as a standard feature on many mid-range models.

In hotels, my nomination for most recent successful innovation in the core product is all-suite hotels, where every guest obtains not only a bedroom and bathroom but also a sitting room. This innovation was pioneered by Granada Royale (a predecessor of Embassy Suites) in 1969.

Finally, what about the most recent major innovation in retail financial products (as opposed to the systems that deliver them)? My vote would go to the cash management account (CMA) pioneered in the United States by Merrill Lynch in 1977 and now available in many different countries. Known generically as an asset management account, this product combines brokerage, checking, and credit (or debit) card services in a single-statement account, with account holders able to borrow automatically against the value of their investments. A slightly more recent innovation—limited to North America—is the home equity account, a form of second mortgage that allows homeowners to tap the equity in their property for automatic loans using checks or a debit card. But even this product dates back to 1983.

Of course, there will be other major innovations. But all in all, significant innovation in core products seems to be an infrequent event in many industries. It is among supplementary service elements that we find much of the action taking place. And it is here that most companies in mature industries should be focusing their strategic thinking for the short and medium term, for it's among supplementary services that forward-looking firms have the best chance to create meaningful product pluses over their more sluggish competitors.

This idea is not a new one by any means. Twenty years ago, Ted Levitt observed, "We live in an age in which our thinking about what a product or service is must be quite different from what it was before. It is not so much the basic, generic, central thing we are thinking about that counts, but the whole cluster of satisfactions with which we surround it."

What this book offers are new ways of thinking systematically about this "cluster of satisfactions" and of implementing improved ways to deliver meaningful benefits.

Competing on Supplementary Service Elements

It's my belief that competitive advantage usually emphasizes performance on the supplementary service elements. After all, if a firm can't do a decent job on the core product—whether it's a manufactured product such as a car or a service such as cable television—sooner or later it's going to go out of business. Let me give you some examples from industries to which anyone can readily relate. We'll start with airline service.

If a firm can't do a decent job on the core product, sooner or later it's going to go out of business.

The core product of the airline business is safe and speedy transportation of passengers between two designated airports. A failure of that core product would probably mean that the aircraft never made it to its destination or, less disastrously, that it landed at the wrong airport. But any airline that loses an aircraft a month or regularly lands at the wrong airports will soon go bust as passengers desert it in droves. Contributing to PanAm's long demise were a series of accidents on Pacific routes in the early 1970s. When the airline later produced advertisements touting its long experience in the region, it used the slogan, "PanAm Knows the Pacific Like Nobody Else." To which the Australians replied, "Well, they certainly should; they've been in it three times!"

The day-to-day choice criteria for business travelers flying within large mature markets such as the United States or the European Community don't normally center around safe arrivals at the right airport—although they may worry about punctuality. Passengers tend to choose between competing airlines on the basis of such supplementary elements as frequent flyer programs, ease of getting through to reservations, speedy check-in at the airport, appetizing meals on board the flight, and safe arrival of their baggage at the other end.

Now let's look at hotels. What's the core product of the lodging industry? Basically, it's a bed for the night. Failure of that core product would probably look something like collapse of your bed in the middle of the night. How often does that happen? It's pretty unusual. After all, hotel beds are built to put up with a great deal of abuse. They have to be.

More likely it's the supplementary services that fail, such as not honoring your reservation when you check in at midnight and it's snowing outside. Have you ever had a hotel "lose" your reservation? If you travel with any degree of regularity, it's highly likely. And if it did happen to you, I'll bet you were pretty mad about it. Whether the problem was due to a data-entry error or to deliberate overbooking is of little interest to the tired traveler who wants to get to bed. Unless the front desk staff promptly found you a better room in another hotel, you probably bad-mouthed the offending hotel to anyone who would listen. Perhaps you even decided to avoid all hotels in that chain for the foreseeable future.

After all, if the chain's reservation system failed you for their hotel in New York, it'll probably fail you for their hotels in Boston, Los Angeles, Singapore, and Paris as well. And yet that reservation system is just a data-based supplementary service element (probably located in a telecommunications center somewhere like Omaha, Nebraska). On the face of it, this service seems far removed from the demanding task of running a nice hotel hundreds or thousands of miles away, yet if its reservations system doesn't deliver what it promises, the would-be guest will never even get to use the core product.

Responding to Problems with the Core Product

Among "all actions and reactions that customers perceive that they have purchased" is quick and effective response to problems with the core product. These problems can range from answering questions about how to use the product to handling breakdowns.

When buying a manufactured product, customers want to be sure that service will be available where and when they want it—and at a reasonable price. In many instances, they expect a warranty period during which problems will be fixed without charge. The availability of service—and the terms of that service—have become key criteria in making purchase decisions.

Consider the personal computer industry. Although the core product is in a continuing state of rapid innovation, it's a crowded field in which numerous look-alike clones compete with more widely known brand names. In a review of 25 of the more powerful models available on the market, *PC Magazine* rated products not only on such features as performance, price, design and construction, expandability, and fast-RAM capacity, but also on service and support. The magazine told its readers to look for a machine with at least a one-year warranty and a support phone number. To test the level and quality of technical support, researchers call each supplier's central support number, ask three questions of varying difficulty, and rate the firm's responses on promptness, courteousness, and accuracy. Other support considerations include free on-site service and toll-free phone support. They rate dealer support by looking at the vendor's policies on dealer training, inventory, and support staff. In coming up with overall evaluations and identifying a "best buy," *PC Magazine* allocates 18 percent of the overall score achieved by each product to its rating on service and support dimensions.

Effective responses are important in service industries as well as in manufacturing. And they are important even when there is no direct competition. Cable TV service is currently a monopoly; as with water, electricity, and other local utilities, there's only one supplier. And it's an information-based service industry where customers normally have no direct contact with the supplier, beyond an electronic signal transmitted through a cable installed to their homes. The cable delivers the core product—more choice of programs and a claim of better reception than from regular broadcast signals or satellite.

Consider the following core product failure. A young couple have invited some friends over to watch the 1000th episode of some top-rated series—call it *Dynasty in Dallas*—in which one of the leading characters is expected to be killed off. It's almost 9 o'clock and time for the show. The beer and the pretzels are ready. But the TV set isn't receiving a clear signal. Instead, jagged lines leap across the screen, and only crackling noises emerge from the speaker. "Quick," say the hosts, "Let's call the cable company to find out what's going on and see if it can fix the problem!"

Now here we have an opportunity for the cable company to demonstrate its problem-solving skills at a critical time for its customers. But horror of horrors, no one picks up the phone at the other end. There's just a recorded message announcing that office hours are from 9 a.m. to 5 p.m. The unavailability of this key supplementary service adds insult to injury. Not only has the core product failed, but the supplier does not see fit to have employees on duty at a time of day when the greatest number of customers are likely to be using the service. Limiting the hours when telephone assistance is available saves money in the short run and makes life more convenient for employees, but it's a sure way to turn off customers.

Let's consider the downside of such a policy from the standpoint of the cable TV firm. This disappointing experience for our group of viewers may have several consequences. At a minimum, there will be much grumbling about the service interruption itself, but also about the fact that the company doesn't care enough about its customers to have someone on duty to help when problems occur. These disparaging comments about the cable TV firm will probably be passed on to other friends and neighbors, some of whom may be thinking of becoming subscribers.

If this problem has occurred before, the couple may decide to terminate their cable TV subscription and install a satellite dish instead. Or they could complain to the regulatory authority that oversees cable TV services. If enough subscribers do that, perhaps the supplier will lose its franchise at renewal time or face opposition to its next proposed rate increase. In either instance, the profit implications could be severe.

Where's the Leverage?

Let me reiterate a point I made earlier: If a firm can't perform satisfactorily on the core product, it's eventually going to go out of business. For customers of a mature industry, the product plus of meaningful differentiation and added value usually comes from a whole bundle of supplementary service elements. Performing on the core service is a matter of "do-or-die" (see Fig. 3-2). But there are some differences in the relative role and importance of various supplementary services.

Do-or-Decline. At the top of the diagram are what I've categorized as "do-or-decline" elements. More and more, service firms are finding that information (by phone or otherwise), order taking, billing, and problem solving are included in this category. If you can't perform well on these tasks—which are generic to almost all service industries—your organization will appear incompetent and uncaring. And you will be setting the stage for a steady decline.

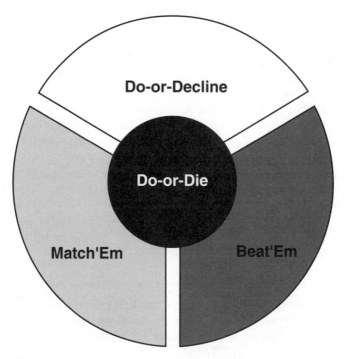

Figure 3-2. Service elements and competitive leverage.

One of the factors that helped to kill a very innovative airline known as People Express—remember it?—was that no one could get through by phone to make a reservation. The lines were always busy. Travel agents quit calling because it was too time-consuming for their agents. Many passengers were lost that way. There are other do-or-decline elements for every service business, but they vary from industry to industry. One must perform at a certain threshold level just to stay in business.

Match 'Ems and Beat 'Ems.   Other supplementary services can be divided into what I call "match 'ems" and beat 'ems." Each firm should decide what the basis for its competitive strategy will be. When targeting a specific market segment, on which attributes will superior performance yield a meaningful competitive edge? And where will it suffice simply to offer the industry standard of performance on a given service element? To answer this question, you will probably have to research what customers think of your firm's products and those of competitors on all relevant service attributes.

Another question to ask is how long it will take before a "beat 'em" is copied by the competition and reduced to the stage of a "match 'em." Innovative extras designed to surprise and delight customers and help distinguish a firm from its competition are often easily copied and have a nasty habit of quickly turning into customer requirements.

Once upon a time, an innovative hotelier had the bright idea of having housekeepers place a mint on the pillow when they were turning down bed covers and checking the room before guests retired for the night. It was a hospitable gesture that also drew customers' attention to the provision of "turn down" service. But it wasn't very long before all hotel chains began copying this idea—after all, the beauty of the concept was that it was both cheap and simple. Some hotels started providing two mints. Others, presumably in league with the dental profession, escalated the war to one or more pieces of expensive chocolate. Evidence that a "beat 'em" had turned into a customer requirement came when the *New Yorker* printed a cartoon of a middle-aged businessman sitting on his hotel bed in his pajamas making a phone call. Scowling, he is saying: "Front desk? I want to know why there's no mint on my pillow!"

> *Innovative extras designed to delight customers and distinguish a firm from its competitors are often easily copied and have a nasty habit of turning into customer requirements.*

Managers must decide for themselves where the opportunities lie for adding distinctive extras and where the focus should be on improving basic performance. A study of customer complaint and suggestion data, plus customized market research studies as needed, represent logical starting points for generating the necessary insights and ideas.

We'll be returning to the topic of supplementary services in Chap. 12, which includes a master checklist of over 80 possible service elements. But before we move on to the next chapter, with its discussion of the tensions that arise between trying to run an efficient operation versus trying to please the customers, let me plant a couple of questions in your head. Doubtless, it will have already occurred to you that many supplementary services are not industry-specific—consider telephone information and order taking, statements and billing, and food and beverage service, for example. To what extent are customer expectations of your firm's service capabilities being shaped by the performance of organizations *outside your own industry?* And do you know who they are?

"Splendid! Then it's agreed. We'll be able to run a much more efficient operation once we get rid of all those pesky customers!"

4 User-Friendly versus User-Hostile

When a service is run for the convenience of operating systems and the personnel who staff them, the result is often a hostile environment for customers. But an organization that gives its customers everything they want without regard to efficiency, cost control, and employee well-being risks ending up in bankruptcy court. Marketers need to understand key concepts in the design of service operations so that they can work with their colleagues in operations and human resources to achieve mutual goals. We look at seven important operational issues—productivity, standardization, batch processing, capacity management, job design, facilities location, and the design of facilities and equipment—and consider how operational goals might be achieved in user-friendly ways.

Have you ever been in a hotel where the attitude of the management and staff seemed to be that they could do a much better job of running the establishment if only guests would stop cluttering up the lobby, messing up their rooms, and constantly calling for room service? Have you ever been told you couldn't ride a bus because you didn't have exact change? Has a postal clerk refused to accept a parcel from you, telling you that it wasn't properly wrapped in accordance with postal regulations? Have you, on visiting a medical clinic, had your name called, been ushered into a small white cell, been asked to strip, and wondered 20 minutes later what is really meant by the phrase "the doctor will be with you shortly"?

If you answered "yes" to any of these questions, then you already know some of the frustrating ways in which operational priorities seem to run counter to achieving customer satisfaction. But don't rush to blame the employees. The issue may go deeper than poor attitudes on the part of front-stage personnel. Like the piano player whom one is not supposed to shoot, they may only be doing their best—in this instance, to follow the dictates of managers and supervisors.

Some managers might claim that each of the situations depicted above reflects a businesslike trade-off of customer satisfaction against the productivity imperative that lies at the heart of keeping costs down. After all, they might tell you, in a competitive market, if prices are too high, customers will take their business elsewhere. And if a firm can't make a profit because its costs are high, then it can't invest for the future.

That's only marginally convincing, but there's worse to come. Customers often complain that service organizations are unresponsive and bureaucratic. They describe confusing facilities in which they had to run from pillar to post in order to complete a transaction, lengthy lines, personnel who decline to serve them on the grounds that "that's not my job" or "I'm not allowed to do that," inconvenient service locations and hours, replacement of service people by complex machines that customers are expected to operate themselves, and seemingly unnecessary rules and regulations concerning the terms under which service will be provided.

These experiences are just a few of the many tedious ways in which operational rules and procedures affect customers. It's clear that operational priorities have a nasty habit of turning into "product minuses."

Customers often complain that service organizations are bureaucratic and unresponsive...operational priorities have a nasty habit of turning into "product minuses."

Get Rid of the Customer and the System Runs Fine

The *reductio ad absurdum* of a managerial mindset that stresses operational efficiency at the expense of the customer is pungently illustrated in this newspaper report from the Midlands of England some years ago:

> Complaints from passengers wishing to use the Bagnall to Greenfields bus service that "the drivers were speeding past queues of people with a smile and a wave of the hand" have been met by a statement [from the bus company] that "It is impossible for the drivers to keep their timetable if they have to stop for passengers."

Great! So now we know how an operations department should define the mission of public transportation service: to operate vehicles in accordance with schedules that are strictly adhered to under all circumstances. If stopping to pick up (or, for that matter, drop off) passengers would violate the sacred schedules, then just keep right on going!

Other benefits of such a strategy include reduced fuel consumption and less wear and tear on clutch and brake linings. But do it nicely, with a smile and a wave of the hand—good relations with customers are *so* important, even if actually serving them gets in the way of running the operation smoothly.

Of course, I jest. But let's look at the other side of the picture for a moment: The situation is not quite as black and white as it first appears. Numerous surveys confirm that punctuality is very important for users of public transport services. Further, if one vehicle arrives late at its destination, it may delay connecting services (or cause passengers to miss those connections) and also depart late for its next run. On the other hand, passengers who arrive at the bus stop before the scheduled arrival time expect to be picked up if space is space available on the vehicle. The problem in this case is that, in its single-minded pursuit of punctuality, the bus company has broken its implicit contract with passengers—to pick them up at designated bus stops—and then compounded the problem by sending out a perfectly dreadful letter of explanation in response to complaints.

All too often, the operational perspective is allowed to dominate service delivery, almost to the point where management and employees sometimes give the impression that they would be happier if all the customers simply disappeared. Yes, efficiency, safety, and productivity are important. But every facet of a service operation should be examined from a customer perspective, too. No one in the organization must ever be allowed to forget that the operation exists to serve customers and not the reverse. After all, it's only by serving customers well that the organization can hope to accomplish its mission.

> *No one in the organization must ever be allowed to forget that the operation exists to serve customers and not the reverse.*

If, as often happens, there is a conflict between efficient operations and serving customers, then changes in both operational procedures and the terms of service should be considered. In the bus company example, rescheduling of the buses would be one solution; this approach could also be combined with changes in routes and bus stop locations, if doing so would lead to better service. But first, consult the passengers.

The bottom line is that service procedures and facilities should reflect a properly researched trade-off of customer needs against the costs of meeting those needs. Operations managers should remember that when customers are physically involved in service delivery, they incur additional costs beyond the monetary price of the service: They are spending their own time and putting in physical or mental effort. A well-designed service operation tries to minimize that time and effort.

Conflict and Compromise in Service Businesses

Managing any type of organization entails conflict between differing goals and agendas. This is particularly true for managers running people-processing services that require a high degree of customer contact, since customers get much closer to the operation than when they are dealing with a firm at arm's length, and they're more conscious of an unsatisfactory delivery process.

Operations versus Marketing

No management function is unimportant in service businesses, but two functions—operations and marketing—drive management strategy in today's marketplace. In turn, the human resources function plays a key role in determining how well that strategy is implemented. Unfortunately, managers who are responsible for these functions are often at odds with one another in terms of how to meet the organization's goals. One result is that employees find themselves caught in the middle, unsure whether their priorities should emphasize operational efficiency or service to customers.

Operations and marketing managers are often at odds about how to meet the organization's goals...employees find themselves caught in the middle, unsure of their priorities.

The operations function sits at the center of any service business, since it creates and assembles the service product, often working under real-time conditions. Historically, operations concerns—which we discuss later in depth—have dominated service management.

Facing increasing competition, many businesses rely on the marketing function to act as a bridge between them and the marketplace. (I use the term *marketing* in its broadest sense, to encompass all management activities concerned with market selection, competitive strategy, and customer relationships.)

Marketing's job is to identify needs and trends within the marketplace, decide which types of customers to target, and craft a strategy to reach these customers and build relationships with them. In their role as customer advocates, effective marketers see their responsibilities as including creation of new product and service concepts, selecting strategies for delivering services at times and in locations that are convenient to customers, helping to make pricing decisions, developing communication programs, and monitoring competitive activities. But introducing a stronger market orientation into service businesses is sometimes resisted by traditionally minded operations executives, who often see marketing as just a costly add-on function that should be confined to consumer research and communication efforts. So, when marketers seek to get involved in product design and service delivery, operations managers may see these efforts as trespassing on their territory.

The issue is not merely a matter of turf: It reflects the operations focus on delivering a smooth-running and cost-efficient service. In a cover story entitled "McRisky," *Business Week* reported on McDonald's plans to broaden menus and add new features to its restaurants. The story noted concerns that such moves, while appealing to customers, could destroy the chain's fabled efficiency. McDonald's executives might do well to consider the earlier experience of Kentucky Fried Chicken (KFC), where a seemingly attractive menu innovation (barbecued spare ribs), championed by marketers, led to serious difficulties. As recalled by a senior operations executive: "It was a big mistake. Our stores are small. They didn't have space for the new equipment that was needed. It was really popular with our customers, but started to mess up the rest of our operation....Marketers are often very creative but should concentrate more on being total business people. Operations people tend to rate the marketing folks on how well they understand the operation."

Eventually, KFC had to withdraw its new menu; not only were spare ribs becoming unprofitable in their own right (pork prices had risen sharply), but this menu item was leading to delays and difficulties in cooking the basic chicken menu that formed the core of the chain's business.

Key Operational Issues

Whatever type of service industry they work in, marketers and other customer advocates need to be familiar with some of the key issues that face their colleagues in operations before rushing to demand service enhancements. Let's consider seven basic operational concerns that are as relevant to marketers and human resource specialists as to operations managers:

1. Improving productivity

2. Standardization versus customization

3. Batch processing versus unit processing

4. Capacity management

5. Job design

6. Location of service facilities

7. Design of facilities and equipment

> *Marketers and other customer advocates need to be familiar with some of the key issues that face their colleagues in operations before rushing to demand service enhancements.*

These issues are key elements in the design of a service operations strategy and are applicable to any type of service process. Table 4-1 summarizes

Table 4-1. Operations versus Marketing Perspectives

Operational issues	Operations goals	Marketing concerns
Improving productivity	Reduce unit cost of production	Customers may feel service quality has declined
Standardization	Keeps costs low and quality constant; simplify operations tasks; recruit low-cost employees	Customers may seek variety, prefer service tailored to their needs and delivered by knowledgeable employees
Batch processing	Seek economies of scale, consistency, efficient use of capacity by processing customers in groups	Customers may be forced to wait, feel "one of a crowd," be turned off by other people in the group
Capacity management	Keep costs down by avoiding wasteful underutilization of resources	Service unavailable when needed; quality may be compromised during high-demand periods
Job design	Minimize error, waste, and fraud; use technology efficiently; simplify tasks and standardize work	Operationally oriented employees with narrow roles may be unresponsive to customer needs
Facilities location	Reduce costs; provide convenient access for suppliers and employees	Customers may find location unattractive and inconvenient
Facilities and equipment design	Control costs; improve efficiency by ensuring proximity of operationally related tasks; enhance safety and security	Customers may see facility as ugly, layout as complicated and time-wasting, and find equipment hard to use

some typical operational goals in each instance and some common marketing concerns relating to the potential impact on customers. Employees often find themselves caught in the middle, trying to serve two masters. So the stage is set for conflict.

The challenge lies in finding the optimal balance between the sometimes conflicting concerns that can bedevil relations between service suppliers and their customers. You'll see some of the problems that can arise in each instance—perhaps you've already had to wrestle with them yourself. But every problem also presents an opportunity.

Improving Productivity

At the heart of most operational strategies is the search for productivity improvements, which occur when the volume/value of output improves relative to the volume/value of inputs. Operational approaches to achieving this goal include:

- Working employees harder
- Recruiting and training more productive employees
- Reducing employee turnover
- Investing in more efficient equipment
- Automating labor tasks
- Eliminating bottlenecks that lead to unproductive downtime in operational processes
- Standardizing both the process itself and the resulting service output

Customer Concerns and Marketing Opportunities. What marketers need to worry about is whether such approaches are received positively or negatively by customers. Among the potential problems: Overworked employees may deliver lower-quality service, automated service delivery may be perceived as inferior to human interaction, and customers may be turned off by a bland and highly routinized process. If the net result of trying to improve productivity is a decline in sales which reduces the value of output relative to input, then the effort is self-defeating.

If the net effect of trying to improve productivity is a decline in sales, then the effort is self-defeating.

In services that involve customers in the production process, there may be opportunities to make customers themselves more productive. What can you do in this respect? Possibilities include efforts to:

- *Change the timing of customer demand* by encouraging use of the service during periods when demand is low and productive capacity is underutilized. Hotels, for instance, offer bargain rates during off-season periods.
- *Involve customers more in production processes* by giving them a chance to serve themselves. Opportunities for self-service exist at some point in

the process of most service businesses, but such shifting to self-service may require installation of new, customer-friendly equipment, availability of help desks and hotlines, and changes in established behavior patterns on all sides.

- *Get customers to use alternative delivery channels* to obtain certain service elements (for instance, using agencies for reservations and payment). Many firms are moving to subcontract some of their activities to specialist intermediaries.

What we're talking about here is the use of marketing insights to help solve operational problems. However, incentives such as time savings and price cuts may be needed to motivate customers, especially when they are being asked to change established habits. A shift to self-service or outsourcing has implications for employees, too.

Standardization versus Customization in Service Delivery

Standardization involves limiting service options and achieving consistency of output by adopting a production-line approach to service creation and delivery—"manufacturing in the field," as Ted Levitt once described it. This approach often boxes employees into narrowly defined job tasks and sharply limits their discretion. It may also involve substitution of technology for people and managing customer behavior to conform with the operating system, rather than vice versa. Seeking greater productivity and the ability to compete on price, some firms have been moving away from personalized service and high client contact toward a "service factory" environment.

Led by franchisers who create standardized business concepts that are easy for entrepreneurial franchisees to replicate, many service suppliers are simplifying, streamlining, and codifying operating procedures. Take a look at the display ads in the Yellow Pages if you want to see just how many different types of consumer and commercial services are available from franchise organizations nowadays. Costs are reduced as a result of economies of scale, since the same tasks are repeated time and time again. Operational problems such as bottlenecks become easier to identify and eliminate, because the entire process has been clarified. Quality control is aided by being able to refer to clear specifications. And simplifying job tasks allows the firm to recruit relatively unskilled, inexpensive workers, who require only limited training to perform highly routinized tasks.

Customer Concerns and Marketing Opportunities. Standardization, however, has its disadvantages: Variations in needs tend to be ignored, and customers may tire of a uniform, homogenized process—consistency is one thing, but many people also appreciate variety. Further, service may start to deteriorate as employees performing highly repetitive tasks become bored and robotlike in their behavior.

Marketers need to understand the forces that drive the search for standardization. Instead of resisting the concept as it relates to the core product, they should look for opportunities to customize supplementary service elements—such as offering personalized advice and consultation, giving purchasers a choice of delivery systems and payment methods, and creating frequent-user clubs that offer special benefits to repeat customers. Just using the customer's name in printed communications or in face-to-face conversations can go some way toward making each customer feel that he or she is being treated as a person rather than as a transaction or account number.

These are some of the approaches that lie at the heart of what Stan Davis has called "mass customizing." Marketers can play a key role in identifying opportunities for combining standardized core products with new service configurations and then working with operations to create them.

Batch versus Unit Processing

Batch processing involves servicing customers or other items in groups rather than singly. This may yield economies of scale as well as make the most efficient use of capacity. Examples include transporting a group of people by bus rather than sending each person individually by taxi, teaching a large class rather than giving personal tutorials, or waiting for a sufficiently large group to form before giving a tour of a museum or historic site. Another example comes from the restaurant chain, Benihana of Tokyo, which seats and serves customers in groups of eight. Repair and maintenance work and handling of college applications are examples of situations in which physical objects are assembled in batches before being processed.

Customer Concerns and Marketing Opportunities. Among the marketing drawbacks of batch processing are that customers feel they are just one of a crowd. In people-processing services, if there is any unsocial or thoughtless behavior among other customers, everybody's service experience may be contaminated by it. Further, service scheduling tends to be less flexible, and customers sometimes have to wait until a large enough batch has been assembled. This may mean standing in line personally or a greater elapsed time before a repair is completed or an application is processed.

Marketing benefits can include lower prices and the fact that other customers may contribute positively to the experience ("meet interesting people"). Not all batch processing requires customers to interact (if you want to keep to yourself on a flight or at the theater, you usually can). But when an organization thrusts people together in ways that require interaction, it's often a good idea to facilitate introductions, such as holding a "get acquainted" cocktail party at the start of a week-long vacation tour.

Batch processing can cause problems for customers even when it applies to their possessions rather than to themselves. Repair businesses often like to wait until several machines requiring the same type of work have been brought in for service before assigning an employee to work on them. This approach allows for more focused work and saves employees from wasting time continually switching from one setup to another. But it delays return of the product to its owner.

American Express used to batch requests by its customers to replace lost credit cards, waiting until a large enough group of requests had been assembled before assigning someone to work on this problem. This policy often led to extended delays in issuing replacement cards. But when marketing research revealed that cardholders were angered by these delays and were switching instead to use of other cards already in their wallets (thus reducing Amex's revenues), the company rethought the process. It abandoned batching in favor of new operational procedures designed to replace lost cards as quickly as possible.

Capacity Management

Many services are capacity-constrained, facing upper limits on the amount of output they can achieve with a predefined level of staffing, facilities, and equipment. As a result, they can't always serve everyone who wants service in a given time frame.

Capacity planning is vital in service businesses that need to match available resources to fluctuating demand levels. The goal is to keep down costs by avoiding wasteful underutilization of people, buildings, and machines when demand is low, and to minimize loss of revenues from customers turned away during peak periods. Good capacity planning reduces the risks that staff and employees will become bored and sloppy as a result of having too little to do or burn out as a result of being overworked and under too much pressure for excessive periods of time.

Capacity planning is vital in service businesses that need to match available resources to fluctuating demand levels.

Possible approaches to managing capacity include using part-time employees who work only in periods of high demand, renting additional capacity as needed, and focusing employee efforts on getting rid of bottlenecks that slow down service delivery throughout the system. These measures are not always feasible, but when they can be implemented, they do increase the firm's capacity to serve more customers at peak times (which is a marketing plus). However, many firms prefer to maintain their capacity at a stable level—which has the virtue of operational simplicity—and let customers wait for service at busy times.

Customer Concerns and Marketing Opportunities.   The above solutions don't always work well for customers. If the extra staff and the supplementary facilities provided at peak periods are not up to scratch, regular customers may perceive service quality as compromised. And nobody enjoys waiting in line. At the root of many capacity problems is the fact that there is too much or too little demand at a particular time. Here's a chance for marketers to develop strategies that can help solve operational problems. Creative marketing solutions to balancing demand and supply include managing demand through pricing and promotional strategies, searching for additional services in periods of low demand for the original service, improving queuing procedures so that waits are less onerous, creating priority lines for regular customers, and introducing reservations systems. We discuss these ideas in more depth and with detailed examples in Chap. 16.

Job Design

Despite advances in automation, many service delivery systems continue to involve interactions between customers and service personnel. Even automated services usually have to be backed up by customer service agents who can intervene—in person or by phone—to help customers who have run into problems. The goal of job design is to study the requirements of the operation, the nature of customer desires, the needs and capabilities of employees, and the characteristics of operational equipment in order to develop job descriptions that strike the best balance between these sometimes conflicting demands.

Many of the most demanding jobs in service businesses are so-called boundary-spanning positions, where employees are expected to be fast and efficient at executing operational tasks as well as courteous and helpful in dealing with customers. In a sense, they have to serve two masters. If the job is not designed carefully or the wrong people are picked to fill it, there's a real risk that employees may become stressed and unproductive.

Customer Concerns and Marketing Opportunities. Marketers often worry that operations-oriented employees may be unresponsive to customer needs. They may argue that customer satisfaction should be paramount in designing and filling customer contact positions; but operations managers are likely to have other agenda. The latter want to develop the most efficient combination of labor and technology, to reduce the potential for human error, to minimize the risk of fraud and waste, and—in certain situations—to create teams of employees working on complementary tasks who will be more productive collectively than if they worked independently (even assuming that they possessed the full array of necessary skills).

As competition in service industries increases, how well a service is delivered in human terms may be as important as good performance on the purely operational components. Training programs may have to be redesigned to ensure that customer-contact employees have the necessary human skills as well as the technical ones. But training has its limits. Sometimes a change is needed in recruitment criteria.

> *How well a service is delivered in human terms may be as important as good performance on the purely operational components.*

When research findings showed that its passengers desired warmer, friendlier service from flight attendants, British Airways first tried to develop these characteristics through training. But human resource managers soon concluded that while good manners and the need to smile could be taught, warmth itself could not. So the airline changed its recruitment criteria to favor candidates with naturally warm personalities.

Going beyond the question of personality is the issue of what responsibilities are delegated to a particular job. There has been much discussion in recent years of the importance of *empowering* employees to use their own discretion to serve customers better. Job designs should reflect the fact that customer-contact personnel may encounter customer requests for assistance in remote sites at any hour of the day and night. Providing employees with greater discretion (and training them to use their judgment) may enable them to provide superior service without referring constantly to rule books or higher authority for any situation that deviates from operational standards.

In the area of job design, both marketers and operations personnel need assistance from skilled human resource managers. Designing job positions, filling them, and providing ongoing training and motivation is too important a task to be handled haphazardly, for employing good people is a major point of competitive differentiation in many service industries.

Choosing Locations for Service Facilities

Have you ever wondered why some discount car rental lots are located in such unattractive, out-of-the-way places? "Call us on arrival at the airport," the reservations agent tells you, "and we'll pick you up outside the baggage claim."

Sometimes it works well. The courtesy bus arrives within minutes, the driver loads your bag, whisks you over to a nice, modern check-in facility on the other side of the airfield, and within a short time you're on your way in a late-model car, content in the knowledge that you're paying substantially less than you would at one of the "majors," whose costs include renting booths in the airport terminals and a car lot within staggering distance of the baggage claim.

But it doesn't always work so smoothly. Perhaps, like me, you've had the experience of a 45-minute wait for the promised courtesy bus to pick you up, followed by a time-consuming drive in busy commercial traffic to a facility several miles away in a dubious neighborhood where you check in at a gloomy office and retrieve your car. Worse still is getting lost in the dark when trying to return the car, and wondering whether the bus will get you back to the airport in time to board your flight. Friendly, courteous employees and a nice car rented at modest rates may be insufficient compensations for the wasted time and mental stress.

Operations and marketing managers are often at odds about where to locate retail service facilities. The former worry about issues such as least cost per square foot, convenient access for delivery trucks and other suppliers, easy maintenance, and good security. Under prodding from the human resources department, they may include access by employees as an additional criterion. Marketers, by contrast, seek a pleasant, safe location that will help define the image of the service organization, often arguing for proximity to other services that the customer may need—especially when their own service is not one that customers would make a special trip to obtain. They usually want a site that customers will find fast and easy to reach from their homes and workplaces by car, public transportation, or on foot, depending on the nature of the business and the local environment.

Common sense should dictate that both marketing and operations viewpoints be considered before a site-selection decision is made in the first place. But it may be a good idea for marketers to research customer reaction to alternative sites so that they can make their case more effectively.

> *Common sense should dictate that both marketing and operational viewpoints be considered before a site-selection decision is made.*

If an existing site is manifestly unsatisfactory, the situation can sometimes be improved by providing customers with better information (maps and signage) or by cosmetic improvements to the exterior of the facilities (trees, flowers, lighting, repainting) to enhance its appearance. But if that is unlikely to solve the problem (cosmetics will do nothing for access time), then the case for a better and more expensive site must be made on the basis of increased revenues and improved customer loyalty.

Design of Facilities and Equipment

A fundamental choice facing all service providers is how to arrange the layout of the work flow with an eye to both efficiency and customer satisfaction. Operations experts identify several alternatives for laying out departments within a service facility. We'll look at three of them.

1. *A job-shop layout*, in which similar equipment or functions are grouped together, requires customers to move from one area to another according to the service activity required. Hotels are a case in point, as are colleges, and many hospitals. Buildings are not always laid out with customer convenience in mind; users may find themselves walking around a lot and even doubling back in their tracks.

2. *A flow-shop or assembly-line layout* is one in which equipment or work processes are arranged linearly according to the progressive steps by which the service is created or assembled. A familiar example is cafeteria service in a restaurant. One marketing challenge is to ensure that the operation has sufficient capacity at each step in the process to avoid bottlenecks and keep the line moving; another is to allow customers to skip steps which they may not need—otherwise they may waste time and become frustrated. Another problem emerges in self-service situations when a customer inadvertently forgets to take a particular step (such as picking up a dessert in the cafeteria line) and is required to repeat the entire process to attend to just one item. Advance instructions, proper signage at each step, sequencing that reflects customers' logic (vegetables after main dishes), and using roving service personnel to assist customers all help to minimize difficulties.

3. A *fixed-position layout* is one where customers remain at a single location and service comes to them. Table service in a restaurant is one example, home shopping services another, and the in-flight portion of airline services (except use of toilets) is a third. It sounds ideal, involving minimal inconvenience for customers. The reality, unfortunately, is not always so rosy. When many customers want service at the same time, there may be insufficient capacity, resulting in extensive delays before service is delivered or even no service at all. Who has not been kept waiting for meal service on board an airliner or in a restaurant? Or for a plumber or an electrician to make a house call?

User-Hostile Facilities and Equipment. Factories are not always very attractive places—they may be noisy, smelly, dirty, ugly, and often vibrate with the pulsing of equipment. That's all very well if employees are not bothered by the situation and good products can be manufactured there efficiently. But it's not good enough for service facilities where customers have to spend time: Given the choice, at equivalent prices, they'll probably select a competitor whose place of business is more welcoming.

Even if they are nicely appointed, service facilities can be confusing for new customers. With clear signage and a layout that is logical to customers, it shouldn't be necessary to ask for directions. And yet, who hasn't become lost in a large airport, department store, or hospital? Perhaps even worse is having to operate confusing pieces of equipment, seemingly designed by technicians for other technicians, rather than for use by technophobic customers in locations where no human assistance is available. User-hostile design of equipment—ranging from ticketing machines to automated banking consoles and from multifunction telephones to hotel clock-radios—is usually a function of inadequate marketing research rather than active contempt for customers, yet it still sends a message that management doesn't care.

A final issue in facilities design has to do with architecture, furnishings, and imagery. Marketers will often argue that service delivery sites should be designed with "atmospherics" in mind, in order to create a desired mood, image, and ambiance for the service organization. Many hotels, for instance, make elaborate attempts to create a dramatic atmosphere in their lobbies and atriums. User-friendly service garages include nicely painted waiting areas with newspapers, a beverage dispenser, a TV, and seats where customers can rest comfortably while their vehicles are being prepared.

The operational mindset may see such efforts as poor space utilization, requiring extra expenditures on climate control and wasteful investment of scarce capital resources in unproductive assets such as coffee machines or artwork and designer furniture. Since operations managers are evaluated on cost control and productivity, they tend to worry about such mundane issues as speed of cleaning, ease of replacing light bulbs in the lobby, fast unloading of delivery trucks, and security from criminals.

But marketers have their eyes focused on the revenue side of the ledger. They will argue for a landscaped exterior with ample parking and for an attractive interior design geared to customer comfort, convenience, and even excitement. They want their customers to feel that they are being served in a friendly environment, rather than being processed like inanimate objects in a hostile factory. They want customers to return in the future and to spread the word to friends and acquaintances. To the extent possible, marketers seek to disguise the factory.

> *Marketers want their customers to feel that they are being served, rather than processed like inanimate objects in a factory. To the extent possible, marketers seek to disguise the factory.*

Both parties should be allowed to have their say in the design and layout of new facilities (or the redesign of existing ones). In high-contact services, the people best equipped to understand the trade-offs may be customer contact employees.

Creative Thinking and Practical Solutions

Historically, operations has been the dominant management function in most service businesses, reflecting its central role in creating and delivering the service. In today's highly competitive service markets, good marketing management has become essential to success. Unfortunately, marketers and operations people sometimes pull in different directions, one advocating improved service features that will appeal to customers, the other emphasizing efficiency and cost control. Coming to terms with the differing and sometimes conflicting perspectives of marketing and operations personnel poses a challenge to both sides.

Even the most ardent customer advocate needs to take time to study operational procedures and to understand the concepts behind them. Understanding how the business works (and why it has been designed to work that way) is a necessary prerequisite to improving customers' satisfaction with service. Employees, too, will benefit from knowing the rationale underlying the ways their work is organized and how it relates to broader goals.

Marketers need to develop an understanding of key operational concepts and strategies, both in general terms and as they apply to specific situations. They must recognize how pursuit of a particular operational strategy contributes to efficiency and results in cost savings, faster service, or other benefits. In addition to determining how a given operational strategy may affect customers, marketers should also ask how a proposed marketing activity may affect operations.

Operations managers should understand that a strategy designed to reduce costs may be equally—or even more—effective in turning off customers and thereby eroding revenues and net profits. Above all, when working in high-contact service environments, operations personnel should recognize that processing human beings is much more complex than processing inanimate objects.

Instead of sticking stubbornly to their own preconceived notions of how to do things, marketers and operations specialists should be looking for creative ways to work together: Marketers may be able to develop customer-oriented strategies designed to make the operation run more efficiently, while operations people can try to reengineer systems to provide better service to customers. Human resource managers may be able to play a pivotal role in designing and filling jobs that serve both objectives without conflict.

Instead of sticking stubbornly to their own preconceived notions of how to do things, marketers and operations specialists should be looking for creative ways to work together.

It takes more than a smoothly running, productive, cost-efficient operation to produce good financial results. The revenues must be there, too. If customers don't like a service because they feel it's tailored more to the supplier's needs than their own, they won't come back. And they'll steer their friends away from it, too. But it's no good overcorrecting and pushing for customer satisfaction at any cost, because that may lead to spiraling costs and operational confusion. The solution lies not in looking for foolish compromises that satisfy no one, but in looking for synergy among operational, marketing, and human resource strategies. We expand on this theme in the next chapter.

"You have reached Galactic Cablevision, offering the best value in home entertainment services. We regret that our antenna tower has collapsed, interrupting reception on most channels, but are happy to reassure viewers that transmission continues on Channel 62 of the West Lakeside City Council meeting. Thanks for calling Galactic and have a nice day!"

5 Product Plus Management: In Pursuit of Compatible Goals

Organizations succeed in the long term by (1) offering their customers better value than competitors; (2) creating a productive operation that offers consistent quality at realistic cost; (3) employing people and suppliers who see value in their relationship with the organization; and (4) creating value for the owners in the form of distributed profits and growing equity in the business. Pursuing congruence among these four goals in an increasingly competitive economy is the essence of product plus management. The common imperative is value.

The Search for Compatibility

One book announces: "The Customer Is Key." Another proclaims: "The Customer Comes Second." Next comes Tom Peters with a *mea culpa*, saying that despite his earlier advocacy of getting close to the customer, you can't really hope to do so until you've first restructured the organization. And then, of course, there's the constant drumbeat from New York and the other bourses of the world, warning executives that unless they improve corporate profits and enhance shareholder equity fast, they'll be in deep doo-doo. What (or whom) is a manager to believe?

If you're running an organization, you're already aware of the potential for conflicts among the differing goals and agendas of the various stakeholders. Senior managers face a continuing challenge as they strive to achieve compatibility among the following four basic forces:

1. *What do we—the organization's management—want?* This question speaks not only to the goals of the owners of the business—profits, growth, and other financially related objectives—but also to the way in which such goals are achieved through marketplace performance, the nature of employee and supplier relationships, impact on the communities in which the firm operates, and expression of the values inherent in the way we choose to do business.

2. *What do our customers want?* What benefits do they expect to obtain from buying and using the goods and/or services that we sell them? What costs are they prepared to incur in return? And what style of relationship are they looking for?

3. *What do our employees and suppliers want?* These two groups provide the labor, skills, and many physical resources we need to run our business. In addition to being paid for their supplies and services, what other benefits do they seek from their relationship with us? What expectations do they have of the process of working with us or for us? (Similar questions can be asked about distributors and other intermediaries who provide services to our own customers.)

4. *What can we do?* With its current resources, what is our organization actually capable of doing?

These forces are shown as four circles in Fig. 5-1. To the extent that the circles overlap, a compatibility exists which bodes well for all parties. Where there is compatibility, there will be synergy in working toward achievement of mutual goals.

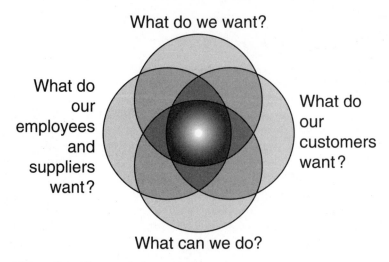

What do we want?

What do
our
employees
and
suppliers
want?

What do
our
customers
want?

What can we do?

Figure 5-1. The search for synergy.

Different Functions, Different Concerns

Traditionally, different management functions have attended to different priorities. When top management asked, "What do we want?," the folks in finance and accounting worried about profit margins, return on investment, and the relative merits of alternative forms of new financing; strategic planners focused on product portfolio and market-share goals; and public affairs specialists took care of investor relations and community outreach. Marketers concerned themselves with responding to the question, "What do our customers want?" Meantime, decisions on "What can we do?" were often seen as the exclusive domain of the powerful operations function. Personnel managers and labor-relations experts tried to deal with "What do our employees want?" (often operating under top-management instructions to give them as little of it as possible, whatever it was); while purchasing and procurement tended to be much more interested in telling suppliers what the firm wanted than in learning what these vendors wanted in return beyond price and payment terms.

Such compartmentalization is totally at odds with the notion of compatible goals and strategic synergy that I call *product plus management*. The "plus" stands for competitive advantage, not only in the market of sales to customers, but also in those other important marketplaces of recruiting and retaining the best employees, building partnerships with the right suppliers and distributors, obtaining new financing on favorable terms, and being seen as a community asset wherever the firm operates.

> *Product plus management stands for competitive advan-*
> *tage in making sales to customers, recruiting and retain-*
> *ing employees, building partnerships with suppliers and*
> *distributors, obtaining new financing, and being per-*
> *ceived as a community asset.*

Happily, the environment of service management has changed and continues to change. Most organizations today express a genuine interest in what customers want (the bigger challenge remains doing something meaningful about giving them just that). The viewpoint on employees is shifting from that of a sometimes troublesome cost center to the organization's most important resource (the change in terminology from "personnel and labor relations" to "human resource management" reflects that shift). Operations managers have closer contact with customers, and some now devote almost as much effort to revenue-enhancing activities as to cost-saving ones. Enlightened firms have also come to realize the value of giving employees extended training and more authority (both confer empowerment), providing them with the resources that they need to make good use of their greater discretion (enablement), and using them as a marketing research tool to feed back ideas on how to serve customers better.

With greater emphasis on core competencies and "back to basics," more companies are now creating partnerships and strategic alliances with suppliers—relationships that require both parties to take a keen interest in what the other wants. Relations with customers are being seen in a similar light. There are signs that some investors are taking a longer-term perspective on the future of the businesses in which they invest, and we seem to be out of the "get rich quick" era of the 1980s with its leveraged buyouts, asset stripping, greenmail, golden parachutes, and penchant for loading up massively on junk bonds. However, the legacy of enormous debt continues to hobble many American service companies at a time when many institutional investors still seem to view their portfolios as little more than a hand of cards in a fast-moving poker game.

How Good Is the Fit in
Your Business?

But enough of the general environment. Let's take another look at Fig. 5-1 and consider your own organization for a moment. Do you see a good fit between the goals of the various players? In the diagram, the four forces driving the business intersect each other at six different points, representing all possible pairings of each force. At each intersection, you need to consider how good the fit is between the relevant pair of forces. I've phrased this issue of compatibility as a series of questions, but of course only you or your colleagues can actually provide the answers. Let's give it a whirl.

- *Is what we (management) want also something that we (the firm) can do?* If not, we are simply whistling in the wind, and our goals are meaningless.

- *Is what we want what our employees and suppliers want?* If not, neither employees nor suppliers will try very hard to help us achieve our corporate goals. And our firm may experience problems in recruitment and retention among both groups.

- *Is what we want what our customers want?* If not, we may gain a reputation as a firm that is unconcerned about customer needs and values; we may come to be seen as a self-centered organization that is interested only in its own goals and agendas and is even willing to ride roughshod over others to get there. (How would you like your firm to be described as "not the sort of company one likes to do business with"?)

- *Is what employees, suppliers, and distributors want what customers want?* If not, customers will quickly detect a lack of interest in recognizing their priorities and the way in which they like to be treated; as a result, they may infer a general lack of enthusiasm for providing customers with quality goods and services.

- *Is what employees and suppliers want what we can do?* If not, we may not be able to pay competitive wages and fees for services rendered, provide satisfactory working conditions and benefits, and offer either the training or the technological leverage that employees require to perform well and at top efficiency; from our suppliers' point of view, we may not be the sort of customer with whom they wish to build a relationship.

- *Is what we can do what our customers want?* If not, then both parties are barking up the wrong tree. Either we must look for different market segments which value what we have to offer, or we must change what we do to bring it into line with what existing customers want. The goal, after all, is to build a base of loyal, long-term customers.

The Key Interest Groups

Underlying these four forces are the needs and concerns of several key interest groups: the *owners* of the business (whose interests may be vested in a board of directors to which senior management is accountable), *employees and suppliers* (who sell their time, talents, or physical products to the organization), and *customers* (who buy and use the outputs of the business).

The distinctions among these interest groups are not necessarily rigid. Senior managers often own part of the business as well as being employees of it. Suppliers, employees, and customers may themselves own shares in the business. In fact, many firms make a practice of encouraging their employees to become shareholders to give them a vested interest in its financial performance, or they create a sense of ownership through profit sharing (some do both). Where provision of labor and expertise is concerned, the distinction between employees and suppliers is sometimes a purely legalistic one—contract workers employed by an external supplier may substitute for employees, while outside professionals, such as consultants and lawyers, may perform work that could also be undertaken by full-time staff.

In any organization, the goal of effective management should be to bring each of the four driving forces into convergence. By doing so, we maximize the shaded area in the middle of Fig. 5-1—the win–win–win–win area where all interest groups enjoy a mutually rewarding relationship.

The Rewards of Loyalty

Relationships that are mutually rewarding lie at the foundation of loyalty. This applies especially to customers and employees.

Customer Loyalty. Economic evidence indicates that serving loyal customers who fit well with the firm's capabilities is more profitable than serving those who soon move on. Frederick Reichheld and Earl Sasser cite industry studies showing steadily rising profits per customer for each year that he or she remains with the same supplier. In year 1, for instance, a new customer of an industrial laundry generates $144 in profits; by year 5, the figure has risen to $256. An automobile service customer is worth only $25 in profits in year 1 but $88 by year 5. For credit card customers the figures are even more extreme: from a net *loss* of $51 to a net profit of $55. Why these differences? The reasons are several:

- New customers cost money to acquire (advertising, sales expenses, credit checks, etc.).

- Customers often make limited use of a service slowly at first and then increase their usage as they become more comfortable with it; in the case of repair and maintenance, older products need more work.

- Operating costs fall as customers become more familiar with the service, are more competent, and need less assistance; selling new services to existing customers is also less costly, since the firm already knows the customers and their needs.

- Established customers may be willing to pay a premium price because of their confidence in the business.

- Satisfied, loyal customers provide free word-of-mouth advertising, generating new referrals without any marketing cost to the company.

The key task, then, is to prevent (or at least reduce) the rate of customer turnover (also known as "churn" in industries such as cable TV). Obtaining new customers to replace lost ones can hit profits hard. In fact, when insurance firms pay high front-end commissions to salespeople, it may take as long as four years for a customer relationship to become profitable.

Many companies experience considerable churn each year. The consulting firm of Bain & Company has found that reducing customer defections by only 5 percent a year may raise the lifetime net present value of an average customer relationship by amounts ranging from 25 to 85 percent. Managers of the credit card business at MBNA, which loses customers at half the overall industry rate, have found that a 5 percent increase in customer retention raises the company's profits by 60 percent by the fifth year.

Employee Loyalty.   Businesses with high employee turnover are frequently stuck in what Leonard Schlesinger and James Heskett call the "cycle of failure." When jobs are low-paying, boring, and repetitive, with minimal training, service is poor and turnover high. Poor service generates high customer turnover, too, making the working environment even less rewarding. As a result, the firm spends all its resources trying to recruit both new customers and new employees. Loyal employees, by contrast, know the job and, in many cases, the customers too. Better service and customer retention should result. We look at the cycle of failure, and its opposite, the cycle of success, in depth in Chap. 20.

Why don't firms try harder to reduce employee turnover? The trouble, says Fred Reichheld, is that "Many companies diminish their economic potential through human resource strategies that ensure high employee turnover, in part because they can't quantify the economics of retaining employees." The same logic applies to independent contractors, such as insurance agents. But he attributes the ongoing success of State Farm Insurance Companies to the interactive effect of both customer and agent retention. According to industry studies, State Farm's customer retention rate exceeds 90 percent, consistently the best performance of all national insurers selling through agents. At the same time, more than 80 percent of newly appointed agents remain associated exclusively with State Farm through their fourth year, compared with only 20 to 40 percent for other companies in the industry. Further, the average State Farm agent has 18 years of tenure compared to between six and nine years for competitors. The fact is, employee retention is central to customer retention, especially where front-line staff are concerned.

> *Employee retention is central to customer retention, especially where front-line staff are concerned.*

The underlying synergy at State Farm arises from the fact that agents who are committed to building a long-term relationship with the company are more likely to build lasting relationships with customers, too. In turn, it's easier for agents to work with (and sell to) loyal customers whose needs, lifestyles, and attitudes to risk they know well. "Agents' experience," says Reichheld, "plus the fact that they spend more time servicing and selling to proven customers, raises agents' productivity to 50 percent above industry norms."

The Value Imperative

So what do all the parties really want, if they are to remain loyal? At bottom, it's *value*. A mutually rewarding relationship implies one in which the benefits outweigh the costs. The term "value" is one that is widely but rather loosely used. Even purchasers of a single product category attach different meanings to the word. For instance, when Valarie Zeithaml asked consumers how they defined value as it related to beverages, she found four broad definitions: (1) value is low price; (2) value is whatever I want in a product; (3) value is the quality I get for the price I pay; and (4) value is what I get for what I give. In my view, the last definition is the most useful, because it implies a trade-off of benefits against costs, yet without limiting costs to just the financial price paid.

The Seesaw of Value

Figure 5-2, which looks like a seesaw with a meter at its axis, tries to capture the trade-off of costs against benefits. On the left end there's a box labeled "Perceived Costs," and on the other end there's a box labeled "Perceived Benefits." In this particular picture, the benefits outweigh the costs of acquiring them, thereby creating positive value. But it could equal-

Figure 5-2. Value = (Benefits − Costs)

ly well have been the other way around, creating negative value. If both ends of the seesaw were totally in balance, then we'd be at the point of indifference.

I emphasize the word *perceived* because people make judgments and decisions based on perceptions, which may differ from what an objective measuring system would define as reality. What one person considers benefits, another may view as a turn off. And what some may see as a burdensome cost, others may ignore.

In most instances, investing in an organization, working for it, supplying it, or purchasing and using its output are voluntary acts. Any decision to engage in a voluntary transaction or relationship involves a trade-off between expected costs and benefits, after factoring in the probability of different outcomes and personal or corporate tolerance for risks.

The most useful way to define the value of a relationship is as the net difference between the streams of perceived costs and benefits that it generates over its lifetime. If the seesaw isn't expected to bump down on the "benefits" side, then there's no perceived value to entering into that relationship. But there's more to the equation. When customers, employees, suppliers, or investors can select just one of several competing alternatives, they'll choose the one that offers them the greatest perceived value. That's why I put the meter in the middle of the seesaw, to indicate that the amount by which benefits are perceived as exceeding costs forms the basis of comparison and choice.

> *The most useful way to define the value of a relationship is as the net difference between the streams of perceived costs and benefits that it generates over its lifetime.*

Real-world seesaws, of course, go up and down as riders shift their weight and flex or straighten their legs. Movement can occur in our model, too. Costs and benefits don't necessarily remain stable over time. As a result, neither does value. A relationship will be broken if, after including switching costs, one of the parties perceives a different alternative as offering better value. This is particularly true of investments, which often change hands with great frequency, especially when the investor has no personal link to the business and no emotional stake in its activities.

In any relationship, it takes two to tango. So value creation cannot be a zero-sum game in which one party wins and the other loses. Both parties—customer and supplier, employee and employer, investor and recipient of funds—must have expectations of receiving value before even an initial transaction can be consummated. The two parties do not sit on opposite ends of the same seesaw; rather they stand observing one of two parallel seesaws in which the monetary elements of the relationship are mirror images: For recipients, it's a benefit; for payers, it's a cost. (Third-party payments may change even this limited symmetry.)

Creating Value for Customers

Goods and services are purchased, of course, for the benefits that customers expect them to deliver. As one observer once put it rather pithily, "People...buy quarter-inch holes, not quarter-inch drills."

Research may tell us what customers think they want. Frequent purchasers of a familiar product can usually tell us exactly what benefits they're looking for and what they're prepared to pay to get them. They will also tell us, rather pointedly, what they don't want. Inexperienced customers or prospective purchasers of new goods and services are more likely to have trouble articulating their needs. Consultation often plays a vital role in helping them clarify what their needs are and what might constitute a satisfactory solution.

But maximizing benefits (which are often highly specific to particular product categories) represents only one side of the value equation: Creating true value also means minimizing perceived costs. The nice thing about costs (from a purely analytical standpoint) is that it's easier to generalize about them across product categories than it is to generalize about benefits, which tend to be highly product-specific.

In most people's minds, costs begin with *monetary prices*, although firms love to use euphemisms for that simple term. Service businesses, in particular, use a wide variety of terms to describe the prices they charge their customers. Colleges and training institutes talk about tuition, professionals set fees, and banks impose service charges as well as calculating the interest payable on loans. Turnpikes establish a toll, magazine publishers a subscription, transport services a fare, brokers a commission, insurance firms a premium, landlords a rent, museums an admission charge, and hotels a room rate.

Customers may incur several other key costs in buying and using goods and services:

- *Time* is a precious commodity for many people. There are no time billionaires, since nobody has more than more than 24 hours a day available. Like me, you probably talk about time in monetary terms: investing it, spending it, wasting it, affording it, and budgeting it. As with money, there's an opportunity cost associated with spending time on any one activity, since we may be taking it away from another. But sometimes we can economize on time by paying more money for a time-saving product that requires less time of its user, subcontracting certain tasks to third parties, or purchasing a faster class of service.

  It's not only time spent by the customer during the service delivery process that matters, but also the elapsed time between starting and completing the service process. People don't always perceive the passage of time in the same way as it's measured by the clock. In particular, time wasted—especially under unpleasant conditions—is typically viewed as more onerous and passing more slowly than time spent doing something useful or pleasant. Psychological studies of public transportation users have shown that travelers perceive time spent waiting for a transit vehicle as passing from 1.5 to 7 times more slowly than the time actually spent traveling on it.

> **There are no time billionaires, since nobody has more than 24 hours a day available.**

- *Physical effort* is involved in using goods and services. Self-service, in particular, often requires customers to substitute their labor (and time) for that of the selling organization. A customer's physical condition may set absolute limits as to the acceptable level of physical effort.

- *Psychic costs* are sometimes attached to the use of particular goods and services—mental effort, feelings of inadequacy, and even fear. These costs may be perceived as especially high by inexperienced new customers.

- *Sensory costs* are those that are experienced physically by customers (over and beyond physical effort). They may include putting up with noise, unpleasant smells, drafts, excessive heat or cold, uncomfortable seats, visually unappealing sights, and even unpleasant tastes from food, drink, or medicine.

To summarize, a strategy of adding value may involve increasing perceived benefits, reducing perceived costs, or both jointly. Money is only one of several costs. There's ample evidence that many customers are willing to trade off money against other types of costs as well as against benefits: They ride expensive taxis on the same route taken by a cheaper bus; they pay a surcharge for express service to get their clothes back faster from the cleaners; and they send packages by "next day" service when two- or three-day service would get it to the same destination for a fraction of the price. I believe strongly that creating value requires rigorous analysis of all possibilities on both the cost and benefit sides of the equation.

> *Creating value requires rigorous analysis of all possibilities on both the cost and benefit sides of the equation.*

The desire to obtain certain benefits and to avoid certain costs is often very situation specific. Let me give you an example. When self-service gas pumps were first being installed in service stations during the late 1970s, some colleagues and I undertook research to determine what incentives drivers would require to switch from being served by a station attendant to pumping their own fuel. Specifically, we were interested in both price incentives and the opportunity to save time.

We tested a draft questionnaire on a small sample of drivers, asking them (1) how many minutes of time per transaction they would need to save before they would use the self-service pumps, and (2) how many cents off per gallon would convince them to make the same switch. To our chagrin, the answers came back loud and clear: "It all depends...." Clearly, more research was needed. "Depends on what?" we asked participants in several, specially convened focus groups. This time, the responses were quite varied. On the weather, said one. On the time of day, declared another. On how I'm dressed, how much of a hurry I'm in, who's with me in the car, what brand of gas the station is selling, stated others.

We concluded that the only way to get a meaningful response was to be very specific in wording the questionnaire. So, in the full-scale survey, this is how we prefaced the question: "It is 10 a.m. on a fine day. You are driving alone in casual clothes and need to fuel your car tank. You drive into a gas station which offers your usual brand and find that it offers two choices...." The upshot was that we obtained an excellent response rate and useful results.

Value Creation for Employees

The same lines of reasoning on costs and benefits also apply to jobs. When people talk about job benefits, we usually think of pay, health insurance, and pension funding. However, most jobs also generate other benefits (otherwise, why would people ever do voluntary work?) Some jobs are seen as learning or experience-building opportunities; some positions provide deep satisfaction because they are inherently interesting or provide a sense of accomplishment; still others provide companionship, a valued chance to meet other people, feelings of dignity and self-worth, opportunities to travel, and the chance to make a social contribution. And let's not forget a sense of fun: Advertising agency founder Jerry Della Femina once described working in advertising as "the most fun you can have with your clothes on."

But working in any job has its costs, too. The most obvious is the time commitment required—not only on the job, but also traveling to and from work. Most jobs also entail some monetary costs, ranging from special clothes to commuting to child care. Stress can be a psychic cost of a demanding job. Unpleasant working conditions may constitute sensory costs, involving exposure to noise, smells, and temperature extremes. And, of course, some jobs require intense physical or mental effort.

Decisions to change the nature of the service operation ("What we can do") frequently affect employees, too. The perceived value of their jobs may go up or down as a result. But not everybody has the same priorities and concerns: There is segmentation among employees as well as among customers. Part of the human resources challenge is to match round pegs to round holes of the right diameter. Savvy human resource managers know that if a job is changed through redesign, it will become more or less attractive to certain types of employees—and they can usually predict which ones.

Job design cannot be restricted just to ensuring that the firm gets its money's worth out of employees. It must also consider the design of the working environment, asking whether employees have the tools and facilities they need to deliver excellent service. To an increasing degree, health and safety legislation is requiring changes in the workplace to eliminate physical and even psychological hazards, but only management can create a positive working climate—and that takes a long time.

Reducing the negative aspects of the job and improving its positive ones may make it easier for firms to hire and retain the best available employees, without having to pay premium salaries and load up on conventional "benefits." Employees who enjoy their work are more likely than unhappy ones to give good service to customers.

> *Reducing the negative aspects of the job and improving its positive ones may make it easier for firms to hire and retain the best available employees.*

Value Creation for Investors and Owners

The value of investments to their owners tends to be easier to assess than the value of products to customers or jobs to employees. It's simpler, after all, to compute and analyze monetary values than to come up with a common denominator for a host of very different costs and benefits that mean different things to different people. But one can't ignore the psychological element. Investors are human, they have different priorities, and they vary in their willingness to accept risk.

The first Lord Rothschild, head of the British branch of the great international banking family, was once approached by a wealthy industrialist seeking advice. A meeting was duly arranged, and, on the appointed day, the visitor was ushered into Rothschild's London office. After opening pleasantries, the banker asked how he might be of service.

"My Lord," the industrialist began, "I have amassed a fortune of 1 million pounds." That was a very substantial amount of money in late nineteenth-century Britain, and Rothschild, although he was worth a lot more himself, nodded approvingly and expressed suitable compliments. "My question to you is this," the visitor continued: "What should I do to be sure of having exactly the same amount of money until the day I die?"

Lord Rothschild looked at the other in astonishment for a moment; then he opened a drawer in his exquisite antique desk and took out a small pistol. Handing it to the industrialist, he replied, "My dear sir, there's only one way. Use this immediately!"

Although reasonable people recognize that some degree of uncertainty surrounds all investments, it's important that managers understand the investment objectives of those who own the business for which they work. At the cost of tying up their capital and foregoing the safe, predictable return of government bonds, the owners—whose share may be small or large—are looking for certain benefits. But have these expectations been clearly articulated? Are the owners' goals long-term or short-term? What level of return are they looking for? How important is consistency of returns in terms of a predictable amount every year? Do they want profits that will be redistributed promptly in the form of large dividends, or are they more interested in long-term capital appreciation, to be achieved by reinvesting all or most of the profits in the business? Are they actively interested in the firm and its particular line of business? Will they stick with their holdings during difficult times as well as good ones, or will they look to sell out the moment they spot a better opportunity? Will they eagerly agree to a takeover or a radical restructuring involving mass lay-offs if that will lead to an immediate increase in the value of their equity?

A special case of investment concerns not-for-profit organizations, where donors and government funders expect some form of social profit to result in return for their gifts and funding. Although such societal benefits may be harder to quantify than cash dividends, it's still important to understand what these "investors" are looking for in terms of the institution's performance.

As many chief executives can attest, life becomes very difficult for a business whose strategic goals are out of sync with investor expectations. Robert Ferris, former CEO of UAL, never got a chance to test his belief that the best long-term strategy for the company lay in integrating the activities of United Airlines, Westin Hotels, and Hertz Rent-a-Car to better serve travelers who required all three services. Investors wanted an increase in equity value, and they wanted it *now*. So Ferris was placed in the ejector seat, as were the company's hotel and rental car subsidiaries, and blasted out of UAL. We'll never know for sure if Ferris was doing the best thing for the long-term future of the company. We do know that UAL got a handsome price for the two subsidiaries and that its stock price rose sharply—in the short run.

Creating a Service That Customers Will Value

When you're starting from scratch in designing a new service, how do you determine what mix of features and price will create the best value for your target customers? Traditionally, innovative new goods and services have been created by artists, architects, designers, and R&D engineers. But these people, however talented, may not know exactly what prospective customers really value. When the Marriott Corporation was designing a new chain of hotels for business travelers (which eventually became known as Courtyard by Marriott), it hired marketing research experts to help establish an optimal design.

Common sense indicates that there are limits to how much service can be offered at any given price, and so the objective of the research was to find out what customers' preferred mix would be—rather than having designers simply prescribe the most "appropriate" mix. The research technique employed by these consultants is called conjoint analysis. Prospective customers are asked to trade off different service features in an effort to determine which ones they value most.

The Courtyard study surveyed both business and nonbusiness travelers. It considered seven sets of attributes, each containing a variety of different features (themselves based on detailed studies of competing offerings):

- External factors (e.g., building shape, pool, landscaping)

- Room features (e.g., size, decor, bathroom design, amenities, entertainment systems)

- Food-related services (e.g., restaurant type and location, menu, room service, vending service)

- Lounge facilities (e.g., atmosphere, policy on nonresident customers)

- Services (e.g., reservations, check-in/out, airport limo, message service, laundry/valet, secretarial)

- Leisure facilities (e.g., sauna, whirlpool, sports, exercise room, electronic games, playground)

- Security (e.g., security guard, 24-hour video, alarm)

Respondents were presented with a number of alternative profiles, each featuring different levels of performance on the various attributes contained in the seven factors; in some instances, certain premium service elements were omitted altogether. They were asked to indicate on a 5-point scale how likely they would be to stay at a hotel with these features, given a specific room price per night. Using a sophisticated research design and powerful statistical techniques, the researchers were able to come up with an optimal design for business travelers in the target market segment. Since the results focused not only on what the travelers wanted, but also identified what they did not want to pay for, the design team was able to meet the specified price while retaining those features most desired by the target market. The corporation then went ahead with the design, creating in Courtyard by Marriott a hotel concept that filled a gap in the market with a product that represented the best balance between price and desired physical and service features.

The success of this project led Marriott to develop additional customer-driven products—Fairfield Inn and Marriott Suites—using the same research methodology. Designers of other services who are interested in creating customer value might usefully employ the same approach. And there's every reason to believe that versions of this methodology could be used to get a better idea of how employees and investors make trade-offs in order to maximize the value to them of jobs and investments.

In Search of Value

The ability to create value is at the heart of product plus management. But it takes more than just good products and great service to customers. Management must work to create value for owners, employees, suppliers, distributors, and other stakeholders, too.

Organizations succeed in the long term by creating loyal relationships with customers, employees, suppliers, distributors, and investors in which each party finds value. That means that the benefits of entering into and maintaining the relationship must exceed its perceived costs (and every relationship, every transaction, has its costs). But it would be a mistake to assume that all value can be reduced to a monetary basis, for as we have seen, benefits and costs are frequently nonmonetary in nature.

It would also be a mistake to assume that product plus organizations immediately lose their crowns if they fail to perform splendidly on every dimension every year. Changing times and the ups and downs of the economy mean that some years will be less successful than others. But such organizations are better placed to ride out rough times. They have a larger reservoir of customer goodwill, greater employee and supplier loyalty, and both the financial reserves and the track record to survive temporary blips in their performance as investments.

6 The Search for Synergy in Service Management

Successful service businesses create operations and delivery systems that simultaneously appeal to their target customers, are well matched to the capabilities of a willing work force, and allow the firm to operate efficiently. To illustrate these principles, we look at two entrepreneurs trying to design a chain of haircutting salons; visit Firstdirect, a British bank with no branches that uses computers and telecommunications to interact with busy customers 24 hours a day; and revisit Southwest Airlines to see how a contrarian approach to operations has created air service that suits its target customers so well that it made Southwest the most profitable airline in America.

A key challenge for designers of new services is to achieve a match between the nature of the operation, the skills and interests of employees, and the desires of target customers, while also meeting the goals of the owners of the business. Success in this endeavor is a function of product plus management by which everybody wins.

When the match is poor (or missing altogether), customers are likely to be turned off, employees may become discouraged, and profits will prove elusive. A good match, by contrast, can provide the innovator with a commanding advantage, even against larger and more established competitors.

To illustrate this point, we'll look at three service companies in three very different industries: haircutting, retail banking, and passenger airline service. Each, through its success or failure, illustrates the importance of seeking synergy in service management.

A Mismatch Between Service Experience and Customer Preferences

Once upon a time, haircutting was a classic cottage industry. There were services for women, who had their hair washed, cut, and styled at hairdressers or beauty salons. And there were services for men, who obtained short-back-and-sides at barber shops. Over time, fashions started to change, especially among younger customers. Many men grew their hair longer and sought to look a little more stylish than their dads. Many women adopted practical, easy styles that took less effort to maintain than traditional styles. Unisex hair salons evolved to serve these needs, but they remained owner-operated businesses.

By the mid-1970s, the success of McDonald's and other fast-food chains in "industrializing" the cooking and delivery of simple menus was laying the basis for business system franchising on a much broader scale. Creative entrepreneurs came to believe that a wide array of proven services could be cloned for profitable replication as company-owned stores or as franchises.

Some years back, two young business school students, Matt and George, developed a plan for a chain of unisex haircutting salons, which they named Flair. Not for them the slow climb to the top of the corporate ladder after getting their MBAs. These prospective entrepreneurs had a bright idea for what was then a new service concept, and they hoped to make a lot of money by putting it into practice.

Reflecting the rigorous training of their operations management course, Matt and George thought carefully about staffing issues, the physical layout of the store, and its decor. They also looked at how customers would move through the service process, from first entering the store and being greeted at reception, through waiting, washing, cutting, drying, and brushing, to payment and exiting.

Operations and Service Delivery

Since the chain would offer only a limited selection of hairstyles for both men and women, customers could expect faster service at Flair than in a conventional hair salon. The two MBA students figured that so long as the end result looked and felt good, speeding up the process would be seen as a competitive advantage by clients. It would also mean that cutters would be more productive.

To customize the experience yet avoid the need for clients to reserve the services of a specific cutter, Matt and George developed a methodology for examining each person's preferred styling according to the quadrants of the head. This analysis would be recorded and filed, so that any cutter could easily retrieve the file and get a good sense of that customer's preferences. Newly hired cutters would, of course, need training in using this methodology; the two MBAs believed that offering this expertise would help them attract younger cutters who could be paid lower wages than more experienced ones, thus keeping down labor costs.

Marketing Considerations

Next, the two budding entrepreneurs put on their marketing hats. They defined the market segments for their chain as middle- and upper-middle-income women and men, aged 18–40, with an average age of 27. Within that group, the most desirable customers were those who either held jobs that allowed them to take time out during the workday or stayed home in the daytime, since they were likely to be more flexible about the timing of appointments and thus enable Flair to make the best use of its cutters' time.

The stores, Matt and George decided, would be located within easy reach of target customers' homes or workplaces, with site selection emphasizing easily accessible urban locations that had an emphasis on retail fashion. Prices for a shampoo, cut, and blow-dry would be set in the middle of the range for the haircutting industry, which should generate sufficient revenues for the chain to cover its costs and generate a satisfactory return on investment.

The Flaw in the Concept

At first blush, the idea looked terrific. Matt and George were very excited. But as they studied it further and discussed it with others, they came to see that the concept had one serious flaw. For they realized that there was a poor fit between the experience and benefits promised by Flair's delivery system and the desires of its target customers. A haircutting store that served both sexes and offered a limited set of hairstyles delivered by inter-changeable cutters was more likely to appeal to students, teenagers, and young clerical workers than to the group they had hoped to attract. But these younger customers would probably be rather price-sensitive.

> *There was a poor fit between the experience and benefits promised by Flair's delivery system and the desires of its target customers.*

Their conclusion? Either the operation would have to be redesigned to better match the preferences of the chosen market segment or, more plausibly, the chain would have to target those market segments that were looking for the benefits offered by the planned delivery system, reduce its prices accordingly, and expect lower profits.

In the upshot, Matt and George chose not to proceed with Flair. However, many of their ideas were subsequently used by a successful chain that focused on a younger market, kept operating costs down by renting space in less expensive locations, and charged lower prices.

Firstdirect: The Branchless Bank

Think of the head office of a sizable bank. What comes to mind? Is it a gleaming skyscraper, the tallest building in town (until a competitor or an insurance company builds something even bigger)? Or is it, perhaps, an impressive neoclassical building that one enters through Corinthian columns into a high-ceilinged banking hall, decorated in marble and mahogany?

To those accustomed to such architectural statements, the head office of Firstdirect—Britain's newest bank—comes as something of a surprise. It's a low, modern shedlike building with reflecting glass windows in an industrial park on the edge of Leeds, 170 miles north of London. By late 1993, Firstdirect was heading toward 500,000 retail accounts throughout the nation, but this unprepossessing building (plus a planned extension) was expected to remain the bank's one and only "branch."

What's going on here? How can a bank operating nationwide survive without a large branch network? And what about the customers? How do they get at their money, pay in deposits, obtain mortgages, and undertake all the other transactions found in traditional retail banking?

Firstdirect is the world's first branchless nationwide bank and the first bank to offer telephone-based, person-to-person service, 24 hours a day, 365 days a year.

Firstdirect is the world's first branchless nationwide bank and the first bank to offer telephone-based, person-to-person service 24 hours a day, 365 days a year.

The Genesis of Firstdirect

Most retail banking services in Britain are provided by large banks and building societies (savings and loan organizations) that operate nationwide. The "Big Four" banks (Barclays, Lloyds, Midland, and National Westminster) control a huge share of the market, and their offices can be found on almost every high street (main street) in the country. If research findings, reports by investigative journalists, and the contents of political debates are any guide, nobody likes them very much. Some of the charges leveled at them are that they are too big, too unresponsive, overly bureaucratic, prone to overcharging, and slow to correct errors.

It was in this context that a group of younger executives at Midland Bank was assigned the task of finding new ways for the bank to increase its market share, especially among professional and managerial customers. Midland was unable to achieve such growth through acquisition and saw that it would be extremely difficult to do so simply by organic growth. Among other things, the industry was oversupplied, profits were hard to achieve, cost cutting was widespread, and hostile customers were demanding higher levels of service.

The task force concluded that there was a need for an altogether new approach to consumer banking: Traditional processes needed to be totally reengineered. As team members researched consumer opinions and studied changing lifestyles, they found that customers were making progressively less use of the retail branch network. A national survey revealed that 51 percent of all respondents preferred to visit their branch as little as possible and that 27 percent wished there were more things they could get their bank to do for them by telephone. But over three-quarters of those interested in a telephone banking service wanted a real person on the other end of the line, not a computer.

In search of more insights, the team surveyed retail banking markets in Europe, North America, and Australia. It found that large numbers of banking transactions were being conducted by telephone, but most such transactions were simply extensions of the branch network and often limited to normal working hours. Other telephone-based services required customers to use a telephone keypad to interact with a voice-activated computer. The team concluded that none of the existing "telebanking" models could be adapted to supply the desired range of banking services. Instead, an entirely new type of bank would have to be created.

A proposal for what would become Firstdirect was presented to Midland's senior management. It would be a branchless 24-hour bank, accessed entirely by telephone (or mail) and offering its customers a full array of retail services, with very competitive charges and interest rates. In autumn 1988, Midland accepted the recommendations and appointed Michael Harris as chief executive to head the new bank. He was given one year to develop and implement the operation.

Implementation: Designing the Technology

Because of the difficulty of obtaining a bank charter from the Bank of England, the new bank was constituted as a division of Midland. For reasons of speed and economy, the development group also decided to use Midland's back office systems and to run account data on its mainframe. And since Firstdirect would have only one branch, which its customers would never visit, their need to obtain cash would be satisfied by the same network of automated machines used by Midland customers. In all other respects, however, Firstdirect was designed as a separate entity, to be operated as independently as possible of its parent.

> *"Normal banking procedures simply did not apply. We had to create a workable system that would be the servant, not the master, of those using it."*

Creating the necessary human and technical systems presented a key challenge. One telephone link had to replace the functions normally delivered by five or six employees in different departments. Moreover, as one officer put it, "We had to be able to respond in seconds, not minutes—normal banking procedures simply did not apply. We had to create a workable system that would be the servant, not the master, of those who would be using it. It had to be a high-performance system that was both flexible and easy to use. To the maximum possible extent, customer transactions, questions, and problems had to be handled within a single phone call."

Several people from Firstdirect visited the United States in search of suitable hardware and software but found none that could meet all their requirements. Instead they selected an automatic call distributor (ACD) switch used by an aerospace firm in Houston, chose video screens (from a telephone company in Atlanta) that would be compatible with a variety of computer sources, and obtained software from a bank in Baltimore.

Job Design, Recruitment, and Training

Providing banking services by telephone was seen as a very different job from traditional branch-office positions. The average teller ("cashier" in British usage) working in a branch has to be something of a jack-of-all-trades, handling large quantities of cash, working with both a computer terminal and paper-based transactions, and spending most of the day in face-to-face contact with customers. Customers with specialized banking requirements have to be directed to an inquiry desk.

Telephone banking would be very different, Firstdirect management concluded. There would be no need for someone who was a whiz at counting out stacks of bank notes, examining customer deposit slips, or spotting forged signatures. Since normal banking methods just didn't apply, neither would normal banking job descriptions.

> *There would be no need for someone who was a whiz at counting out stacks of bank notes, examining customer deposit slips, or spotting forged signatures.*

"Banking representatives"—as Firstdirect decided to call its front-line employees—would need strong communication capabilities and excellent listening skills. These skills would be more important than banking experience. Neither customers nor banking representatives (BRs) would see each other, let alone know the other person, so it was all the more vital to create trust and confidence. BRs would have to sound friendly and well informed over the phone and be able to access and input data accurately and efficiently. Speed would be important, not only to achieve productivity goals but also to meet customers' expectations of prompt service. However, a customer must not feel unduly rushed.

Hiring criteria stressed maturity; Firstdirect would not employ recent high school leavers since they lacked good telephone presence. What recruiters looked for was confident people with a positive attitude who could project themselves well and convey a sense of energy. "If you're not putting that over," remarked one human resource manager, "You're lost!" Strong listening skills were seen as particularly important, because customers wanted reassurance that their needs were understood, particularly when seeking advice as to what type of service would best meet their own situations. Finally, recruiters were looking for systematic, well-organized people who could work together in teams.

As it turned out, Firstdirect found itself deluged with job applications. Many people were attracted by the excitement of working for an innovative organization; others liked the opportunity to work full-time outside normal 9–5 hours, and still others were looking for part-time work; the presence of a child-care center in the building was a particular plus for working parents with small children. Subsequent recruitment in later years has been equally productive.

Successful applicants (then and now) receive six weeks of intensive training, three of which are classroom-based. Topics include product knowledge, relevant banking procedures, and technical skills in using the equipment and understanding the screens—the different displays that appear on the monitors.

New recruits also learn personal skills to help them develop effective telephone techniques. Voice control involves the development of physical skills in pitch, tone, and authority. After all, telephone-based personnel are like actors in a radio drama who never see their audience; everything from friendliness to competence must be conveyed through the voice. And finally they learn customer-development skills, such as spotting potential opportunities to sell new services. In this task, they are aided by the computer, which prompts for certain products based on analysis of that customer's characteristics.

The First Three Years

Firstdirect opened for business in October 1989. Its initial marketing actions were designed to set it apart from traditional banks. Innovative advertising included two television "firsts." One involved interrupting a car manufacturer's ad (by prior permission!) with a special bulletin promoting Firstdirect. The other involved running specially synchronized ads on two separate TV channels. At the end of the ad, viewers watching on one channel were invited to tune to the other channel to see an alternative perspective on Firstdirect. And in a pointed reference to its 7-day-a-week operation, the bank first opened its phone lines for business on a Sunday.

Growth was rapid and steady. In late 1992, Firstdirect announced that it had reached breakeven with 350,000 accounts and that it was adding new accounts at the rate of 10,000 to 12,000 a month. Customer surveys showed high levels of satisfaction with service and found that some 28 percent of new customers came from word-of-mouth recommendations.

Reflecting this rapid expansion, the offices in Leeds are in a constant state of change. "We started with 200 people, now we have 1400," Mike Siddons, director of operations, told me. "At any given time, we currently have up to 600 working on site, but that number drops to under 50 when calls are at their lowest levels during the middle of the night. One of our challenges is to keep up the level of energy and enthusiasm as we grow."

An Inside Look

Upon arriving at the bank's offices in Leeds, I was struck by the sheer scale of the operation. The building is huge—100,000 square feet of space on a single open floor, with an additional 80,000 square feet planned for a nearby site. Although Firstdirect employees never see their customers, everyone is smartly dressed. There's no one here in sweaters and jeans. "We want to maintain a sense of professionalism," explains Siddons. On the other hand, professionalism does not mean stuffiness. The building has an open plan, with just low partitions to baffle the sound of numerous conversations. The mood is friendly and democratic, with everyone—from BR to chief executive—on first-name terms. That's quite a contrast from traditional banking culture, especially in Britain.

Most staff members appear to be in the 25–45 age range, although some are older, and at least one is in a wheelchair. When taking calls, employees are seated in stations that handle a cluster of four people. These clusters, in turn, are grouped on the floor into different areas of specialization, such as customer service, financial services and lending, mortgages, investment services, Visa credit cards, and foreign services.

Large electronic screens on the wall display current performance levels. The goal is to answer 80 percent of calls within 20 seconds or less. The screens display for all to see the percentage of calls meeting that time goal during the past five minutes, together with the number of customers currently waiting to speak with someone in that group.

About 85 percent of calls (20,000 a day in late 1993) can be handled by BRs; most calls last between two and six minutes. More specialized needs are referred to one of the other groups. In a nice touch, customers are told how long they may expect to wait on the line to speak with someone in another group, asked whether they wish to hold or be called back later, and—if they elect to hold—given a choice between listening to recorded music or simple silence.

When a prospective customer inquires about opening an account, the new accounts representative first answers the caller's questions and then offers to send out a package containing more information and an application form. If the caller agrees, the employee immediately downloads the person's name and address to the mailing area, where a personalized letter is automatically printed, bundled with a brochure and application form, and inserted into an envelope for mailing.

How about security? I ask. To verify his or her identity and mailing address, the applicant is asked to provide a copy of a recent utility bill. The information requested on the application includes date and place of birth. If the application is accepted, the new customer will be asked to supply three other pieces of personal information: a memorable date (other than birthday), a memorable address (other than the current one), and mother's maiden name. In turn, Firstdirect's computer will assign the customer an account number and a secret four-digit code. These various pieces of information are then used randomly as a screening device. I learn how when I'm invited to listen in on several calls.

Julia has been a banking representative for 15 months. Her previous experience includes several years as a police officer, followed by two years' hotel work abroad. She puts on her headset and presses the button that connects her to the system. Immediately, a call comes through. "Hello, Firstdirect, how may I help you?" she asks. The customer, who is obviously experienced in use of the system, begins by giving his name and account number. Julia enters the number, and the account flashes on the screen. The computer prompts her to ask for the second and fourth digits of his code. Julia enters these without seeing anything but x x x x on the screen. These digits entered and accepted, the computer now prompts for his mother's maiden name, which is displayed for Julia to see. The caller provides the name, and Julia checks that it's correct. Now the customer is free to proceed with his request, which involves payment of several bills and transfer of funds between accounts.

Each of the calls that follows is different. Julia handles them all pleasantly and knowledgeably, putting one caller on hold (with his permission) while she asks a product specialist about a specific problem. Calls come in from all over the country. The extent of the customer's banking relationship varies from one account to several, including loans and Visa cards. And each has a different request to make. One customer inquires about opening an additional account; Julia answers several questions and offers to send him an information package. He hems and haws for a moment and then agrees. Julia thanks him and promises to get it to him promptly, downloading his name, address, and request to the mailroom as she speaks.

Another Eternal Triangle

Back with Mike Siddons again, I asked him about what, other than a rapid growth rate, constitutes success for Firstdirect. He responded by sketching an inverted triangle, standing on its apex, which he labeled "quality." Against the other two corners he wrote "costs" and "income," respectively. "These three things are forever interacting and fighting against one another," he stated. "We must keep the three in balance, otherwise the business—the triangle—will topple over. We have to manage recruitment, training, work flow, and systems for optimum efficiency at the same time that advertising and referrals are generating a steady flow of new business. And we have to maintain the quality of our services in order to retain and grow the income we get from our existing customers. That has everything to do with the quality of telephone service at our front desk."

> *"Quality, costs, and income are forever interacting and fighting against one another....We have to keep the three in balance, otherwise the business will topple over."*
>
> **MIKE SIDDONS**

How well is 24-hour person-to-person banking working? One piece of evidence is that other banks in Europe and North America are adopting the concept. In Spain, for example, Banco Directo has become Europe's second all-telephone bank. And in the United States, Boston-based BayBank has added full-service personal contact to its existing 24-hour automated services. Others plan to follow.

And what about Firstdirect's own performance relative to its competitors? Perhaps the best evidence as I write comes from the November 1992 issue of *Which?* (the British equivalent of *Consumers' Report*), which studied 15 banks and building societies that together account for nearly all retail banking activity in Britain. Firstdirect was listed among the five best in terms of overall satisfaction. Yet Midland (recently merged with the Hongkong & Shanghai Banking Group), along with two of the other "Big Four," was listed among the three worst performers. Not long afterwards,

Mike Siddons was transferred back to Midland to help transfuse it with the insights gained at Firstdirect. With luck, the child shall lead the parent.

Swimming Profitably Against the Tide at Southwest Airlines

Southwest Airlines, which I introduced in Chap. 1, has always been a maverick in the airline industry. At the outset, what turned heads was Southwest's then-unconventional marketing strategies, with its zany promotions, outrageous stewardess uniforms, off-peak discount prices, creative advertising, and attention-getting public relations activities.

When the Dallas–Fort Worth (DFW) Airport opened in 1974, far from the center of town, it was not immediately popular with Dallas-based passengers used to the convenience of nearby Love Field. Other airlines moved out to DFW, but Southwest refused, stating that its flights would continue to use Love Field until the runways were plowed up and seeded with cotton.

One small but sore point among DFW users was that not only did phoning downtown Dallas cost 25 cents rather than a dime, but the mean-spirited airport authority had installed dollar-bill changing machines next to the public phones that returned only 95 cents in change. Upon learning this fact, Southwest's president arranged for the dollar-bill changers at Love Field to give out $1.05 in change, as a way of promoting the better value offered by his airline. The press covered this news with enthusiasm, and the DFW machines were soon reprogrammed to provide their hapless users with a better rate of return.

But communications, however clever, deliver only a promise. Southwest Airlines owes its long-term success to continuing efforts to provide customers with better value than competitors. Through organic growth it has expanded to become America's seventh largest passenger airline and the only one to post a profit for 20 years in a row (no mean feat when competitors have been losing hundreds of millions or even seeking the protection of the bankruptcy courts).

How do they do it? you wonder. Perhaps it's through high fares and lavish standards of service? No, it's not high fares: Southwest has positioned itself since its founding as a low-fare airline. And it's not lavish service either—at least not in terms of lobster-and-champagne meals, individual video screens with a choice of 40 channels, or luxurious leather seats. After all, Southwest has the lowest costs per seat mile of any American carrier (and perhaps the lowest in the Western world). You don't achieve that ranking by splurging on frills. Well, then, are they nonunion, working their employees like dogs for rotten wages and no benefits? To the contrary, the great majority of employees are unionized, earning good wages, and 30 percent of them collectively own 10 percent of the company's outstanding shares.

> *Over the past 20 years, Southwest's management has spent at least as much time courting its employees as it has the passengers they serve.*

Part of the secret lies in the fact that, over the past 20 years, Southwest's management has spent at least as much time courting its employees as it has the passengers they serve. As CEO Herbert Kelleher says, "If you don't treat your employees right, they won't treat other people well." An equally important secret of Southwest's success lies in the nature of its operations strategy.

A Contrarian Approach to Operations

From an operational perspective, Southwest refuses to play by the rules of conventional airline wisdom (except those relating to safety, of course). It will not interline with other carriers, which means that it will not transfer passenger baggage to or from flights on other airlines, nor will it accept tickets written on other carriers. It offers no assigned seating. And it serves only the most basic of refreshments.

There's more. Southwest declines to build its operations around large-scale hub-and-spoke systems that would allow it to offer a wide array of connecting flights from almost any airport in its system; instead, the vast majority of its routes are designed around short-haul, point-to-point services. It prefers to avoid mega-airports such as DFW or Chicago's O'Hare in favor of secondary airports such as Love Field or Midway. It has resisted the temptation to become an international carrier, offer transcontinental service, or even to fly to Hawaii. And its fleet consists of only one type of aircraft: Boeing 737s; at last count, Southwest had over 150 of them and continues to expand its fleet.

Each of these deliberate choices has implications for productivity and cost reduction. Lower costs allow Southwest to charge lower fares. Lower fares attract more passengers. More passengers mean more frequent flights, which in turn attracts more passengers, especially business travelers who appreciate the convenience (flights depart every 15–30 minutes on the busy Dallas-to-Houston route). More flights, more passengers, and lower costs have meant profits even in bad years. And that translates into lower financing costs when the airline wants to buy or lease new aircraft—which it does with great frequency.

Elements of Operating Strategy

Let's now take a closer look at the elements of Southwest's operating strategy and at their implications for passengers and employees as well as for cost control.

No Interline.   Some airlines with complementary routes like to feed each other with business, issuing through-tickets on flights with well-matched schedules. Southwest won't do this because such a strategy would make all its passengers dependent on the on-time performance of another carrier. Refusing to transfer bags between its own flights and those of other airlines may seem churlish, but it speeds up the turnaround time between arrival and departure. And declining to accept another carrier's ticket for a trip on the same route greatly simplifies Southwest's accounting. In 1989, the airline estimated that not interlining saved it $25 million a year. That figure is undoubtedly higher today.

No Assigned Seating.   Don't ask for a window or an aisle seat when booking a Southwest flight, because they can't give it to you. The airline operates on the principle of "first come, first to board." Your boarding pass is a color-coded plastic card with a number on it. The first passenger to check in gets card number 1 and will be boarded with the first batch of passengers, thus getting the choice of almost any seat. Receive card number 101 and you'll probably have to make do with a middle seat. The cards are collected as you board, and are reused hundreds of times, which is good for the environment. More significant, Southwest has no need to store seat assignments in its reservation system, no need for equipment to print paper boarding passes, and no need to verify seating arrangements at check-in. The net result is simpler procedures for employees, faster service at the check-in desk—and more costs savings.

No Meals.   Although advertisements for first and business class service on international flights often depict gourmet meals, most airline food in domestic economy class is pretty mediocre. But storing, heating, and serving it still require galley space, heavy food carts, and sometimes more cabin crew to serve it than the minimum number laid down by safety regulations. Provisioning at the start of the flight takes time, and there's more to unload at the destination. All of which raises costs. When mediocrity is the standard, why try to compete? Southwest doesn't. The flight attendants just serve beverages and peanuts or similar dry snacks and have more time to take care of other passenger needs. One of Southwest's TV ads begins with a shot of peanuts and a soft drink; the announcer says, "Because most of Southwest Airlines flights are short, we serve you snacks..." (*cut to shot of typical airline meal*) "...which saves you money because you don't have to pay for an airline meal..." (*cut to shot of hand dropping antacid tablets in glass*) "...or anything associated with an airline meal." (*Cut to shot of Southwest aircraft*) "Southwest Airlines. We save you time *and* money."

Point-to-Point Rather Than Hub-and-Spoke.   Operating a big hub-and-spoke system enables airlines to offer passengers a large number of city-pair destinations, with an intervening change at the hub. Aircraft descend in droves on a hub airport during a relatively brief period, passengers change flights, and then all the aircraft depart again in quick succession. The downside is that the amount of ground-service capacity—airport gates, ground personnel, and ramp equipment—required is determined by these peak periods of intense activity. If one incoming flight is delayed, then all departing flights may have to leave late in order to protect connecting passengers. The net result is that both equipment and personnel spend less time in productive activity. But point-to-point flights can be spaced more evenly over the day (as long as flight departure times are convenient for passengers), and no one aircraft need be held for another.

Targeting Secondary Airports.   The biggest and busiest airports often suffer the greatest congestion. There are delays in the air, delays at the airport, and delays on the access roads. Flying through secondary airports offers Southwest a better chance of maintaining on-time schedules, turning aircraft around quickly, and attracting customers who either want to avoid the hassle of using a mega-airport or simply find its location inconvenient to their homes, offices, or downtown destinations.

> *Flying through secondary airports offers Southwest a better chance of maintaining on-time schedules, turning aircraft around quickly, and attracting new customers.*

No Long-Distance or International Service.   Long-distance flights would involve flying new types of aircraft with which Southwest has no experience. Crews would have to stay in hotels, rather than being able to return home at night, as most are currently able to do. Meals would have to be provided.

Passengers would travel with far more baggage than they usually do on short-haul trips. International flights would require dealing with distant suppliers, foreign currencies, customs officials, and foreign government agencies.

Only Boeing 737s. This unique commitment (for a relatively large airline) simplifies maintenance, spares, flight operations, and training. The 737 is particularly well suited to and cost-effective on short- and medium-range routes. It is also very easy to service at intermediate stops, as we'll see in a moment.

Secrets of the 15-Minute Turnaround

Jet airliners are very expensive to purchase. Fully equipped, a new Boeing 737 costs around $25 million. Its big brother, the 747, costs upwards of $120 million. An aircraft earns money for an airline only when it is flying with paying passengers. So the more hours per day an aircraft is in revenue-producing service *in the air*, the greater is its earning capacity. Southwest does well by domestic industry standards: On average, its 737s are in revenue service 11 hours per day.

Fielding a team of highly skilled, well-motivated mechanics is one way that Southwest keeps its fleet ready to fly. Good maintenance reduces departure delays due to emergency repairs. A related way to obtain high utilization rates is by selling off older aircraft and replacing them with new ones. Southwest operates the youngest fleet in the U.S. airline industry, which means that its aircraft require less maintenance and are less likely to experience failures than older ones. That can save costs, too (although servicing the later-model 737s does require more expensive equipment and greater technical expertise). But perhaps the simplest way of increasing revenue hours per aircraft is to minimize the time it spends on the ground in between flights by turning it around more quickly. These procedures allow Southwest to operate its schedules with far fewer aircraft than a competitor would require. I asked the airline to show me how it achieves this.

Love Field, in suburban Dallas, is Southwest's home base and still one of its busiest airports. All other carriers have moved to DFW (it took intensive lobbying and an act of Congress to allow Southwest to remain there and operate interstate flights from this location). "We routinely turn our 737s around in 15 minutes or less," Audy Donelson, the station manager at Love Field, tells me when we meet. "Our competitors usually take 30 to 50 minutes—or more. Let me show you how we do it"

He leads me through a door in the busy flight operations room that opens onto the parking apron. A bright red and orange aircraft is parked at a nearby gate, and another is taxiing toward the runway. As we watch, a third 737 lands and quickly taxies toward the gate nearest to us.

In contrast to its siblings, this aircraft is painted red, white, and blue, with an enormous white star on the side of its nose. It bears the name *Lone Star*, in tribute to the Texas state flag. Three other aircraft, not at Love Field today, are painted to look like Shamu the Killer Whale. We emerge from the doorway as soon as *Lone Star* rolls to a stop, while the jetway above us swings out to embrace the front cabin door. Even before the passengers have unbuckled their seats, a team of ramp agents and mechanics has moved in to service the aircraft. Each has an assigned task.

As modern jetliners go, the 737 is relatively small and its fuselage is only a few feet off the ground, making it easy to service without the need for large and expensive equipment. The "lav driver" swings in with a tiny tank truck to connect a hose to the rear belly of the fuselage and vent the aircraft's toilets. Meanwhile a mechanic sets a small stepladder underneath one wing, lifts a hose attached to the fuel hydrant set in the parking apron, stands on the lowest step of the ladder, and hooks up the hose to the aircraft's fuel tank. The process will be repeated for the tank in the other wing.

It takes only minutes to pump in the 1350 gallons of jet fuel the 737 needs for its flight to New Orleans, thanks in part to a peculiar-looking contraption called a pumper, which is equipped with several large bottles of compressed nitrogen and is parked next to the hydrant. Donelson gives it a friendly pat. Behind him, a ramp agent is unloading bags from the hold.

"We have one of these pumpers at every gate hooked up to the fuel hydrant," the station manager explains. "The pressurized gas works the fuel valves, allowing the jet fuel to pass through the hose and into the aircraft. Most other airlines use a fuel truck which drives around from gate to gate. It takes time for them to tie onto the hydrant and more time to disconnect again. If the truck is late, the aircraft can be delayed. Any time you drive a vehicle around an aircraft, there's a risk of hitting it and causing damage. You've got to maintain the trucks, and they need fueling, too. They cost around $60,000 each. The pumper is always there, requires almost no servicing, and uses bottles of nitrogen which are dirt cheap and last for months." He chuckles and pats the pumper again. "These things are Air Force surplus and cost us just $10,000 each."

We climb a mobile stairway and enter the 737 through the galley door, where another ramp agent has been unloading used beverage cans and snack containers and is about to begin reprovisioning the galley with new ones. The last of the passengers are filing out. One flight attendant wishes them good-bye as they leave, but her two colleagues are busy behind the departing passengers. They have been following the end of the line, as it moves forward from the rear of the cabin, and picking up trash such as discarded newspapers and paper napkins. "By the time the last passenger leaves, the cabin will be clean," says the station manager. "We keep a small carpet sweeper on board in case the floor gets dirty. Other airlines use separate cleaning crews. But now it's time we got moving. The new passengers will be boarding any moment." As we follow the last departing passenger out, he pauses to crack a joke with the two pilots in the cockpit, who are preparing for the next flight.

In the departure lounge, the gate agent is collecting the plastic boarding cards. "Getting the passengers on quickly is the final step," says Donelson. "Not having advance seat reservations speeds our boarding process, since passengers have an incentive to check in early, to get a low boarding number, and then to board as soon as their number's called to get a better seat."

Key Insights

Southwest Airlines and Firstdirect were both launched in response to customer dissatisfaction with existing services. Both have benefited from creative thinking and a willingness to risk doing things differently. Based upon their experience, I'd like you to consider the following four propositions.

Challenge Established Procedures.   Just because all other firms in your industry do things in a certain way, don't assume that you must follow sheeplike. In order to meet consumers' preferences for avoiding visits to the bank, Firstdirect was willing to undertake a radical reengineering of existing retail banking processes. Southwest has taken a contrarian approach to a whole host of airline industry procedures, even returning to the "old-fashioned" practice of a point-to-point route structure instead of the "modern" hub-and-spoke approach.

Use Appropriate Technology.   Like most businesses today, both Southwest and Firstdirect depend on technology for many aspects of their operations, yet each has taken care to select technologies appropriate to its operational strategy and market positioning. Firstdirect has innovated by using the best *proven* telecommunications and computer technology to serve its customers and steal an advantage on competitors. Southwest, by contrast, has opted for a back-to-basics approach for certain operational tasks, using plastic boarding cards and surplus Air Force fuel pumpers to speed service, keep things simple, and lower costs. Although later chapters spotlight new technologies, you should remember that "high" technology may not always offer the only—or even the best—route to competitive advantage.

Dont't Try to Please Everybody.   For all their virtues, telephone banking and no-frills airline service aren't to everyone's taste. Firstdirect believes the current potential for telephone banking in Britain is about 15 percent of the market—suggesting that, in the near term, 85 percent of all retail bank customers will prefer to remain with a branch they can visit in person. And not everyone loves Southwest Airlines. "I hate Southwest!" an executive told me recently, following a class in which I'd described the airline's strategy. "Why's that?" I asked, wondering what ghastly experience he was going to describe. "The planes are like cattle cars!" he said. "They're always full, and you can't reserve the seat you want in advance. All they serve to eat is peanuts. I call them Southworst!" "Why on earth do you fly them?" I inquired. "Well, often they're the only choice I've got at the times I want to travel."

So is Southwest a bad airline? Of course not. It's safe, speedy, reliable, clean, friendly, and frequent; and it offers customers excellent value. The problem in question results from a poor fit between one traveler's preferences and the product that Southwest has chosen to offer to a large and growing market segment. Southwest shouldn't refuse this man's business and should treat him as well as any other passenger. But management would make a grave mistake if it were to abandon its successful operating concept and market niche in an attempt to woo more customers like him from another market segment. Sometimes the customer is wrong...for your company, that is.

Create Strategic Synergy. By dovetailing marketing, human resource, and operations strategies, both firms have achieved the synergy that Matt and George realized was missing from their proposed haircutting chain. Southwest and Firstdirect have created a synergy between the benefits they offer customers, the design of their operations, and the way in which their employees' jobs and operating environments have been designed.

Taken collectively, these three elements have created product plus service that is the envy of competitors. The owners' needs are being fulfilled, too. Both organizations are in business to make money—one for its parent, the other for its shareholders (many of whom are also employees). As Firstdirect's parent, Midland Bank also expects a second return on its investment: new learning on how to transform its own business.

In the chapter that follows, I expand on this theme of integrating different activities to create customer-pleasing performances. Let's see what insights we can draw from the performing arts.

The failure of Flavius Bernstinus' new musical comedy was widely attributed to problems with the advertising medium.

7 Service as an Art Form

Creating and delivering service involves a series of processes that customers experience as a performance. The theater provides a good analogy for service delivery, with actors, stage sets, scripts, costumes, and even music. Backstage activities (which the customer doesn't see) exist only to create and support good performances on stage. Front-stage activities involve customers in service delivery and may require them to interact with facilities, equipment, employees, and even other customers. Mounting and stage managing service performances require an integration of many different activities, including recruiting the right actors and backstage workers and giving them the tools and skills they need to perform their roles well.

"All the world's a stage and all the men and women merely players," wrote Shakespeare in *Henry V*. "They have their exits and their entrances and each man in his time plays many parts."

The stage is an apt metaphor for services. What is being offered to customers, after all, is a *performance* rather than some physical thing. Some service dramas are tightly scripted and highly ritualized; others are improvisational.

> **The stage is an apt metaphor for services. What is being offered to customers, after all, is a performance.**

Customer-contact personnel are members of a cast, playing roles as *actors* in a drama, and supported by a backstage production team. In some instances, they are expected to wear special costumes when on stage (uniforms supplied by management) or to conform to grooming standards and a dress code. Depending on the nature of their work, they may be required to learn and repeat specific lines, ranging from a basic telephone greeting to a singsong sales spiel, or from recitation of government-mandated safety information to a parting salutation of "Have a nice day!"

Actors need training, coaching, and direction. So do employees. Elocution and voice control can be taught (use of the voice is especially important for service personnel who make public announcements or who deal with customers by telephone). Scripting often prescribes actors' behavior as well as their lines. Eye contact, smiles, and handshakes may be required in addition to a spoken greeting. Other rules of conduct may include bans on smoking, soda drinking, or gum chewing while on duty (very welcome, in this audience member's opinion).

Service facilities constitute the theater, containing the *stage* on which the drama unfolds; sometimes the setting changes from one act to another, as (say) when airline passengers move from check-in, to boarding lounge, to aircraft cabin, and ultimately to the interior of the destination terminal and the baggage claim area. The stage may have minimal props or elaborate scenery. In highly ritualized services, such as dining in a restaurant, "blocking" may prescribe how the actors should move relative to the stage, items of scenery, and other actors.

Customers may be cast as a passive *audience*, of whom little is demanded except that they pay the price of admission and show their appreciation in appropriate fashion. Or they may be asked to take an active role, participating in the unfolding of the drama, even to the extent of influencing its denouement.

Viewed from an unromantic perspective, theaters are simply entertainment factories where dramas are produced for immediate consumption by customers. But not all theater companies require each customer to attend performances at their "factory." In many instances, the customer's own facilities provide the stage on which the actors will perform with their props—and they will even put on a show for an audience of one. Telecommunication linkages offer an alternative performance environment, allowing customers to be involved in the drama from a remote location, much as in radio or TV theater.

Staging the Service Drama

Any service business represents a system, comprising *service operations*, where inputs are processed and the elements of the service product are created; and *service delivery*, where final "assembly" of these elements takes place and the product is delivered to the customer. Parts of this system are visible (or otherwise apparent) to customers; other parts are hidden from view in what is sometimes called the technical core, and the customer may not even know of their existence.

Some people use the terms "front office" and "back office" in referring to the visible and invisible parts of the operation. Others talk about "front stage" (or "on stage") and "backstage." I prefer using the theatrical analogy because it suggests performance rather than administration and bureaucracy. Purists will fault me for using the term "front stage" rather than "on stage," but I do so deliberately. The customers' attention is nearly always focused on what is happening in the front of the stage rather than to its rear. In participative services, customers like to see themselves as being located front and center, rather than as secondary players positioned side stage.

The Service Stage

As in a play, the visible components of the service operations system can be divided into those relating to the actors (or service personnel) and those relating to the stage set (or physical facilities and equipment). What goes on backstage is of little interest to most customers. Like any audience, they evaluate the production with reference to those elements that they actually experience during service delivery and, of course, on the perceived service outcome.

If backstage workers fail to perform their support tasks properly, the impact will quickly be felt by the audience. For instance, restaurant patrons may find that certain menu items are not available because some-one forgot to go to the fish market that morning, or that food is overcooked because the ovens were not adjusted properly. Users of repair services may experience delays in getting their equipment back if technicians fail to report for work or needed spare parts are out of stock. And hotel guests may be awakened early by banging noises as thoughtless maintenance personnel start work on repairs to the heating system.

If backstage workers fail to perform their support tasks properly, the impact will quickly be felt by the audience.

The Product Shapes the Play

The four broad categories of services described in Chap. 2 each require a different type of involvement by customers in the core activity. When customers have no choice but to be physically involved in the service operation, as in people-processing services, then the process should be designed around them. The longer they remain at the service facility, the greater their need for other services (including such theater basics as coatroom, food, beverages, toilets, and telephones). When delivering other types of services, providers have the option of maintaining an arm's-length relationship with customers.

The proportion of the overall service operation that is visible to customers varies according to the nature of the service. In people-processing services, a large part of the physical facility is open to customers, although there may still be some backstage activities that customers don't see. So just like a theater, the factory needs to be given a reasonably appealing design and equipped with whatever amenities and creature comforts customers have come to expect.

Retailers of consumer goods use many different "stages" to market their products, ranging from glamorous, full-service department stores to utilitarian factory outlets. Some choose to minimize interactions with customers by instituting mail-order operations. The design of building exteriors and interiors provides customers with tangible clues about the nature and quality of the service that they are buying. Similarly, the appearance of the employees themselves, and that of their vehicles and tools, also serves to create an image.

Because the customer is less involved in the delivery of repair and maintenance services—there's no need to hold your computer's little electronic hand while it is having transplant surgery for a diseased hard disk—the visible component of the service operations system tends to be proportionately smaller. Yet, customers may still be looking for clues concerning competence and professionalism.

Information-based services directed at customers' minds (education, entertainment, religion, consulting) may not require the customer to be physically present at the site where delivery originates. But they do require the customer's *mental* presence. Telecommunications provide the means of maintaining that mental link even when customer and provider are widely separated. Services delivered by telephone are like radio theater in that everything must be conveyed by inflexions in the actors' voices, with props limited to noises such as background music.

> *Services delivered by telephone are like radio theater, in that everything must be conveyed by inflexions in the actors' voices.*

Information-processing services, such as banking, insurance, consulting, and legal services do not require the customer's physical presence at all from a purely operational standpoint. That's because there may be no operational reason for the customer to visit the "factory" where the work is actually performed. When necessary, interactions between customer and service provider can often be conducted at arm's length by mail, telephone, fax, or electronic terminal.

However, some people do feel more confident, especially with financial and professional services, if they can meet the service provider in person at least once. And suppliers of such services often like to meet customers because they find it easier to obtain needed information from them once a personal relationship has been established. But this is a cultural issue and there are signs that such attitudes are changing as people become more comfortable with technological linkages. In the meantime, many professionals continue to define themselves for clients by how they dress and what their offices look like.

Service Delivery Systems

Service delivery is concerned with where, when, and how the service product is delivered to the customer. It represents an extension of the front-stage operations system, embracing not only facilities, equipment, and personnel, but also, in some service performances, exposure to other customers, too. Figure 7-1 tries to capture these elements in graphic form. On the left, you can see that the service operations system is divided into an invisible backstage (or technical core) and a front stage comprising interior and exterior facilities, equipment, and service people. The front stage is coupled to the service delivery system, where we find the customers.

Mary Jo Bitner has coined the term "servicescape" to describe the physical surroundings in which service delivery takes place. She argues persuasively that their design influences the behavior of both customers and employees. Responsibility for designing and managing the service delivery system has traditionally fallen to operations managers, but marketing needs to be involved, too, since a good understanding of customer needs and concerns is important if the system is to work well. What's more, if we're dealing with a service facility where customers may interact with each other—such as a hotel or post office—people's behavior has to be managed discreetly. Ideally, we want all customers to behave in ways that will enable the system to work efficiently and deliver the level of service that they are looking for.

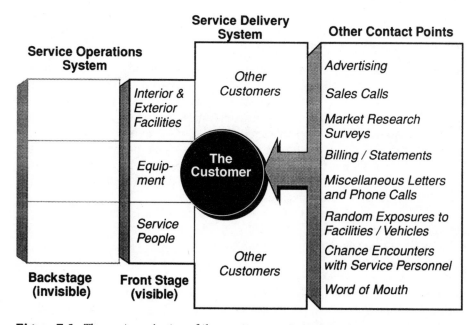

Figure 7-1. The customer's view of the service organization.

Shrinking the Stage

Traditionally, the interaction between service providers and their customers has been a close one. However, for reasons of both operational efficiency and customer convenience, people seeking services that don't require their physical presence are finding that the amount of direct contact with the service organization is being reduced nowadays. As we saw in Chap. 6, Firstdirect customers actively prefer less contact. In short, the visible component of the service operations system is shrinking as the delivery system changes to emphasize more self-service and arm's-length transactions.

Electronic delivery often offers greater convenience than face-to-face contact. Self-service equipment, such as automated teller machines, is available in numerous locations and accessible 24 hours a day, 7 days a week. But there are potential disadvantages, too. Customers sometimes find the shift from personal service to self-service disconcerting: The nature of the play has been radically altered. Research can provide insights into how best to redesign the service in order to maintain or even improve its appeal to customers. And implementing any radical change in the delivery system will probably require an information campaign to educate customers, as well as a responsive attitude toward consumer concerns, and even some promotional incentives.

Other Points of Contact

Moving beyond the theatrical analogy, elements outside the service delivery system may contribute to the customer's overall view of the service organization. As shown in Fig. 7-1, these elements include communication through advertising and sales calls, participation in market research surveys, telephone calls and letters from service personnel, billings from the accounting department, random exposures to service personnel and facilities, and word-of-mouth comments from current or former customers. News stories and editorials in the mass media may also affect the image that customers have of the organization.

Collectively, the different elements in this diagram represent an overall *service marketing system*, comprising all the different ways in which the customer may be touched by the organization, as well as capturing impressions during service delivery. Each element offers clues about the nature and quality of the service product. Inconsistency between different elements may weaken the organization's credibility in the customers' eyes.

I've expanded on all these elements in Table 7-1, which can serve as a checklist to help you think through the nature of the service marketing system for your own business.

Table 7-1. Components of the Service Marketing System

1. *Service personnel.* What types of contact does your firm have with its customers? Possibilities may include: face to face, telecommunications (telephone, fax, telegram, telex, electronic mail), or mail and express delivery services. And which people from your firm have personal contact with customers? Consider each of the following categories and add any others:

   - Sales representatives
   - Customer service staff
   - Accounting/billing staff
   - Repair personnel
   - Operations staff who do not normally provide direct service to customers (e.g., engineers, janitors, security)
   - Designated intermediaries, such as retailers and agents, whom customers perceive as directly representing the service firm

2. *Service facilities and equipment.* First take an inventory of all physical elements with which customers may come in contact, then take a hard look at each through a customer's eyes. Do you like what you see as you examine:

   - Building exteriors, parking areas, landscaping
   - Building interiors and furnishings
   - Self-service equipment operated by customers
   - Vehicles and other equipment

3. *Nonpersonal communications.* There are many other ways in which customers and prospects learn about your firm and the goods and services that it sells. These include:

   - Form letters and direct mail
   - Brochures/catalogs/instruction manuals
   - Advertising
   - Signage
   - News stories/editorials in the mass media

4. *Other people* also shape customer perceptions in important ways. These influences include:

   - Fellow customers encountered during service delivery
   - Word-of-mouth comments from friends, acquaintances, or even strangers

Why the Customer's Viewpoint Is Important

Customers view service businesses through different lenses and from a different perspective than do managers and service personnel. For members of a theater company, whether they are actors, stagehands, wardrobe mistresses, or directors, the play's the thing, and thinking about the theater consumes much of their waking day. For customers, each service drama (even if an ongoing one like a soap opera) is probably only a small part of their daily lives. And rather like Lyndon Johnson, who had a special three-screen television installed in the White House so that he could watch three programs at once, busy customers sometimes find themselves dealing with more than one service at once (for example, a "power breakfast" at a hotel restaurant with an investment banker, during which several cellular phone calls are made).

The scope and structure of the service marketing system may vary sharply among different organizations. As an exercise, you might like to try using the list in Table 7-1 to develop a system profile for a variety of services—a hospital, an airline, a college, a hotel, a dry cleaner, a bank, an automobile service shop, and the postal service. Recognize, though, that some interactions may be random rather than planned. For instance, what impression does it create for a prospective customer to see a truck belonging to an express delivery service broken down by the side of the road? Or to be buying stamps at the post office and observe a uniformed employee (say, a doorman) from a nearby hotel shouting rudely at the postal clerk at the adjacent window?

Although it's clearly the function of operations to manage the service operations system—and of human resources to ensure that this system is staffed with trained and motivated personnel—it's the marketer's task to ensure that the overall service marketing system runs in ways that balance customer satisfaction against operational concerns with efficiency and cost control.

Much operations work is done behind the scenes and is relevant to customers only to the extent that it results in creation and delivery of a good product. But the visible elements of the operation, where service delivery takes place, must be seen in the context of the broader service marketing system. In short, there's an overlap between the marketing and operations spheres of influence. As I have emphasized before, all managers need to understand both perspectives and then to think about how service employees can be managed to achieve optimum results.

Service employees often find themselves in what are termed "boundary-spanning roles," where they are expected to be responsive to the concerns of different departments. Customer-contact personnel, in particular, may find themselves being evaluated on both operational efficiency and customer satisfaction. Often, however, they receive little guidance on how to resolve conflicts between these two goals. Human resource managers need to clarify responsibilities and priorities when preparing job descriptions. They can also help by recruiting employees who are comfortable in making judgments when presented with ambiguous situations and in training them through scenario building and role playing to resolve conflicting priorities.

About the Actors...

As any performer will tell you, acting (or other types of performing in public) is hard work. The hours can be long and antisocial, the pay meager, and working conditions unappealing, with inadequate props or backstage support. Fellow employees who behave like classical prima donnas and insensitive directors who throw tantrums at the slightest provocation (or even without it) add to the stress of the job.

Audiences are often hard to please and critics unkind. Many shows play to small and unappreciative audiences and fold early. The late theatrical impresario, Sol Hurok, was once asked to explain the failure of what had seemed like a promising Broadway play. Sol spread out his hands, palms up, and said simply: "If the audience doesn't want to come, you can't stop them!"

Scientific management has its place in services, but it is no longer enough in dealing with the human side of the enterprise. Managing people is more art than science. The theatrical analogy has its limits (like any analogy), but it's worth thinking about how good directors get great performances. The task starts with casting: recruiting the right actors for specific roles. The Walt Disney Company, which is in the entertainment business, actually uses the term "casting" and assesses prospective employees in terms of their potential for on-stage or backstage work. On-stage workers, known as cast members, are assigned to those roles for which their appearance, skills, and personalities provide the best match.

Few actors advance immediately to leading role positions (and most never make it). They go through a period of training, perhaps in theater school, and apprenticeship, gaining experience in minor roles, before they are ready for more demanding roles. Putting an inexperienced and poorly trained actor into a key role is not fair to either the actor or the audience. Nobody benefits when someone is set up to fail. Yet it seems to happen all the time in service businesses. And then management whines, "you just can't get good help, nowadays!"

Theater directors are concerned not only with the technical aspects of an actor's performance—moving correctly, using appropriate gestures, getting the right voice inflections—but also in the human and psychological dimensions. They try to get each actor to enter into the mindset of the character that she or he is playing and to project that understanding in interactions with other players. Any play requires teamwork: Actors must not upstage each other (beyond the behavior mandated by the script), timing must be coordinated carefully, and all the backstage workers must perform their assigned tasks on cue.

Participative types of theater involve the ability to interact with the audience. Requisite skills include reading the mood of the audience in general and of individual customers in particular, flexibility, empathy, a penchant for improvisation, and the ability to recover gracefully when the performance doesn't go as smoothly as expected. Most services have at least an element of improvisation (if they didn't, the employees would turn into programmed robots). But the ability to improvise well is a learned skill. Just turning workers loose with the instruction to "go do it" may result in their misreading the customers and doing the wrong thing, such as acting in a stiff and stilted manner that makes customers uneasy.

A final point is that performers sometimes depend on technical props, ranging from a magician's box of tricks to a musician's instrument or a singer's microphone. Without the right props, in good working order, they simply cannot give a high-quality performance. Service workers are often in the same boat: There are limits to their ability to perform well without the tools of their trade, and there are limits to their ability to please customers when they must contend with poor working conditions and inferior or improperly maintained equipment. Understanding employee needs in this respect is vital. So is taking the necessary corrective action.

Conductor André Previn likes to tell the story of the nightclub owner whose pianist complained repeatedly about the piano. "It's awful," the pianist told him time and again, "you've got to get it fixed!" Despite her protests, nothing was done. But then, one evening as she was entering the club, the owner came rushing up. "I fixed it, I fixed it!" the latter declared excitedly, grabbing the pianist by the arm. "Ya gotta come and see the pianner!" They entered the performance area and there was the piano. It had been repainted bright red.

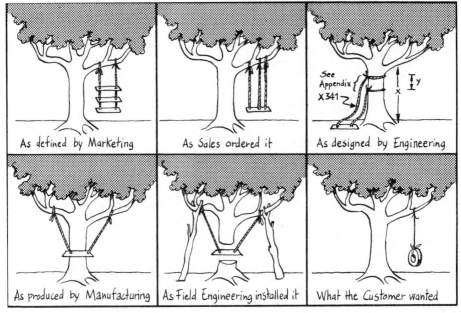

As defined by Marketing | As Sales ordered it | As designed by Engineering

As produced by Manufacturing | As Field Engineering installed it | What the Customer wanted

Based on an anonymous original.

8 Who Defines Quality: You or the Customer?

Historically, quality was defined by operations managers. It's only recently that quality has come to be defined with reference to customer needs and expectations. Since the evolution of the quality movement has been largely dominated by manufacturing concerns, not all quality concepts are equally useful for services. But researchers have developed some frameworks and measurement systems that recognize the role played by the human element in service delivery processes. Many quality improvement programs have not met expectations; we consider some of the possible reasons why.

"Quality Programs Show Shoddy Results" trumpeted the headline in *The Wall Street Journal*. Some months later, a story appeared in *Newsweek*, titled: "The Cost of Quality: Faced with Hard Times, Business Sours on 'Total Quality Management.'"

The *Newsweek* story cited a survey of 500 companies by Arthur D. Little, which found that only 36 percent felt that "total quality management" (TQM) was having a significant impact on their competitive abilities; the magazine cattily observed that it was seminar organizers, consultants, and book publishers who had reaped the biggest quality rewards. The *Journal* referred to an Ernst & Young/American Quality Foundation study of quality improvement efforts by 584 American, German, Japanese, and Canadian firms, concluding that "among most U.S. companies, virtually no quality boosting practices have reached lasting and meaningful levels." Something has clearly gone awry with the TQM movement that was so highly touted during the late 1980s and early 1990s. In management, as in most other areas of human activity, there are fads and fashions. There are also good concepts and practices whose potential is overblown and whose costs are underestimated by their enthusiastic promoters. Finally, the same word often means different things to different people. Let's dig a little deeper.

In management there are fads and fashions. There are also good concepts and practices whose potential is overblown and whose costs are underestimated by their enthusiastic promoters.

Defining and Measuring Quality

What *is* quality? The word is bandied around so much, yet it means different things to different people in different contexts. David Garvin has identified and described five alternative perspectives (to which I've added my own observations).

- The *transcendent* view of quality is synonymous with innate excellence, a mark of uncompromising standards and high achievement. This viewpoint is often applied to the performing and visual arts. It argues that people learn to recognize quality only through the experience gained from repeated exposure. However, suggesting that managers or customers will know quality when they see it offers little practical guidance.

- The *product-based approach* sees quality as a precise and measurable variable. Differences in quality, it argues, reflect differences in the amount of some ingredient or attribute possessed by the product. Since this view is entirely objective, it fails to account for differences in individual tastes, needs, and preferences. What if you (or any other prospective customer) is not interested in the attribute in question?

- *User-based definitions* start with the premise that quality lies in the eyes of the beholder, equating quality with maximum satisfaction. This subjective, demand-oriented perspective recognizes that different customers have different wants and needs. That's useful.

- The *manufacturing-based approach*, in contrast, is supply-based and is concerned primarily with engineering and manufacturing practices. (In services, we would say that quality was operations-driven.) It focuses on conformance to internally developed specifications, which are often driven by productivity and cost-containment goals. On the other hand, many customers do value consistency and reliability.

- *Value-based definitions* define quality in terms of value and price. By considering the trade-off between performance (or conformance) and price, quality comes to be defined as "affordable excellence." This perspective makes clear that one can have a high-quality motel as well as a low-quality five-star hotel (which will soon lose that fifth star if it doesn't shape up). Quality, it implies, is relative.

Garvin suggests that these differing views of quality help to explain the conflicts that sometimes arise between managers in different functional departments. But he argues that "Reliance on a single definition of quality is a frequent source of problems....Because each approach has its predictable blind spots, companies are likely to suffer fewer problems if they employ multiple perspectives on quality, actively shifting the approach they take as products move from design to market...."

> *"Reliance on a single definition of quality is a frequent source of problems...each approach has its predictable blind spots."*
>
> **DAVID GARVIN**

The Dimensions of Quality

Another of Garvin's contributions has been to identify eight dimensions of quality that might be useful as a framework for both analysis and strategic planning:

- *Performance* on the core product's primary operating characteristics
- *Features:* secondary characteristics ("bells and whistles" or supplementary service elements)
- *Reliability:* low probability of malfunction or failure
- *Conformance to specifications:* the degree to which the product's design and operating characteristics meet preestablished standards
- *Durability:* how long the product continues to be useful
- *Serviceability:* speed, courtesy, competence, and ease of repair; satisfactory handling of complaints
- *Esthetics:* appeal of the product to the five senses
- *Perceived quality:* image and reputation of the product and the firm responsible for it

Although many of these characteristics can be applied to services, most are derived from experience with manufactured goods and notably downplay the human side of service. However, a group of researchers in marketing (Valarie Zeithaml, Leonard Berry, and A. Parasuraman) have come up with quality dimensions of their own. Based on research among users of various types of services, they identified five groups of characteristics that customers use to evaluate service quality:

- *Tangibles:* appearance of physical facilities, equipment, personnel, and communication material
- *Reliability:* ability to perform the promised service dependably and accurately
- *Responsiveness:* willingness of staff to help customers and provide prompt service
- *Assurance:* competence, courtesy, and trustworthiness of staff; freedom from danger, risk, or doubt
- *Empathy:* ease of making contact, good communications, and understanding of customers' needs

In each of the different services that were studied, Zeithaml and her associates found that reliability was consistently the most important characteristic.

As you can see, this second set of characteristics is customer-focused. That's not surprising, since the researchers asked customers how they defined quality. But the first set is somewhat more ambiguous. With conformance, for instance, much depends on who sets the specifications: Do they reflect customer desires, or is it one more case of Father knows best? The history of the quality movement (discussed below) suggests that the notion of allowing customers to define quality is a relatively recent one. Many firms still need to make the connection.

A Short History of Quality

In his book, *Managing Quality*, Garvin reminds us that, as a concept, quality has been with us for millennia, but its emergence as a management function is more recent. Writing in 1988, he broke down modern approaches to quality into four "quality eras," which he called inspection, statistical quality control, quality assurance, and strategic quality management. To these, I add a fifth of my own, which I'll come to in a moment. First, let's look at Garvin's historical analysis, which also embraces many of the key terms and concepts used in quality management.

Inspection

Garvin traces quality's beginnings to the rise of formal inspection procedures during the early nineteenth century. *Quality control* implies some uniform model of the product against which to measure actual performance. Such uniformity became possible in manufacturing with the development of rational jigs and fixtures, designed to ensure accurate machining operations in order to produce identical (and therefore interchangeable) parts. Inspections of this output, previously performed by eye, were now undertaken with the aid of gauges, designed to measure physical output against a uniform standard. By the early twentieth century, inspection activities were being linked more formally to quality control, and quality itself was being viewed as a distinct management function.

Statistical Quality Control

The quality movement gained a scientific footing for the first time in 1931 with the publication of the work of W. A. Shewhart, one of a group of quality researchers at Bell Telephone Laboratories. In Garvin's words, "He was the first to recognize that variability was a fact of industrial life and that it could be understood using the principles of probability and statistics." The issue was no longer the existence of variation—that was certain to continue at some level no matter what actions were taken—but how to distinguish acceptable variations from fluctuations that indicated trouble. A key contribution was the *process control chart* for plotting production values to determine whether they fell within the acceptable range.

Two of Shewhart's colleagues developed statistical techniques for sampling a limited number of items in each production lot. Their goal was to trade off the high cost of 100 percent inspection against the risks of either (1) approving a lot that actually contained too high a percentage of defective items or (2) rejecting a lot that, in reality, met quality standards. Large-scale refinements of these techniques were undertaken during World War II to speed the production and delivery of military supplies, where inspection created serious bottlenecks.

Quality Assurance

The third quality era saw the development of four important new concepts: the costs of quality, total quality control, reliability engineering, and zero defects.

The costs of quality was a term coined by Joseph Juran in an effort to answer the question, "How much quality is enough?" Juran's premise, published in 1951, was that the costs of achieving a given level of quality could be divided into *avoidable* and *unavoidable* costs. The latter costs were those associated with inspection and other quality control initiatives designed to prevent defects from occurring (or at least from reaching the customer).

Avoidable costs were those of product failures—wasted materials, labor hours spent on rework and repair, complaint processing, and the financial losses resulting from unhappy customers. Juran regarded failure costs as "gold in the mine," because they could be extracted by investing in quality improvement efforts. The payoff from such investments, he declared, could be substantial. The managerial implication of Juran's work is simple: Additional expenditures on improvement are likely to be justified as long as failure costs remain high.

Total quality control (TQC) was the brainchild of Armand Feigenbaum, who argued in 1956 that "control must start with the design of the product and end only when the product has been placed in the hands of a customer who remains satisfied...the first principle to recognize is that *quality is everybody's job*." He declared that quality activities could be grouped into three categories: new-design control, incoming-material control, and product/shop floor control. Success required the cooperation of multiple departments, so that designers did not create products that were hard to manufacture, assemble, ship, or use. Quality systems now included new-product development, vendor selection, and customer service—as well as manufacturing control.

Reliability engineering emerged during the 1950s, driven by the needs of the Armed Forces to have electronic and aerospace equipment that could be relied on to keep on working, and so avoid the need to maintain expensive stockpiles of replacements. In addition to designing out the weakest links in a product, procedures also required detailed reporting and analysis of failures in the field to facilitate redesign.

Zero defects, which originated with the Martin Company in 1961–1962, was driven by the needs of a military customer for a product that would not only work right the first time (it was a missile) but could also be delivered on time, despite an accelerated schedule. Rather than emphasizing engineering skills, zero defects focused on management expectations and human relations. The key objective was to expect perfection the first time, rather than inspecting out imperfections, and the focus was on identifying problems at their source, with particular attention to correcting such common causes of employee errors as

- Lack of knowledge
- Lack of proper facilities
- Lack of attention to employee awareness and motivation

This third era of quality management marked a watershed. It had taken almost 150 years for the concerns of customers to be addressed and for employee initiatives to be seen as a critical input to quality improvement programs. As Garvin notes, the zero defects movement, with its emphasis on employees, emerged at the same time as other new thinking on human resource management. Concepts such as Theory Y and the Scanlon Plan, which encouraged managers to offer greater autonomy to workers, were similar in spirit to the way in which zero-defects strategies focused on motivation and employee initiative.

> *It had taken almost 150 years for the concerns of customers to be addressed and for employee initiative to be seen as a critical input to quality improvement programs.*

Strategic Quality Management— The Japanese Experience

Despite the changes generated by the quality assurance era, the field remained largely defensive in the United States during the 1950s and 1960s, with application of new concepts diffusing only slowly. As Garvin writes, "Quality was still seen as a problem to be solved rather than as a potential competitive weapon." In Japan, by contrast, the quality movement was progressing much more rapidly toward a strategic perspective.

Ironically, three American quality specialists were responsible for capturing the enthusiasm of Japanese executives from the 1950s onwards. W. Edwards Deming, a disciple of W. A. Shewhart, lectured on the importance of a rigorous, systematic, statistically based approach to solving quality problems. He was especially concerned with separating *special causes* (assignable to individual operators or machines) from *common causes* that were management's responsibility. He also encouraged adoption of a systematic approach to problem solving—the so-called Deming cycle of Plan, Do, Check, Action. Finally, he introduced the Japanese to modern methods of consumer research. Meantime, Juran and Feigenbaum awakened the Japanese to the less statistical aspects of quality management. Juran lectured on planning, goal setting, organizational issues, the need to set goals and targets for improvement, and management's responsibility for quality. Feigenbaum argued for a systemic (or total) approach to quality.

Government-sponsored industrial standards and a nonprofit organization, the Union of Japanese Scientists and Engineers (JUSE), proved to be key vehicles for consolidating the Japanese quality movement and for promoting diffusion of new ideas and success stories on a national basis. Innovations included Kaoru Ishikawa's *cause–effect diagram* (first used in 1952 and described in more detail in Chap. 14), quality control circles (1962), companywide quality control (1968), and quality function deployment (1972).

Quality control circles (QCC) consist of small groups of workers, trained in quality-solving skills, who are encouraged to take the initiative in identifying and solving problems and in suggesting improvements to management.

Companywide quality control (CWQC) represents an extension of Feigenbaum's TQC ideas. Its components are fourfold:

- Involvement of all functions in quality activities.

- Involvement of all levels, from top executive to shop-floor employees, in a shared concern for quality (backed up by extensive training). QCCs became one important element of this involvement.

- A philosophy of continuous improvement.

- A strong customer orientation—quality is defined from the customer's point of view, so that design and production processes can be focused accordingly.

Quality function deployment (QFD) is a set of planning and communication routines which originated at Mitsubishi's Kobe shipyard. QFD focuses on developing skills to design, create, and market products that customers want to buy and will continue to repurchase. It uses elaborate charts to translate perceptions of quality into product characteristics, which are then turned into engineering and production requirements. The basic design tool is a chart called the *house of quality*. Building the house begins with marketing research to determine the specific product attributes desired by customers from a given market segment, their relative importance, and how customers perceive competing products performing against one's own on each attribute.

Strategic Quality Management— The American and European Experience

It wasn't until the early 1980s that significant numbers of American and European companies started waking up to the strategic role of quality that had been adopted by the Japanese more than a decade earlier. For many, the rude awakening came from the dramatic competitive inroads made by Japanese manufacturers because of their superior quality and reliability. Product liability suits, government-mandated product recalls, and the consumerist movement also provided an impetus for change, by increasing sharply the cost of selling defective products. Thus arrived in the West what Garvin calls the fourth quality era, strategic quality management.

Three important books captured broad public attention and galvanized managerial interest in quality during the decade of the 1980s. The first was Philip Crosby's *Quality Is Free* (actually published in 1979), which claimed that perfect quality was both technically possible and economically feasible. Crosby, who had worked earlier for Martin, where "I created the concept of Zero Defects," went on to found a training and research institute called Quality College.

Next came *In Search of Excellence* (1982) by Tom Peters and Robert Waterman, which highlighted successful American companies and identified common success factors. In a long chapter called "Close to the Customer," the authors devoted 10 pages to the topic of "quality obsession." Finally, there was David Garvin's *Managing Quality* (1988), which reviewed the historical evolution of quality (as summarized here), offered a comprehensive understanding of quality from philosophical, economic, marketing, and operations management perspectives, and presented important examples from different industries, including his own research on quality in air-conditioner manufacturing.

The Fifth Quality Era: Total Quality Obsession

In August 1987, an act of the U.S. Congress established the Malcolm Baldrige National Quality Award (named after one of its advocates, the late

Secretary of Commerce, who had died the previous month in a rodeo accident). The Award's broad goals have been described by the Department of Commerce as "to promote quality awareness, to recognize quality achievements of U.S. companies, and to publicize successful quality strategies." The preamble to the act also made explicit note of lagging productivity growth in the United States. Up to six awards may be given annually, limited to two each among three categories: manufacturing, service, and small business.

The establishment of this award was seen, in part, as an American counterpoint to Japan's distinguished Deming Award, created in 1951 in honor of W. Edwards Deming. The Baldrige Award quickly captured public imagination as well as the attention of business leaders. Some speakers and media commentators began referring to it as the "Nobel Prize" for business (conveniently overlooking the fact that it was restricted to American companies).

Certainly, the time was ripe for such an initiative. After a decade of losing market share to Japanese entrants, a few innovative American companies such as Xerox and Hewlett-Packard were starting to show results from reinventing their organizations and their philosophies along quality lines. The Xerox experience was particularly noteworthy, since the company had made a striking comeback and was also credited with popularizing the notion of *benchmarking* (identifying and studying top performers on each of a series of important product attributes).

Recent years had also witnessed a veritable explosion of discontent with the quality of service. This topic even rated a major story in *Time* magazine: "Why Is Service So Bad?" its title asked plaintively; "Pul-eeze! Will Somebody Help Me?" *Time*'s cover for that issue depicted a customer groveling in front of a smirking service rep as the latter placed a sign on the counter reading "Out to Lunch." More and more, the "quality" theme began to dominate speeches, articles, and news stories—succeeding the "excellence" theme of a few years earlier, which was beginning to sound a bit shopworn.

Unfortunately, all this media attention proved a bit too rich. In retrospect, 1987 can be seen as the start of the fifth quality era, which I call *total quality obsession* (TQO). Underlying this was the notion, promoted by Philip Crosby and many consultants, that the only acceptable performance standard was the "quality absolute" of zero defects, which some called "total quality." The sole way of achieving such an absolute, inevitably, was total quality control, itself driven by *total quality management* (TQM).

Those who enjoy semantic distinctions might like to compare the Japanese-originated "companywide quality control" against its Euro-American offspring, "total quality management." When Arthur

Feigenbaum spoke of total quality control in the 1950s, he used the term in its systemic sense of comprising every aspect of the process. David Garvin says, "There's a good reason for using the word 'total.' It means you're supposed to run the shop in a totally different way." However, I worry that the term "total quality management" may have come to symbolize the absolute perfection inherent in zero defects. After all, there's a big difference between applying quality control to every aspect of the process and achieving 100 percent perfect output.

> *There's a big difference between applying quality control to every aspect of the process and achieving 100 percent perfect output.*

The term *empowerment* also came into vogue about this time. The theory was that if you trained workers rigorously in quality improvement techniques and gave them the authority to take action on solving quality problems, this in itself would lead to substantial gains. Many firms bought this notion, and a large training industry soon grew to supply the necessary courses.

It wasn't long before TQM took on the aura of a religion. Evangelistic speakers popularized the 100 percent perfect goal in conferences and corporate training seminars by arguing that doing it right 97, 99, or even 99.9 percent of the time wasn't good enough. "What would happen," they liked to ask, "If an airline reported that 99.9 percent of all flights had landed safely or a hospital boasted that 99.9 percent of all newborn babies in the maternity unit had not been dropped on their heads?" As a fairly frequent flyer and the father of two children, I can relate very well to such statements. But there's a fundamental difference between the implications of a one-in-a-thousand failure rate that results in a smoking hole in the ground or an accidentally brain-damaged baby versus a similar chance of experiencing a delayed flight arrival or receiving a lukewarm cup of coffee in the hospital cafeteria. If there is any absolute, it's surely that we should keep things in proportion.

Why TQM Programs Fail

Why has TQM failed to meet expectations? I believe that there are nine basic reasons.

Insufficient Time Frame. In many instances, it takes a long time to implement new process changes, even longer for such changes to have a measurable impact on quality, and longer still before changes in product quality are perceived by customers and start to affect brand choice behavior. Some of the reported "failures" may, in fact, simply need a little more time before they start to show the hoped-for results. However, it's a good strategy, when designing a quality program, to pick some early applications that are likely to yield positive results quickly.

Unreasonable Expectations. Quality improvement programs have often been oversold and overbought. Some chief executives have embraced them in the expectation of a quick fix that will promptly yield competitive advantages and positive financial results. But quality improvement is not a magic ingredient that is guaranteed to work. In particular, firms that are followers may not be able to expect the same gains in profits and market share won by the leaders. In fact, the benefit of quality programs to "follower" firms may take the form of preventing further decline rather than harvesting new gains. Overall, I suspect that some firms had expectations that were simply too high, and so disappointment was inevitable.

Premature Empowerment. Many firms misunderstood the notion of empowering employees. They believed that, given training in quality techniques and new authority to take action, employees would become self-directed and positive results would soon occur. In practice, employees often had no idea what to do next; they weren't given clear goals and were afraid to stick their necks out. So nothing happened. Successful programs begin by empowering employees to take action in tightly prescribed areas, such as complaint resolution, and build slowly from there.

Misnomer and Misrepresentation. Many so-called quality programs have, in fact, been internally oriented, focusing on cutting costs and enhancing productivity rather than on improving the quality of goods and services that the customers receive. Employees who participate in quality improvement efforts in the belief that they are helping the company to improve its competitive position and achieve greater customer satisfaction soon become disillusioned when they perceive that their contributions are actually leading to large-scale layoffs. Under such circumstances, employee resistance to imposition of so-called quality programs is predictable and understandable.

Quality from the Neck Down. Having once commissioned a quality program, senior managers often remain aloof. Some see their job as "running the company"; promoting and facilitating a quality program is somebody else's job. The result is that top management remains uninvolved and doesn't know what is going on. In companies with a strongly directive, top-down management style, middle managers may become paralyzed while waiting for Mr. Big's reaction. Consultants become very frustrated under such circumstances, since they know that it takes ongoing top-management involvement to legitimize a companywide quality program and move it forward. "Daily, consistent, relentless leadership is what it takes," says Rob Evans of ODI, an international training and consulting firm.

It takes ongoing top-management involvement to legitimize a companywide quality program and move it forward.

High Costs in Hard Times. The costs of quality improvements, especially when these involve new capital expenditures and investments in employee training, are very substantial. Even when a program starts to have an impact on improving service quality, it may be some time before a positive financial impact results. In situations where top management is under great pressure to improve financial results (as during periods of extended recession), it's extremely tempting to cut quality expenditures when they are not showing any financial payoff.

Low Threshold for Pain. Even if top management knows all the arguments for seeking to improve quality, what the potential payoffs are, and how to go about it, the fact remains that working day in and day out on quality improvement is hard work and not necessarily much fun. David Maister likens it to someone with a weight problem who says, "I know all the reasons why I should lose weight—I'll look better, feel better, and live longer. I also know what I have to do to lose weight: eat less, change my diet, and exercise more. But I tried it for a few days and it was just too painful. Besides, I've got lots of other, more pressing priorities, like giving up smoking. One thing at a time is enough!"

Activities-Focused versus Results-Focused. Much of the cost of TQM programs is centered on employee training; conducting research studies and developing new information and measurement systems can also be expensive. But unless there is continuing emphasis on *results*, especially those that will be meaningful to customers, these activities can become totally detached from the task of actually running the business. Just spending money on training, research, and measurement doesn't necessarily mean that management is bringing about meaningful improvements in quality that customers will notice and respond to.

Too Much, Too Soon. Not every company is ready to try to emulate the quality initiatives of world-class performers. The Ernst & Young/AQF study concluded that firms which rank relatively low on profitability and productivity should not be overly ambitious. Trying to adopt cutting-edge techniques used by the leaders may actually make matters worse in the short run.

Don't get me wrong: I do believe strongly in the importance of trying to improve quality. My concern is with the overselling and resulting misunderstanding of TQM. Obsession is an unhealthy word, implying excessive preoccupation with one topic to the exclusion of others. As David Garvin put it to me, "Anyone who believes that quality or, for that matter any other management process, is an answer to all their prayers is suffering from self-delusion."

And I don't want to denigrate (as some do) the value of the Baldrige Award. In many respects, establishment of this award has been an immense success. It has energized companies by providing a goal to shoot for, it has codified criteria that place as much emphasis on the process by which quality results are achieved as on the actual results themselves, and it has publicized the work of winning companies by requiring them to share what they have learned about achieving outstanding quality. Expectations are similarly high for the recently established European Quality Award, first offered in 1992. As for the doubts expressed about TQM, I think they're healthy. A period of questioning and skepticism may be what is needed to put quality programs into perspective and restore them to the right track.

Understanding Service Quality

When researchers began to study service industries, they argued that new ways of thinking about quality were needed, reflecting the intangible nature of many services and the all-too-fallible human dimension in service delivery. The Finnish researcher, Christian Grönroos, argued that a distinction should be drawn between the process of service delivery ("functional quality"), which relates to how service is delivered and is often strongly people-based, and the actual service output, which he termed "technical quality."

One of the problems with manufacturing-based approaches to quality improvement is that they are difficult to apply to front-stage processes, especially where service delivery is being provided by employees for immediate consumption by customers. There are limits, for instance, to how well managers can apply reliability engineering to service personnel.

When customers are engaged in the production process, either in collaboration with employees or through self-service, the task becomes even more difficult: Zero defects is essentially unattainable. What takes place backstage, by contrast, lends itself much more readily to engineering analyses and statistical quality control. The output of many possession-processing services, in particular, can usually be inspected before being delivered to customers.

Measuring Service Quality

Relative to work in manufacturing, research into service quality has been strongly customer-driven. In part, of course, this reflects the greater involvement of customers in service delivery systems (especially in people-processing services). To a large extent, service-based definitions equate quality with customer satisfaction, as defined by the formula

$$\text{Satisfaction} = \frac{\text{Perceived Service}}{\text{Expected Service}}$$

In theory, it's quite simple. If customers perceive the actual delivery of service as better than expected, they'll be happy. If it's below expectations, they'll be mad. This approach has its limitations: What if you don't know what to expect or don't feel qualified to evaluate the outcome? However, it seems to work reasonably well for services with which customers are somewhat familiar (and therefore have realistic expectations) and are also able to form reasonable judgments about what was actually delivered.

To predict satisfaction, we've got to know two things. First, how did the customer perceive the service? Perception is all in the mind. Two different customers might perceive the same service in very different ways. Second, what were the customer's expectations? Were they in line with the firm's ability to deliver service, or were they unrealistic? In an attempt to create a standardized approach to measuring service quality along these lines, the team of Zeithaml, Berry, and Parasuraman developed a survey research instrument called SERVQUAL.

Customers are asked to complete a series of scales which measure their expectations of a particular company (or product) on a wide array of specific service characteristics. Then they record their perceptions of actual service performance on those same characteristics. When perceived performance ratings are lower than expectations, this is a sign of poor quality; the reverse indicates good quality.

Zeithaml and her colleagues have identified various potential shortfalls

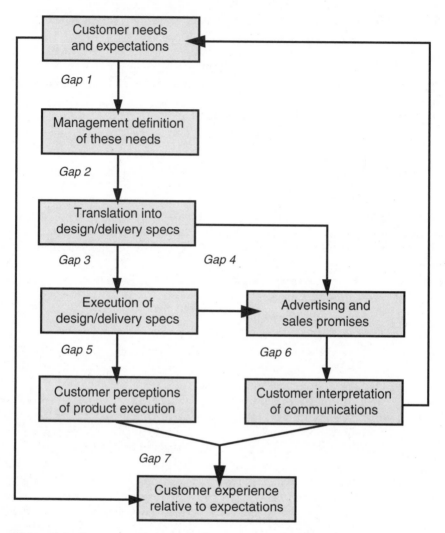

Figure 8-1. Seven gaps that may lead to customer disappointment.

within a service organization that might lead to a gap between what customers expect on a particular service characteristic and what they receive. I've expanded their framework to include a total of seven gaps (see Fig. 8-1), each of which is discussed below.

Gap 1 is not knowing what your customers need and expect. This is really inexcusable. A logical response is to undertake research to find out.

Gap 2 is not using knowledge of customer needs and expectations as the basis for defining and specifying service quality standards. This is what I call the "Father knows best" phenomenon: Even if the kids tell you what they want, you ignore it and prescribe what you think will be good for them.

Gap 3 results when execution fails to match the predefined standards. This is the conformance problem and often reflects poor internal communications and lack of quality controls.

Gap 4 comes from a failure on the part of advertising and salespeople to portray the service accurately in their communications to customers; most commonly they overpromise. This problem could result from being poorly briefed about the service or from a tendency to exaggerate performance in order to capture customer interest. Excessive claims are just asking for trouble, since they may raise customers' expectations to heights that cannot possibly be met.

Gap 5 results when the customer misperceives the quality of service performance. One of the characteristics of good quality is that it's often unobtrusive: A customer may simply not realize the quality of work performed, especially with an infrequently used service such as heath care, consulting, or specialized repair work.

Gap 6 occurs when a customer misunderstands what a salesperson says, or misinterprets the nature of an advertising message, and expects something different from what was actually promised.

Gap 7, finally, comes when the customer compares what he or she experienced with what was expected (initial expectations as modified by marketing communication messages).

With so many potential gaps, it may seem like a miracle that anyone is ever satisfied with any service! Improving quality, then, requires identifying the specific causes of each gap and developing strategies to close them. In some instances, the solutions don't involve changing service delivery at all; rather, they focus on managing expectations, insisting that all communications about the service be accurate and clearly presented, and trying to ensure that customers understand exactly what it is that they have received. The strength of this gap methodology is that it addresses some of the communication and perceptual issues underlying quality.

To summarize the basic lessons:

- Ask your customers what they need (this requires research).
- Translate those needs into service specifications.
- Employ training and quality control procedures to make sure that execution conforms to service specs.
- Brief marketing communications people carefully so that they promise only what you know you can deliver.
- Manage your customers' expectations, so that they do not have unrealis-

tic ideas about any aspect of service delivery or the resulting costs and benefits.

- Make sure that customers recognize what they are getting—if necessary, toot your horn and draw their attention to the quality of work that you have performed for them.

A number of firms have taken the basic SERVQUAL methodology and added some specific questions of their own to measure performance on specific characteristics. They have also weighted different service attributes to reflect their relative importance to the customer. Other firms have chosen to develop their own, specialized measuring instruments and to create company-specific quality indexes. We look at Federal Express's approach in Chap. 9.

Service Guarantees

A small but growing number of companies have chosen to offer customers an unconditional guarantee of satisfaction, promising an easy-to-claim replacement, refund, or credit in the event of dissatisfaction. Christopher Hart argues that such guarantees represent powerful tools to promote and achieve service quality, for the following reasons:

1. Guarantees force firms to focus on what their customers want and expect from each element of the service.
2. Guarantees set clear standards, telling customers and employees alike what the company stands for. Payouts to compensate customers for poor service will encourage managers to take guarantees seriously, because they highlight the financial costs of quality failures.

Service guarantees set clear standards, telling customers and employees alike what the firm stands for.

---

3. Guarantees require the development of systems for generating meaningful customer feedback and acting on it.
4. Guarantees force service organizations to understand why they fail, encouraging them to identify and overcome potential fail points.
5. Guarantees build marketing muscle by reducing the risk of the purchase decision and building long-term loyalty.

The notion of service guarantees has now been extended to relationships between internal customers and suppliers: Both sides agree on what service is to be provided and on what terms.

The Way Ahead

So where do we go from here? In dealing with service businesses, perhaps the most important point to bear in mind is that different types of organizations should consider different approaches to quality management. Three distinctions are especially relevant.

1. *What type of service is involved: people processing, possession processing, or information-based services?* The more that customers are personally involved in the service process, the greater are the number of elements that enter into their evaluation of service quality, and the more likely they are to be exposed to the human side of quality. Moreover, the behavior of customers themselves may have a significant effect on quality performance. Quality improvement in such organizations must include a focus on employee–customer interactions. With their greater emphasis on backstage operations, possession-processing and information-based services should be more able to control their operational environments and to focus on technical processes.

2. *How systemic is the service process?* If you determine that your processes are not highly interdependent, but instead involve an assembly of discrete elements, created and delivered separately from one another (as in hotels), then you may be able to adopt a strategy of working to improve the quality of one element at a time. Even in highly systemic processes (such as transportation or telecommunications), improvement of supplementary service elements can often be tackled without affecting the core process. Such an approach involves a fraction of the cost, risk, and disruption of going immediately to a full-blown, companywide quality program. In fact, by picking a project with a high probability of early success, you may find it easier to gain support for broader-based efforts later. If there are several potential projects from which to choose that meet this criterion, pick one that addresses an area of competitive weakness.

3. *How much quality progress has the firm already made?* The Ernst & Young/AQF study suggests strongly that inexperienced firms, typically characterized by weaker performance on profitability and productivity, should adopt different techniques from firms with prior experience in quality management. Table 8-1 documents the approaches suggested by this

Table 8-1. How to Make Your Company a Quality Master*

	NOVICE Getting started
Measures	
Profitability	Less than 2% return on assets (ROA)
Productivity	Less than $47,000 value added per employee (VAE)
Techniques	
Employee involvement	$ Train heavily. Promote teamwork, but forget self-managed teams, which take heavy preparation. Limit employee empowerment to resolving customer complaints.
Benchmarking	Emulate competitors, not world-class companies.
New products	Rely mainly on customer input for ideas.
Supply management	Choose suppliers mainly for price and reliability.
New technology	Focus on cost-reduction potential. Don't develop it—buy it.
Manager and employee evaluation	Reward front-line workers for teamwork and quality.
Quality progress	$ Concentrate on fundamentals. Identify processes that add value, simplify them, and move faster in response to customer and market demands. Don't bother using formal gauges of progress—gains will be apparent.

$ Activities that should reap the highest paybacks

SOURCE: Reprinted from December 7, 1992, issue of *Business Week,* pp. 64–65, by special permission. Copyright © 1992 by McGraw-Hill Inc. (Data: Ernst & Young/American Quality Foundation.)

JOURNEYMAN	MASTER
Honing new skills	Staying on top

2% to 6.9% ROA	ROA of 7% and higher
$47,000 to $73,999 VAE	VAE of $74,000 and up

$ Encourage employees at every level to find ways to do their jobs better—and to simplify core operations. Set up a separate quality assurance staff.

Imitate market leaders and selected world-class companies.

Use customer input, formal market research, and internal ideas.

Select suppliers by quality certification, then price.

Find ways to use facilities more flexibly to turn out a wider variety of products.

Base compensation for both workers and middle managers on contributions to teamwork and quality.

$ Meticulously document gains and further refine practices to improve value added per employee time to market, and customer satisfaction.

$ Use self-managed, multiskilled teams that focus on horizontal processes such as logistics and product development. Limit training, mainly to new hires.

$ Gauge product development, distribution, customer service versus the world's best.

Base on customer input, benchmarking, and internal R&D.

Choose suppliers mainly for their technology and quality.

Use strategic partnerships to diversify manufacturing.

Include senior managers in compensation schemes pegged to teamwork and quality.

Keep documenting gains and further refine practices to improve value added per employeee, time to market, and customer satisfaction.

---

*Novices that try to match the techniques used by world-class performers may actually make things worse by trying to do too much, too soon. So finds a three-year study of 580 companies in North America, Germany, and Japan by Ernst & Young and the American Quality Foundation. Instead, they suggest making gradual progress toward excellence.

Start by measuring your existing performance. Two key measures are return on assets, which is simply aftertax income divided by total assets, and value added per employee. Value added is sales minus the costs of materials, supplies, and work done by outside contractors. Labor and administrative costs are not subtracted from sales to arrive at value added.

study for three types of company, characterized by varying levels of performance. In which group would you characterize your firm?

Putting Things in Perspective

Although minimizing defects is important, let's not go overboard on the concept of zero defects. A more important objective, in fact, is *zero defections*, that is, avoiding loss of existing customers due to dissatisfaction with quality. Product plus firms are realistic. They accept that all defects are bad, but know from research and complaint data that some defects are much more important to customers than others.

If you don't already know what turns your customers off, do some research to find out. Further, you should recognize that some defects cost more money to fix than others. Despite what Phil Crosby has said, not all quality improvement efforts will necessarily pay for themselves. If your resources are limited and your operation is not highly systemic in nature, it may be best to invest in fixing those defects that will yield the greatest financial returns. Also, try to find out how much more (if anything) customers are prepared to pay for better quality on specific characteristics—particularly for higher reliability—and set your priorities and pricing policies accordingly. Improving *value* is the real objective.

Finally, if you're in an industry where service processes involve frequent interactions between employees and customers, or use of the public infrastructure, or are subject to natural phenomena such as changes in the weather and acts of God (or a combination of all of the above), you should accept that achieving zero defects is probably impossible. But this doesn't mean that zero defections is also unachievable (after all, your competitors presumably face the same constraints). Your goal should be to hold on to all customers that you consider desirable ones. Achieving this goal will require continuous improvement to eliminate controllable errors, plus development of contingency plans for handling problems outside your control.

You'll find the issue of quality improvement coming up again and again throughout this book, together with presentation of several simple tools and frameworks that anyone can use. In the next chapter we look at how one famous service company developed a systemic approach to quality management and won a Baldrige Award for its efforts.

"Actually, my birthday's not until next Tuesday. Would you mind holding on to it until then? I love surprises!"

9 Absolutely, Positively: Systemic Quality at Federal Express

Few companies have made such concerted efforts to improve quality as Federal Express (FedEx), the first company to win America's coveted Malcolm Baldrige National Quality Award in the service category. We look at how FedEx's highly systemic operation works backstage, including a visit to its Memphis SuperHub, and examine the information technology that supports the company's physical operations. Key components of FedEx's quality improvement program include a "service quality index" based on measuring failures that could irritate or disappoint customers; employee evaluations of their manager's performance; a training program that emphasizes thought processes over statistical techniques; use of quality action teams to study and resolve service problems; publicizing and replicating service successes; and efforts to better align internal customer–supplier relationships.

Federal Express has never been shy about promoting its competitive advantages. When the company first launched its overnight package service in 1973, it competed for business against airfreight forwarders, who shipped packages in the cargo holds of passenger aircraft. The leading firm was Emery Air Freight, which traffic managers saw as setting the industry standard. FedEx decided to tackle Emery head-on.

Convinced that their service was superior, FedEx managers commissioned an independent research firm to send identical packages between 47 cities, using both company's services at regular rates. No employees were aware of the test. The researchers reported back that only 42 percent of Emery's packages had arrived the following day, versus 93 percent for FedEx whose rates were also cheaper. FedEx promptly used these findings in a TV and press advertising campaign, headlined: "Federal Express. Twice as Good as the Best in the Business."

There would be more of these implied quality claims as the company grew and grew. In 1978, the company adopted a slogan that became almost a national byword: "When it absolutely, positively has to be there overnight" (later amended to "on time" for use with second-day and international service). Another ad asked: "Why fool around with anybody else?" And then there was, "It's not just a package, it's your business."

When I first learned that Federal Express had started a companywide quality improvement program, I was intrigued. After all, there was no Japanese competitor to worry about, FedEx was already the industry leader, it was profitable, and quality had been implicit in the company's approach to operations and marketing since the beginning. I knew that as CEO, Fred Smith constantly set goals of improving reliability, productivity, and financial performance, promoting the corporate imperative of People–Service–Profits. The company also had a reputation for being an excellent place to work; it rewarded and celebrated outstanding achievements among its employees, who were well trained and highly motivated. So why did FedEx even need such a program? The basic answer was to help it achieve its goal of 100 percent customer satisfaction and ensure that the company remained the industry leader in both good times and bad.

The company's first attempt to address quality improvement techniques at the corporate level quickly fizzled. In 1985, top management brought in a consultant to conduct an off-site meeting with top management. But this individual's statistically driven, manufacturing-oriented approach did not sit well with service-oriented managers. Thomas R. Oliver, then senior VP–marketing (and later the company's executive vice president–worldwide customer operations) recalled: "Everyone walked away with a calculator and a statistics book, but our interest had not been captured. The senior managers didn't believe it would work in a complex service environment." Some improvements were made, but nothing significant happened, and the idea lost momentum. By mid-1987, however, the sales and customer service division was struggling with service problems that were becoming increasingly serious as the company continued to expand. As the new head of that division, Oliver decided it was high time to reexplore the quality issue.

Disappointed with the previous consultant, Oliver selected Organizational Dynamics, Inc. (ODI), an international consulting firm, to help FedEx in its efforts. ODI's great advantage, from Tom Oliver's perspective, was that it paid little attention to statistical techniques but a lot more to the thought processes and involvement of a company's people in developing quality improvement programs.

> *ODI's great advantage was that it paid little attention to statistical techniques but a lot more to the thought processes and involvement of a company's people.*

No quality improvement effort can be discussed in a vacuum. So, rather than launching straight into a description of the program, let's first take a look at the operating system behind FedEx's advertising promises. Then we'll examine the company's approach to quality, which includes training, improved alignments between internal suppliers and customers, quality action teams to identify and eliminate root causes of problems, replication of successful innovations, and measurement against demanding performance goals. Lastly, we'll see what can be learned from the FedEx experience.

The Federal Express System

Federal Express is an all-freight operation, specializing in the time-definite, reliable transport of high-value goods and documents. Every weeknight, some 500 aircraft and over 37,000 vans and trucks transport an average of nearly 1.8 million packages on both domestic and international routes, as well as carrying heavy freight shipments.

The system works in much the same way around the world, although FedEx uses subcontractors for local transport in some countries. In the United States, the highly standardized package operation calls for couriers to pick up packages and transport them to a local station; there, they are loaded onto aircraft (or sometimes large trucks) and shipped to a hub for sorting, reloading, and shipping to destination cities, where couriers deliver them to addressees. Three classes of service give customers in most locations a choice of delivery speeds: next business-day morning, next afternoon, and two days.

The Role of Information

One fascinating aspect of Federal Express is that it's in the information business as much as in the physical business of package handling. The company runs three information networks: a traditional, commercial revenue system for such tasks as accounting, finance, and payroll; a line-haul flight operations system; and COSMOS, perhaps the world's most sophisticated customer service system.

> *Federal Express is in the information business as much as in the physical business of package handling.*

COSMOS—which stands for Customer, Operations, Service, Master Online System—was first installed in 1979 and has been constantly upgraded to add capabilities, exploit new technologies, extend geographic reach, and cope with the increasing volume of business. It has evolved into a worldwide electronic network, transmitting critical package information to the customer service database at world headquarters in Memphis, Tennessee. Its major components are an order-entry system for customers to request package pickups, a continuously updated record of each package's progress through the FedEx system, financial records for billing purposes, and a huge relational database of customer transactions that is invaluable for analysis and planning.

To request a pickup in the United States, customers telephone a toll-free number that connects to a customer service agent (CSA) at one of 16 call centers around the nation. Calls can be diverted from one center to another to maintain the company's response-time standards. Since most calls are received in the mid- to late afternoon, peak volumes can be shifted to centers in other time zones. The CSA requests the shipper's account number and enters this on an electronic order blank on the video screen. The system then automatically displays the account name, address, phone number, location, contact name, and other relevant data.

Once a pickup request is entered, COSMOS alerts the nearest dispatch center, which, in turn, transmits the information to a courier serving that specific area. The request is displayed on a video screen in the courier's van or on a portable unit the size of a slim briefcase used by walking couriers.

This entire process can be undertaken without human intervention if the shipper places the order by touch-tone telephone through FedEx's "Automatic Pickup" service.

Tracking the Package Through the Federal Express System

Each step in the physical flow of package movements is paralleled by an information flow (Fig. 9-1). A FedEx package is identified by a unique 10-digit bar code on its accompanying airbill label. Each time the package changes hands, the bar code is scanned by an infrared light pen, and information on its movements is transmitted to COSMOS.

The first scan takes place at the pickup location. Using a hand-held terminal called a COSMOS IIB SuperTracker (a little bigger than the remote control for a TV and VCR), the courier scans the bar code and then enters the type of service, handling code, and destination zip code. The SuperTracker records this information and adds the time of pickup. The courier then places the SuperTracker in a specially designed thermal process printer and generates a bar-coded label with all the required package routing information for automated sorting. This first scan is known as PUPS (for Pick-Up Package Scan). Packages picked up from drop boxes are also scanned. As one senior executive noted, "Miniaturization has enabled us to stretch the communications system right to the customer's doorstep."

On returning to the van, the courier plugs the SuperTracker into a shoe within the dispatch computer, which promptly transmits its information to COSMOS. (In many overseas countries, this data transfer takes place when the package arrives at the Federal Express station.) After the van is unloaded, each package is scanned again before being reloaded into a container for transport to a sorting hub. Any exceptions—such as packages that are damaged or miss the aircraft—receive a P.M. eXception (PMX) scan, which records additional information such as shipper's and recipient's names and addresses. The package will be scanned four more times: before leaving the hub, upon arrival at the destination station, before being loaded into a local delivery van, and finally, at the delivery point.

The information provided by the scans enables the company to offer full custodial care of all packages and also provides an important tool for measuring quality. Provided that the package has been properly scanned at each stage, a trace of a missing package will reveal in seconds the time and location of the most recent scan. Although competitors such as UPS have invested enormous sums to develop their own tracking systems, none can match the level of tracing capability offered by Federal Express, which has even developed a humorous advertising campaign around this product plus.

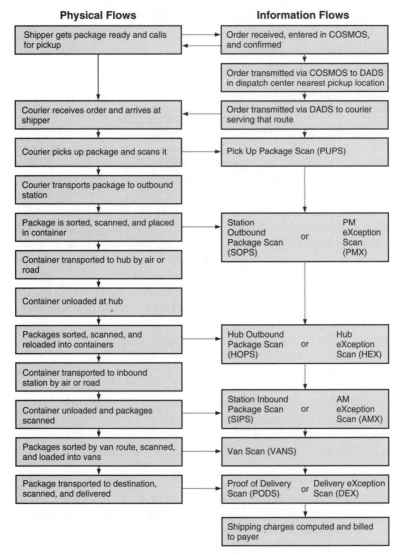

Figure 9-1. Physical flows and information flows for Federal Express packages. (*Source:* C. H. Lovelock, *"Federal Express: Quality Improvement Program,"* Case GM-456. Copyright © 1990 by the International Institute for Management Development (IMD), Lausanne, Switzerland. IMD retains all rights. Not to be reproduced or used without written permission directly from IMD, Lausanne, Switzerland.)

Senior executives emphasize the importance of accurate information for the company's success. Says one: "The notion of picking up and delivering a package without being able to offer the customer total information on it is unacceptable to us."

Front Stage and Backstage

As a possession-processing service, FedEx's business has a relatively small "front stage." The only activities that are "visible" to customers are calls to request pickups (not needed if the shipper has a standing daily order), pickup by a courier or deposit of the package in a drop box, and delivery by another courier to the destination address. All that remains is billing, and even this may be highly automated (we discuss it in Chap. 17). Other formal contacts with service personnel are few and far between: requesting a trace, making a complaint, or meeting with an account executive. In fact, most people's exposure to Federal Express is primarily random: We see their vehicles and couriers on the streets, their aircraft at airports, and their ads in the press or on TV.

Quality issues at FedEx revolve around how well backstage physical and informational processes work to ensure the high level of service that customers expect from the company. FedEx's operation is highly leveraged: A problem with a single van may affect all customers on that route (although substitution will be arranged promptly); a problem with a single station may affect all customers within the city or region that it serves (although, here again, there are contingencies for backup operations); but a sudden problem at the SuperHub in Memphis one night could affect half of the company's worldwide package volume. The Friday before Christmas, 1989, is graven in FedEx minds. For that was the day that the coldest weather in Memphis in 50 years caused burst water pipes in the SuperHub and, to make matters worse, the SuperHub sorting operation was shut down by a computer foulup. Packages, many of them last-minute Christmas presents, had to be sorted by hand. Managers and employees alike spent much of Christmas Day making home deliveries throughout their local areas in a dramatic bid at service recovery.

With this in mind, let's go backstage for a moment to see what goes on at the SuperHub, where three-quarters of a million packages are sorted every work night. Then we'll look in more detail at how the company approaches quality improvement.

Backstage at the SuperHub

It's almost one o'clock in the morning at Memphis International Airport. Aircraft are landing practically every minute, and the sky is full of lights as still more of them circle and make their final approaches. Yet the passenger terminal, where my host met me earlier, has long since shut down for the night. Once they have landed, the aircraft head toward the airport perimeter, in the direction of a long, massive structure.

The SuperHub building covers a million square feet (that's 23 acres!) on a 280-acre site. Inside is an automated matrix of 83 conveyor belts, moving at right angles to one another. Between 11 p.m. and 1:15 a.m. more than 100 aircraft, about 80 percent of them large jets such as Boeing 747s and 727s and McDonnell-Douglas MD-11s or DC-10s, arrive from 98 locations all over the United States, together with flights from Asia, Europe, Canada, Mexico, and South America. Parked in lines outside the structure, they wait while their cargoes, totaling over 900,000 packages, are unloaded and sorted inside the SuperHub. Reloaded, they will depart between 2:15 and 3:45 a.m. Additional packages, many of them scheduled for second-day delivery, will be sorted during the daytime. The balance of FedEx's 1.8 million daily packages will be sorted at three smaller domestic hubs in the continental United States and at hubs in Alaska, Tokyo, and Paris.

On the way by car to the SuperHub, we pass the company's private oil tank farm, capable of storing 1,050,000 gallons of fuel, pumped through pipelines from a terminal on the Mississippi River, 7 miles away. My eyebrows rise at the next sight: A large fleet of snowplows, snow blowers, and other snow-removal vehicles, smartly painted in FedEx colors, is parked in a lot beside the perimeter road. My host explains that the company purchased this equipment at a cost of over $2 million in 1988 after a heavy snowstorm—unusual for Memphis, which then had almost no snow-removal equipment—badly disrupted operations one night. "We only need this equipment about once every two years," she explains, "But when we need it, we really need it!"

Tour groups are already forming at the entrance to the SuperHub. Working in and around the vast building, where the dull roar of machinery fills the air, are some 6500 employees, neatly dressed in dark blue uniforms. The company is now the largest employer in the region, but still draws heavily for part-time workers from local colleges.

My private tour begins with the unloading process. At one of the loading bays beside the building, we come to an already empty DC-10 and clamber inside. And it really *is* empty: a hollow shell with no seats, no baggage containers, no movie screens, no interior partitions, no galleys, no carpets, no windows even. Just a cockpit at the head of a huge empty hull with giant entry doors and a reinforced floor designed to accept containers full of packages. Leaving the aircraft, we move on to watch a crew of 14 workers attack a Boeing 727 freighter. Using specially designed equipment, it takes them 12 minutes to unload 22 tons of freight. Containers are opened and the packages removed. The packages now begin their journey through the SuperHub on a wide belt known as the Primary Matrix.

We pause for a moment on a catwalk above the Primary Matrix, which is moving at 10 mph. It seems to move very quickly for a conveyor belt. Watching packages of different sizes, shapes, and colors rush by in their dozens and hundreds creates an almost hypnotic effect. I'm reminded of a mountain torrent in full flood. My guide taps me on the shoulder. "There's a lot more to see yet," she declares.

At intervals along the incoming belt to the Primary Matrix, packages are being diverted down the slide by automatic guide arms which control the flow. At the bottom are smaller belts, which move at right angles to the main belt. Fast-paced workers funnel the packages down these belts as one employee keys the routing information into the automated sorting system. As the packages move on these belts, now more slowly, mechanized pistons—driven by the computerized routing information—leap out at intervals to push specific packages aside, sorting them automatically yet again onto yet another set of belts, which now run parallel to the Primary Matrix incoming belt. These belts travel to the Secondary Sort, where the destinations are further narrowed by three-letter identifiers. The end results of this remarkable process are clusters of packages sorted by destination airport and ready for reloading into containers and thence into aircraft. But first, employees scan each package to record its departure from the hub.

We move on from aircraft reloading, this time to take a look at the large flight operations room, which boasts global weather-forecasting capabilities unequaled by any organization outside the armed forces. Uniformed captains and first officers are obtaining briefings for their return trips, and the flight status screens show that the first aircraft are already departing. It's now almost 2:30 a.m. Within the next hour, the SuperHub will start to shut down as the last remaining flights are loaded and depart. But the night is still young, and the average package is only halfway to its final destination point, where the courier's arrival will signal a return to front-stage operations.

Setting Goals for People–Service–Profits

By June 1988 (the beginning of fiscal year 1989), Tom Oliver and fellow managers working with ODI had concluded that for quality improvement efforts to succeed in the sales and customer service division, it was critical to involve domestic ground operations—FedEx's largest division, which then employed 25,000 couriers and 15,000 others. Most problems at Federal Express, says Oliver, are cross-divisional in nature. One division creates a certain output and passes it on to the next, whose problems often relate directly to what has happened earlier, up the line. Many companies face such a problem, but difficulties are compounded if there are rigid demarcation lines between departments or divisions. How is your own business placed in this respect?

> *Most problems are cross-divisional: one division creates a certain output and passes it on to the next division, whose problems often relate directly to what has happened earlier.*

The systemic nature of FedEx's operations requires a systemic approach to quality improvement. So the program devised by Federal Express and ODI included the following key elements:

1. Measuring performance on each of the three elements underlying the company's "People–Service–Profit" philosophy
2. Training both managers and employees
3. Creating quality action teams to work on resolving specific quality problems
4. Publicizing quality success stories and replicating them throughout the company
5. Promoting internal customer–supplier alignments

Measuring Performance

Prior to the quality improvement program, FedEx had measured service quality primarily in terms of on-time deliveries. Profits, of course, were measured through standard financial accounting procedures. Performance on the other P–S–P element, FedEx's people, was measured through a companywide survey of employee opinions, known as Survey–Feedback–Action (SFA). Each division and department also had its own specific goals and measures, as did many individual managers.

Survey–Feedback–Action. FedEx has conducted this confidential, annual employee survey for many years. It serves as a basis for airing concerns and resolving work-group problems. The survey today consists of 32 statements with which all employees are asked to agree or disagree on a five-point scale, ranging from "strongly agree" to "strongly disagree." Participation exceeds 99 percent. Scores are reported only for work groups, so no one knows the responses made by an individual employee. The first 10 questions (see Table 9-1) concern an employee's view of his or her manager; firmwide, the percentage of favorable responses on these 10 items constitutes what is known as the SFA Leadership Index. The remaining items include questions about pay,

Table 9-1. Survey–Feedback–Action (SFA) Leadership Index

---

1. I feel free to tell my manager what I think.
2. My manager tells me what is expected of me.
3. Favoritism is not a problem in my workgroup.
4. My manager helps us find ways to do our jobs better.
5. My manager is willing to listen to my concerns.
6. My manager asks for my ideas about things affecting our work.
7. My manager lets me know when I've done a good job.
8. My manager treats me with respect and dignity.
9. My manager keeps me informed about things I need to know.
10. My manager lets me do my job without interfering.

NOTE: Employees respond to each item on a five-point scale, ranging from "strongly agree" to "strongly disagree" (alternatively, they can check "undecided/don't know"). The term *workgroup* means "all persons who report to the same manager as you do, regardless of job title."

SOURCE: Federal Express.

working conditions, views on senior management, feelings about the company, and the importance of quality in the work group.

Take a look at the statements in the Leadership Index for a moment and consider how they relate to helping employees improve quality. At least six items concern the ease and content of communications between manager and employees (who might themselves be managers of other employees). The other items deal with behavior—both positive (helpfulness, respect) and negative (favoritism, interference). A number of companies have similar evaluation systems in place. Does yours? If so, are the findings being used as an input to quality improvement? If your firm does not have such a system, how do you think employees would rate their managers? And how would you predict that your own subordinates would rate *you?* Most managers find the concept threatening at first, but come to welcome the insights that these ratings, and follow-up discussions, provide.

"The more each unit tried to maximize its own performance, the more it tended to send difficult problems downstream."

TOM OLIVER

Establishing Common Goals. "One of the big difficulties in getting cross-divisional cooperation," notes Tom Oliver, "is the multiplicity of different goals. These goals might individually maximize the performance of each division, but collectively result in a deterioration of performance for the system. We realized that the more each unit tried to maximize its own performance, the more it tended to send difficult problems downstream. So we concluded that what we needed for Federal Express were three very simple goals.

"First, we took the existing SFA Leadership Index. The leadership a manager provides has a tremendous impact on the positive attitudes of the employees. We determined to use this index as the single goal in our people-management process, and established a goal of 72 for FY1989, up from 71 the previous year.

"People–Service–Profit implied a profit goal, so we set a goal of a 10 percent operating margin on the domestic business. That goal was regardless of individual department performance. Service had historically been defined in terms of couriers' on-time delivery efforts—what percentage of packages were delivered by 10:30 a.m. There were a lot of problems with that service level measurement; specifically, we could get that package delivered by 10:30 a.m. on the wrong date! It was also a limited measure, suggesting that Federal Express could be successful simply by delivering packages on time. That was no longer true.

"We found that the information associated with packages had as much to do with customer satisfaction as did delivery. For instance, 'don't know' answers to questions upset customers. As we reviewed customer correspondence, we found that the angriest of all the letters we got were those where our information processes failed us as opposed to those where we didn't deliver on time. What was needed was a broader measure that addressed other shortcomings that upset customers, such as failure to answer the phone quickly, damaged packages, etc."

> *"We found that the angriest of all the letters we got were those where our information processes failed us as opposed to those where we didn't deliver on time."*
>
> **TOM OLIVER**

Creating a Better Measure of Service. Oliver met with several other senior vice presidents to decide what service measures to use. ODI stressed the danger of using percentages as targets. In an organization as large as Federal Express, they argued, delivering 99 percent of packages on time or having 99.9 percent of all flights land safely would still lead to horrendous problems. Instead, they sought to approach quality from the standpoint of zero failures. Oliver emphasizes:

> It's only when you examine the types of failures, the number that occur of each type, and the reasons why, that you begin to improve the quality of your service. For us, the trick was to express quality failures in absolute numbers. That led us to develop the *Service Quality Index* or SQI, which takes each of 12 different events that occur every day, takes the numbers of those events, and multiplies them by a weight from 1 to 10 points, based on the amount of aggravation caused to customers— Fred Smith calls it our "hierarchy of horrors."

Table 9-2 shows the components of the SQI (pronounced "sky"), which is computed as a daily total and as a cumulative daily average. Each of the 12 items is measured each day (most of it automatically, through systems such as COSMOS), and the raw number of occurrences is weighted by a factor of 1, 5, or 10, depending on how seriously it upsets customers; the choice of components and weightings reflects detailed customer research. Like a golf score, the lower the index, the better is the performance.

Table 9-2. Computing the Service Quality Index (SQI)

Failure type	Weighting factor	$\times$	Number of occurrences[1]	$=$	Daily points
Wrong date, late service failures	5				
Right day, late service failures	1				
International[2]	1				
Invoice adjustments	1				
Traces (not answered by COSMOS)	1				
Abandoned calls	1				
Damaged packages	10				
Missing proofs of delivery (PODs)	1				
Overgoods[3]	5				
Complaints reopened by customers	5				
Lost packages	10				
Missed pickups	10				
Total failure points (SQI)					xxx,xxx

[1]Targets are set each year for the number of occurrences in each failure category in order to achieve an improvement over the previous year, relative to total volume. These occurrences are multiplied by the relevant factor to create points that are totaled to create the SQI goal.

[2]A composite score of service quality indicators from the company's international operations, including customs clearance delays.

[3]Packages that lack or have lost labels identifying the sender and addressee.

SOURCE: Federal Express.

Based on internal records, it was calculated that the average score during FY1988 (ending May 31) would have been 152,000 points per day—out of a potential maximum of 40 million per day if everything possible had gone wrong. The goal set for FY1989 was the same—152,000 points—but since package volumes were expected to rise by 20 percent, it actually represented a 20 percent improvement. The average daily score was reported on a weekly basis, both for the most recent week and the year to date. Employees were urged to "Reach for the SQI!" At the same time, they were being given the tools and the focused assignments needed to tackle problems and prevent failures.

To reinforce the significance of these three corporatewide goals, senior management tied the entire management bonus process to achievement of the three goals: SQI, Leadership Index, and domestic profits. Simply put, there would be no bonus for any manager at the end of FY1989 unless the company achieved all three goals. "Needless to say, that caught everyone's imagination," says Oliver, smiling wryly. He adds, "It was very different from our previous approach of having managers' bonuses based on their ability to meet individual management-by-objective goals without regard to whether that did or didn't help the corporate process."

In the upshot, fiscal year 1989 turned out to be a great year. The company achieved the profit goal, despite some difficult circumstances, and the SQI came in at 133,000 points. The Leadership Index reached 76, representing the largest single jump in the history of the SFA process, in terms of managers' relationships with employees. As a further check on quality, every quarter FedEx surveys 2100 customers, drawn randomly from each of several market segments, and gauges their satisfaction against a detailed list of service attributes.

The notion of evaluating all managers simultaneously against three corporatewide criteria—profits, service quality, and employee appraisal of leadership skills—is unusual. Tying every manager's bonus to achieving a corporatewide target on all three measures simultaneously is extraordinary. But look at Fig. 9-2 and consider the implications. A myopic focus on immediate profits often results in cutting corners on service and short-changing employees; singlemindedly trying to please customers can cause ballooning costs and lead some managers to berate employees for service failures rather than getting at root causes; and emphasizing employees' satisfaction to the exclusion of all else risks not pushing them to go the extra mile to serve customers better and avoid waste. Success in the long run, as I emphasized in earlier chapters, requires a continuing search to achieve synergy among goals, so that success in meeting the needs of one group of stakeholders leads naturally to success with the others.

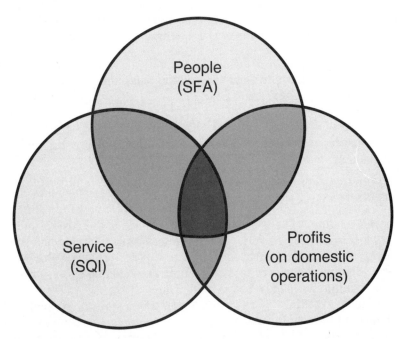

Figure 9-2. "People–Service–Profits" at Federal Express: three synergistic measures of managerial performance.

Training Through the Quality Advantage Program

On-the-job training has always been a major priority at Federal Express. So instituting new quality-related training programs fit well with the existing culture. Unlike job-specific courses, however, these programs were designed to reach FedEx's people at all levels. ODI began at the top, designing and leading quality planning workshops for FedEx's senior vice presidents, their direct reports, and managing directors from all divisions. The product of each workshop was a series of action plans, setting priorities for problem resolution. Training was then rolled out to managers and employees.

A key goal of ODI's Quality Advantage Program is to get people to take the time needed to analyze what are often complex problems, rather than shooting from the hip with instant solutions. Under the leadership of ODI vice president Rob Evans, consultants trained all managers in the Sales and Customer Service division to understand the quality process, then began training employees and facilitators from other divisions, including Ground Operations. Different versions of the programs have been developed for managers and employees.

The program begins with a module on "The Meaning of Quality," introducing the five pillars on which ODI believes that a quality organization must be built:

- *Customer focus*—a commitment to meeting customer needs
- *Total involvement*—"improving quality is everyone's job"
- *Measurement*—where and when to take action; documenting progress
- *Systematic support*—applying strategic planning, budgeting, and performance management to quality improvement efforts
- *Continuous improvement*—always reaching for new and better ways to perform one's job

A second module, "The Cost of Quality," identifies the costs of not doing quality work, including rework, waste, unnecessary overtime, and job dissatisfaction. The goal is to help participants estimate their own cost of quality, breaking this down into avoidable and unavoidable (necessary) costs, and then planning ways of reducing the former.

The third module, "You and Your Customer," describes the customer–supplier chain and helps participants to see that everyone in Federal Express is both a customer and a supplier. Participants learn to identify their own key customers and suppliers within the company—and how they are linked—and then to understand how to align customer needs and supplier capabilities in order to meet agreed requirements.

Everyone in Federal Express is both a customer and a supplier.

The "Continuous Improvement" module emphasizes that it's everyone's responsibility to fix and prevent problems, and it shows how to identify early warning signals of certain problems. Continuous improvement requires everyone to strive to meet customer needs in innovative ways. The fifth module, "Making Quality Happen," is directed at managers, supervisors, and professionals; it describes how to take a leadership role to implement quality programs.

Quality Action Teams

A related program, Quality Action Teams (QATs), focuses on how quality improvement should be implemented. Each QAT typically consists of four to 10 members, formed on either an ad hoc or ongoing basis to attack specific problems. Membership often comprises both hourly employees and management personnel, and a team may be drawn from multiple work groups or divisions. ODI breaks the problem-solving process into four phases:

- Focusing on a particular problem or opportunity
- Analyzing data
- Developing solutions and action plans
- Executing these action plans to implement the solutions

To help QATs perform each of these tasks, ODI has taught participants how to apply 20 problem-solving tools, including fishbone (cause-and-effect) analysis, flowcharting, and cost–benefit analysis.

ODI's Evans believes that one reason for the company's SQI successes is that FedEx immediately set up 12 QATs, each headed by a senior manager, to focus on each of the specific SQI components. Results were posted weekly, and every three months each QAT reported out to Smith and other senior executives. Subsequently, hundreds of other QATs were formed throughout the company to tackle specific problems.

Quarterly awards are given to QAT participants in four categories: (1) greatest impact on SQI results; (2) best use of the quality process (using tools that had been taught); (3) best understanding of root causes (identifying and working on underlying problems rather than superficial effects; and (4) best use of line employees (gathering information from the people closest to the process who know it best).

Publicizing and Replicating Successes

Federal Express and ODI have also made efforts to facilitate a bottom-up movement in quality improvement within the divisions. The aim is to create a network of first-line employees and shared approaches to problem solving. Quality professionals from each of FedEx's 14 divisions form a quality advisory board which holds regular meetings to discuss failures and successes. The challenge is to coordinate the replication of successes by getting people to describe what they have actually done and how they did it—as opposed to simply talking about the results. Forms and electronic mail systems have been created to make it easy to record this information, while a reward system encourages people to turn in details of their successes.

"Recognition programs have a mutual benefit," says Linda Griffin, manager of regional customer automation. "They motivate and reward employees and create some peer pressure. At the same time, management gets to see the value of the training programs, which reinforces the belief that training is the right thing to do."

> *"Recognition programs have a mutual benefit: They motivate and reward employees and create some peer pressure. At the same time, management gets to see the value of the training programs."*
>
> LINDA GRIFFIN

Two Success Stories. Couriers in a QAT at one station were frustrated with the problems (such as missed pickups) caused when the regular courier on a route was absent—due to vacation, sickness, or other reason—and had to be replaced by a substitute unfamiliar with the route, obscure addresses, hidden building entrances, location of freight elevators, pickup or delivery locations on different floors, etc. So they designed an informational sheet or booklet describing each route. The result was a sharp increase in on-time delivery and productivity. This idea has now been incorporated in the "Policy and Procedures" manual for all stations.

Another example concerns a sorting table designed by employees in the Phoenix station to prevent missorts caused when envelopes slide across a smooth surface and into the wrong destination piles. The Phoenix employees videotaped their new table design and passed it on to the company's industrial engineers, who developed several versions of the sort table targeted at different-sized stations.

Sharing success stories is seen as a way to get more people involved in QATs and to improve working relations within the company through customer–supplier alignments. One concern is that people tend to gravitate toward QATs, which are often seen as more fun. "We really have to push the notion of customer–supplier alignment," says one manager. "People and departments don't always work well together!"

Promoting Customer–Supplier Alignments

The notion of customer–supplier alignments is designed to build effective working relationships both within the company as well as between FedEx and its external customers. All employees are invited to view themselves as suppliers when they provide services to another employee, department, or outside customer; similarly, they should see themselves as customers when obtaining information, materials, or services from another employee or outside vendor.

A workbook has been developed to walk "customers" and "suppliers" through three key alignment questions. The process culminates in a written document that spells out the customer's expectations and the supplier's service guarantee. The three key questions that a supplier asks the customer are:

- What do you need from me?
- What do you do with what I give you?
- What are the gaps between what I give you and what you need?

To encourage clear communication of needs and expectations FedEx has been using its own satellite broadcast network, FXTV, in both a sharing and training role. For instance, ODI's Rob Evans participated in a program entitled "Customer/Supplier Alignment: The First Step in Quality," designed to reinforce earlier quality training. Evans began his segment of the live broadcast by reminding viewers of the "right things right" grid, a simple four-cell matrix developed by ODI (Fig. 9-3).

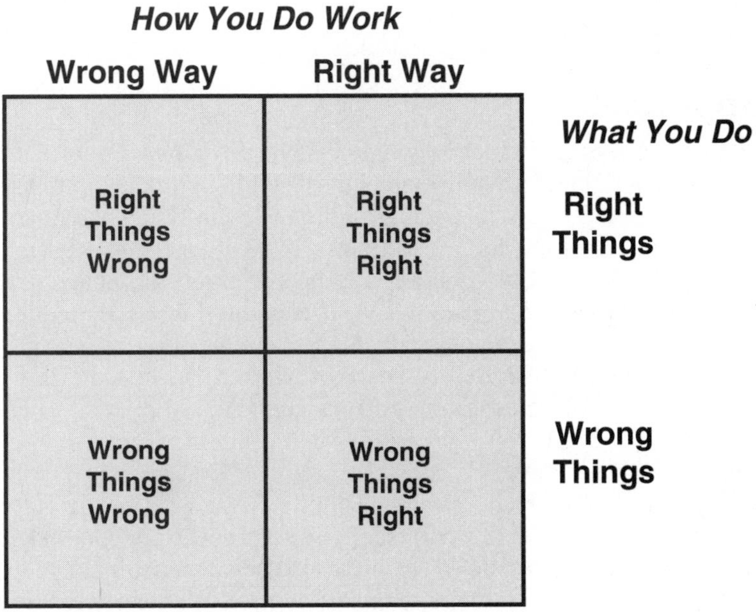

How You Do Work

Wrong Way	Right Way	
		What You Do
Right Things Wrong	Right Things Right	**Right Things**
Wrong Things Wrong	Wrong Things Right	**Wrong Things**

Figure 9-3. The "right things right" grid. (*Copyright © 1992 by Organizational Dynamics, Inc. Reprinted by permission.*)

"That grid," said Evans as the diagram appeared on the screen, "is a simple way to look at the work we do from two different angles. The first angle is *how* we do the work we do. We either do things wrong or we do things right. The second angle has to do with *what* work we actually do—doing the right things or the wrong things. When we put these two together, we have four possibilities:

- We could be doing *the right things wrong*—that's the old way of looking at quality problems...and of course that happens.
- We could be doing *the wrong things wrong*—really wasting our time.
- Or we could be doing *the wrong things right*—things that don't matter to our customers, internal or external—but doing a very good job of them.
- The fourth possibility is doing *the right things right*. This is the only one that adds value to our customers and our company."

Evans continued: "In a quality organization, people spend the great majority of their time doing the right things right. What we've found at ODI is that most managers spend 45–60 percent of their time doing the right things right, but the rest is wasted—time, effort, money. Of that wasted time, about half seems to fall into the wrong things right category."

An Appraisal

Continuous improvement means what it says. How has Federal Express performed in the light of its enormous investments in quality improvement? Despite ongoing increases in package volumes, the SQI has continued to decline. The final average for FY1993 was 149,303 (see Table 9-3), slightly below the FY1990 plan, but substantially better given the near doubling of packages handled since the index was first computed in FY1988. Meantime, the Leadership Index target was 79. Although corporate financial results were in the red in FY1992, due to restructuring in Europe, FedEx continues to make profits on domestic operations and FY1993 results will be $200 million better.

In October 1990, Federal Express became the first company to win the prestigious Malcolm Baldrige National Quality Award in the service category. "What are the secrets to your company's success?" people asked CEO Fred Smith. In a keynote speech at a national conference held in conjunction with the award ceremonies, Smith declared: "There is no secret to whatever success Federal Express has enjoyed. What we do is all in the books. Our secret, if there is one, is just doing what they say."

Table 9-3. Service Quality Index (SQI): Actual versus Goal FY1993

FY1993
Average Daily Failure Points
June 1992–May 1993

Failure type	Weighting	Goal	Actual[1]
Wrong date, late service failures	5	51,764	63,286
Right day, late service failures	1	32,169	37,031
International	1	29,372	22,941
Invoice adjustments	1	8,057	7,981
Traces (not answered by COSMOS)	1	4,314	4,430
Abandoned calls	1	4,127	4,194
Damaged packages	10	2,609	2,995
Missing proofs of delivery (PODs)	1	1,504	2,450
Overgoods	5	1,331	1,180
Complaints reopened by customers	5	1,319	1,207
Lost packages	10	899	972
Missed pickups	10	535	636
Total average failure points (SQI)		138,000	149,303

[1]Includes failures created by Hurricane Andrew in 1992 and a massive snowstorm in March 1993 that disrupted transportation in numerous states.
SOURCE: Federal Express.

But doing what the books say isn't necessarily easy. Nor are quality programs fast or cheap to implement. Says Tom Oliver: "Most companies need four to five years of continuous effort before employees and managers alike really understand that this is the way to approach problems." In 1990, Oliver estimated that quality training one employee could cost $200 in the first year and $100 in each subsequent year. Add in the value of time away from the regular job, multiply the yearly total by over 80,000 employees, and the bill really starts to mount up. In some respects, the easiest tasks have already been completed. Continuous improvement may pose tougher problems.

Quality alone doesn't guarantee success. Being a leader also means that people love to point out instances where you dropped the ball. The company now admits that it made a strategic miscalculation in Europe, overestimating the potential for market growth and its ability to take share from already entrenched competitors. It also underestimated the difficulties associated with acquiring established, non-express-type trucking companies in a variety of different countries and molding them into a unified, pan-European organization sharing FedEx's distinct culture. Since 1992, FedEx has withdrawn from intra-European shipments, subcontracted local operations in several countries, and refocused its European activities to build

> **"What we do is all in the books. Our secret, if there is one, is just doing what they say."**
>
> *FRED SMITH*

traffic for EXPRESSfreighter service on intercontinental routes and to develop long-term business logistics contracts.

Commenting on Federal Express's ongoing progress (as of early 1993), Tom Oliver observed:

> We've come a long way from 1988. Volume is more than double and SQI is still down. Profits are getting better in a tough, worldwide economy. But Quality isn't "sexy" for us anymore. Like a good marriage, you have to believe that continuous commitment and strong communications yield the desired rewards. Quality works because people at the very first level want to make a difference and be contributors. This is true even when management seems intent on preventing them from doing so because management sees profit as the overriding objective, rather than seeing profit as the outcome of superior customer service and employee creativity. When management is truly supportive, the sky is the limit.

Federal Express is an impressive company, offering many learning insights. Its model of quality improvement cannot, of course, be transferred wholesale to any type of service business. After all, its program is designed for a large, sophisticated firm whose business emphasizes what this book calls possession-processing and information-processing services, with most operations taking place backstage. Still, any service organization would do well to ponder the following points:

- *Quality training must be results-oriented*, not technique-oriented. Building awareness and handing out tools is not enough: The process must speak to improving results.

- *Create and train quality action teams*, and give employees real service problems on which to put quality tools to relevant use. As employees (and the company) gain experience, encourage them to take initiative on problem solving.

- *Reward, publicize, and replicate service improvements*. Multisite operations, in particular, offer fertile opportunities for taking solutions developed at one site and implementing them companywide.

- *Avoid percentage-based service quality measures*. Instead of reporting percentage of "good" performances, emphasize raw numbers of "bad" incidents that are known, from research and complaints, to upset customers.

- *Create a single composite index* (if practicable) that consolidates all major negative performance components, with each suitably weighted to reflect the degree to which it turns off customers; publicize changes in this index regularly; and use it as a corporate rallying point.

- *Look for opportunities to use technology* to measure performance automatically, to minimize internal paperwork.

- *Recognize that quality improvement takes time.* Even if you seek a long-term goal of zero defects, set realistic (but challenging) goals for incremental improvement.

- *Study internal customer–supplier relationships.* Get "customers" to clarify their needs, and encourage "suppliers" to develop guaranteed service agreements.

- *Work on improving managers' leadership skills.* Leadership can be taught at every level of supervision, but managers and supervisors need feedback. Consider implementing a form of FedEx's Survey–Feedback–Action program (there are several commercially available versions of this type of survey), but recognize that successful application requires a degree of trust between employees and managers.

- Finally: *Identify the right work to do—and do it right.*

"Idiots! You were supposed to pick up the skier, not the skis!"

10 Process and Progress: Understanding the Customer Experience

To obtain the benefits they seek from a particular service, customers move through a series of steps over a period of time that can range from minutes to years. Their role may be passive or active (or both). By flowcharting the process, step by step from start to finish, managers can understand the service drama from the perspective of a particular type of customer. We visit a hospital emergency room for insights into how flowcharting helped managers and medical personnel reengineer and improve a very demanding service process.

Plays that feature a huge cast of characters, numerous subplots, and constant changes of scene are sometimes hard to follow. The audience gets lost and confused. "What's going on?" they wonder. "Who's that character—have we seen him before? Where are we? When are they going to get to the point?"

The service drama is often highly compartmentalized, especially when a series of different activities are performed in sequence by numerous different players. As a result, it's easy for customers to get "lost" in the system and to feel that nobody knows who they are or what they need. And here's the rub: That perception may be quite accurate! How many times have you, as a customer, had to explain who you are and what you want to several different employees of the same organization, because there seems to be a complete lack of internal communication? Inanimate objects, from shirts at the laundry to customers' orders in the computer, can also get lost.

Lack of communication is not the only problem. Poorly designed physical facilities and employees who don't understand how their part contributes to the unfolding service "drama" lead inevitably to an unsatisfactory experience for customers, particularly when the latter are personally involved in people-processing services.

A well-designed service process, by contrast, appears seamless and logical, even when it involves multiple steps and service is delivered by a variety of employees performing specialized functions. What's needed is to begin with a vision of the overall process and then to weave together its constituent elements. Redesigning an existing service requires determining what the process currently looks like and then comparing the reality with a new vision. There can be no hope of progress without knowledge of the process.

> *There can be no hope of progress without knowledge of the process.*

By flowcharting a service process step by step from start to finish, managers and employees alike can start to understand the service drama from the varying perspectives of different types of customers. But it's also vital to understand how backstage activities (which the customer doesn't see) help to create and support good performances front stage.

Experiencing a Hospital Emergency Unit

Moviemakers and TV producers love medical emergencies. Apart from the human drama, the audiovisual opportunities are terrific: Helicopters dropping out of the sky with a chop-chop-chop noise as windswept medical personnel wait below; sirens in the night and flashing lights on rain-soaked surfaces as ambulances screech to a halt at the floodlit entrance to a massive building; orderlies rapidly pushing a prone figure on a stretcher down a long corridor to the sound of beeping monitors while doctors and nurses run alongside urgently giving and taking instructions; police officers and loved ones anxiously awaiting news of a colleague critically injured in the line of duty. It's hot stuff.

The emergency unit (EU) of a hospital is usually the point of entry for any patient who unexpectedly requires medical assistance because of an accident or sudden onset of a medical problem. The human drama inherent in this most variable of all health-care environments lends itself well to Hollywood movies and television soap operas. And drama there is in real life, too—although often of a quieter and more intimate nature than the scenarios I sketched. From the staff's perspective, times of intense activity in the EU may be interspersed with periods when nothing happens. From the standpoints of patients whose problems are not medically urgent, the experience of a visit can be depressing: long waits in harshly lit rooms filled with a cross section of society—sad-faced old people, an unshaven person talking to himself, a parent comforting a frightened child.

But what of the task of managing such an operation? Like police and fire services, EUs offer service 24 hours a day, 365 days a year. The work is unpredictable. Nobody can say who will need care, or when, or what medical intervention will be required. Will several ambulances arrive bringing victims of an MVA (motor vehicle accident) involving traumatic injuries? Or will someone walk in with a painfully infected finger? Will the next one be a potential miscarriage, or chest pains, or asthma, or a broken toe, or a psychiatric case? And then there are the friends and family members who often accompany patients; they, too, may need attention to alleviate their fear and distress.

The potential for confusion, stress, and error is high. For an EU to function well, it needs dedicated, well-trained medical staff and orderlies who trust each other. The better its facilities and equipment are, the more responsive an EU can be to a wide mix of cases, without having to transfer patients to another hospital for more specialized treatment. But people and facilities, while important in themselves, are not enough: The process by which patients are received and treated must itself be well conceived and executed. For the consequences of any failure in this process may be nothing less than fatal.

EUs must be among the most difficult of all service operations to manage efficiently. Opportunities for standardization are limited, since a wide array of multifaceted services must be tailored to the needs of each patient and delivered by many different employees. Units must be staffed 24 hours a day, 365 days a year, by employees with specialized skills who work together in teams. The capacity to serve must be sufficient to meet an unpredictable level of life-threatening emergencies, where work has to be performed under tight time constraints. For the most part, EUs can't select their patients, they can't require advance reservations, and (unless they have collaborative arrangements with other hospitals), they can't be picky about which types of ailments they will choose to treat. Let's look at how one large hospital approaches the challenge.

> *Emergency units must be among the most difficult of all service operations to manage efficiently.*

Beth Israel Hospital

Boston's Beth Israel Hospital, locally known as "the BI," is a 504-bed teaching institution affiliated with Harvard Medical School. As a tertiary-care center, treating patients with relatively serious or unusual problems, it draws patients from all over the country. But it also serves as a community hospital for local residents whose medical needs may be quite commonplace. The BI has been cited as one of the 101 best service organizations in America. In January 1993, it was also named as one of the 10 best employers in the nation.

Under the leadership of its long-term president, Mitchell T. Rabkin, M.D., the BI was the first American hospital to issue a "Statement on the Rights of Patients." In 1975, the BI became the first major medical center to introduce primary nursing. Each patient is assigned a primary nurse who is responsible for managing that person's hospital experience from admission through discharge or transfer to another unit of the hospital. The primary nurse, who is both care giver and care manager, works closely with the patient's doctors and develops a 24-hour nursing-care plan for each assigned patient. When the primary nurse goes off duty, she or he meets with incoming nurses or leaves instructions for the next shifts.

During the 1980s, the BI undertook a major construction and renovation program to improve its inpatient facilities. Then the hospital turned its attention to renovating its emergency unit, a very visible facility that was often the first point of entry for new inpatients, as well as a treatment center for many outpatients from the local community. The old EU was a gloomy, congested facility. Because of crowding, its customers lacked privacy. Indeed, on busy days, patients whose condition had stabilized might have to lie on stretchers in the corridors; meantime, service for nonemergency cases could be painfully slow.

"Before the renovation," observed Dr. Rabkin, "The EU was immensely jammed. All kinds of activities—medical, administrative, and passers-by—were blended into a welter of confusion." Management's challenge was to bring order to the process, enhance the quality of care, and improve each customer's experience, while also keeping within tight cost constraints.

> *Management's challenge was to bring order to the process, enhance the quality of care, and improve each customer's experience, while also keeping within tight cost constraints.*

Flowcharting the Process

An important, but widely ignored, architectural precept is that no building should be constructed (or renovated) without a good understanding of the activities that will be taking place within and around it. If interior space isn't designed to accommodate a desired process, then it will simply shape that process—perhaps in undesirable ways. But how do you go about sorting out what needs to be done?

Dr. Rabkin describes how managers and board members approached the task of renovation:

> In order to understand what was going on and exercise some judgment on whether we wanted that to continue in the new Beth Israel emergency unit, we developed flowcharts. The purpose was simply to follow the patient—and all that which derived from the patient's visit—through its various stages to see whether that visit was being processed in the most appropriate manner.
>
> In a hospital particularly—and probably in many other industries as well—what begins with a rational process on day 1 probably evolves over time into something that is less than rational, due to changes in technology, changes in procedure, new imperatives, and the inevitable deterioration of verbal messages passed from one person to another over the months or years.
>
> And so we thought it was terribly important to stand back and evalu-

ate by means of flowcharting precisely what was happening to the patient and to information about the patient that was needed for decision making. A variety of insights developed out of this flowcharting, ranging from the lengths of time, for example, that patients might wait on the front bench before they were fully evaluated to the number of different providers that particular types of patients interacted with during their visit to the emergency unit. Another issue was whether those who were the most sick were cared for the soonest.

In a multiservice environment such as an EU, different types of patients require different treatments, although there will be some common elements. One flowchart traced what might happen to a patient who arrived complaining of chest pains. Alternative outcomes are possible in such a situation, depending on diagnosis and response to treatment. By way of illustration, I've shown the first few steps in the flowchart in Fig. 10-1.

Let's say the patient is a middle-aged man who arrives alone by taxi at the hospital. The flowchart begins with his arrival at the EU, where at the front desk he sees a young woman who is the triage nurse. Her job is to learn the apparent nature of his problem and quickly determine its acuity level. If she concludes that the problem is not urgent—perhaps she suspects indigestion—then the patient is sent to the registration assistant, who requests the basic information needed to create a medical record, including personal data, insurance coverage, and name of personal physician. This done, the patient is asked to take a seat and wait until his name is called.

Alternatively, the triage nurse may conclude that the patient is suffering cardiac problems that could be an acute heart attack and that his case should be classified as urgent (or emergent). In this instance, she will call for another nurse to take the patient by wheelchair to an examining room. The flowchart shows the next two steps, in which this second nurse helps the patient to get changed and onto an examining table, and then starts to undertake a more thorough analysis and provide preliminary treatment. Information is then entered onto a patient record.

Different activities have been coded in different ways according to traditional process chart conventions: A rectangle denotes an activity, a diamond denotes a decision, and the third shape indicates recording of information. The balance of the chart (not shown) includes another six action steps and four decision points in the EU, up to the point where a decision is made either to discharge the customer or admit him for inpatient treatment.

These additional steps on the flowchart include a visit from a registration assistant to collect information (if the patient or a companion is able to provide it), and a telephone call to the patient's private physician (if he has one); next the nurse briefs an EU resident (physician), who reviews the electrocardiogram, examines the patient, and studies his historical record (if available). The resident then decides what orders to place for medications,

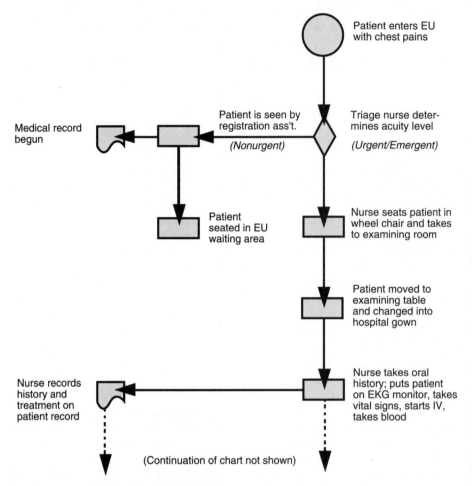

Figure 10-1. Flowcharting initial steps in treating an emergency unit patient. (source: *Beth Israel Hospital, Boston, MA.*)

lab tests, and X rays, consults with the patient's own physician (if that doctor can be reached), and with a specialist from the hospital's own cardiac-care unit; the latter may also wish to examine the patient. Finally, a decision is made on treatment, which could involve discharge to the care of his private physician or admission as an inpatient. The latter branch of the flowchart continues with over 20 more steps, following the customer through an overnight stay, with additional tests, treatment, meals, prescriptions, and on to final discharge. All these actions and decisions involving the patient are paralleled by updates to his records.

There's nothing very dramatic in this flowchart—no sudden cardiac arrest, for instance, leading to heroic efforts to save the patient's life (there are, of course, well-established procedures for dealing with such an event). For the task facing planners of the new EU was not to create a movie script but to examine a wide array of routine procedures. In practice, this flowchart simplifies the real-world environment. As you can see from the text accompanying the diagram, one box sometimes combines a cluster of activities performed by the nurse ("takes oral history, puts patient on EKG monitor, etc."). This illustrates the point that flowcharting should be only as detailed as the nature of the analysis requires.

Insights from this flowchart and other studies were helpful to Beth Israel's management and board at two levels. First, they provided essential inputs to designing the physical layout of the new EU facility. Second, they led to important changes in the procedures for processing patients.

One significant innovation was to extend the primary nursing concept to the emergency unit. So a specific nurse is now assigned to follow each patient's progress and provide ongoing care, with the goal that no patient be forgotten and left unattended for long periods of time. A second innovation was to assign certain nurses and physicians to the roles of what were called "flow nurse" and "administrative physician." Their task is to monitor the overall flow of patients through different steps in diagnosis and treatment and to help speed that flow by assisting at any relevant stage in any process where there seems to be a bottleneck that delays service to customers.

A Visit to the Emergency Unit

One problem that I see with flowcharting and other technical descriptions of processes is that they can become bloodless models, divorced from the daily reality of creating services for customers. Behind the charts and the terse descriptions are real people working in real buildings with real equipment. And in front-stage situations, these people are interacting directly with their customers. So to bring this point home, let me take you on a short tour of Beth Israel's Emergency Unit.

The BI is located about 2 miles from the center of downtown Boston, within what must be one of the world's largest medical complexes. Loosely described as the Longwood Medical Area, it includes the Harvard Medical School, the BI, Children's Hospital, the Brigham and Women's Hospital, New England Deaconess Hospital, the Joslin Diabetes Center, and the Dana-Farber Cancer Institute, plus an enormous, dedicated power plant to supply energy. The BI itself comprises a cluster of 12 buildings, at one end of which a big red sign announces the Emergency Unit.

As I arrive, I can see a couple of ambulances parked outside; two emergency medical technicians are unloading a stretcher from one of the vehicles. Although it's a wintry day in Boston, with leaden skies and snow flurries, the EU is bright and cheerful inside, with walls painted in a variety of pastel colors, lots of light oak woodwork, and floors either carpeted or covered in red tile.

Twin desks face the glass entry doors. One is occupied by the triage nurse, the other by a uniformed hospital information representative. Nurses at Beth Israel dress very casually—there's no starched cap and white uniform. In fact, there's no dress code at all; the only requirement is that they wear a name badge; in practice, most nurses choose to wear something white and something colored, or put on a white jacket. The triage nurse on duty today is wearing a white knit sweater.

I've come to see Kathy Carr, R.N., who holds the position of Nurse Manager of the EU. At the moment, she's talking reassuringly to a middle-aged woman whose husband, I learn later, has just been admitted after collapsing at a nearby museum. As I wait, two police officers emerge from behind a pair of double doors and exit the building. They had brought in a psychiatric patient who was acting in a disturbed manner on a Boston street.

After a couple of minutes, Carr is free to join me and give me a tour. To the right of the desks is an open doorway to the waiting area, which has comfortable armchairs but no sofas ("once one person sits on a sofa, it's full!"). There are also three registration booths, where assistants obtain relevant information from waiting patients or their companions. These booths are separated by glass partitions, designed to provide patients with some privacy while they discuss sensitive information. A corridor behind the triage desk leads to the adjoining walk-in clinic and on toward the main lobby of the hospital. To the left, double doors lead to the medical (or acute) area of the EU, while a second set of doors leads to the surgical area.

It's quite easy to relate the first steps of the flowchart to the layout of the unit. The triage nurse and the information representative are located at a natural focal point for the beginning of the process, acting as traffic cops for patients and other visitors alike. It would be hard to get lost here; even if you were feeling very confused, someone would be sure to see you and offer to help.

It's quite easy to relate the first steps of the flowchart to the layout of the unit. The triage nurse and the information representative are located at a natural focal point for the beginning of the process.

Kathy Carr has held her position for 15 years, during which time both the unit and her job have evolved tremendously. With her experience and qualifications (which include a master's degree), she could easily move to a more senior administrative post. But she loves her job at the EU, because it combines management—including mentoring of younger staff—and clinical practice. Once a week, she devotes a full day to nursing in the unit, which keeps her involved in patient care. But at any time extra help is needed, she can don a white coat and assist. As we chat, a patient who has just arrived by ambulance is wheeled through the double doors on a stretcher. I glimpse a shock of white hair. Carr explains that the patient's condition had been radioed in by the ambulance driver, so there was no need to visit the triage nurse first.

On a typical day, the EU sees about 110 patients, excluding those with relatively simple problems who are triaged to the BI's Walk-In Clinic down the corridor. Roughly 20–25 percent of them arrive by ambulance. Perhaps 60–70 percent of patients have been in the EU before; some of them suffer from chronic conditions. Less than 1 percent die while in the unit, although some are terminally ill, including an increasing number of AIDS sufferers. Since the BI does not normally treat children, pediatric patients and their companions will be directed (or, if necessary, personally escorted) to nearby Children's Hospital. A very sick child, however, may be stabilized first at the BI and then transferred by ambulance. About 55 percent of cases will be treated in the "medical" area, the physical location that handles all acute cases, including major trauma; the most common problems involve malfunctions of the heart or lungs. Other patients, mostly suffering from injuries to their extremities, such as sprains and fractures, or from gynecological problems, will be treated in the adjoining "surgical" area.

The peak hours for patient visits are between 11 a.m. and 11 p.m. During those times, there will be four medical physicians on duty, two surgeons, one administrative physician, nine nurses, two orderlies, and two unit coordinators. As many as 16 nurses will be on duty during the shift-overlap period, so that outgoing nurses can brief the incoming team about the various patients under treatment. At other hours, fewer staff are on duty, although additional personnel can be summoned from other parts of the hospital in the event of a major influx of patients. It's hard to predict the patient mix, although the EU does get a greater number of alcohol-related cases on Friday and Saturday nights (largely reflecting the local student population).

As we walk through the double doors into the medical area, the scene is busy but also calm and deliberate. The walls and ceiling are painted in pastel colors, with curtains striped in blue and gray. In the middle of the long, rectangular room is an "island" containing countertops, space for storing certain materials and equipment, and two workstations with telephones, video monitors, and keyboards for the unit coordinators. Walking over to the island, Carr points out a doctor who is briefing an ambulance technician by radio on appropriate care for a seriously injured patient en route to the hospital; a team of care givers will be ready for him when he arrives. The unit coordinator's job is to track the progress of all patients and to coordinate requests for medicines, supplies, equipment, and specialized staff. At one of the workstations, Carr scans the patient list on the monitor to determine the mix of cases.

Patients are being cared for in treatment areas that line the sides of the section and can be closed off by glass doors or by curtains. The areas are large enough to hold an array of equipment and a medical team in addition to a bed; all are easily visible from the central island. One of these little rooms is empty, most have their curtains closed, but medical staff are moving in and out. Patients have some choice as to whether curtains are left open or drawn while they rest after treatment. As I watch, the curtains screening one room are drawn open, several medical staff emerge, and an orderly wheels a woman on a stretcher toward the exit; she's being admitted as an inpatient.

Another room has its doors and curtains open to reveal an elderly man propped up in a sitting position; despite being connected to an intravenous drip and having transparent oxygen tubes inserted in his nose, he's looking around, quite alert. A doctor in a white coat (or maybe she's a nurse—it's hard to tell without reading the name tag) comes up to him with a smile and they share a joke. Apparently he's going to be discharged soon. In one room, a frail-looking old woman is lying very still behind closed glass doors with a younger woman, perhaps a daughter, beside the bed, holding her hand.

About 50 percent of patients arrive with a companion. Unless it would interfere with treatment, these visitors are allowed to accompany patients and to sit with them; often, they are in a position to give valuable information about the patient's background or the circumstances surrounding the current problem. Visitors, too, often need care and attention; the BI has developed an evening program for EU volunteers, who sit with family members and friends in the waiting area and provide support.

We move on to the surgical area, which appears quiet (although who knows what might be occurring behind closed curtains). Carr points out a group of nurses who, she explains, are engaged in a change-of-shift report. One nurse is briefing the other about current patients. "Here, we've got an elderly man with…" (the medical jargon describing his condition and treatment is unintelligible to me). She shakes her head and continues. "He's real anxious. We've called his wife, and she's on her way over." Carr and I listen for a while, then make our way out to the lobby.

Although I've observed no dramatic events (slightly to my relief), I've seen advanced medical technology, information being given, stored, and retrieved, touching little human vignettes, and task-oriented teams of care givers constantly forming and unforming. I've also seen an attractive, custom-designed facility that reflects the needs of both the providers and recipients of service. But sooner or later, as processes and technology change, it will need another redesign.

The Rationale for Flowcharting

Flowcharting is not exactly a new tool. It has been used in industrial engineering and in computer programming for decades. But its application to service processes, particularly those involving people processing, is rather more recent. The simple flowcharting shown in the Beth Israel example can usefully be applied to any type of service where management wants to gain a better understanding of the customer's experience of service delivery.

> *Simple flowcharting can usefully be applied to any type of service where management wants to gain a better understanding of the customer's experience of service delivery.*

More complex flowcharts, sometimes referred to as "process flow diagrams" or "service blueprints," depict not only what is happening to the customer front stage, but also what is taking place backstage in order to support front-stage activities. Often, a single action at the customer interface needs to be supported by a whole chain of backstage activities, involving a series of internal supplier–customer interactions.

Creating a Flowchart

Flowcharting the customer experience (or any other process) requires discipline and the willingness to do some research. Creating a broad overview of a process is usually relatively simple: How does it start (does the customer initiate the process or does somebody else; is there a causal event)? What happens next? What are the key steps thereafter, and in what sequence do they occur? What are possible end points (often there is more than one), and what are desirable outcomes in each instance?

Flesh can be added to the bare bones by asking: Where does each step in the action take place (at what location, in what type of facilities)? Who serves the customer at each step, and what precisely do they do? What actions must the customer undertake in person (as opposed to being waited upon)? What supporting equipment is needed at each step? Next come questions relating to backstage activities: What actions must take place behind the scenes in support of the steps that the customer experiences in person?

The task becomes more complex once you get into detailed service blueprinting, involving microanalysis of backstage processes. Assistance from an operations specialist may be needed, for the output soon starts to look like a diagram of complicated electrical circuitry. My focus here is on gaining a good understanding of front-stage processes, together with some insights into the backstage activities that support them. Table 10-1 provides a basic overview of how to go about creating a simple flowchart.

The service delivery process is rather like a river flowing through time: Some activities take place upstream, others downstream. Tributary streams, in the form of backstage processes, feed into the main flow. What happens upstream, whether in the main stream or in a tributary, can have a bearing on subsequent activities. Mistakes and mishaps made in real time frequently have real-time consequences, not least when delays in completing a particular step slow down the rest of the process.

As you analyze each step in a completed flowchart, you need to bear in mind what the customer seeks to obtain from the overall process. Useful questions to ask include:

- What would be the customer's ideal scenario at this point in the front-stage process? (Perhaps it would be to avoid that step altogether!)

- Where are the potential fail points and what could go wrong, both front stage and backstage?

- How might failures at any point be identified in a timely fashion and corrected—or better yet—prevented?

- What employees, equipment, and facilities are being used to serve the customer at each point in the process?

- What actions must take place backstage to deliver each specific service element to the customer?

Developing flowcharts can be a good team-building exercise, helping individuals who are involved in different aspects of a particular service delivery process, both front stage and backstage, to understand better how their work contributes to the overall customer experience. It may also help them appreciate the role played by each of the other members of the service team.

For many employees, the most important single learning point from creating a flowchart may be the realization that they are actually members of a

Table 10-1. A Basic Overview of Flowcharting the Customer Experience

Key Steps

1. Define the purpose of the flowchart clearly: What do you wish to learn (and why) about what type of service, involving what sorts of customers, and under what types of usage conditions?
2. Compile a list of the activities that constitute the experience of the relevant customers. Initially, keep these activities aggregated (e.g., do not decompose "board aircraft" into "hand boarding pass to agent, walk down jetway, enter aircraft, find seat, stow carry-on bag, sit down").
3. Chart each step in the customer's experience in the sequence in which it is normally encountered (alternative charts may be needed if sharply different sequences are encountered—they may be evidence of segments with differing needs or of alternative versions of the service).
4. For every front-stage activity, chart backstage supporting activities. Validate your description—solicit inputs from customers and be sure to involve relevant personnel. (Each may have his/her understanding of the process—look for consensus.)
5. Supplement the flowchart by a narrative that succinctly describes the activities and their interrelationships; be sure to identify the different players clearly.

General Advice

- Remember that there is no one correct way to do a flowchart: Two differently structured descriptions may serve your purpose equally well.
- Complaints by customers and personnel concerning problems at specific points in the process provide good clues as to where you should go into greater detail and disaggregate broad steps such as "board aircraft" into more specific components. (The term "granularity" is often used to describe level of detail; the desired level is achieved when all questions have been answered.)
- If informational processes are an issue, you may wish to show a parallel flow indicating points at which information is collected and records/databases are created, accessed, or updated.

team. It's very important to involve employees in creating flowcharts that concern their own activities, rather than delegating the task entirely to specialist staff or consultants. At a minimum, you have to show them the chart and ask: "Is this, in fact, the way we do it?" Otherwise, you run the risk of portraying the process the way you guess it currently works, rather than the reality.

As a warm-up exercise, I like to suggest that people begin by flowcharting some services that they use frequently in their own role as customers. Possibilities include going out to dinner, renting a car, staying in a hotel, taking an adult education course, getting a car repaired, and ordering a pizza for home delivery. Bear in mind that flowcharts are often situation-specific: A hotel stay as part of a business trip is a slightly different process

> *For many employees, the most important single learning point from creating a flowchart may be the realization that they are actually members of a team.*

from staying in a hotel while on vacation with the family; an emergency car repair resulting from a breakdown far from home is not the same as a scheduled visit to your local service garage to repair an oil leak.

Key Insights from Flowcharting

Flowcharting is applicable to any type of service process involving people, physical objects, or intangibles such as information. With the aid of a flowchart, we can follow the progress (or lack thereof) of a customer receiving service or that of some inanimate object being processed, from cars to pizzas to financial transactions.

Some flowcharts describe several different types of processing in combination, as when a customer takes a defective car to a service garage, describes the problem, and then leaves. Backstage (from the customer's perspective), the mechanics move to examine the vehicle, diagnose the problem, and propose the remedy. A service rep then calls the customer with a cost estimate and obtains approval. Parts are ordered, delivered, and used to effect repairs. Later, at a preagreed time, the action returns to front stage as the customer returns, pays the bill, collects the car, drives away, and tries to determine whether the car is now working properly. The garage manager must knit together both front- and backstage processes if mechanics are to work efficiently on the right problem, cars are to be repaired promptly and within the estimated cost, and customers are to feel that they were treated properly. (Now I've given away some of the key elements in preparing the car-repair flowchart!)

Flowcharts can present a wide-angle view of the big picture or macroanalysis. For instance, you could chart participation in an executive development program, beginning with a would-be participant learning about the program, obtaining information, applying for admission, being accepted, registering, taking classes, completing a program evaluation, graduating, and returning to the job. Alternatively, you could zoom in to create a microanalysis, flowcharting the process of a single day. This could begin at breakfast with other participants, move on to study-group meetings, class, coffee break, visit to the toilet, another class, lunch, individual study, a physical exercise program, a shower, meeting with a study group, a late afternoon class, a visit to the library before dinner, and so forth.

Flowcharts can also be used to study backstage processes that involve providing internal services to internal "customers." For instance, doctors rely for X rays on the services of radiologists and X-ray technicians, garage mechanics depend on the parts department to respond to requests for spare parts, loan officers in a bank ask clerks to run a credit check on a customer who has applied for a mortgage, and television news producers pray daily that reporters will get their stories in on schedule.

There are further applications to flowcharting in addition to gaining a better understanding of the customer's experience. They include: reducing cycle time by reengineering the process, improving capacity planning, and rethinking job design. We take a brief look at each.

> *Further applications to flowcharting include reducing cycle time by reengineering the process, improving capacity planning, and rethinking job design.*

Business Process Improvement. Improving productivity in services often requires speeding up the overall process (or cycle time); another objective may be to provide faster service to customers. The cost of creating a service is often a function of how long it takes to deliver each step in the process, plus any dead time in between these steps. Customers may view the time that they spend personally in process as a cost to be minimized (although there are some instances, such as entertainment, where their objective is to spend a certain amount of time in a pleasing activity). Even when customers aren't involved in the process, the time that elapses between ordering a service and receiving it may be seen as costly if they're in a hurry for the output—repair of a broken machine, installation of a new computer system, receipt of legal advice, delivery of a consulting report, or whatever.

Reducing the overall cycle time of a process involves identifying each step, examining how long it takes, looking for opportunities to speed it up (or even eliminate it altogether), and cutting out dead time. Running tasks in parallel rather than in sequence is a well-established approach to speeding up processes that lies at the heart of critical path management and PERT charts.

Capacity Planning. One of the most irritating situations facing customers is a bottleneck in the service delivery process. There you are, moving nicely through the cafeteria line, when you run into a 5-minute wait at the cashier's station. Why does this dead time occur? Perhaps the two cashiers on duty can't process customers as quickly as can the meal servers and self-service stations farther up the line. The solution may lie in adding a third cashier at busy times or finding faster ways to process each transaction (such as better training for cashiers, installing cash registers that operate more rapidly, or rounding all prices to make for faster change giving). Similar problems arise when processing inanimate objects. The goal should be to have a balanced system. By calculating average processing times at each step relative to the capacity available, potential bottlenecks can be identified and possible solutions considered. However, an average implies some variability, so if a clump of customers arrives, and each customer requires above average in-process time, temporary delays will still occur.

As you may remember, Beth Israel Hospital dealt with the problem of bottlenecks in its emergency unit by adding to the staff a flow nurse and an administrative physician who could contribute needed capacity at any point in a particular patient's treatment cycle.

Job Design.   How many different people should have face-to-face contact with a customer during service delivery? Specialized tasks sometimes require several personnel, but the more there are, the more anonymous the service becomes. Flowcharting helps to clarify what *types* of employees meet the customer and how often, but it may require further research to determine whether the same job holder always performs a specific task for the customer, or whether several people do. A key goal of introducing primary nursing at Beth Israel Hospital was to reduce the number of different nurses who might serve a single patient.

Buoyed by the success of improvements to patient care in the Emergency Unit, BI managers are continually reexamining the experience of hospital inpatients. One study involved a survey of which personnel came into a patient's room. Flowcharts examined typical days in the lives of different categories of patients. Everyone was surprised by the findings.

"It was just unbelievable, the numbers of different people involved!" exclaimed Dr. Rabkin. Not only were medical and technical personnel popping in and out of patient rooms, but also nurse's aides and employees responsible for housekeeping, meal service, and transporting patients. Seeing this parade of different faces depersonalized the patient's experience, felt Dr. Rabkin and his colleagues. So, to improve efficiency and provide deeper personal contact with the patient from fewer people, the hospital has begun blending the jobs of housekeeper, nurse's aide, dietary tray server, and transporter into a new position of "support assistant."

Dr. Rabkin describes the rather striking result:

> We said to these people: Now that you're a support assistant, you're going to have these 7 rooms and 10 patients. And all 10 patients are going to have these two nurses. All of a sudden, the support assistants

were part of a team. They had nurses and patients with whom they identified—these patients were now "their" patients—and they started to show more concern for the patients' comfort and welfare, because they were better able to identify with the patients and form personal relationships. And the patients, too, started to get to know the support assistants and were even complimenting them *by name* in letters to management after being released from the hospital—something that had virtually never happened before.

You could see the reflection of the change also in the sociology of the nursing unit. These assistants were people who, in the past, would never have brown-bagged lunches with the nurses. Now they do. They're part of the team!

Back to the Drawing Board

This chapter has been about getting a better understanding of your current service operations. Flowcharting is basically a generic term for an array of different process-charting tools, including blueprinting and structured analysis and design techniques (SADT).

These tools are every bit as useful for designing a new service as for improving an existing one. Flowcharting is to service design what architectural sketches and detailed blueprints are to the design of buildings and equipment. Different configurations of the service can be examined from the perspective of cycle time, costs, labor requirements, and the need for specialized equipment and facilities design. You can also evaluate how well alternative approaches are likely to satisfy customers—not only in terms of creating desired outcomes, but also with reference to financial and time costs and the demands placed on the customer during the service delivery process. In fact, such analysis may reveal opportunities to offer alternative versions of the process to meet the needs of different customer segments.

In the next chapter, I offer a slightly more detailed example of flowcharting a complete process. This one involves a couple going out to dinner at a restaurant. The goal of Chap. 11 is to help you envision good service by thinking carefully about the customer's own situation at each stop in the front-stage process, as well as considering what your own definition of good service might be at that point. We also examine all the horrible things that might go wrong, both front stage and backstage (well, not all, but quite a few anyway). Your eyes opened to the complexities of this process, you will probably never again be able to look at the dining experience in quite the same light!

Monsieur O'Hara, manager of Chez Jean, enjoyed dreaming up new challenges for would-be patrons wishing to reserve a table.

11 From Turn-Offs to Turn-Ons

At each step in the unfolding of the service drama, the firm has many opportunities to screw things up and turn off its customers. But savvy managers understand their customers' expectations; they are aware of what customers are looking for, not only in terms of end benefits but also in terms of the process of service delivery itself. A humorous example of going to dinner at a restaurant likens meal service to theater, portraying the process in flowchart form as a three-act drama. The chapter shows how to use some commonsense analytical procedures to prevent turn-offs caused by service failures and instead turn on your customers by giving them the quality and value they are looking for.

OTSUs and ISSOs

Have you ever heard of the ancient and not-so-honorable art of OTSU or the splendid art of ISSO?

No, these are not yet another set of new Japanese management techniques. The term OTSU was coined by my friend and former Harvard colleague, David Maister. It stands for the *Opportunity To Screw Up*. At every step in the service delivery process, there are probably at least half a dozen different opportunities to screw up. Many service firms seem to know them all and to delight in practicing them on their hapless customers.

In sharp contrast to the evil OTSU is the ideal way that the service ought to be performed at each step if the customer is to be truly satisfied. I call this the *Ideal Service ScenariO*—or ISSO for short.

Let's Go Out to Dinner!

You'll find it easier to grasp the significance of these two concepts if I provide a detailed illustration to which you can relate in your own role as a customer—dinner for two at what you hope will be a nice restaurant.

Earlier (in Chap. 7) I argued that the stage is an apt metaphor for any service that entails direct contact between customers and service providers. Let's look at what's entailed in visiting an institution that advertises itself as a fine restaurant. Here the eager audience will find a cast of dozens, sometimes incredible sets and costumes, and even musical accompaniment ranging from a soulful-eyed violinist playing sentimental classical favorites to a medley of hits from when the customers were young, nicely taped by Muzak. After the meal, I'll suggest a methodology for applying these concepts to any type of service. *Bon appetit!*

Act I of a Three-Act Drama

The Restaurant Experience is a drama in three acts, each divided into several scenes or steps in the service process. The play opens with Act I, "Appointment with Destiny" (Fig. 11-1). In this particular drama, the act comprises six scenes, beginning with selection of the restaurant and concluding with being seated at table (other restaurant dramas might have more or less scenes, depending on the circumstances).

These six steps constitute our customers' initial experience of the restaurant performance. They all take place front stage, as it were. But much is

The Restaurant Experience:

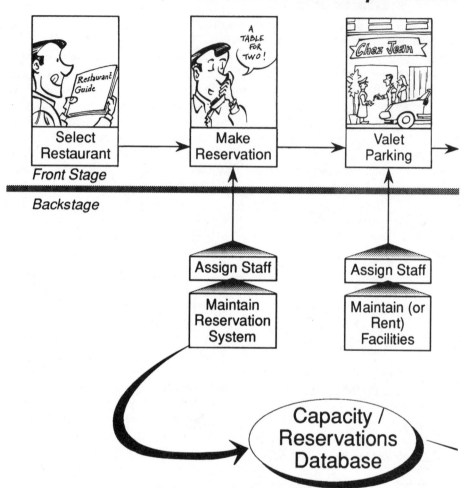

Figure 11-1.

also taking place backstage. Each element of the front-stage action is supported by a series of backstage activities, including assignment of staff, delivery and preparation of food, maintenance of facilities and equipment, and storage and transfer of data—depicted here by the broad arrows which link requests for tables to the seating capacity and reservations database.

Act I: "Appointment with Destiny"

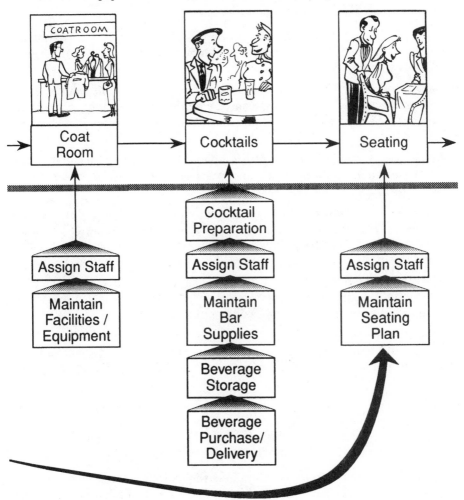

Figure 11-1. (*Continued*)

Screwing Up Creatively

Let's follow the customer through each step. Then we can start to think about the accompanying OTSUs (later we'll consider the ISSOs).

In the first scene, one of our customers selects a restaurant, then proceeds in Scene 2 to try to make a reservation. But lots can go wrong, for

OTSUs can be found everywhere. Put yourself for a moment in the position of a restaurant manager who is looking for juicy ways to screw up the reservations process. Here are some helpful hints:

- Don't list your phone number in the telephone directory, restaurant guides, or your ads. That way nobody but your family and close friends will know how to reach you.

- Let the phone ring 10 or 15 times before answering—you want to make sure that you deal only with the most committed customers, rather than wasting time answering dumb questions from folks who are just shopping around.

- Better yet, leave the phone off the hook. It gets rid of that distracting ringing noise in the background and gives the impression that the restaurant must be immensely successful.

- If you feel that someone must occasionally answer the phone, assign the task to somebody who doesn't speak English; perhaps one of the cooks has recently arrived from overseas? That way, neither party will understand the other. After all, customers always enjoy a challenge!

- Alternatively, put the reservations phone in the kitchen, next to the potato-peeling machine or the dishwasher. The background noise may make meaningful communication impossible, but so what?

- To show prospective customers who's boss, pick employees with naturally rude and offhand manners to take reservations, but give them no training, and don't monitor their performance (you wouldn't want to spoil their act).

- Don't bother to have a reservations book anywhere near the phone. That way, employees taking calls will have to guess the times when tables might be free and will need to keep the reservations in their heads until they have a moment to record them. It's good memory training.

OTSUs are funny when you talk about them. John Cleese made millions laugh with his portrayal of an inept hotel manager in the British television series *Fawlty Towers*. But customers don't always see the funny side when the joke is on them. It's only by identifying all the possible OTSUs associated with a particular task that service managers can put together a delivery system which is explicitly designed to avoid all possible screwups.

> *OTSUs are funny when you talk about them, but customers don't always see the funny side when the joke is on them.*

Identifying ISSOs

By thinking through the ideal service scenarios, or ISSOs, managers can design each aspect of a system to deliver that ideal, and then assign appropriate personnel to specific tasks. Among other things, employees must themselves be well informed as to what constitutes an ideal scenario for the types of customers their organization seeks to serve. If staff members don't understand that, or lack the necessary training and support systems, how can they possibly be expected to deliver a superior service performance?

What do you expect when you are making a restaurant reservation? I don't know the answer because I've never asked you—and I'm not about to guess. But if a restaurant owner were to ask me, I would happily tell that person what my ISSO would be for Act I, Scene 2. First, there would be a boldface listing in the phone directory so I could run my finger down the page and find the number quickly. And the telephone line would be staffed during normal business hours as well as during the specific hours when meals were being served. The phone would be picked up within three rings by a pleasant-voiced person who would answer with the name of the restaurant and his or her own name. That person would be able to check my desired reservation date and time and give me a response within 15 seconds. At no point in the process would I be put on hold.

If my preferred time were not free, the reservation taker would volunteer other times available on the same date. He or she would also be able to respond knowledgeably and cheerfully to any questions I might have about the restaurant—how to get there, the nature of the menu and descriptions of some of the chef's specialties, prices, availability of tables with a view, presence or absence of a no-smoking section, suitability of the restaurant for children, and so forth. Finally, when taking the reservation, the person would get my name right, would not address me as "Chris," would confirm the agreed time and size of party, then thank me for my reservation and conclude by telling me, "we look forward to your visit."

Am I being unreasonably demanding? No, I don't think so. Am I ever disappointed? Yes, regularly. But a few restaurants do get it right, and I appreciate that.

Creating More OTSUs in Act I

Assuming that our customers get past the reservations hurdle, they arrive outside the restaurant where, as an extra service to its patrons, the management provides valet parking. Assignment of the right staff here is rather important for anyone who takes pride in his or her car. How would you feel, as you sweep in, driving your late-model Mercedes or Jag (or even your lovingly cared-for family Ford) to be greeted by a couple of 17-year-old boys in leather vests and cutoff jeans? One has long greasy hair, the other has shaved all his off. There's a funny smell in the air—a combination of marijuana and burnt rubber. One of the lads has a tattoo on his bare arm, reading "Born to Race." Do you want to give them the keys to your car? Or might you just decide to leave, there and then?

Playing the customer role, imagine yourself proceeding through each of the three remaining scenes depicted in Act I of our play:

- Dropping off coats at the coatroom
- Ordering cocktails in the lounge
- Being seated at your table

You know what would be your ideal scenario in each case, and you have some expectations as to what constitutes a minimum acceptable level of service.

Unfortunately, there are innumerable opportunities for the restaurant to screw up: The coatroom is locked, the drinks in the bar are warm, and the maitre d' or hostess has still not arrived to show you to your table long after the confirmed time of your reservation.

A customer's impressions tend to be cumulative. If a couple of things go wrong and you haven't walked out yet, you'll be looking for other things that aren't quite as they should be—the background music is a bit loud, there's a dirty smudge on the mirror behind the bar, and one of the waiters looks as though he needs a shave. On the other hand, if the first steps go really well, you may be willing to overlook a slip-up later on.

A customer's impressions tend to be cumulative. If a couple of things go wrong, you'll be looking for other things that aren't quite as they should be.

I'll bet that you—along with every other reader of this book—has walked out of some restaurant at some point during Act I, because you were so turned off by your experience or impressions up to that point. Too bad, because you might have missed the best meal of your life. But even worse for the restaurants concerned, because they may have lost forever their chance to show you just how good their core product really is.

Experiencing the Core Product in Act II

In Act II, "Banquet of the Gods," customers are finally exposed to the core product for which they came—a good meal and perhaps a fine wine to accompany it. If the restaurant fails to satisfy the customer's expectations on this core product, then it's clearly in serious trouble. For simplicity, I've depicted the action in just six scenes in Fig. 11-2, rather than showing it in greater detail, course by course. In practice, if you were actually running a full-service restaurant, you might want to go into fuller detail.

The curtain rises as our two customers are engaged in reviewing information about the food and wine offered by Chez Jean. Is this information complete? Is it intelligible? If the menu is in French, can the staff provide translations into English or other languages? Will explanations and advice be given in a helpful and noncondescending manner for guests who have questions about specific menu items or are unsure about which wine to order?

Decisions made, the next step is to place the order with the server, who will then have to pass it on to personnel in the kitchen and wine cellar and at the billing desk. Mistakes in transmission of information are a rich source of OTSUs in many organizations. Bad handwriting or unclear verbal requests can lead to delivery of the wrong items altogether—or of the right items, wrongly prepared.

A tavern that I patronized when I lived in Montreal had a simple solution to ensuring that patrons received hamburgers cooked the way they wanted them. We'd order our burgers and the waiter would later return with a trayful for our group. "Who ordered theirs well-done?" he would ask. I'd raise my hand and he would take a cocktail stick bearing a little flag saying "well-done" from his tray, stab it into one of the burgers and place it in front of me. "Now who wanted medium?" Two more hands might be raised, whereupon a pair of burgers would be labeled with the relevant flags and served to my colleagues. And so on to "rare." Since there was no discernible difference between the insides of the burgers, this on-the-spot labeling provided a neat way of customizing your order.

But our customers front stage at Chez Jean are probably ordering something a little more elaborate, with higher expectations of the core product. In subsequent scenes of Act II, they will be evaluating not only the quality of food and drink, but also how promptly it is served (not too promptly, for that would suggest frozen foods cooked by microwave) and how graciously. A technically correct performance by the server can still be spoiled by such human failures as an offhand, cold, or ingratiating manner.

As before, a great deal of activity is taking place behind the scenes, much

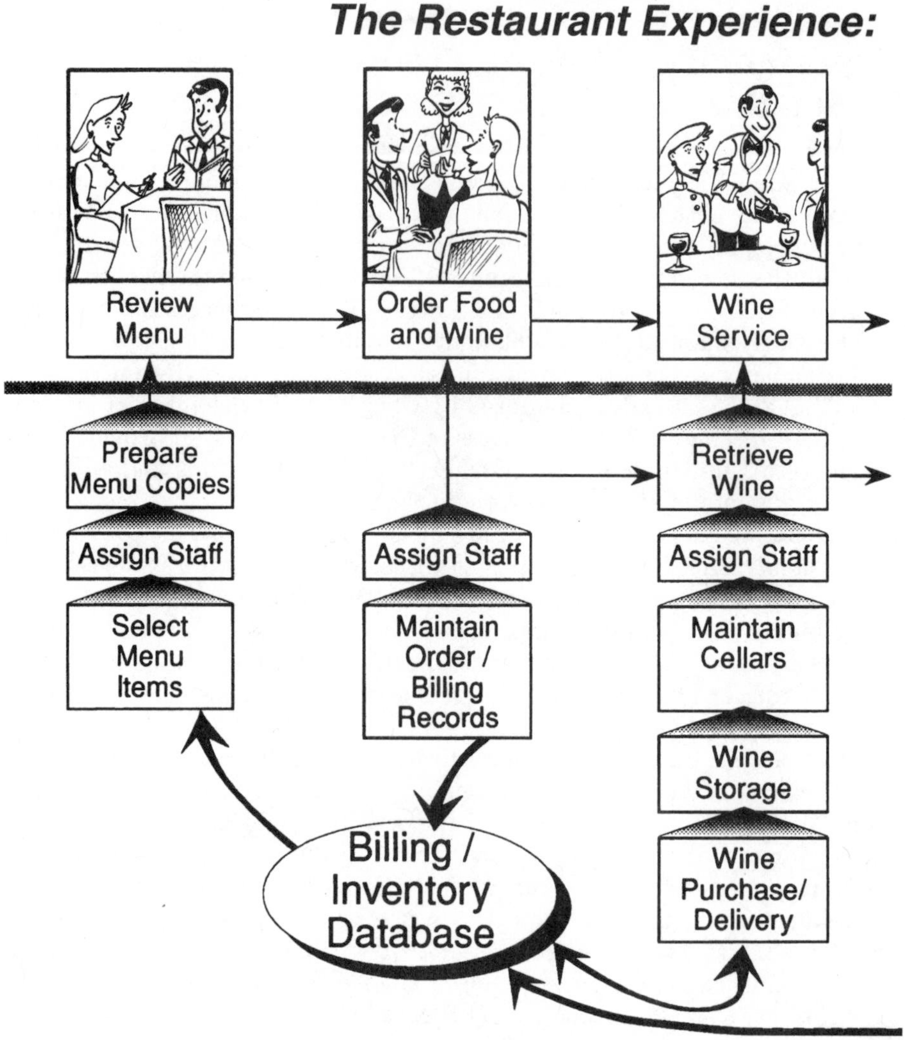

The Restaurant Experience:

Figure 11-2.

of it far removed from direct customer contact, and some of it necessarily occurring long before the customer's arrival. For instance, when preparing the day's menu, a check should be made of what foods are already in inventory and what should be purchased on the day itself. Keeping daily records of what menu items are ordered by customers, and in what numbers, is not only useful logistical information but also good marketing research data.

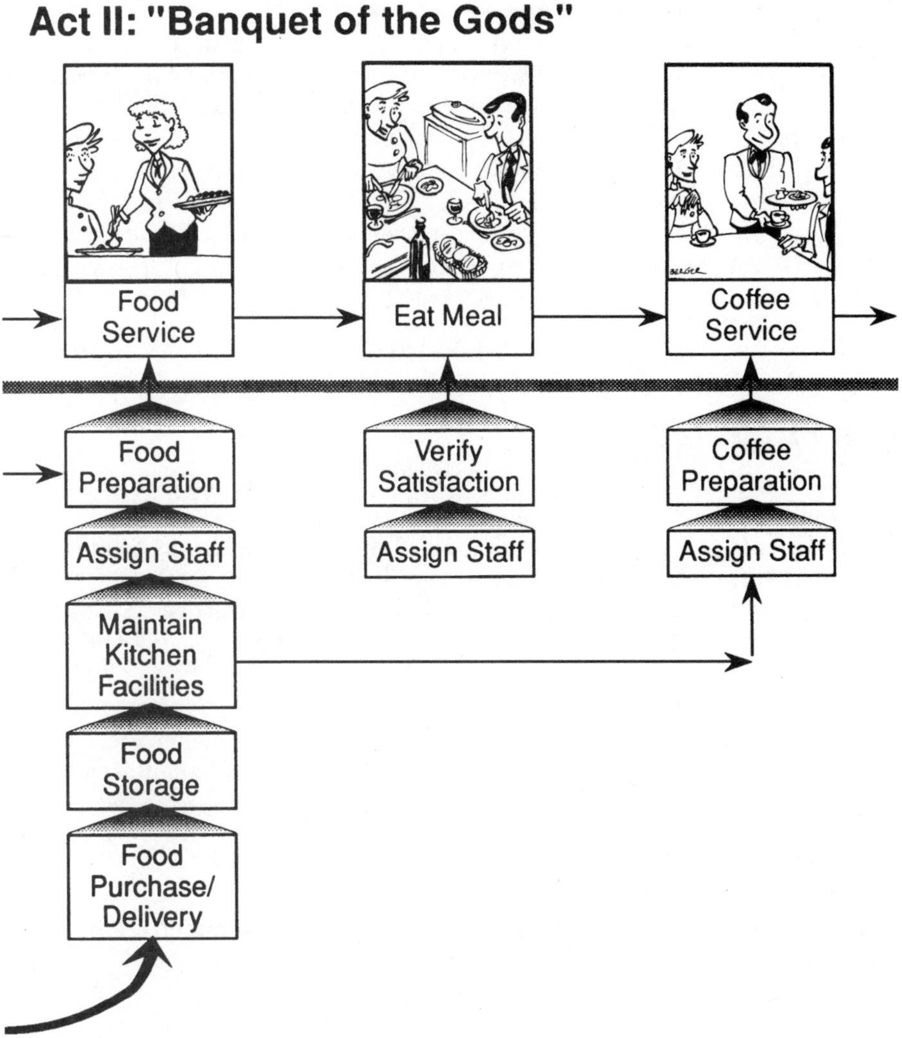

Act II: "Banquet of the Gods"

```
→  Food          →  Eat Meal      →  Coffee        →
   Service                            Service
```

```
→  Food             Verify            Coffee
   Preparation      Satisfaction      Preparation
```

```
   Assign Staff     Assign Staff      Assign Staff
                                          ↑
   Maintain
   Kitchen ─────────────────────────────┘
   Facilities

   Food
   Storage

   Food
   Purchase/
   Delivery
```

Figure 11-2. (*Continued*)

Determining How, When, and Where OTSUs Occur

A persistent OTSU in food service is that a menu item is no longer available. Eliminating such an OTSU, so that it doesn't happen in the future, requires yanking it out by its roots. But where are those roots? Tracing this problem back to its source may reveal that somebody in purchasing screwed up, forgetting to order a certain type of food in sufficient quantity for the anticipated demand. Alternatively, maybe the necessary food spoiled because it wasn't stored properly, or maybe the cooks burned it all because the oven controls were inaccurate due to lack of proper maintenance.

In Chap. 14 we look at *fishboning*, a specific quality control technique for tracing problems to their source. It starts with a team of managers and staff brainstorming all possible reasons why a particular type of failure might occur, grouping them into various categories, and then documenting actual practice to determine, through a Pareto analysis, which of these possible causes are most frequently the source of the problem in question.

The Final Act

Since this isn't a murder mystery or a Shakespearean tragedy, we won't kill off any of the actors by poisoning them or drowning them—like the unfortunate Duke of Clarence—in a butt of Malmsley wine (what a way to go!). The only life at stake here is that of the restaurant itself, since too many OTSUs may weaken its heart. So let's move on to Act III, "Return to Reality," which continues to be a busy time both front stage and backstage (Fig. 11-3).

The core service has now been delivered (and our customers are, let's say, happily digesting it). But a variety of supplementary service elements remain to complete the experience. Ideally, the scenario should look like this:

- An accurate, intelligible bill is presented as soon as the customer requests it.
- Payment is handled politely and expeditiously, and all major credit cards are acceptable.
- Customers find the restrooms clean and properly supplied.
- The right coats are promptly retrieved from the coatroom.
- A staff member opens the door, thanks the guests for their patronage, bids them goodnight, and expresses the hope that they will come again.
- And finally, the customer's car is brought promptly to the door in the same condition as when it was left.

But how often is this ideal achieved in Act III? How often do OTSUs intervene to ruin the customers' experience and spoil their good humor? How many times do you, I wonder, remember occasions when the experience of a nice meal in Act II was completely spoiled by one or more OTSUs in Act III? I have asked this question of more than a thousand executive program participants and MBA students. On each occasion, virtually every hand has gone up, and the most commonly cited OTSU has been inability to get the bill when one has finished the meal and is ready to leave. It's such a surefire recipe for indigestion (especially at lunch time, when businesspeople need to get back to work) that I find myself wondering how many restauranteurs also run a pharmacy on the side.

Act III should be short. The action in each of the remaining scenes should move smoothly, quickly, and pleasantly. There should be no unexpected denouement, no shocking surprises at the end. But the curtain should come down to thundering applause from members of the audience. After all, the goal is to have them return soon for an encore.

Critics Corner

Looking at the overall restaurant performance, it's clear that, even in the simplified form presented here, the service delivery process is very complex. As you've seen, the core product in Act II is surrounded on either side by supplementary service elements in Acts I and III. (You may even want to photocopy the three acts and paste them together to view the full performance.)

If a restaurant can't provide good food and drink, its patrons won't come back. Negative word-of-mouth comments will spread, and eventually the organization will fail. The turnover in new restaurants is very high. But I suspect that as many fail as a result of deficiencies in the supplementary elements as do because of poor food or sour wine.

Our restaurant example was deliberately chosen to illustrate a high-contact service with which all readers are likely to be familiar. But many services, such as repair and maintenance, insurance, or accounting, involve much less contact with customers, since a high proportion of the service operation is located backstage. In such instances, of course, an OTSU committed front stage is likely to represent a higher proportion of the customer's exposure to the organization and may therefore be viewed even more seriously.

Broader Insights

Eliminating OTSUs and creating ISSOs for your target customers is a deadly serious business. OTSUs are to service organizations what germs and viruses are to human beings: At a minimum, they will debilitate; at

The Restaurant Experience:

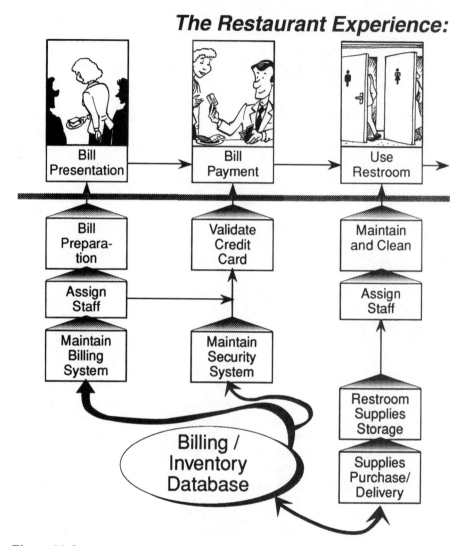

Figure 11-3.

worst, they may kill. Achieving and maintaining an OTSU-free environment is not easy. And in some cases, where the organization must coexist with the external environment, it is almost impossible. But to the extent that OTSUs can be identified, they can be controlled and contingency plans developed to finesse those that cannot be eliminated.

OTSU control begins with developing a detailed flowchart, showing each step in the service delivery process, both front stage and backstage.

Act III: "Return to Reality"

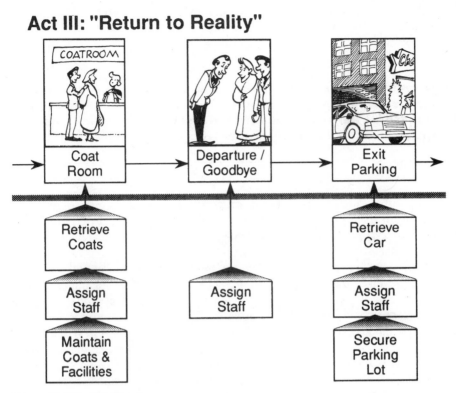

Figure 11-3. (*Continued*)

Operations experts talk about "fail points" in a flowchart to indicate where things can go wrong. The OTSU concept goes one further by trying to identify *every possible thing that might go wrong* at that point. And complementing the analysis is a determination of the ISSO or ideal service scenario at that point. The worst OTSUs are those that affect external customers directly as they wait for service front stage. But other OTSUs, even when their impact is confined backstage, may still hinder employee productivity, leading to increased costs and lower morale.

Among the key insights from our discussion in this and the previous chapter are three that relate to teamwork. First, all employees and managers, whatever their own responsibilities, must understand the service delivery process as it's experienced by customers. Teams must be process-oriented in services, and the most important process of all is the customers'.

Second, backstage personnel must understand how their work relates to their colleagues working front stage. In a very real sense, backstage personnel provide a series of internal services, represented by the vertically stacked boxes that support front-stage activities. If they do their jobs poorly, the folks backstage increase the chance for OTSUs by their colleagues who have customer contact responsibilities.

> *All employees and managers must understand the service delivery process as it's experienced by customers. Backstage personnel must understand how their work relates to their colleagues working front stage.*

Finally, all personnel, both front-stage and backstage, must understand how their job fits into the total process. Someone working upstream in the process can affect the way the customer interacts with service personnel downstream.

Perhaps you have worked as a waiter or waitress at some point in your life (in my student days, among the many jobs I held was working as a bar-waiter in a Butlin's Holiday Camp on the south coast of England). If you've ever waited tables, you know what it is like to serve an angry customer who has experienced a series of mishaps before reaching the point of being ready to order. Such customers are hard to please, hard to sell on special menu items or extra desserts, and—worst of all—they're likely to be stingy tippers. If the serving staff know that customers are mad because of poor service earlier in the process, they are going to be upset with their coworkers in the restaurant, and both morale and efficiency are likely to decline. Parallel situations occur all too frequently in other types of service situations, where employees in one department blame those in another for making their jobs more difficult and sending problems downstream.

ISSOs concern not only *what* is done, but *how* the customer would prefer it to be done. Unfortunately, many service businesses don't bother to ask. Perhaps they believe that their expertise enables them to deliver what is best for the customer ("trust me, this will be good for you!"). Surveying customers to determine their ISSOs has to be undertaken on a segment-by-segment basis, since needs and expectations often vary widely from one category of customer to another. And since people's ideal scenarios may change over time, this type of research has to be repeated periodically.

It's not always possible to give customers exactly the service that they would like (some medical treatments, for example, are necessarily unpleasant), or to give it at a price they are willing to pay. In such instances, the answer may lie in explaining the situation and managing expectations, so that customers know what they can reasonably expect.

OTSUs and ISSOs also apply to "internal customers," that is, employees and suppliers who provide service for others working within or for the organization. To the extent that employees are given the chance to discuss how they would like to interact with external suppliers and with support personnel, managers will be able to determine areas for potential improvement.

Improving and Reengineering Service Processes

As we've seen, flowcharting yields the best results when it is applied to analysis of specific situations. This chapter emphasizes the importance of preventing failures at each point in an existing process and making sure that each step is delivered in ways that will match customer expectations. But polishing existing processes until they shine, both front stage and backstage, is not the only (or even always the best) way to go.

Instead, managers may need to rethink and reengineer the processes that underlie service delivery. Such rethinking should include reappraising what supplementary elements are included in the package, as well as how the core product itself is defined. This analysis should also extend to "make-or-buy" decisions relating to outsourcing and supplier relations.

For ideas on product repositioning, consider the restaurant flowchart. We have illustrated a relatively expensive, high-service restaurant. A variety of different forms of food service could be created by eliminating, adding, or rearranging various process elements. Many of the supplementary service elements, moreover, could be eliminated. Knock out reservations, valet parking, the cocktail lounge, and the attended coatroom, for example, and you have repositioned a fancy restaurant as something more modest. Shrink the menu and replace table service by self-service, and you're moving into fast-food territory. Get rid of the tables and you're left with take-out. Or you can remove the customers from the premises altogether and replace take-out by home delivery. Pursuing that avenue, why not expand the menu options and add servers back into the equation? Then you'll have custom catering! Most options will, of course, require a redesign of backstage operations.

You might also want to think about reengineering the information flows that accompany or complement physical activities. The databases depicted in the restaurant flowchart, for example, are not fully integrated. If you are operating a full-service restaurant and want to build relationships with valued customers, it will help to link reservations data with menu selection and payment data. Then you can build profiles of "frequent guests" in terms of who they are and where they live or work; how far in advance they normally reserve; how often they visit (and with what size of group); what seating, menu items, and beverages they prefer; what payment medium they like to use; and how much they spend in total. Integrating backward into suppliers' information networks is a second direction to explore.

Whatever your business, it's important not to lose sight of broader issues in service development, including competitive analysis and ongoing customer research. But you also need to think systematically about all available options. How do you decide what mix of supplementary service elements should surround your core product? In the next chapter, we examine a framework that should stimulate your thinking about how to enhance (or simplify) the package of supplementary services that you select to surround any of your firm's core products.

"This is just our little way of saying that customers like you, Ms. Jensen, are Megabank's most important asset."

12 Product Plus Service: Like Petals on a Flower

Core products vary widely from one type of business to another, but supplementary services are often common to a great many seemingly different industries. These supplementary services can be clustered into eight groups: information, consultation, order taking, hospitality, caretaking, exceptions, billing, and payment. Collectively, they can be likened to the petals of a flower. Even if the core is fine, wilted petals will spoil the impression for customers.

"Take time to smell the flowers" is advice often given to busy people whose heavy work load and hectic pace leave them little time to enjoy some of life's simpler pleasures.

Flowers provide yet another good metaphor for services. To be worth smelling—and, even more important, worth looking at—they should appeal to the senses. Ask a child to draw a flower, and she or he will probably sketch the classically symmetrical daisy or marigold, with a corona of petals radiating from a disk in the middle. It's usually the petals that first attract attention, since they provide the form and color that make each type of flower distinctive. But the "business" part of the flower lies in the center, where pollination and seed production take place.

We can think of supplementary services as akin to a circle of petals around the core product. In a well-designed and well-managed service organization, the petals and core are fresh and well formed. They complement each other. Badly designed or poorly executed service is a bit like a flower with missing, wilted, or discolored petals. Even if the core is perfect, the overall impression of the flower is unattractive.

Eight Groups of Supplementary Services

The more you examine different types of services, the more you will find that most of them have quite a few supplementary services in common. Try drawing flowcharts for a variety of services: You will soon notice that although the core product differs, common supplementary elements—from information to billing and from reservations to problem resolution—crop up time and again.

There are potentially dozens of different supplementary services, but almost all of them can be classified into one of the following eight clusters:

- Information
- Consultation
- Order taking
- Hospitality
- Caretaking
- Exceptions
- Billing
- Payment

In Fig. 12-1, these eight clusters are displayed as eight petals surrounding the center of a flower, so why not call it the "flower of service"?

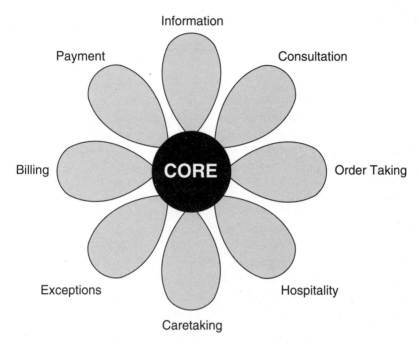

Figure 12-1. The flower of service.

Not every core product is surrounded by supplementary elements from all eight clusters. In fact, the nature of the service process helps to determine which ones need to be offered. For instance, when you visit a service facility, managers must pay attention to hospitality and perhaps caretaking services, but these won't be needed if you (and other customers) deal with the organization only at arm's length.

Another determinant of what supplementary services to include is the market positioning strategy that management has selected. A strategy of adding benefits to gain a competitive edge will probably require more supplementary services (and also a higher level of performance on all such elements).

In the balance of this chapter, I discuss each of the eight petals on the flower of service, considering what types of supplementary services are included within each category. You'll find a complete summary in Table 12-1, which can also serve as a checklist for evaluating each of your own products.

As you review these eight groupings of supplementary services, you might also want to think about your own experiences as a customer or when purchasing on behalf of an organization. When you were dissatisfied with a particular purchase, was it the core that was at fault, or was it a problem with one or more of the petals?

Table 12-1. The Eight Petals of the Flower of Service: Classifying Supplementary Services

---

Information
  Directions to service site
  Schedules/service hours
  Prices
  Instructions on using core product/supplementary services
  Reminders
  Warnings
  Conditions of sale/service
  Notification of changes
  Documentation
  Confirmation of reservations
  Summaries of account activity
  Receipts and tickets

Consultation
  Advice
  Auditing
  Personal counseling
  Management/technical consultancy

Order taking
  Applications
    Membership in clubs or programs
    Subscription services (e.g., utilities)
    Qualification-based services (e.g., colleges)
  Order entry
    On-site fulfillment
    Mail/telephone order for subsequent fulfillment
  Reservations
    Seats
    Tables
    Rooms
    Professional appointments
    Admissions to restricted facilities (e.g., exhibitions)

Hospitality
  Greeting
  Food and beverages
  Toilets and washrooms
  Bathroom kits
  Waiting facilities and amenities
    Lounges, waiting areas, seating
    Weather protection
    Magazines, entertainment, newspapers
  Transportation
  Security

Table 12-1. The Eight Petals of the Flower of Service: Classifying
Supplementary Services (*Continued*)

Caretaking
  Caring for possessions customers bring with them
    Child care
    Pet care
    Car parking
    Valet parking
    Coatroom
    Baggage handling
    Storage space
    Safety deposit/security
  Caring for goods purchased by customers
    Packaging
    Pickup
    Transportation
    Delivery
    Installation
    Inspection and diagnosis
    Cleaning
    Preventive maintenance
    Repairs and renovation
    Upgrades

Exceptions
  Special requests in advance of service delivery
    Children
    Diet
    Medical needs
    Religious observances
    Accident
    Deviations from standard operating procedures
  Handling complaints/compliments/suggestions
  Problem solving
    Warranties and guarantees against product malfunction
    Difficulties that arise from using the product
    Difficulties caused by service failures, including problems with staff or other
      customers
  Restitution (refunds, compensation, etc.)

Billing
  Periodic statements of account activity
  Invoices for individual transactions
  Verbal statements of amount due
  Machine display of amount due
  Self-billing

(*Continued*)

Table 12-1. The Eight Petals of the Flower of Service: Classifying Supplementary Services (*Continued*)

Payment
  Self-service by customer
    Exact change in machine
    Cash in machine with change returned
    Prepaid card
    Insert credit/charge/debit card
    Insert token
    Electronic funds transfer
  Customer interacts with payee personnel
    Cash handling and change giving
    Check handling
    Credit/charge/debit card handling
    Coupon redemption
    Tokens, vouchers, etc.
  Automatic deduction from financial deposits (e.g., bank charges)
  Control and verification
    Automated systems (e.g., machine-readable tickets)
    Personal systems (e.g., gate controllers, ticket inspectors)

In Chap. 13 we use this framework to evaluate a successful small company which works hard to enhance the value of its high-quality core product by providing superior supplementary services.

Information

To obtain full value from any good or service, customers need relevant information about it, especially if they are first-time users. Such information may include directions to the site where the product is sold (or details of how to order it), service hours, prices, and usage instructions. Other information, sometimes required by law, might include conditions of sale and use, warnings, reminders, and notification of changes. Finally, you and your customers may want documentation of what has already taken place, such as confirmation of reservations, receipts and tickets, and summaries of account activity.

Firms that are enthusiastic about their products and have a strong service orientation often take an educational perspective toward providing information. (Ask yourself how many more customers your firm might attract—and keep—if everybody knew about your product, what its capabilities were, where and when to obtain it, and how to obtain maximum value from using it.)

> *To obtain full value from any good or service, customers need relevant information about it, especially if they are first-time users.*

Information can be provided in many forms, including preprinted brochures, signs, or prerecorded messages. Alternatively, information may be provided by service personnel (who had better be prepared to answer questions!) either face to face or by phone. More recent innovations include providing information through touch-screen video monitors or computer-driven voice systems accessed by telephone, but these must be user-friendly if management expects people to use them.

Consultation

Providing information suggests giving a simple response to customers' questions (or pre-prepared information that anticipates their needs). Consultation, by contrast, involves a dialogue to probe customer requirements and then develop a tailored solution.

At its simplest, consultation consists of immediate advice from a knowledgeable service person in response to the request: "What do you suggest?" Effective consultation requires an understanding of the current situation, before suggesting a suitable course of action. Good customer records can be a great help in this respect, particularly if relevant data can be retrieved easily from a remote terminal.

Counseling represents a more subtle approach, since it often involves helping customers to understand their situation better and encouraging them to come up with their "own" solutions and action programs. This approach can be a particularly valuable supplement to services such as health treatment, where part of the challenge is to get customers to take a long-term view of their personal situation and adopt behaviors which may involve some initial sacrifice.

Finally, there are more formalized efforts to providing management and technical consultancy. The "solution selling" associated with marketing expensive industrial equipment and services is a good example: The sales rep researches the customer's situation and then offers objective advice about what particular package of equipment and systems will yield the best results for the customer.

Order Taking

Once you are ready to buy, a key supplementary element should come into play: accepting applications, orders, and reservations. Unless your service organization—or its designated intermediaries—is easily accessible when and where customers want to place an order, you may lose their business.

Some service providers like to establish a formal membership relationship with customers. Banks, insurance companies, and utilities, for instance, require prospective customers to go through an application process designed to gather relevant information and to screen out those who do not meet basic enrollment criteria (bad credit record, poor health, and so forth). Unfortunately, this policing function sometimes becomes excessively bureaucratic, involving lengthy forms in quadruplicate or extended delays while references are checked. The risk is that efforts to weed out poor prospects may turn off good ones and take so long that applicants lose interest and turn to a faster and more responsive competitor.

In other instances, where the customer is making a single purchase, the process is (or should be) much simpler. Whatever the circumstances, the process of order taking should be polite, fast, and accurate. And is it too much to suggest that order takers show at least a little enthusiasm? After all, what is happening now will contribute to their future paychecks!

Reservations (including appointments) represent a special type of order taking which entitle the customer to a specified unit of service—an airline seat, a restaurant table, a hotel room, time with a qualified professional, or admission to a facility such as an exhibition hall with restricted capacity. The scheduling aspect introduces an extra need for accuracy, since reservations on, say, the wrong flight to the right place are likely to be unpopular with customers. Many types of reservations provide printed confirmation. Dentists and other professionals often make a point of reminding customers a day or two in advance, either by phone or mail, so that they don't forget appointments.

Hospitality

When you purchase people-processing services—such as transportation, or lodging, or health care, or a haircut—you have to enter the service factory to get them, and stay there until service delivery is complete. A well-managed business tries, at least in small ways, to treat customers as guests—especially if they have to spend a long time on site. After all, the marketing folks invited you there!

Hospitality—taking care of the customer—is potentially a very pretty petal, reflecting pleasure at meeting new customers and greeting old ones when they return. Courtesy and consideration for the customer's needs apply to telephone interactions, too, but it is in face-to-face encounters that they find full expression.

> *A well-managed business tries to treat its customers as guests, especially if they have to spend a long time on site. After all, the marketing folks invited you there!*

In some cases, hospitality starts (and ends) with an offer of transport to and from the service site, as with courtesy shuttle buses to and from distant parking lots or transportation terminals. If you must wait a while before the service can be delivered, then a thoughtful service provider will offer weather protection (wherever service takes place outdoors) or an indoor waiting area with seating and even entertainment (TV, newspapers?) to pass the time. When you spend more than an hour or so in a service facility, you may become thirsty, hungry, or need to use toilets and washrooms. Providing such supplementary services is an act of hospitality that may also increase your satisfaction with the core product. Charging for use of toilets tends to be seen as mean-spirited (at least in America), but it may be fine to offer food and beverages at a price. Good hosts also worry about the safety of their guests (and the latters' possessions); reflecting a more uncertain social fabric, increasing attention nowadays must be paid to security services.

Caretaking

Looking after the customer's possessions may be an important part of providing service. In fact, unless certain caretaking services are provided (notably parking for cars), customers may not come at all.

The list of potential caretaking supplementary services when customers come to visit the service site is a long one. It includes provision of coatrooms; baggage transport, handling, and storage; safekeeping of valuables; and even child care and pet care.

Another set of caretaking services relates to physical products that customers buy or rent. These services are particularly applicable to products ordered by mail or phone. Caretaking services of this nature may include packaging, pickup and delivery, assembly, installation, cleaning, and inspection. Customers who are purchasing durable goods—such as cars, cameras, or computers—may also want to know about the availability (and cost, if any) of repair and maintenance services, and whether they can purchase maintenance contracts as a form of insurance.

Exceptions

Exceptions involve a group of supplementary services that fall outside the routine of normal service delivery. However, astute managers anticipate exceptions and develop contingency plans and guidelines in advance. In that way, employees know what to do and so do not appear helpless and surprised when customers ask for special assistance.

> *Astute managers anticipate exceptions and develop contingency plans and guidelines in advance.*

There are several different types of exceptions.

1. *Special requests:* There are many circumstances where an individual or corporate customer may request some degree of customized treatment that requires a departure from normal operating procedures. In the case of people-processing services, advance requests often relate to personal concerns, including care of children, dietary requirements, medical needs, religious observances, and personal disabilities.

2. *Problem-solving* situations arise when normal service delivery (or product performance) fails to run smoothly as a result of accidents, delays, equipment failures, or customers experiencing difficulty in using the product.

3. *Handling of complaints/suggestions/compliments* requires well-defined procedures. When customers want to express dissatisfaction, offer suggestions for improvement, or pass on compliments, it should be easy for them to do so, and the service provider should be able to make an appropriate response quickly.

4. *Restitution* is concerned with compensating customers for performance failures. This compensation may take the form of repairs under warranty, legal settlements, refunds, an offer of free service in the future, or other forms of payment in kind.

Managers need to keep an eye on the level of exception requests. Too many may be a sign that standard procedures need revamping. For instance, if you are running a restaurant and your staff frequently receives requests to serve special vegetarian meals, this might be an indication that it is time to revise the menu to include at least one vegetarian dish.

A flexible approach to exceptions is generally a good idea, because it reflects responsiveness to customer needs. On the other hand, some types of exceptions should be discouraged, because they may compromise safety, have a negative impact on other customers, or place an unrealistic burden on employees.

Billing

Billing is common to almost all services (unless the service is provided free of charge). Inaccurate, illegible, or incomplete bills offer a splendid opportunity to disappoint customers who may, up to that point, have been quite satisfied with their experience. Of course, such failures add insult to injury if the customer is *already* dissatisfied. Billing should also be timely, because it will probably result in faster payment; if customers are actually on site, waiting for a bill can be a frustrating waste of their time.

> *Inaccurate, illegible, or incomplete bills offer a splendid opportunity to disappoint customers who may, up to that point, have been quite satisfied with their experience.*

There are various forms of billing procedures, ranging from verbal statements ("that'll be $12.50, please,") to a machine-displayed price, and from handwritten invoices to elaborate monthly statements of account activity and fees. More and more, billing is being computerized. Despite its potential for improving productivity, computerized billing has its dark side, as when an innocent customer tries futilely to contest an inaccurate bill and is met by an escalating sequence of ever larger bills (compounded interest and penalty charges), accompanied by increasingly threatening, computer-generated letters.

Perhaps the best sort of billing of all is self-billing, where the customer tallies up the amount of an order and either encloses a check or signs a credit-card payment authorization. In such instances (which range from penciled figures on a paper form to sophisticated electronic procedures), billing and payment are combined into a single act. All the seller needs to do is check that the customer's arithmetic and credit are both good.

Payment

In most cases, a bill requires the customer to take action on payment (and such action may be very slow in coming!). One exception is bank statements which detail charges that have already been deducted from the customer's account. Ease and convenience of payment (including credit) are increasingly expected by customers when they purchase many types of goods and services.

Self-service payment systems require customers to insert coins, bank notes, tokens, or cards in machines. But equipment breakdowns destroy the whole purpose of such systems, so good maintenance and rapid-response troubleshooting are essential. Much payment still takes place through hand-to-hand transfers of cash and checks, but charge cards and electronic systems are growing in importance. Use of tokens, vouchers, coupons, or other prepaid tickets represent still other alternatives.

A final supplementary element that I've included under the payment category is verification and control. Ticket collectors at points of entry to a service facility, roving inspectors on public transport, and security personnel at retail store exits work to ensure that all users pay the due price. Despite that oft-repeated slogan, "the customer is always right," a small minority of customers do not always behave rightly. Hence the need for control systems. However, these tasks need to be well organized so that lines do not back up at entry and exit points. Inspectors and security officers must be trained to combine politeness with firmness in performing their jobs, so that honest customers do not feel harassed. But a visible presence often serves as a deterrent.

Let Service Flourish!

The eight categories of supplementary services that form the "flower of service" collectively embrace a wide array of possible augmentations of the core product. Some of these elements—notably billing and payment—are, in effect, imposed by the marketer. But even if they are not actively desired by the customer, they still form part of the overall service experience. Any badly handled element can create a product minus, with consequent negative impact on competitive advantage.

Most supplementary services do (or should) represent responses to customer needs. Others are facilitating services (such as information and reservations) that enable customers to use the core product more effectively. Still others are "extras" that enhance the core or even reduce some of its nonfinancial costs (for example, meals, magazines, and entertainment are hospitality elements that help pass the time on what might otherwise be very boring airline flights). But not every core product will be surrounded by all eight petals. People-processing services are the most demanding of supplementary elements, especially hospitality, because they involve the closest, and often most protracted, interactions with customers. However, when customers do not need to come to the service factory, the need for hospitality may be limited to simple courtesies in letters and telecommunications. Possession-processing services tend to be heavy on caretaking elements, but there may be no need for the caretaking petal when providing information-based services in which customers and suppliers deal entirely at arm's length.

Managerial Implications

As a manager, you have lots of decisions to make concerning what types of "flower" to offer your customers. One key question is whether to offer certain supplementary services as optional extras (and whether or not to charge an extra price for them), or whether to bundle all service elements together at a single price. There are no simple rules governing such pricing decisions, but you should continually review your own policies and those of your competitors in this regard. One option is to offer customers a menu featuring both a la carte items and fixed-price combinations, and let them make the choice.

You can use Table 12-1 as a checklist in your search for new ways to augment existing core products (either goods or services), as well as to help you design new offerings. Of course, if you choose to compete on a low-cost, no-frills basis, there will be fewer supplementary elements in each category than if you are offering an expensive, high-value-added product. Different levels of supplementary service around a common core may offer the basis for a product line of differentiated offerings, similar to the various classes of travel offered by an airline on the same flight. The list does not claim to be all-encompassing, since specialized products may require specialized supplementary elements, but it does provide a good departure point.

Customer research, evaluation of competitive offerings, and feedback from employees can all provide important inputs to (1) designing the right mix of supplementary service elements, (2) establishing appropriate performance standards for each, and (3) establishing supplementary prices as needed. As emphasized in Chap 5, the key criterion is *value*.

There is, of course, little point in adding elements that customers do not want: The flower of service should be cultivated with the customer's pleasure in mind rather than the provider's. But it's even better if you can manage to please both parties simultaneously. All the elements that make up each petal should receive the care and attention needed to consistently meet defined service standards. In that way, the resulting flower will always have a fresh and appealing appearance. After all, neither you nor your customers would want it to look wilted or disfigured by neglect.

One key insight from the flower-of-service concept is that different types of core products often share use of similar supplementary elements. As a result, customers may make comparisons across industries. For instance,

"If my stockbroker can give me a clear documentation of my account activity, why can't the office supplies store where my firm has an account?" Or, "If my favorite airline can take reservations accurately, why can't the French restaurant up the street?"

Questions such as these suggest that managers should be studying businesses outside their own industries in a search for "best-in-class" performers on specific supplementary services. This is the basis of benchmarking; however, as noted in Chap. 8, slavishly pursuing world-class performers may be inappropriate for firms with limited experience in quality management: They should simply focus on well-managed local businesses.

> *Managers should be studying businesses outside their own industries in a search for "best-in-class" performers on specific supplementary services.*

Opportunities to Use Information Technology

As you look at the eight petals that make up the flower of service, you can see that the majority of petals are data-based or information-dependent: Information, consultation, order taking, and billing all involve information processing. Certain types of exception handling and payments may also be information-based. Hospitality, however, involves physical things—either performing physical actions for customers or providing them with certain physical facilities. The same is broadly true for caretaking.

The fact that so many supplementary elements are information-based has enormous significance for both innovation and competitive advantage. Why? Basically, it's because there are more and more opportunities to enhance service (and also to improve productivity in some instances) through intelligent applications of information technology—a topic we look at further in Chap. 17.

To summarize, the important managerial issue is not how many petals the flower has, but ensuring that each petal is perfectly formed and adds luster to the core product in customers' eyes. In the following chapters, we look in more depth at each of the petals and present examples of both good practice and interesting new technological innovations. We begin, in Chap. 13, by applying the flower of service framework to a successful small business whose core product, rather fittingly, consists of the genetic material needed to grow flowers.

"I just don't understand it! Either they're freaks or somebody secretly dumped a load of fertilizer on them!"

13 Cultivating the Flower of Service

In today's economy, manufacturing firms need to be hybrids. Not only must they excel at the physical aspects of production, they also need to be skilled service providers. Some firms deal with this problem by subcontracting key tasks, but outsourcing is not for everyone. Firms that want to stay at the cutting edge of product innovation while also retaining close contact with their customers may prefer to operate as integrated manufacturing and service organizations. This strategy does offer tighter control over the quality of both the core product and associated supplementary services. Rather appropriately, we illustrate the "flower of service" concept with a close look at White Flower Farm, a high-quality nursery which sells plants throughout the United States and Canada from a single growing location in rural New England.

White Flower Farm is picturebook New England. An eighteenth-century, white, wooden house and neat horse barns stand among trees and flowering shrubs atop one of the gently rolling hills of Litchfield, Connecticut. Around the buildings are manicured lawns, brilliant banks of flowers, climbing shrubs, many species of trees, and a series of both formal and informal gardens that come into their prime at different points in the growing season.

If you were to pass by White Flower Farm, you'd recognize it as a work of love—and of art—by dedicated people possessing both skill and impeccable taste. You might, however, be surprised to learn that this is also a highly successful small business, serving a quarter of a million customers throughout the continental United States and Canada, promising an exceptional commitment to quality, and achieving annual sales in excess of $10 million. Closer investigation of this family-owned business would reveal, among other things, acres of flowering fields, a retail garden center, and a computerized fulfillment center with a refrigerated warehouse in the nearby town of Torrington.

An Integrated "Manufacturing" and Service Business

Unlike most mail-based suppliers of bulbs and live garden plants, White Flower Farm is a fully integrated company. Other suppliers (some of which are significantly larger) buy from growers, mark up the products, and redistribute them in response to mail and telephone orders. White Flower, by contrast, is vertically integrated and does everything, from growing almost all its own stock—bulbs purchased from carefully selected growers in the Netherlands, roses from California, and a special strain of begonias from England are among the few exceptions—to picking and packing orders. Only the actual transport and delivery of orders to customers is entrusted to an outside supplier.

The Early Years

White Flower Farm began as a hobby of Jane Grant, a writer for *The New Yorker*, and William Harris, an editor at *Fortune*, who purchased the then 50-acre property in 1939. Harris and his wife would leave Manhattan on Friday afternoons and head for the hills of western Connecticut to tend the gardens of their weekend cottage. Harris turned this avocation into a small mail-order operation in 1950, but continued to run it more as a hobby than a business. By the mid-1970s, Harris was nearing 80 and in failing health. Enter a young business school graduate, Eliot Wadsworth II, who was looking for something significant and rewarding to do with his life.

Then in his early thirties, Wadsworth had worked as a research assistant at the Harvard Business School, as a New York investment banker, as co-owner of several Kentucky Fried Chicken restaurants in Maine—where his role included building new stores, training staff, and holding the marketing reins—and finally as an acquisitions analyst for a Boston-based distributor of garden products. But the job he decided he really wanted was running a nursery. Enchanted by White Flower Farm, which he saw as "significantly undermanaged," he signed on with Harris as general manager. Having gained the latter's trust, he bought the business in a leveraged buyout in January 1977.

Vision and Focus

In 16 years, Wadsworth has expanded White Flower Farm from 4 cultivated acres to over 100, with another 200 acres in reserve. And he has increased annual sales from $750,000 to $10 million, plus another $4.5 million from Shepherd's Garden Seeds, an independently managed seed business purchased in 1987. He has also increased his staff, attracting "smart, experienced people" for each specialized slot. "We have a lot in common," he says of the staff. "We love what we're doing, we're all high energy, we like process and seasonality and plants. We're metabolically in sync with one another."

Wadsworth expects further growth, but places more value on the sheer pleasure he and his associates (who also share 25 percent of the profits) draw from the business itself.

> I'm in this business because I love it, not for the money. We could easily extend into selling clothing, as so many mail-order companies eventually seem to do. But I don't want to be in the fashion trade. A more contemporary model would be to promise everyone the moon, grow like mad, and sell out. But I like plants. I think you should stick to what you know and like. I don't believe that the vitality of an organization is measured only by its ability to grow at a certain rate each year. I prefer the 3M model, which is that 15 percent of sales each year must come from products which are new that year. The diversity of plant material is so enormous that there's no danger of running out!

The firm's catalog—from which I've been buying for my own garden for many years—is a work of art in its own right. Published in the spring and fall and running 80–110 pages, *The Garden Book*'s hundreds of color photographs are matched by elegant, informative prose. Wadsworth himself writes much of the copy, including a friendly introduction, which he signs pseudonymously as "Sincerely, Amos Pettingill." His own long-haul view of the business is captured in Amos's observation on trees (see box).

> ### *Amos Pettingill on Trees*
>
> *Trees are not usually offered by mail-order nurseries because they are large, and expensive to ship, and can be awkward for the amateur gardener to install. But there are times when this sensible principle does not apply, and this is one. We are offering two different kinds of trees this spring...a new strain of hybrid American Chestnut that is blight-free and promises to restore this glorious tree to our landscape...[and] a short list of old-fashioned apple varieties...*
>
> *Planting trees is not a pastime consistent with the current American insistence on instantaneous gratification, but it's an opportunity to do something significant for the next generation. Visitors to the nursery will notice that we have been planting Elms for almost a decade and are now setting out a small grove of Chestnuts for our grandchildren to enjoy. It may not meet the test of rational economic behavior, but it's enormously satisfying.*
>
> From "Once Over Lightly,"
> The Garden Book, Spring 1993

Some Management Challenges

"The nature of our business is odd," concedes proprietor Wadsworth, "because it incorporates so many different disciplines. We run a farm, a million-dollar-a-year export–import operation, a retail store, a computerized warehouse and fulfillment center, and an in-house advertising agency to handle photography, copywriting, and catalog production. These many discrete activities are highly interrelated and seasonally synchronous."

Wadsworth compares his operation to another highly successful New England mail-order business, L. L. Bean, which he admires.

> Our business is more challenging, because there are more uncertainties. Their operation is indoors in a warehouse. It's theoretically possible to manage against any chosen level of customer expectation. We can't. A late harvest, disease problems, or heavy rains will inevitably lead to variations in our service. Those sorts of problems don't affect the production and sale of boots and turtlenecks.

White Flower Farm prides itself on growing almost all its own stock rather than outsourcing, as most mail-order plant retailers now do. Wadsworth recognizes the disadvantages in this strategy but believes it's the best way to maintain quality. In a number of instances, White Flower claims to offer genetically superior versions of widely available species. Its Rudbeckia plants, for instance, are vegetatively propagated (that is, grown from cuttings). You can buy the most popular form of Rudbeckia, the black-eyed Susan, from any garden store or mail-order firm, but it will almost always have been grown from seed. White Flower's research shows that their version, which is relatively expensive at $5.25 per plant (because propagation is labor-intensive), will produce more and better flowers on stronger stems over a longer blooming season.

Constraints on Capacity Planning

With a single production facility, Wadsworth knows that White Flower Farm is rolling the dice a little every year, despite its intensive research and quality control efforts:

Our manufacturing process is frozen in a seasonal pattern and substantially governed by the laws of Nature. We can manipulate this a little bit by temperature control in greenhouses and storage areas, but it's expensive and has its limits when you're cultivating a hundred acres, and growing many different varieties of over 200 species. We pass along to our customers the uncertainties of agriculture in New England. There can be no absolute perfection in our business: To pretend otherwise is foolish and invites disappointment among our customers. Enough disappointment is built in by God.

"There can be no absolute perfection in our business: To pretend otherwise is foolish and invites disappointment among our customers."

Manufacturing uncertainties range from underproduction to overproduction. Specific crops can be reduced by unseasonal frosts, extreme variations in rainfall or temperature, record-breaking storms, new disease mutations, or pests in epidemic quantities. Since White Flower Farm will not sell substandard merchandise or meet any shortfall by buying in from other growers, such an event inevitably means that some orders cannot be met. The firm's philosophy is to manage customer expectations in this respect. The catalog warns its readers that "surprises can and do occur with living things," and offers a choice between providing close substitutes in the event of shortfalls in supplies, or receiving a refund instead. Says Wadsworth, "We're saying, in effect, that we'll occasionally have to disappoint you in order to meet your expectations."

On the other hand, some conditions will lead to bumper harvests, far exceeding demand. Live plants cannot be stockpiled for long in a stage of development suitable for mailing, planting seasons are often short, speculative packaging for shipment is expensive and risks damage to live products, and warehouse space is limited. Special offers at the retail store or to telephone customers may help move some of the surplus, but the balance will have to be recycled and plowed under.

The uncertainty extends to those plants that are shipped, too. Refunds and replacements in response to plants that fail to perform as promised tend to run 2 to 3 percent of sales, but three-quarters of all such problems tend to occur with just a few types of plant, and these are different every year. "We're testing all the time," says Wadsworth, "but sometimes there's an undetected disease or a particular type of plant will have suffered a hidden systemic shock (such as exposure to extreme temperature during harvest) whose impact doesn't show up until after the customers plant it. Learning is a continuous process for us."

A current research project involves developing a proprietary packaging system to ensure temperature control in transit, when plants and bulbs are no longer under White Flower's constant care. Aiding the company in its research is a group of 40 "regional garden advisers"—experienced customers who volunteer their efforts to try out plants in their areas, provide feedback on how well plants travel, and generally keep abreast of local horticultural and competitive activities.

Products That Outlast Their Owners

Another uncertainty involves customers themselves. White Flower Farm has 250,000 active accounts, defined as anyone who has purchased from the company within the last five years. All receive two editions of *The Garden Book* each year, at an average unit cost of $1.10 per copy. Some 200,000 additional copies are mailed out in response to requests from people exposed to advertising that appears in publications such as *The New Yorker* and *House and Garden* or to names on purchased mailing lists.

Although White Flower seeks to create loyal, repeat purchasers, not every existing customer purchases every year. When a nursery deals in perennials (which live for years) rather than annuals (which grow, bloom, and die within a single season), there may be limits to a single customer's needs. Ironically, the higher the quality, the better the plant performs and the longer it lives. "Unfortunately, there's no product obsolescence and no fashion change in herbaceous peonies," sighs Wadsworth. "They last 80 to 100 years. Unless you pour gasoline on them, they will outlive you. Our business is really very different from selling stylish turtleneck sweaters!"

> *"Unfortunately, there's no product obsolescence and no fashion change in herbaceous peonies....Unless you pour gasoline on them, they will outlive you."*

Eventually, successful gardens fill up with healthy plants. At that point, the only hope is to persuade a gardener to remove or give away some existing stock to make room for interesting, newly available varieties. In his search for new varieties to offer, Eliot Wadsworth has traveled to Britain, Germany, France, Switzerland, the Netherlands, and Canada. When I interviewed him, he was planning a trip to Japan and China, with the intention of finding exciting plants not previously available to his customers in North America.

Existing species imported from abroad offer more potential than new hybrids, which are relatively few in number. But White Flower first tests new species intensively in its own gardens and laboratories. At any given time, it has some 600 new varieties on trial. After a one- to two-year trial, another two to five years is required to build up a salable stock.

The White Flower of Service

The core product of White Flower Farm is, of course, the plants that it sells—a broad selection of extremely healthy, clean, high-quality stock, including some newly available or enhanced varieties that are not offered by competitors. However, there's a big difference between what customers buy and what White Flower Farm actually sells. Drooling over the gorgeous catalog, keen gardeners envisage magnificent blooms. They mail, phone, or fax their orders to the farm and some while later—often much later—a package arrives at their home.

Eliot Wadsworth grins as he describes what awaits recipients when they open one of these carefully prepared packages:

Our customers have in mind lovely flowers. Instead they get little brown things in a box. There's no instant gratification. What we deliver is genetic material that is capable of producing what you *really* want. So we have to accompany the orders with substantial information. Like the computer business, most of the genetic material we offer is, broadly speaking, a commodity, although we're always introducing new varieties ahead of the competition. Our real competition is not so much other mail-order firms (which are often cheaper than we are) but garden centers, where you can select a growing plant, sometimes already in bloom. Our value-added activity has to be a mix of information and service, including how to care for each plant and how to combine plants in pleasing ways. We don't have to create the warm desire to garden that so many people already feel, because that comes with the change of seasons, but we do need to give them confidence in their ability to combine plants to make a beautiful garden.

> *"Our customers have in mind lovely flowers. Instead they get little brown things in a box....Our value-added activity has to be a mix of information and service."*

At the risk of mixing metaphors, let's now look at some of the ways in which White Flower Farm uses the petals of supplementary services, as described in Chap. 12, to enhance its own core product.

Information

Among its many other roles, White Flower Farm is also an educational organization. Lesson One begins with *The Garden Book*, which helps customers select plants that will be right for their own environment. A map at the back identifies plant hardiness zones across the United States, ranging from Zone 2 (average annual minimum temperature of −50°F to −40°F) to Zone 11 (40°F to 50°F). Detailed information and growing hints on each genus and variety are accompanied by one or more photographs, so that customers will know what the plants will look like in bloom. A summary table helps readers to compare different species against such characteristics as color, height, blooming season, hardiness zone, preferred soil conditions, amount of sun required, spacing between plants, and suitability of flowers for cutting.

The book also offers many ideas for how to obtain effective displays. Consider these examples. On hardy bulbs: "[B]egin with the notion that bulbs, like most plants, look best in clumps or clusters, not set out as lonely sentinels. Nature does it this way and she's a reliable guide." On delphiniums: "In choosing plants for a border, we suggest 'Blue Mirror' for the front, the other species in the middle, then a thick wall of the hybrids in the back. Because no two of these plants will bloom at exactly the same time, the blooming period will be relatively long." And on 'Johnson's Blue' geraniums: "For a magnificent carefree planting, combine with pink and white ever-blooming shrub roses."

When you've made your selection from the catalog, you'll find a pull-out order form, on the back of which is ordering, shipping, and service information. And when you receive your shipment, you'll find enclosed a *Cultural Instructions* booklet, containing advice on planting and caring for your purchases, plus summary information on the name labels shipped with the plants.

For the future, White Flower is hoping to test a CD-ROM catalog, containing text and pictures for individual plants, and also pictures of each plant in combination with others. In another use of computer technology that will be applicable to every customer, the company plans to print out custom-prepared growing instructions keyed to your plants, your zip code, and the current stage in the growing season.

Consultation

Suppose you're still not sure what to order and wondering about the suitability of certain plants for your garden. Or perhaps you're concerned about the performance of some plants you purchased previously from White Flower Farm. Can you turn to anyone for customized advice? Indeed you can. *The Garden Book* advises: "Our phone staff is trained to handle many questions, but are not professional horticulturists. For complicated questions or problems, please call our staff horticulturist, Mr. Landon Winchester....There is no charge for his assistance." Winchester, who consults to customers three days a week, came to the farm after a long career with the Brooklyn Botanical Garden and a stint as superintendent of horticulture for the City of New Haven. On a busy day, he may take as many as 50 calls.

Order Taking

White Flower Farm receives about 150,000 orders each year from some 90,000 different customers (not every customer buys every year). A core group of some 50,000 customers buy two to three times a year, for an annual total of as much as $250 each. The very largest orders, usually of a one-time nature, may reach as high as $5000.

About 65 percent of all orders are received by mail, 1 to 2 percent by fax, and the balance by telephone. Although 75 percent of customers live in the northeastern United States, the company caters to people clear across the continent, including Canada, and its telephone ordering hours of 9 a.m. to 9 p.m. Eastern time on weekdays reflect that fact. Phone lines are also open for shorter periods on Saturdays and Sundays (after all, that's when busy people have the time to get fired up about their gardens, just like the original founders). At peak times, there are 12–14 operators on duty.

However, the company has bucked the trend of toll-free telephone numbers. Wadsworth explains:

> We tried it twice, once before deregulation and once afterwards. But we gave it up because it was too expensive. The second time around it cost us $150,000 a season. Many people used this number to call and chat as opposed to just placing orders. We couldn't find a civilized way to control the length of dialogue, so were having to add more phone staff. Another interesting phenomenon was that the availability of this number seemed to encourage customers to place orders at the last possible moment, which is brutal in a seasonal business. Since we discontinued the 800 number, call times have dropped.

What the company has done is to find ways of enhancing the value of service actually provided to customers who are paying for a phone call. As in many other telephone-based ordering systems, the operators work with keyboards and video screens. The data available on the screens go beyond supplying details of in-stock positions, for the software combines information on individual stock-keeping units (plants) with the customer's zip code, which is categorized by hardiness zone. If the customer orders plants that are unsuitable for his or her specific zone, the screen will automatically prompt the operator to ask whether the customer is aware of this discrepancy (some expert gardeners rejoice in the challenge of growing plants under difficult conditions; most prefer not to). The computer also assists the operator by offering, on command, summary horticultural information about each plant and suggestions for other plants that will work well in combination with it.

Hospitality

"Please visit the nursery" urges the catalog (the pictures make it look enormously inviting). Visitors are always welcome, in season (April–October), to stroll through the display gardens and what are referred to as the "production fields." About 15,000 people a year accept this invitation, including a number of tour groups, but "we cannot accommodate tours traveling by bus on weekends due to limited parking." There's also a retail store, selling plants, seeds, and selected garden equipment. "Our store staff are knowledgeable and courteous," promises *The Garden Book,* "and are happy to assist with your selections." About 10 percent of all sales are made through this store. One weekend each summer, Eliot Wadsworth, accompanied by his family and staff members, hosts an open house at which iced tea and cucumber sandwiches are served.

Caretaking

Once you have placed an order with White Flower, the company believes that its first responsibility is to the plants in question. For this reason, it will not ship a plant until the time comes to plant it in the customer's hardiness zone (all zip codes are keyed to these zones). Where necessary, plants are maintained in a state of suspended animation in refrigerated sections of the warehouse. Sometimes, an order must be broken into two or more shipments so that each plant arrives at its own best planting time. "These split shipments are expensive," concedes Wadsworth, "but they're the right thing for the plants."

Although inexperienced customers may be dismayed not to receive plants in bloom (except for a few Christmas specials), the reality is a bit more encouraging than Wadsworth's description of "little brown things in a box." Inside the box is protective filler, and then the plants that you ordered, packaged to keep them dry (as with bulbs) or moist (as with rooted plants). The latter are likely to be individually wrapped in labeled, shrink-wrapped packages, with their roots surrounded by sphagnum moss to keep them moist.

Accompanying instructions urge rapid planting and tell you how to do it (also how to store the plant for a short period if you're unable to plant immediately). As with many physical products, the primary responsibility for caretaking shifts to the customer on delivery. White Flower will advise on installation, maintenance, and troubleshooting, but it won't do them for you—this is self-service gardening, not contract landscaping!

Exceptions

If you have special requests—such as delayed or expedited shipments, White Flower will do its best to oblige, providing this doesn't harm the best interests of the plants. If you need help of a technical nature, you can call Mr. Winchester, the horticulturist. If you find a problem with your shipment, you're invited to call the Customer Service Department. As for complaints or suggestions, "If there is any way we can improve our products or services to better meet your needs, please let us know." All complaints are followed up to determine if there is a systemic problem.

The company stands by its products, but its guarantee is not exactly unconditional. "We guarantee to ship plants that are true to variety and in prime condition for growing, to deliver at the proper time for planting (presuming timely receipt of orders), and to provide clear and reliable information regarding the proper use and care of every item offered," reads *The Garden Book*. "We will cheerfully refund or replace, one time, any plant that has been properly cared for but has failed to grow....Adjustments... cannot be considered beyond one year from shipment."

Why not offer one of those unconditional guarantees that have become so popular in recent years? It's not just the nature of the product that drives White Flower's chosen approach, but also the nature of the partnership that it undertakes with its customers. This is made clear in the statement that appears below the guarantee, "Our Shared Responsibility" (see box).

Our Shared Responsibility

The relationship between you, the gardener, and us, the grower, is important to understand because we are dealing with living things that will occasionally fail despite our mutual best efforts. Our job is to provide vigorous, healthy plants and to get them to you in top shape. Your job is to plant these promptly in an appropriate site, paying attention to the cultural advice that we provide. If our plants get proper care and do not grow, it is our responsibility and we will make good. But if they arrive in good health and are lost to extreme weather or neglect, that is your responsibility and while we may share your disappointment, we cannot share your loss. We promise to do our job to the highest standards we know and count on you to do the same.

From **The Garden Book**
(White Flower Farm's catalog)

This is, by any standards, a remarkable statement. It captures, like none other I have ever seen from supplier to customer, the true meaning of partnership. But White Flower Farm also trusts its customers: If they state that they did their best but the plant died or performed poorly, the firm will take them at their word and cheerfully give a refund or replacement.

Billing and Payment

The company has made life easy for itself on this score by combining these two "petals" into one. The rationale for requesting advance payment (as many mail-order firms do) is that any order involves reserving stock from a limited and perishable inventory. If you order by mail, you are expected to tally up the value of your purchases and include payment with your order—in effect, it's self-service billing. White Flower will let you pay by check, money order, or credit card. If you order by phone, the customer service representative tells you how much you owe and asks for your credit card number.

What Can We Learn from White Flower Farm?

Forty years of successful operation are ample testimony to the quality of White Flower Farm's core product: the genetic materials that it sells. Any gardener can tell you what a core product failure looks like in a plant: Either it dies in the ground where you so lovingly planted it, or it grows too big or too small, or turns the wrong color, or fails to flower properly (if at all), or falls victim to diseases that it was supposed to resist. Word-of-mouth travels quickly among gardening enthusiasts, and businesses that supply poor-quality stock will soon suffer a fate similar to their products: withering and dying on the vine as their bottom lines turn the wrong color.

But it's not the quality of the core product alone that has enabled White Flower Farm to survive and prosper. The quality of the supplementary services surrounding that core help it to maintain a competitive advantage against garden centers that can offer instant gratification. As we saw in the previous chapter, the eight petals of the "flower of service" collectively embrace a broad array of possible service elements (please refer back to Table 12-1). The mix of services offered should reflect the nature of the core product, the nature of the customers at whom the product is targeted, and the competitive niche—or corner of the garden if you prefer—that management seeks to stake out.

A key lesson to be drawn from looking at White Flower Farm's activities is simply the importance of selecting the right mix of supplementary service elements—no more and no less than you need—and creating synergy by ensuring that they are all internally consistent. After all, you wouldn't want to try grafting petals from a rose, a chrysanthemum, a daisy, a tulip, and host of other different flowers around the center of a giant sunflower. It would look most peculiar!

White Flower's philosophy of operation reinforces certain basic principles that management experts have been making for years: Stick to your knitting, be a learning organization, manage expectations, make intelligent use of information technology, and keep close to your customers. But there are a few points that jumped out at me as I studied this organization, and I'd like to conclude this chapter by sharing them with you.

1. *Recognize the inherent variability of service environments.* Don't pretend to yourself or your customers that perfection is attainable when it isn't. If the core product or key supplementary services (or both) involve natural elements, human beings, and the public infrastructure, then there are finite limits to the degree of perfection that can be attained. Go for zero defects on those process elements where reason, resources, and research say it is feasible and meaningful. Then develop contingencies to handle those circumstances on which you cannot, realistically, impose your will.

2. *Become a teaching organization as well as a learning one.* The best customers are the best educated—not in the sense of how many degrees they have, but in terms of their understanding of the capabilities of your product and your company. Investments in customer education are as necessary as investments in employee training and in product research. Knowledgeable customers buy the right products in the right way from the right suppliers and use them right. These customers know how to draw the best value from the relationship. In the process, they will probably enable you to do the same.

Knowledgeable customers buy the right products in the right way from the right suppliers and use them right.

---

3. *The true meaning of partnership is shared responsibility.* Firms need to clarify, in a positive and affirming manner, that customers have responsibilities, too. Managing customers' expectations is not limited to what they can expect of product performance. You should educate customers to understand the role you would like them to perform, however passively, in working with your organization and its products to obtain the best results. But try to be collegial about it, in the spirit of partnership; don't appear patronizing or authoritarian.

4. *Turn your customers into teachers and create your own faculty.* You can learn from your customers in many different ways: by encouraging com-

plaints and suggestions, by conducting surveys, and by observing how they actually use your products (whether these be goods or services). But consider formalizing the process on a group basis, by creating panels, advisory boards, or ongoing users' groups. Their role—which should be made explicit rather than left vaguely open-ended—can range from "beta testing" of new products (before they are ready to be generally released) to feedback on the long-term results achieved from existing products, and from suggesting or brainstorming new ideas to providing market intelligence on competitive activities in their local environments.

A Warning on Conventional Wisdom

Finally, looking at White Flower Farm's performance reminds me of the dangers of one-track conventional wisdom, however new. Specifically, this firm's experience suggests that:

- Outsourcing is not for everybody: There is still a role for the vertically integrated firm, especially in a niche market. The key criterion is whether such integration creates superior value for customers and owners, and generates greater satisfaction and involvement for employees.

- Toll-free (800) numbers are not for everybody. They may change customer behavior in undesirable ways.

- Mail-order companies are generally created to serve narrow niches. As they grow larger, things get blurry; they can easily end up selling commodities for razor-thin margins.

- There are better strategic goals for some firms than growth. Indeed, a single-minded pursuit of growth for its own sake may be unhealthy; it can blind a firm to other ways of creating value for its stakeholders. In particular, a strategy of continuous innovation may stand you in better stead competitively, as well as creating more satisfying challenges for management and employees.

"That's the third time this month you've made the same complaint! Can't you think of something more original?"

14 Problem Solving and Service Recovery

When customers' expectations aren't met, they're going to be disappointed. But many don't complain, figuring it's not worth the effort. They vote with their feet, tell their friends, and take their business elsewhere. If things have gone wrong, it's very important that management learn about it, take prompt action to solve the problem, and try to regain the customer's goodwill. Contingency plans for service recovery are best made and rehearsed in advance. Collecting complaints also provides an input to strategy. By learning about problems, management can take steps to find out what causes them and thereby prevent a recurrence. When an airline was troubled by late flight departures, it used a fishbone chart to identify all possible causes, undertook Pareto analysis to determine which reasons caused the most delays, and then focused on fixing the principal causes.

Even businesses that generally perform well still have to deal from time to time with dissatisfied customers. Although the first law of quality might be defined as "do it right the first time," no quality-minded business can afford to be without contingency plans for how to act when things go wrong. Many problems result from internal failures—faulty merchandise, rude personnel, lengthy delays, defective execution, or billing errors. Others are caused by factors outside the firm's immediate control, such as failures in the public infrastructure (phone lines are cut), weather (service facilities are flooded), criminal activities (arson, break-ins, vandalism), or personal troubles for customers (a missing child, a medical emergency, a lost wallet).

How well a firm handles complaints and problem resolution will have a major impact on whether it retains or loses the customers in question. If a company has thought through all such possibilities, developed contingency plans, and then trained its employees accordingly, its people will know what to do and have the authority to take action toward solving the problem.

Complaining Behavior and Complaint Handling

Recently, I stayed in a relatively expensive British hotel which had not kept up with changing customer expectations. Although it was housed in an attractive modern building, it had made no accommodation to nonsmokers: no smoke-free sections in the restaurant, no rooms set aside for nonsmokers. In fact, my room smelled of smoke and boasted a giant ashtray within which an open book of oversized matches pointed skyward like a battery of miniature Scud missiles. After a colleague and I were driven from our dinner table by a veritable bonfire of smoke from the adjoining party of four, cutting short our meal without coffee or dessert, I asked to speak to the hotel's duty manager and told her of my disappointment. She was pleasant, but expressed amazement: "That's the first time anybody has complained about this in the 18 months I've worked here!" she replied.

The fact is, around the world, most people do not complain, especially if they don't think it will do any good. And managers may not hear about complaints made to customer-contact personnel. These were some of the key findings of the landmark Technical Assistance Research Programs Institute (TARP) report of 1986, which studied consumer complaint handling in America. Let's take a closer look at some specific findings.

What Percentage of Problems Are Reported? From its own research and detailed literature studies, TARP found that for manufactured consumer products, only 25 to 30 percent of customers complained. For problems with grocery products or their packaging, A. C. Nielsen found a complaint rate of 30 percent. Even for problems with big-ticket durables, TARP determined that the complaint rate was only 40 percent. Similar findings come from other countries. A Norwegian study found that the percentage of dissatisfied consumers who complained ranged from 9 percent for coffee to 68 percent for cars. A German study showed that only a small fraction of customers expressed dissatisfaction, but among this group the complaint rates ranged from 29 to 81 percent. And finally, a Japanese study found complaint rates of 17 percent among those experiencing a problem with services and 36 percent for those experiencing a problem with goods.

Where Do People Complain?   Studies show that the majority of complaints are made at the place where the product was bought or the service received. Very few dissatisfied consumers complain directly to the manufacturer or the head office. In fact, industry-specific studies conducted by TARP suggest that fewer than 5 percent of complaints about big-ticket durable goods or services ever reach corporate headquarters, presumably because retail intermediaries fail to pass them on.

Industry-specific studies suggest that fewer than 5 percent of complaints about big-ticket durable goods or services ever reach corporate headquarters.

Who Is Most Likely to Complain?   In general, research findings suggest that consumers from high-income households are more likely to complain than those from lower-income ones, and younger people are more likely to complain than older ones. Complainants also tend to be more knowledgeable about product and complaint mechanisms. Other factors that increase the likelihood of a complaint include problem severity, importance of the product to the customer, and whether financial loss is involved.

Why Don't Unhappy Customers Complain?   TARP found three primary reasons why dissatisfied customers don't complain. In order of frequency, customers stated:

- It's not worth the time or effort.
- They decided no one would be concerned about their problem or interested in doing anything about it.
- They did not know where to go or what to do.

Unfortunately, this pessimism seems justified, since a large percentage of complainants (40 to 60 percent in two studies) reported dissatisfaction with the outcome of their complaints. There is one other reason why people don't complain, and it's sometimes a reflection of culture or context. A study in Japan found that 21 percent of dissatisfied customers felt awkward or embarrassed about complaining. In some European countries, there is a strong guest–host relationship between service providers and customers (especially in the restaurant industry), and it's considered bad manners to tell the provider that you are dissatisfied with the service (or the meal).

Impact on Repurchase Intentions.   When complaints are resolved satisfactorily, there's a much better chance that the customer involved will remain brand-loyal and continue to purchase the good or service in question. TARP found that intentions to repurchase different types of products ranged from 69 to 80 percent, among complainers who were completely satisfied with the outcome, to only 17 to 32 percent for complainers who felt that their complaint had not been settled to their satisfaction.

Although TARP reported significant improvements in complaint handling practices between 1979 and 1986, many customers remain dissatisfied with the way in which their problems are resolved. A 1988 study, investigating the performance of five companies that were among the largest and most marketing-oriented in their respective industries, found that between 33 and 50 percent of customers surveyed were not satisfied with the way in which their service problems had been resolved. Commenting on this finding, Leonard Berry and A. Parasuraman observe: "The rates of satisfactory resolution for services in general probably were lower than for the five companies investigated."

The truth is, many industries are still a long way from meeting their customers' expectations on service. Consider what business users of personal computers want from service providers by way of speed of delivery on each of seven different service elements. Table 14-1 compares their preferred and maximum acceptable response times with what they claim they experienced. In every instance, actual response times are closer to maximum than to preferred, and in two instances they exceed these maximums.

Complaints as Market Research

There are two ways of looking at complaints. One is as a series of individual customer problems, each of which requires a resolution (I'll return to this in a moment). The second is as a stream of information that can be used to help measure quality and suggest improvements to service design and execution. Product plus organizations see complaints both ways. In the latter case, it's

Table 14-1. Outside Service Providers' Typical Time
to Deliver Service

	Actual (N = 306)	Prefer (N = 304)	Maximum acceptable (N = 303)
First telephone support call-back	3.8	1.6	4.2
Telephone support problem resolution	7.5	2.8	7.4
On-site response—remedial service	12.0	6.4	12.5
On-site service repair—elapsed to resolution	13.4	6.5	12.9
On-site response for multivendor service	12.5	7.5	13.2
On-site multivendor service—elapsed to resolution	14.9	7.8	15.4
LAN installation/implementation (weeks)	7.9	5.2	9.8

NOTE: Times are in mean business hours except where noted.

SOURCE: Ledgeway/Dataquest, *PC/End-User Computing Services: User Wants and Needs*, 1991 Annual Edition, p. 89. Reprinted by permission.

only realistic to include suggestions and inquiries, too. A suggestion usually indicates an opportunity to move a customer from "somewhat satisfied" to "very satisfied." Inquiries often reveal weaknesses in providing information or point to a need for improved customer education.

For complaints/suggestions/inquiries to be useful as research input, they have to be funneled into a central collection point, logged, categorized, and analyzed. That requires mechanisms for capturing complaints wherever they are made—without in any way hindering resolution of each specific problem—and transmitting them to a central location.

> *There are two ways of looking at complaints: as individual customer problems, each of which requires a resolution, and as a stream of information that can be used to measure quality and suggest improvements.*

Consider for a moment how and *to whom* your own customers might register a complaint, and then check off which of the following "entry points" might apply to your own organization:

- Employees who deliver service to customers face to face, either in a retail location or at a customer site
- Employees who serve customers by telephone from either a local office or a central facility

- Employees whose role is primarily that of an information provider or "traffic cop" (receptionist, triage nurse, inquiries coordinator, security guard, telephone operator)

- Intermediary organizations whose own employees serve your customers on your firm's behalf in any of the above capacities

- Managers who are in contact with customers as part of their normal routine

- Managers who normally work backstage but who are summoned by a customer seeking higher authority

- Senior managers contacted by name (or by job title) by mail, fax, or phone

- Suggestion or complaint cards mailed or placed in a special box

- Complaints to third parties—consumer groups, legislative agencies, trade organizations, and other customers

It's not surprising that TARP found such a low percentage of complaints getting through to the head office, since many firms lack the mechanisms to record complaints (especially when they are made verbally) and then funnel them back to a central point. Moreover, employees, managers of local service outlets, and intermediary organizations must be persuaded to share information that might seem to be an indictment of their own performance. To the extent that a complaint can be solved locally, local managers may see little perceived value in passing the information along.

Encouraged by TARP findings—as well as by motivational speakers whose theme seems to be "the more complaints you can generate, the better"—many companies have indeed improved their complaint collection procedures, with special toll-free phone lines and prominent displays of customer comment cards. But just collecting complaints doesn't necessarily help resolve them; in fact, accepting complaints and then ignoring them may make matters worse.

What if your goal in centralizing complaint records is to generate input for research? Follow-up may be needed to obtain more insights as well as to resolve the customer's problem. Southwest Airlines is a great believer in using customer complaint, compliment, and suggestion letters to monitor airline performance and stimulate internal research and self-analysis. About 1000 customers write to the airline every week, and a staff of 45 people in two departments is kept busy researching problems and responding to customers. These are not form-letter responses: Explaining why a flight was late has sometimes required as much as seven pages! Herbert Kelleher, the airline's humorous CEO, responds to many letters personally. He once responded to a smart-aleck protest that toilet paper was inserted upside down in a 737 toilet by asking the complainant, "What the hell were you doing upside down in our lavatory?"

Analysis of centralized logs often provides a useful input to more formal marketing research, with questions targeted at a broad cross section of customers, including those who for cultural or other reasons might be reluctant to initiate a complaint. Personal or telephone interviews offer much better opportunities than mail surveys to dig deeper and probe for what lies behind certain answers: "Can you tell me why you feel this way? Who (or what) precipitated this situation? What was their response? What action would you like to see the firm take to prevent a recurrence of such a situation?"

Complaint data alone may not be a good index of service quality, either. Singapore Airlines used to base its quality measure, known as the Service Productivity Index, on such indicators as punctuality data, the ratio of baggage mishandled/recovered per 1000 passengers, and the ratio of complaints to compliments addressed to management. In recent years, however, it has added data from multilingual in-flight surveys to this index. Why? Because it found that Japanese and other Asians were less willing to send in written complaints to management than were Americans, Australians, and Europeans (notably Germans).

In my view, the most useful research roles for centralized complaint logging are (1) to serve as an early-warning indicator of perceived deterioration in one or more aspects of service—either in general, or at a specific location; and (2) to indicate topics and issues that deserve more detailed research.

Problem Resolution

Some complaints are made while service delivery is still taking place; others are made after the fact. The advantage of getting "real-time" complaints is that there may still be a chance to correct the situation before service delivery is completed (and perhaps major damage is done). Such recovery efforts can be absolutely vital when the service involves an extended process with significant consequences. The downside of real-time complaints (from a staff perspective) is that hearing them is demotivating and dealing with them immediately may interfere with the smooth delivery of service. But that's the old operations mindset coming to the fore again! The real difficulty for employees is often that they lack the authority and the tools needed to resolve customer problems, especially when it comes to arranging alternatives at the company's expense or authorizing compensation on the spot.

> *Employees often lack the authority and the tools needed to resolve customer problems.*

When complaints are made after the fact, the options for recovery are more limited, being confined to apologizing, repeating the service to achieve the desired solution (in situations, such as repair, where that is still possible), or offering some other form of compensation. In both instances, how the complaint is handled and how the problem is addressed are likely to have an important influence on whether the customer remains with the firm or seeks new suppliers in the future.

TARP has argued that complaint handling should be seen as a profit center, not a cost center, and even created a formula to help companies relate the value of retaining a profitable customer to the overall costs of running an effective complaint-handling unit. Plugging industry data into this formula yielded some impressive returns on investment: from 50 to 170 percent for banking, from 20 to 150 percent for gas utilities, over 100 percent for automotive service, and from 35 to 400 percent (*sic*) for retailing.

Designing an effective problem-resolution process for your own company must take into account its specific environment and the types of problems that your customers are likely to encounter (flowcharting and OTSU analysis will help here—see Chap. 11). However, as a result of discussions with executives in many different industries, I offer the following basic guidelines.

1. *Act fast.* When the complaint is made in real time, then speed is of the essence if full recovery and a successful outcome are to be achieved. When complaints are made after the fact, many companies have now moved to follow IBM's long-standing policy of answering every customer complaint within 24 hours. Even when full resolution is likely to take longer, fast acknowledgment remains very important.

2. *Admit mistakes but don't be defensive.* Acting defensively may suggest that the organization has something to hide or is reluctant to explore the situation fully.

3. *Show that you understand the problem from the customer's point of view.* Seeing the situation through the customers' eyes is the only way to understand what they think has gone wrong and why they are upset. Jumping to conclusions with your own interpretation of what the problem "really" is may simply compound an already bad situation.

4. *Don't argue.* The goal is to gather facts so as to reach a mutually acceptable solution, not to win a debating contest or prove that the customer is an idiot. Arguing gets in the way of listening and seldom defuses anger.

5. *Acknowledge the customer's feelings.* Acknowledging feelings, either tacitly or explicitly ("I can understand why you're upset"), helps to build rapport, which is the first step in rebuilding a bruised relationship.

6. *Give the customer the benefit of the doubt.* If you're not certain whether

customers are telling the full story or whether the complaint is fully justified, there's still a good chance that they are in the right. So treat them as though they are, until such time as you have clear evidence otherwise. If a lot of money is at stake (as in insurance claims or potential lawsuits), careful investigation will be warranted; if the amount concerned is small, then it's not worth the cost of haggling over a refund or other compensation—but check your records and see if there is any past history of dubious complaints by the same customer.

7. *Clarify the steps needed to solve the problem.* When instant solutions aren't possible, tell customers how you plan to proceed. Not only does this let them know that the gears are being put in motion, but it also sets expectations as to what sort of time frame is involved (but don't overpromise!).

8. *Keep the customer informed of progress.* Nobody likes being left in the dark. Uncertainty breeds anxiety and stress. Customers tend to be more accepting of disruptions if they know what is going on and receive periodic progress reports (even acknowledgments that a particular solution has not worked and that another will have to be tried are helpful— unless there is manifest evidence of incompetence—because they indicate that the supplier still cares and is trying hard to resolve the problem).

9. *Consider compensation.* When financial loss is involved (that is, customers did not receive the service outcome that they paid for, or they lost money because the service failed), then either a monetary payment or an offer of equivalent service in kind is not only appropriate, it may even be necessary to avoid the risk of legal action. Service guarantees often lay out in advance what such compensation will be. Significant loss of a customer's time because of service delays also merits compensation in some form. Gifts may mollify upset customers, too, but there may be a judgment call involved here. In many cases, what customers really want is an apology and a commitment to avoid similar problems in the future.

10. *Persevere to regain customer goodwill.* The problem may not be fully solved, even when it appears to have been solved. What do I mean by this conundrum? Simply that a key challenge lies in retaining customers whom you've disappointed but with whom you want to maintain a relationship. Often this takes perseverance and follow-through. J. W. Marriott, Jr., CEO of the hotel chain, told me of personally making numerous phone calls to an angry customer who controlled a lot of business, and even following up with face-to-face discussions over lunch in an effort to win business back (which he did). And he added: "Sometimes those customers whom you make that extra effort to gain back become the most loyal customers that you have."

> *A key challenge lies in retaining customers whom you've disappointed but with whom you want to maintain a relationship.*

11. *Prevent recurrence.* When a problem is caused by controllable, internal forces, there's no excuse for allowing it to recur. In fact, maintaining the goodwill you have so painfully regained in the previous step depends on your ability to keep the promises that were made to the effect that "we're taking action to make sure it doesn't happen again!"

With prevention in mind, let's look at some simple, but powerful, quality tools for determining the root cause of specific problems.

Getting Flights Out on Time

A useful example of tracking a problem to its source (and then fixing it) comes from the airline industry. The company in question, Midway Airlines, is a regional carrier which is based at Chicago's secondary airport, from which it takes its name. Demonstrating effective use of control charts, cause-and-effect analysis, and Pareto analysis, the story comes from the late Daryl Wyckoff, who held the James J. Hill Chair of Transportation at Harvard and was also a director of the airline.

Most of Midway's flights last 2 hours or less in length, and the airline targets business travelers in particular. Early one spring, Midway faced a serious punctuality problem. An excessive number of its flights were arriving late at their destinations. Research quickly showed that most of these delayed arrivals were caused by delayed departures. Company records, captured in the control chart in Fig. 14-1, showed that the number of flights leaving on time was declining. In fact, only about 75 percent of flights departed "on time" (which was rather loosely defined as within 15 minutes of schedule).

Concerned that its personnel didn't understand the importance of getting flights out on time, Midway deputized one of its senior officers to visit all stations and to exhort employees to work harder on ensuring that flights were able to leave on schedule. He was a great motivational speaker and the initial results were most encouraging, with the percentage of on-time departures rising to almost 95 percent over the next 6 months.

Management was delighted with the success of the motivational cam-

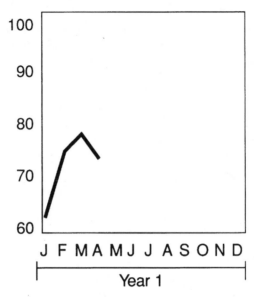

Figure 14-1. Control chart for departure delays showing percentage of flights departing within 15 minutes of schedule during the first 4 months of the year.

paign, congratulated the officer responsible, and returned him to his usual duties. However, their pleasure was short-lived, for on-time departures promptly nose-dived again during the next few months (Fig. 14-2).

The Fishbone Chart

At a subsequent board meeting, Daryl Wyckoff theorized that perhaps there were some systemic problems causing late departures, as opposed to an unmotivated work force. Following his recommendation, management decided to employ cause-and-effect analysis, using a technique first developed by the Japanese quality expert, Kaoru Ishikawa. Groups of managers and staff brainstormed all the possible reasons that might lead to the late departure of an aircraft from the gate. The resulting factors were then categorized into one of five groupings—Equipment, Manpower, Material, Procedures, and Other—on a cause-and-effect chart, popularly known as a fishbone chart because of its shape.

I've reanalyzed the data, as originally reported by Wyckoff, and extended the original chart to comprise eight rather than five groupings—breaking down "Manpower" into Front-Stage Personnel and Backstage Personnel,

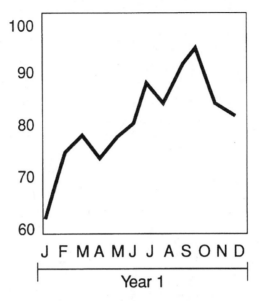

Figure 14-2. Control chart of departure
delays showing percentage of flights departing
within 15 minutes of schedule, extended to 12
months.

splitting out "Information" from "Procedures," and adding a new category,
"Customers." My version of the chart, now even more fishlike, is shown in
Fig. 14-3. It displays a total of 27 possible reasons for late departures.

Pareto Analysis

The next step in Midway's analysis was to study late departures of flights
from all airports served by the carrier, identify the reason(s) in each case,
and conduct a Pareto analysis to determine what proportion of delays were
caused by what factors. Pareto analysis underlies the so-called 80/20 rule,
because this analysis often shows that around 80 percent of the value of one
variable (in this instance, the number of service failures) is accounted for by
only 20 percent of the causal variables (i.e., number of possible causes). In
this instance, the ratio was even higher; findings showed that 88 percent of
late departures from airports other than the hub at Midway Airport in
Chicago were caused by only four (15 percent) of all the possible factors.

In fact, more than half the delays were caused by a single factor: acceptance of late passengers (when the staff held a flight for one more passenger
who was checking in after the official cutoff time). On such occasions, the

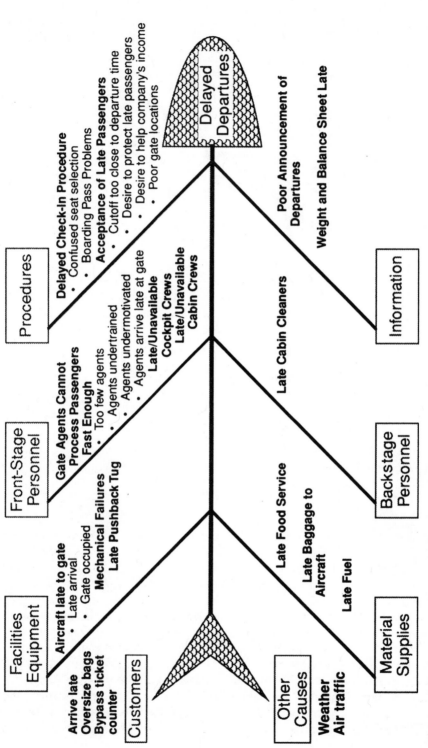

Figure 14-3. Cause-and-effect chart for airline departure delays.

airline made a friend of that late passenger, but enemies of the other 119 sitting on the aircraft waiting impatiently for it to leave. Other major causes of delays included waiting for pushback (the tug that pulls the aircraft away from the gate), waiting for fueling, and delays in signing the weight and balance sheet (a safety requirement that the captain must observe on each flight).

Midway then took analysis one stage further by examining the causes, station by station. It found some interesting variations from the system-wide averages (Fig. 14-4).

In Newark, for instance, late passengers accounted for only 23 percent of delays. Waiting for pushback was more of a problem (23 percent), as was waiting for fueling; late weight and balance sheet actually dropped off the list of the top four problems, being replaced by late arrival of the cabin cleaners. At Washington National Airport, waiting for pushback and late passengers each accounted for 33 percent of delays. Other major problems were late weight and balance sheet and waiting for fueling. Further analysis then probed for any deeper root causes underlying those already identified. (In the case of acceptance of late passengers, for instance, the problem is that passengers themselves arrive late. Next question: Why?)

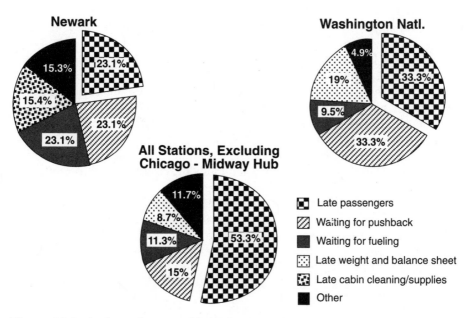

Figure 14-4. Analysis of causes of flight departure delays.

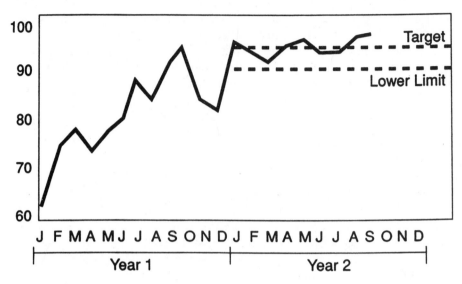

Figure 14-5. Control chart of departure delays showing percentage of flights departing within 15 minutes of schedule over a 2-year period.

Actions and Results

Armed with these insights, Midway's management moved quickly to correct each of the major problems identified—revamping procedures such as delivery of the weight and balance sheet to the cockpit, changing policies on acceptance of late passengers (and informing both staff and passengers), pressing service suppliers (such as fuel and cleaning) to perform at a higher level or lose their contracts, and reexamining the deployment of personnel and vehicles allocated to the pushback task. The result? An immediate and sustained improvement during the following year, with on-time departures remaining around 95 percent, as shown in the control chart reproduced in Fig. 14-5. Subsequently, management revamped the standard of on-time departure, redefining "on-time" rather more precisely as within 5 minutes of schedule.

One important insight from this story is that customers themselves often cause service problems. It was for this reason that I developed an enlarged fishbone chart, featuring a separate category for customers. In this instance, the revised chart shows that customers cause three problems for gate agents: They arrive late, they try to carry on board oversized bags which should have been checked and stowed in the baggage hold, and they bypass the ticket counter (where they could have checked the bag and received a boarding pass).

Like most quality tools, fishbone charts were developed for use in manufacturing, where customers have little impact on day-to-day operational processes. My fishbone also separates backstage personnel from front-stage ones, to highlight the fact that front-stage activities are often dependent on backstage support: Gate agents can't board passengers until the cleaners have finished work in the aircraft cabin. Finally, I believe that many service problems result from information failures, especially failures by front-stage personnel to tell customers what to do and when. In this instance, poor announcement of departures may be one of several underlying reasons why passengers arrive late at the gate.

A New Quality Goal: Zero Defections

"Defector" was a nasty word during the Cold War. It described disloyal people who sold out their own side and went over to the enemy. Even when they defected toward your side, rather than away from it, they were still suspect. Today, the word is being used to describe customers who drop off a company's radar screen and transfer their brand loyalty to another supplier. This time, though, there's a difference: Almost everyone's sympathies are on the side of the defector. These modern-day defectors do share one characteristic with their old political counterparts: They're potentially great sources of information—about why they defected from your firm (or from a competitor's to yours). Holding exit (or arrival) interviews can be very enlightening.

Frederick Reichheld and Earl Sasser popularized the term *zero defections*, which they describe as keeping every customer the company can profitably serve (there are always some you're not sorry to lose!). Not only does a rising defection rate indicate that something is already wrong with quality (or that competitors offer better value), it also signals a probable profit slump ahead. Large customers don't necessarily disappear overnight, but they may signal their mounting disaffection by steadily reducing their purchases as they head toward the border crossing. If you're observant, you may be able to catch them before they go and try to persuade them to stay.

Putting Service Recovery Programs into Perspective

Fred Reichheld, who leads Bain & Company's loyalty/retention practice, has studied both customer and employee retention in several dozen industries and has worked on retention issues with more than 30 clients around the world. He says that it's much harder to engineer higher loyalty into a business system than most managers suspect. At the root of the problem, he says, is that:

> Most business people don't recognize the full economic implications of loyalty; they agree intuitively with the concept, but they have not made the required investments. The trouble is, they underestimate the value of loyalty and overestimate the ease of creating it.
>
> Typically, managers tend to look for a few ad hoc solutions, such as better recovery efforts, pricing and promotional incentives, and reward programs for regular customers of the "frequent flyer" variety. But the impact of such efforts is often quite modest, particularly if they're easily copied by competitors. At Bain, we've found that we obtain our best successes with clients when their top managers come to recognize that building and maintaining loyalty is a systemic challenge, not just a tactical embellishment. They view loyalty as the core of sustained competitive success.

"Most business people don't recognize the full economic implications of loyalty...they underestimate the value of loyalty and overestimate the ease of creating it."

FREDERICK REICHHELD

Clearly, to the extent that you can uncover customer dissatisfaction and resolve it promptly, your chances of retaining desirable customers are improved. But having a good complaint-handling mechanism is doing little more than treating symptoms which, in many cases, have avoidable causes. So it's imperative that you work continuously to improve your overall service system as well. That means getting to the bottom of service problems and making sure they don't recur.

What do you do when your research shows that customers themselves are the source of the problem? For some answers to that question, turn to the next chapter.

The right/wrong customer–right/wrong behavior matrix.

15 Sometimes the Customer Is Wrong

Nobody really believes that the customer is always right. In truth, the customer is sometimes horribly wrong, and it's silly to pretend otherwise. There are two types of wrong customers. First are those whose service needs cannot easily be met by the organization and who should not, therefore, be part of the target market. Second are what I call "jaycustomers," who may meet the desired profile except that they behave stupidly, irrationally, or illegally toward service personnel, facilities, and other customers. Effective marketing and screening (within the constraints of what is legal and ethical) can minimize the presence of the first type. But there have to be contingency plans for dealing with the several different types of jaycustomers, ranging from diplomatic handling by well-trained employees to taking legal action.

There, I've gone and done it. I've used the W-phrase. I've made the statement that nobody in service management is even supposed to think, let alone utter. It's probably going to get me into trouble, but no matter: In your heart, you know I'm right. The fact is, when the customer is wrong, it's very hard to achieve product plus service: Both quality and productivity are compromised, employees' jobs are made that much tougher, and profits are jeopardized.

But let's be clear up front and recognize that there are two broad categories of wrong customers. First, there are customers (both individual and corporate) who are wrong for the supplier, because their needs, consumption patterns, willingness to spend, or other characteristics do not fit the supplier's goals or capabilities. And then there are customers who, although they match the target profile, behave in wrong ways. Both groups are likely to cause problems—not least for front-stage personnel, and even for other customers—but the root causes are very different and so are the remedies.

The Wrong Customer

At various points in this book, we've talked about the importance of *focus*, of zeroing in on certain types of customers, of matching customer needs and preferences to the firm's operational processes and human capabilities (and vice versa). If you know what to focus on, you also know what to avoid.

Six Situations to Avoid

There are basically six categories of wrong customer:

- The fit between product and customer is poor.
- There are differences in personalities and style.
- The relationship doesn't offer mutually good value.
- The customer lacks sufficient resources.
- The cyclicality of customer demand is wrong.
- The customer lacks needed skills and technologies.

All six situations should be approached with care and preferably avoided. However, their potential for destabilizing the supplier organization may vary widely from one type of business to another.

Poor Product–Customer Fit.   One size does not fit all. Nor is a broad product line helpful when the customer specifically wants something different from what you're offering. Unless the basic characteristics of the core product and accompanying supplementary services match the customer's underlying needs, there's going to be disappointment. Don't pretend that you can satisfy a customer when you know you can't (and have good reason not to change your product line-up). Why set people up for disappointment? You may do more for your firm's reputation by directing such customers to another supplier.

Sometimes, however, inexperienced customers may not fully understand their own needs; they may even ask for the wrong product. Through careful probing and analysis, you may be able to help such customers clarify their requirements. Traditional-minded buyers who have not kept up with new developments may also be candidates for objective advice and consultation. Both parties stand to benefit when expressed needs can be usefully redefined in the light of changing market conditions, technologies, or solutions. Taking the time to educate customers is often the key to successful relationship building. But pushing the wrong product-service package isn't likely to lead to fruitful relationships or positive referrals.

Differences in Personalities and Style. In some lines of business, providers need to develop close working relationships with their customers at a personal level. Successful relationships are built on trust, which implies similar working styles, including a shared set of values and ethical standards. All parties need to agree on their priorities and stick to them, until such time as they mutually agree that a change is needed. Bad customer-supplier relationships, like bad marriages, often result from differences in style, personality, and values that neither party manages to resolve.

Bad customer-supplier relationships, like bad marriages, often result from differences in style, personality, and values that neither party manages to resolve.

Personality differences at the individual level can sometimes be resolved by switching the players on your side (you may have to change the account manager or other team members to accommodate the client). But differences in corporate personality are much harder to resolve. If, after careful review and some heart-searching a firm concludes that it cannot (or does not wish) to do business with a prospective customer, then it's rightly admitting that this is "the wrong customer for us."

The Relationship Offers Inadequate Value. Even when the product seems to fit the customer well and the customer has made an initial purchase, no extended relationship is going to work if the customer is unwilling or unable to incur all the associated costs—monetary and nonmonetary—over the long term. Doctors and consultants often see clients losing interest when the latter learn the full implications of working toward a desired solution: They don't perceive sufficient value. Although it's tempting to try to preserve the relationship, there's an opportunity cost for the supplier in investing time in lukewarm clients who may eventually drift away anyway. The reverse also holds true: Some customers demand more free service and support than the supplier can afford to give. Learning when and how to say "no" often spells the difference between red and black ink on the bottom line of a relationship.

> *Learning when and how to say "no" often spells the difference between red and black ink on the bottom line of a relationship.*

Insufficient Resources. Many promising customer relationships go belly up when the customer runs short of working capital and is forced to curtail activities as part of a major cost-paring exercise. In a more serious scenario (which occurs all too frequently during recessions), customers themselves go belly up, often leaving a trail of uncollectible bills behind them. In the worst case, a series of such fiascoes brings the supplier to its knees, too. There's a difference between agreeing to supply a new customer whose creditworthiness is questionable and helping an existing customer "work things out" during a period of financial difficulty. Prospective customers can be deficient in resources other than money, too. Colleges screen applicants for intellectual potential; organizers of rugged physical activities such as trekking in the Himalayas may screen for past experience and medical condition. Whatever the missing resource, there's no point in setting up customers for failure, however enthusiastic and committed they may be.

When Air BP, the aviation-fuel division of BP Oil, decided to enter the business of aviation service centers (described by some as "truck stops for executive jets"), it formed a partnership with a family firm in California that already ran two successful operations of this nature, and for which Air BP supplied the fuel. This firm—let's call it Chuckair— agreed to a 50–50 partnership with Air BP to build one new service center and purchase a second. BP put in its share of the money and the venture got under way. As the months passed, however, Chuckair found banks unwilling to lend the full amount of money it required for its own share. Trying to make the investment out of its own resources, the little firm fell seriously behind in payments to Air BP for fuel purchases. Eventually, the big oil company withdrew from the venture and dissolved the partnership.

Wrong Cyclicality. Service firms and other suppliers that cannot produce for inventory often find themselves cycling constantly between feast and famine as far as demand levels are concerned. Knowingly accepting new business from customers who want delivery when your capacity to serve is already stretched to its limits is a guaranteed recipe for indigestion. An accounting firm, for example, whose auditors are working flat out between January and March but have little to do between July and October would be foolish to take on new clients whose fiscal year coincides with the calendar year. Service firms of this nature should try to build a balanced portfolio of customers whose most intense demands will come during complementary periods, rather than simultaneously. The alternative is low quality at peak seasons and low productivity at other times.

Lack of Needed Skills and Technologies. When customers and suppliers need to work closely together from an operational perspective, both sides should bring compatible skills and technological systems to the partnership. Customers and suppliers can and do educate each other (Japanese auto manufacturers, for instance, are well known for teaching their suppliers how to meet quality and delivery standards). But like college admissions, certain basic competencies may be needed of would-be students before further education can take place. The growing trend to integrate supplier–customer information networks requires compatible systems. Although new systems can be installed from scratch, it's cheaper and faster to do business with people who already have the appropriate systems in place.

Common Sense versus Bureaucracy

Dr. Samuel Johnson once described remarriage after an unsuccessful first attempt as "the triumph of hope over experience." Starry-eyed optimism in the marketing department that problems previously encountered with customers or suppliers will not be repeated in the future is certainly no recipe for creating profitable, long-term relationships. But neither is it helpful to allow once-bitten accountants, systems designers, and lawyers to lay down inflexible terms under which new customers will be "accepted."

Nevertheless, common sense does dictate a certain caution, especially when moving into new or less familiar markets. As in defensive driving, an ounce of caution is worth a pound of cure. So, as a supplier, do ask yourself what types of customers will generate mutually satisfactory relationships for your organization. And as a customer, turn the question on its head and ask yourself what sort of suppliers can provide the relationships you seek.

In both instances, it's helpful to consider failed relationships and think about the underlying causes. If, with the benefit of hindsight, these failures could have been predicted, then you already know something about "wrong customers" (or "wrong suppliers") and can use those insights to prevent a future occurrence of the same type of problem.

> *It's helpful to consider failed relationships and think about the underlying causes. If these failures could have been predicted, then you already know something about "wrong customers."*

But what of relationships that sour or fail because what looked like the "right" customer proceeds to behave wrongly? This set of problems leads to consideration of what I call the "jaycustomer." But first, let me explain where I got the term.

Jaycustomers

You'll know you're in Venice as soon as you step outside the station!" an Italian friend told us. He wouldn't elaborate further, but just smiled enigmatically and said: "You'll see for yourselves!" A few weeks later, we did.

The train crossed a causeway from the mainland and came to a stop in a modern station that could have been almost anywhere. Our family strode through the station concourse, out the exit doors, and came to an abrupt halt. There, across a narrow pedestrian piazza, lay the Grand Canal, a hundred yards wide with stuccoed buildings in pastel colors lining the far bank. The contrast with the traffic-choked squares or streets that lie outside most major railroad stations around the world was simply astonishing, for Venice is free of cars and trucks.

We walked to the edge of the canal and watched the busy water traffic moving by. *Vaporetti* (water buses) were stopping to load and unload passengers. There were police launches and ambulance launches, water taxis in polished wood, and motorized trash barges looking rather less elegant. A gondola threaded its way between two barges bearing produce and building supplies, respectively, and disappeared into a small side canal. An Italian postal service launch chugged past, followed by a construction barge moving debris from a building site and sporting three discarded urinals perched incongruously atop a pile of bricks. There was even a United Parcel Service vessel carrying several dozen neatly stacked parcels on its decks. Instead of the normal roar of city traffic, there was just a soft sound of splashing water and chugging motors.

As I was reflecting—rather unromantically—on the logistics of supplying a city where canals replaced streets, my son, Timothy, spoke up. "Well," he said, "One thing they don't have to worry about here is jaywalkers!" "Yes," his sister, Elizabeth, agreed, "But what about jay*swimmers?*"

Jaywalkers. That distinctively American word used to describe people who cross streets at unauthorized places or in an unusual manner. Why not apply the prefix "jay" (a slang term for a stupid person) to swimmers, too? If the Venice canal traffic didn't get you, the water certainly would.

And why not take this word game one step further, as the Germans like to do with their compound words, and create a whole new vocabulary of derogatory terms by adding the prefix "jay" to a variety of other words? How about *jaycustomer*, for example, to denote someone who *jayconsumes* a product (or *jayuses* a service) and then *jaydisposes* of it afterward? In fact, the entire management lexicon would probably lend itself to application of this prefix. But let's not digress.

Jaycustomers Are Everywhere—
No They Aren't

Every product that has ever been made, every service that has ever been offered, has encountered its share of jaycustomers. But opinions on this topic seem to polarize around two opposing views of the situation. One is denial: "The customer is king and can do no wrong." The other view sees the marketplace of customers as positively overpopulated with nasty people (and even nastier corporate purchasers) who simply cannot be trusted to behave in ways that self-respecting suppliers should expect and require. The first viewpoint has received wide publicity in gung ho management books and in motivational presentations to captive groups of employees. But the second often appears to be more widely believed among cynical managers who have been burned at some point in their professional lives. As with so many opposing viewpoints in life, there are important grains of truth in both perspectives, with the reality lying somewhere in the gray area in between.

Since defining the problem is the first step in resolving it, let's start by considering the different types of jaycustomers who may plague or prey upon suppliers of goods and services. I've identified six broad categories and given them generic names, but many customer contact personnel have come up with their own terms of endearment for these charming folks. As you read, you can think about which apply to your own organization—it will depend in some degree on what type of product/service packages you offer.

And, perhaps, reflecting on my categories may stimulate you to add a few more of your own.

Some Common Species

The Thief. This jaycustomer has no intention of paying for your product or service and sets out to steal it. Another variant of the thief is *the discounter*, who pays less than full price by such devices as switching price tickets or contesting certain entries in an itemized bill on baseless grounds.

The best-known variety of thief is the shoplifter. What American retailers euphemistically call "shrinkage" is estimated to cost them billions of dollars every year. Some shoplifters are professionals who steal to resell, but the great majority want the goods for themselves. Not all are evil people. Some, such as kleptomaniacs, are acting out psychological compulsions; others, at the bottom end of the economic ladder, steal out of desperation.

And thieves do not limit themselves to shoplifting goods. Many services lend themselves to clever schemes for avoiding payment. For those with a technical bent, it is sometimes possible to bypass electrical meters, access telephone lines free of charge, or circumvent normal cable TV feeds. Riding free on public transportation is also a popular pastime. And we mustn't forget the use of fraudulent forms of payment such as stolen credit cards or checks that are guaranteed to bounce.

The challenge for managers of afflicted enterprises is to devise schemes for protecting themselves against thieves, while avoiding the temptation of employing Gestapo-like tactics against the bulk of honest customers. As a graduate student, I well remember using a university library that was run with all the finesse of a concentration camp. Admittedly, this was during the campus disturbances of the late 1960s and early 1970s. But the underlying fear seemed to be that terrorist students would seek to "liberate" the collection. The measures taken to prevent such an occurrence were so draconian—beginning with rigorously enforced proof of identity at the single entry point and ending with a near strip search on departure—as to discourage all but the most committed user from ever darkening the building's door. What's a library for, anyway?

> *The challenge for managers is to devise schemes for protecting against thieves, while avoiding the temptation of employing Gestapo-like tactics against honest customers.*

A happier memory from the same period is of a meeting I had with two managers from the regional office of Greyhound Bus Lines as part of a research project. At the end of our meeting, the regional manager asked me diffidently if I knew of a book by Abbie Hoffman, a well-known radical activist, called *Steal This Book!* Wondering if he were pulling my leg, I replied that I recognized the author's name but not the book. Why was he interested, I asked, unable to contain my curiosity. The man from Greyhound, a model of conservative respectability in his gray suit, white shirt, and short haircut, shuffled his feet and looked embarrassed.

"Well," he finally blurted, "this book apparently tells you how to avoid paying for almost everything, and it seems there's a chapter on how to ride Greyhound for free. I figured that if it were selling anywhere, it would be at the Stanford University bookstore. As a favor, would you be willing to get us one? Of course," he added hastily, "we'll reimburse you" (at least he didn't expect me to steal it!).

The next day, I went to the infamous bookstore. And there, indeed, was the book, invitingly displayed. Furtively, I peeked inside and found a veritable encyclopedia of tips on how to rip off capitalist-pig, Establishment-run enterprises. Greyhound was indeed featured, complete with a host of ideas for riding free and avoiding detection. Feeling a little foolish, I ignored the invitation on the cover and took the priceless volume to the checkout station, wondering if I were the first to actually pay for it. A few days later I delivered the book, discretely hidden in a brown paper bag, to my contact at Greyhound, who did indeed reimburse me (on delivery of a receipt).

The folks at Greyhound had the right idea. Finding out how people steal your product is the first step in taking preventive measures to stop it, or corrective measures to catch them at it and, where appropriate, to prosecute. But please try not to alienate your honest customers by degrading their own service experience. And provision must be made for honest but absent-minded customers who forget to pay. Many stores now attach electronic tags to their merchandise, which can only be removed at a cashier's station. If the customer passes a point near the exit door with merchandise that still bears a tag, it sets off an alarm, thus offering a clear choice between returning to the register or making a break for it.

The Rule Breaker. Just as highways need safety regulations (including "Don't Jaywalk"), so do many businesses find it necessary to establish rules of behavior for employees and customers. Some of these rules are imposed by government agencies for reasons of health and safety. Air travel is perhaps the best example; there can be few other environments outside prison where healthy, mentally competent, adult customers are quite so constrained (albeit with good reason).

In addition to enforcing government regulations, suppliers often lay down their own set of rules to facilitate the smooth functioning of the operation, avoid unreasonable demands being placed on employees, prevent misuse of products and facilities, protect themselves legally, and discourage individual customers from behaving in ways that would have a negative impact on others. On top of formal rules are the unwritten norms of social behavior to which customers are expected to adhere without being told.

There are risks attached to making lots of rules. They can make an organization appear bureaucratic and overbearing. And they can transform employees, whose orientation should be service to customers, into police officers who see (or are told to see) their most important task as enforcing all the rules. A third problem is that there are always going to be some customers who break the rules anyway—either because they haven't bothered to take note of them or just for the hell of it.

> *There are risks attached to making lots of rules. They can make an organization appear bureaucratic and overbearing. And they can transform employees into police officers.*

How should you deal with rule breakers? Much depends on which rules have been broken. In the case of legally enforceable ones—theft, bad debts, trying to take guns on aircraft—the courses of action need to be laid down explicitly, as much to protect employees as to punish or discourage wrongdoing. Company rules are a little more ambiguous. Are they really necessary in the first place? (If they aren't, get rid of them.) Do they deal with health and safety? If so, advance education and reminders will reduce the need for taking corrective action. The same is true for rules designed to protect the comfort and enjoyment of all customers using the same facility. And then there are unwritten social norms, such as "thou shalt not jump the line." Other customers can often be relied upon to help service personnel enforce rules that affect everybody else, or even to take the initiative in doing so. The fewer the rules, the more explicit the important ones can be.

The Belligerent. We've all seen him (or her)—in a store, at the airport, in a hotel or restaurant. Red in the face and shouting angrily, or perhaps icily calm and mouthing off insults, threats, and obscenities. Things don't always work as they should: Machines break down, service is clumsy, customers are ignored, flights are delayed, an order is delivered incorrectly, staff are unhelpful, a promise is broken. Or perhaps the customer in question is expressing resentment at being told to abide by the rules.

Front-stage employees are often subject to verbal abuse under such circumstances, regardless of whether they bear any responsibility for the situation. If they lack the authority to resolve the problem, that often just makes the belligerent madder still, even to the point of physical attack. Drunkenness and drug abuse add an extra layer of complication.

Organizations that care about their employees go to great efforts to develop skills in dealing with these difficult situations. Training exercises that involve role-playing help employees to develop the self-confidence and assertiveness that they need to stand up to upset customers. Employees also need to learn how to diffuse anger, calm anxiety, and comfort distress (particularly when there is good reason for the customer to be upset with the organization's performance).

Consider the following scenario. A well-dressed business traveler in his mid-thirties is having a hard time getting home, due to weather-related delays. His flight from Dallas, on which cabin service was poor and the meal uninviting, arrives late at Philadelphia. There, he finds that the airline's connecting flight to Boston has already departed. The carrier's next flight is not for another two hours, and it will be one o'clock in the morning before he gets home. Then he hears an announcement on the public address system that this last flight is fully booked—would-be passengers should put their names on the standby list. Tired and frustrated, he seeks out a customer service agent, insists that he's got to get home that night (without specifying where home is), and starts to let her know in no uncertain terms what he thinks about her airline.

The agent, who is about 10 years younger than the traveler, listens to his little tirade for a minute or so. Finally, since it shows no sign of ending, she interrupts. "Sir," she says, looking at him sternly, "Will you please calm down! Until you do, I cannot help you." The traveler is momentarily astonished at the young woman's response. His mouth opens and shuts, but nothing comes out. Then he shakes his head. "I'm sorry," he apologizes. "I know it's not your fault. But I do need to get back to Boston tonight." She is sympathetic, helps him find a flight on another carrier, and he makes it home.

I was the traveler, and I've never forgotten that incident. It demonstrated to me the importance of selection and training for service jobs that might involve stressful contact with customers. Employees have to be able to stand up to angry customers and try to calm the situation rather than escalating it. Poise, assertiveness, politeness, firmness, empathy, and competence were some of the characteristics that this young agent displayed. (Ever since, I have tried to be nicer to service personnel in situations where their employer has failed me but it's clearly not their personal fault.)

But what is an employee to do when an angry, belligerent customer—what airline personnel call an "irate"—brushes off attempts to defuse the situation? There are limits to the abuse that any firm should allow its employees to endure. Supervisory personnel must be prepared to intervene. In a public environment, one priority should be to move the "irate" to a location away from other customers. A car dealer told me he makes a point of inviting upset customers into his office, offering them a cup of coffee or a soda, and asking them to tell him exactly what the problem is. Sometimes supervisors may have to arbitrate disputes between customers and staff members; at other times, they need to stand behind the employee's actions. If it's one of those rare instances where an employee has been physically assaulted by a customer, then further action may be needed, including summoning security officers or the police. Some firms prefer to minimize such events because of the publicity. But Southwest Airlines stands up for its employees. "If subsequent investigation shows that a customer has made an unprovoked physical assault on one of our employees, we will prosecute," declares Audy Donelson, station manager at Dallas's Love Field. "We don't sweep these things under the rug."

Abusive behavior by customers over the telephone poses a different challenge. Service personnel have been known to cut off angry customers by simply hanging up on them. But that action doesn't resolve the problem. Bank customers tend to get upset when they learn that checks have been returned because they are overdrawn (they've broken the rules) or that a request for a loan has been denied. At Firstdirect, the all-telephone bank, one recommended approach for handling customers who continue to berate a banking representative even after the reasons for an action have been carefully explained is to say firmly: "This conversation isn't getting us anywhere. Why don't I call you back in a few minutes when you've had time to digest the information?" In many cases, a breathing space for reflection is exactly what's needed.

The Family Feuders. A subcategory of belligerents are those who get into arguments (or worse) with other customers (often members of their own family). Employee intervention may calm the situation or may exacerbate it. Sometimes the trick is to get other customers on your side. My favorite story of this nature is based on a real incident, captured for posterity in a business school case study by John Haywood-Farmer of the University of Western Ontario.

Put yourself for a moment in the position of business school students faced in class with the following problem. The scene is a large and expensive restaurant. It's about 9 p.m. on the busiest night of the year—New Year's Eve. Every table is filled. This is a wonderful opportunity for the restaurant to really show its stuff and build its reputation for the future.

Then a waitress comes up to the manager. "Excuse me," she says, "I've got a problem in my section. This couple are having a knock-down argument. They're screaming and yelling at each other. Everyone in the section, that's about 50 diners, has stopped eating and is watching them. It's just awful. You've got to come and do something about it!"

With a sinking feeling in his stomach, the manager strides over with the waitress following him. He can hear the sound of shouting even before he enters the section. Every diner is watching a man and a woman at a table for two in the corner. As the manager approaches, the woman picks up her plate, which is filled with food, winds back her arm, and shouting, "Take that, you creep!" hurls the plate at her companion. The latter ducks and the plate smashes upside down on the floor and breaks into pieces. Prime rib, baked potato, greens, and gravy splatter in all directions. The other diners gasp. The atmosphere is electric.

Now, the question facing the students is this: What action should the manager take? For that matter, what would you do? This is a real-time problem; there are about 10 seconds to do something before you completely lose control of the situation. There's no time for a market research study, no time to build a simulation model, no time even to call managers at other restaurants and ask for their advice. Students fumble. "Ask the couple to leave," they suggest. "Call in the cleaning staff from the kitchen." "Tell the other diners you're sorry."

The manager at the center of the storm gave an inspired response. Approaching the woman, he asked in a loud but polite voice that could be heard by every diner, "Excuse me, madam, but was there something wrong with your dinner?"

The other diners roared with laughter, the couple rose shamefacedly from their table, paid their bill, and left quickly. History does not record what subsequently happened to their relationship. Some management challenges require detailed analysis, advance planning, and careful implementation. Others, like this one, require almost instantaneous response. Where necessary, service managers need to be prepared to think on their feet and act fast.

The Vandal.   It's astonishing the level of physical abuse to which service facilities and equipment can be subjected. Coke is poured into a bank's ATMs; graffiti are scrawled on both interior and exterior surfaces; cigarette burn holes in carpets, tablecloths, and bedcovers; bus seats are slashed and hotel furniture broken; telephone handsets are torn off; customers' cars are vandalized; glass is smashed and fabrics torn. The list goes on and on.

> *It's astonishing the level of physical abuse to which service facilities and equipment can be subjected.*

Not all of the damage is done by customers, of course. A lot of exterior vandalism is done by bored youth. And disgruntled employees have been known to commit sabotage. But much of the problem does originate with wrong-behaving, paying customers. Alcohol and drugs lie at the bottom of some of it, psychological problems may contribute, and plain carelessness plays a role. And there are occasions when unhappy customers, feeling mistreated by the service provider, try to get back. Finally, there are those charming folks with a constant urge to carve their name on something, so that posterity may remember the visit of Bud and Jeanie to Podunk's Honey Moon Inn in May 1992. Bud and Jeanie are in good company; Lord Byron, for instance, carved his name on the dungeon wall when he visited the Château de Chillon on Lake Geneva in 1820. It's now carefully preserved under Plexiglas. (Bud and Jeanie's names were removed by a carpenter, who refinished the furniture at a cost of $63.40.)

The best cure is prevention. Improved security can prevent some vandalism. Good lighting helps, as does open design of public areas. Consultants can suggest pleasing yet vandal-resistant surfaces, protective coverings for equipment, and rugged furnishings. Better education of customers on how to use equipment properly (rather than fighting with it) and warnings about fragile objects reduce the likelihood of abuse or careless handling. And then there are economic sanctions: security deposits or signed agreements in which customers agree to pay any subsequent damage charges for which they are responsible.

And what do you do if prevention fails and damage is done? If you catch the perpetrators, first clarify whether there are any extenuating circumstances (accidents do happen). Sanctions for deliberate damage can range from a warning to prosecution. As far as the physical damage itself is concerned, fix it fast (within any constraints imposed by legal or insurance considerations). A former general manager of AC Transit in Oakland, California, had the right idea years ago. "If one of our buses is vandalized," the late Alan Bingham told me, "whether it's a broken window, a slashed seat, or graffiti on the ceiling, we take it out of service immediately, so nobody sees it. Otherwise you just give the same idea to five other characters who were too dumb of think of it in the first place!"

The Deadbeat.   Aging receivables is a favorite pastime in accounting offices: 30 days, 60 days, 90 days, 120 days...and so on to "charge off." Leaving aside those who never intended to pay in the first place (see under "Thief"), there are many reasons why customers end up as delinquent accounts. But once again, prevention is better than cure.

A growing number of service businesses insist on prepayment, many ticket sales being a good example. Direct-marketing organizations ask for your credit-card number as they take your order. The next best thing is to present the customer with a bill immediately upon completion of service, as most dentists now do. If the bill is to be sent out after the fact, send it fast, while the service is still fresh in the customer's mind.

As we saw in Chap. 12, billing and payment are supplementary services—two of the petals in the flower of service—and the underlying systems are worth designing properly to encourage and facilitate prompt payment. Any good accountant can advise on appropriate techniques and schedules for pursuing delinquent accounts.

However, not every apparent delinquent is a hopeless deadbeat. Perhaps there's good reason for the delay, perhaps mutually acceptable payment arrangements can be worked out. A key question is whether such a personalized approach can be cost-justified relative to the results obtained by purchasing the services of a collection agency. If you don't know, why not try a scientifically conducted experiment to find out? But there may be other payoffs, too. If the client's problems are only temporary ones, what is the long-term value of maintaining the relationship? Will helping the customer work things out create positive goodwill and word-of-mouth? These decisions are judgment calls, but if creating and maintaining long-term relationships is your goal, they bear exploration.

Some Final Words on the Topic of Wrongness

This has been a depressing chapter, hasn't it? *Caveat venditor* it seems to say—let the seller beware of entering into relationships in the first place. And if you do, beware of that seething mass of cheats and swindlers out there. But my intentions are not to create paranoia and encourage a police-state mentality, nor to provide excuses for treating customers badly on the grounds that security takes precedence over service. Instead, I want to inject a positive sense of realism into that well-worn slogan, "The customer is always right."

Creating and maintaining mutually rewarding relationships with customers requires that you pick the right partners in the first place. So you have to clarify what characteristics make for a good fit. There are only two caveats here. First, be careful not to lay down any criteria for customer selection which are potentially illegal or might be viewed as unethical. Second, recognize that both your firm and your customers change over time and may grow apart—today's good fits may become tomorrow's misfits, unless you make a conscious effort to evolve and grow together or agree to a friendly separation.

> *Creating and maintaining mutually rewarding relationships with customers requires that you pick the right partners in the first place.*

The problem of wrong behavior is likely to have different implications for different types of businesses. But several generic principles apply to dealing with the problem:

- Prevention is always better than cure. Try to identify all factors that stimulate the wrong behavior. Then determine what it would take to design them out of the front-stage service environment. Perform a cost–benefit analysis to determine which steps are worth taking.

- Remember that the bulk of your customers are "right" and behave "right." Don't treat them all like suspected criminals or incompetents.

- Wrong behavior often results from ignorance of how to do it right. Educating customers may save embarrassment and improve productivity.

- Remember that front-stage employees bear much of the burden of dealing with wrongly behaving customers. Clarify what constitutes appropriate action on their part to deal with difficult situations, and teach them the skills they will need. Take steps to ensure their personal safety, and provide for supervisory and security assistance where needed.

- The better a company's information system, on an account-by-account basis, the better is its ability to identify persistent offenders, understand the reasons for wrong behavior, and develop customized solutions to specific problem situations.

- All else being equal, give the customer the benefit of the doubt.

A firm that tells employees "the customer is always right," and leaves it at that, insults their intelligence and invites their cynicism. But so, too, does any firm that by word or deed sends the message, "the customer can't be trusted."

"But sir, you must understand, guaranteed reservations aren't valid on nights when the computer overbooks!"

16 Getting the Most Out of Your Productive Capacity

Most service operations have upper limits to their productive capacity. When demand exceeds supply, business may be lost or customers forced to wait; and when supply exceeds demand, productive capacity goes unutilized. Ways of bringing demand and supply into balance include adjusting capacity to "chase" demand, managing demand levels through price changes and other strategies, or using queuing and reservations systems to inventory demand until the supplier is able to take the business. Many firms use a combination of approaches. The starting point lies in understanding what factors limit capacity to serve and why demand levels vary in the first place. But it's not enough just to fill capacity. Service firms need to ensure that their resources are employed in the most productive manner. Yield management involves decisions on how much to sell, when, at what rates, and to what customer segments.

Cape Cod is a remarkable peninsula of narrow land, jutting out into the Atlantic Ocean off the Massachusetts coast like a long arm, bent at the elbow. With its beaches and salt marshes, sand dunes and fishing harbors, picturesque towns and lobster dinners, it's a destination resort...in season, that is.

In summer, the Cape is a busy place. Colorful umbrellas sprout like giant flowers along the miles of sandy beaches. The parking lots are full. There are lines outside most restaurants. Stores are busy (especially when it rains). The Mid-Cape Highway is clogged. Hotels sport "No Vacancy" signs. Fishing trips have to be booked well in advance, vacation cottages are rented, and the visitor centers at the National Seashore are crowded with tourists.

Return for a weekend in mid-winter, and what do you find? A few walkers brave the chill winds on the otherwise empty beaches. You can park in almost any legal space you wish. Many restaurants have closed (their owners are wintering in Florida), and only the most popular of the remaining establishments even bother to suggest reservations. The stores have laid off seasonal workers and, in some cases, cut their hours. The main problem on the Mid-Cape Highway is being stopped for speeding. If a motel sports a "No Vacancy" sign, that means it's closed for the season; others offer bargain rates. Recreational fishing: Are you crazy? There's ice on Cape Cod Bay! Owners of vacation cottages have drained their water systems and boarded up the windows. And the visitor centers are open during limited hours—and only on weekends.

Welcome to a problem that besets a huge cross section of businesses serving both individual and corporate customers: fluctuating demand that plays havoc with efficient use of productive assets.

Unlike manufacturing, service operations create a perishable inventory that cannot be stockpiled for sale at a later date. That's a problem for any capacity-constrained service that faces wide swings in demand. The problem is most commonly found among services that process people or physical possessions—such as transportation, lodging, food service, repair and maintenance, entertainment, and health care. It also affects labor-intensive, information-processing services that face cyclical shifts in demand. Accounting and tax preparation are cases in point.

Unlike manufacturing, service operations create a perishable inventory that cannot be stockpiled for sale at a later date.

Effective use of productive capacity is one of the secrets of success in such businesses. However, the goal shouldn't be to utilize staff, labor, equipment, and facilities as *much* as possible, but rather to use them as *productively* as possible.

From Excess Demand to Excess Capacity

The problem is a familiar one. "It's either feast or famine for us!" sighs the manager. "In peak periods, we're turning customers away. And in slow periods, our facilities are idle and our staff stand around looking bored."

At any given moment, a fixed-capacity service may face one of four conditions (see Fig. 16-1):

- *Excess demand.* The level of demand exceeds maximum available capacity, with the result that some customers are denied service and business is lost.

- *Demand exceeds optimum capacity.* No one is actually being turned away, but conditions are crowded and all customers are likely to perceive a deterioration in the quality of service delivered.

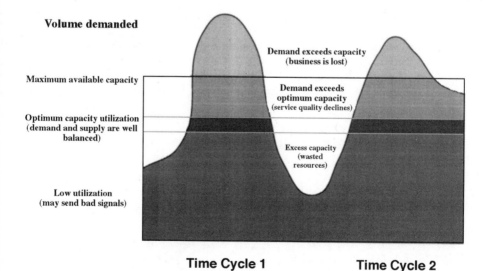

Figure 16-1. Implications of variations in demand relative to capacity.

- *Demand and supply are well balanced at the level of optimum capacity.* Staff and facilities are busy without being overworked, and customers receive good service without delays.

- *Excess capacity.* Demand is below optimum capacity and productive resources are underutilized. In some instances, this poses a risk that customers may find the experience disappointing or have doubts about the viability of the service.

You'll notice that I've drawn a distinction between maximum available capacity and optimum capacity. When demand exceeds maximum capacity, some potential customers may be turned away and their business lost forever. But when demand is operating between optimum and maximum capacity, there's a risk that all customers being served at that time may receive inferior service and thus become dissatisfied.

Sometimes optimum and maximum capacities are the same. At a live theater or sports performance, a full house is grand, since it stimulates the players and creates a sense of excitement and audience participation. The net result? A more satisfying experience for all. With most other services, however, you probably feel that you get better service if the facility is not operating at full capacity. The quality of restaurant service, for instance, often deteriorates when every table is occupied, because the staff is rushed and there's a greater likelihood of errors or delays. And if you're traveling alone in an aircraft with high-density seating, you tend to feel more comfortable if the seat next to you is empty. When repair and maintenance shops are fully scheduled, delays may result if there is no slack in the system to allow for unexpected problems in completing particular jobs.

There are two basic solutions to the problem of fluctuating demand. One is to adjust the level of capacity to meet variations in demand. This approach, which entails cooperation between operations and human resource management, requires an understanding of what constitutes productive capacity and how it may be increased or decreased on an incremental basis. The second approach is to manage the level of demand, using marketing strategies to smooth out the peaks and fill in the valleys so as to generate a more consistent flow of requests for service. Some firms use both approaches.

> *There are two basic solutions to the problem of fluctuating demand. One is to adjust the level of capacity, the second is to manage the level of demand. Some firms use both approaches.*

Measuring Capacity

What do we mean by productive capacity? In a service context, it can take the form of *facilities* that physically contain people or things, such as medical clinics, hotels, buses, supermarket shelves, coaxial cables, pipelines, warehouses, or railroad freight wagons. A second form of capacity concerns *equipment*—telephones, hair dryers, computers, diagnostic equipment, airport metal detectors, cooking ovens, and cash registers that process people, things, or information. *Labor* is the third type of productive capacity and may be used for both physical and mental work. Professional services are especially dependent on highly skilled staff to create high-value-added, information-based output. Abraham Lincoln captured the concept well when he remarked that "a lawyer's time and expertise are his stock in trade."

Measures of capacity utilization include the number of hours (or percentage of total available time) that facilities, labor, and equipment are employed productively in revenue operation, and the percentage of available space (e.g., seats or cubic freight capacity) that is actually being utilized in revenue-producing operations. Human beings tend to be far more variable than equipment in their ability to sustain consistent levels of output over time. One tired or poorly trained employee staffing a single station in an assembly-line service operation such as a cafeteria restaurant or a motor vehicle license bureau can slow the entire service to a crawl.

In a well-planned, well-managed service operation, the capacity of the facility, supporting equipment, and service personnel will be in balance. Similarly, sequential operations will be designed to minimize the likelihood of bottlenecks at any point in the process. In practice, however, it's difficult to achieve this ideal all the time.

Stretching and Shrinking the Level of Capacity

Some capacity is elastic in its ability to absorb extra demand. A subway car, for instance, may offer 40 seats and allow standing room for another 60 passengers with adequate handrail and floor space for all. At rush hours, however, perhaps 200 standees can be accommodated under sardinelike conditions. Service personnel may be able to work at high levels of efficiency for short periods of time, but would quickly tire and begin providing inferior service if they had to work that fast all day long.

Even where capacity appears to be fixed, as when it's based on the number of seats, there may still be opportunities to accept extra business at busy times. Some restaurants, for instance, increase their capacity by cramming in extra tables and chairs. Upper limits to such practices are often set by safety standards or by the capacity of supporting services, such as the kitchen.

Another way of stretching capacity is to utilize the facilities for longer periods—for instance, flying aircraft 11 hours a day instead of 9, opening a medical clinic in the evenings, and asking employees to work overtime. Alternatively, efforts may be made to reduce the cycle time required to process customers or other objects. You can do this either by speeding up delivery of the service itself (by using new techniques, better-trained employees, or faster equipment) or by minimizing slack time, as when the check is presented to diners as soon as they finish their meals, in the hope that they will vacate their tables promptly.

Beyond these "elastic" strategies there's the strategy known as "chase demand." Actions that managers can take to adjust capacity to match fluctuating levels of demand include the following.

1. *Using part-time employees.* Many service businesses recruit extra workers during their busiest periods. Examples include postal workers and store clerks hired for the Christmas season and hotel employees hired during vacation periods. Employment agencies that specialize in "temporaries" have become important service businesses in their own right, supplying employees for a wide range of short-term jobs.

2. *Renting or sharing extra facilities and equipment.* Are you worried about overinvesting in fixed assets that won't be fully utilized? Then consider renting extra space or equipment for use at peak times. Organizations with complementary demand patterns sometimes enter into formal sharing agreements. One unusual but sensible example involves suburban churches, whose large parking lots for Sunday worshippers and participants in evening programs have been made available to transit authorities on weekdays for use as commuter park-and-ride lots.

3. *Scheduling downtime during periods of low demand.* To ensure that 100 percent of capacity is available during peak periods, building renovations and preventive repairs should be conducted at times when demand is expected to be low. Likewise, employee vacations and training programs should logically be arranged for these same periods.

4. *Cross-training employees.* Even when the service delivery system appears to be operating at full capacity, some employees may be underutilized. If staff are trained to perform a variety of tasks, they can be shifted to bottleneck points as needed, thus increasing total system capacity. You can see this happening in well-managed supermarkets.

When the checkout lines start getting too long, the manager calls upon stockers to operate cash registers. Likewise, during slow periods, the cashiers may be asked to help stock shelves. Effective service managers keep a watchful eye on the service flow and are prepared to reassign workers or even lend a hand personally if they see bottlenecks occurring.

Changing the Capacity Mix

Sometimes the problem lies not in overall capacity but in the mix that's available to serve the needs of different market segments. On a given flight, for instance, an airline may have too few seats in economy even though there are empty places in the business-class cabin; or a hotel may find itself short of suites one day when standard rooms are still available.

One solution lies in designing physical facilities to be flexible. Some hotels build rooms with connecting doors. With the door between two rooms locked, the hotel can sell two bedrooms; with the door unlocked and one of the bedrooms converted into a sitting room, the hotel can offer a suite.

The Boeing Co., facing stiff competition from Airbus Industrie, received what were described, tongue-in-cheek, as "outrageous demands" from prospective customers for its new 777 airliner. The airlines wanted an aircraft in which galleys and lavatories could be relocated, plumbing and all, almost anywhere in the cabin within a matter of hours. Boeing gulped but solved this challenging problem. When the first B-777 rolls off the production line in May 1995, its owners will be able to rearrange the passenger cabin within hours, reconfiguring it with varying numbers of seats allocated among one, two, or three classes.

Understanding the Patterns and Determinants of Demand

Now let's look at the other side of the equation. If you want to control variations in demand for a particular service, you need to determine what factors govern that demand. Be prepared to obtain answers to some key questions.

If you want to control variations in demand for a particular service, you need to determine what factors govern that demand.

1. *Do demand levels follow a predictable cycle?* If so, is the cycle duration:

   - One day (varies by hour)
   - One week (varies by day)
   - One month (varies by day or by week)
   - One year (varies by month or by season; or reflects annually occurring public holidays)
   - Some other period

   Often, multiple cycles operate simultaneously. Thus, demand for passenger transport may vary by time of day, day of the week, and season all at once.

2. *What are the underlying causes of these cyclical variations?*

   - Employment schedules
   - Billing and tax payment/refund cycles
   - Wage and salary payment dates
   - School hours and vacations
   - Seasonal changes in climate
   - Occurrence of public or religious holidays
   - Natural cycles, such as coastal tides

3. *Do demand levels seem to change randomly?* If so, could the underlying causes be:

   - Day-to-day changes in the weather (Consider how rain and cold affect the use of indoor and outdoor recreational or entertainment services.)
   - Health events whose occurrence cannot be pinpointed exactly (Heart attacks and births affect the demand for hospital services.)
   - Accidents, acts of God, and certain criminal activities (These require fast response not only from fire, police, and ambulance personnel, but also from disaster-recovery specialists and insurance firms.)

Random fluctuations are usually caused by factors beyond management's control, but analysis will sometimes reveal that a predictable demand cycle for one segment is concealed within a broader, seemingly random pattern. This fact illustrates the importance of breaking down demand on a segment-by-segment basis.

For instance, a repair and maintenance shop that services industrial electrical equipment may already know that a certain proportion of its work consists of regularly scheduled contracts to perform preventive maintenance. The balance may come from "walk-in" business and emergency repairs. While it might seem hard to predict or control the timing and volume of such work, further analysis could show that walk-in business was more prevalent on some days of the week than others and that emergency repairs were frequently requested following damage sustained during thunderstorms (which tend to be seasonal in nature and can often be forecast a day or two in advance).

Keeping good records of each transaction helps enormously when it comes to analyzing demand patterns based on past experience. Computer-based services, such as telecommunications, can track customer consumption patterns by date and time of day automatically. When it is relevant, it's also useful to record weather conditions and other special factors (a strike, an accident, a big convention in town, a price change, launch of a competing service, etc.) that might influence demand.

> *Keeping good records of each transaction helps enormously. Computer-based services can track consumption patterns by date and time of day automatically.*

Not all demand is desirable. Have you ever wondered what it's like to be a dispatcher for an emergency service such as 911? People differ widely in what they consider to be an emergency. Imagine yourself in the huge communications room at police headquarters in New York. A sergeant is talking patiently to a woman who has dialed 911 because her cat has run up a tree and she's afraid it's stuck there. "Ma'am, have you ever seen a cat skeleton in a tree?" the sergeant asks her. "All those cats get down somehow, don't they?" After the woman has hung up, the sergeant turns to a visitor and shrugs. "These kinds of calls keep pouring in," he says. "What can you do?" The trouble is, when people call the emergency number with complaints about noisy parties next door, pleas to rescue cats, or requests to turn off leaking fire hydrants, they may be slowing response times to fires, heart attacks, or violent crimes. Discouraging undesirable demand through marketing campaigns or screening procedures will not, of course, eliminate random fluctuations in the remaining demand. But it may help to keep peak demand levels within the service capacity of the organization.

No strategy for smoothing demand is likely to succeed unless it's based on an understanding of why customers from a specific market segment choose to use the service when they do. It's difficult for hotels to convince business travelers to remain on Saturday nights, since few executives do business over the weekend. Instead, hotel managers may do better to promote weekend use of their facilities for conferences or pleasure travel. Attempts to get commuters to shift their travel to off-peak periods will probably fail, since such travel is determined by people's employment hours. Instead, efforts should be directed at employers to persuade them to adopt flextime or staggered working hours.

Strategies for Managing Demand

Getting the best use out of available capacity requires looking at the business mix as well as the total volume. Some market segments may be more desirable than others for a variety of reasons: The customers represent loyal relationships, or fit particularly well with the organization's mission, or reinforce the ambience that a service facility is trying to create, or have needs that match the professional skills and interests of staff members, or pay higher rates and are more profitable (or a combination of these factors).

There are five common approaches to managing demand. The first, which has the virtue of simplicity but little else, involves *taking no action and leaving demand to find its own level*. Eventually, customers learn from experience or word of mouth when they can expect to stand in line to use the service and when it will be available without delay. The trouble is, they may also learn to find a competitor who is more responsive.

More interventionist approaches involve influencing the level of demand at any given time, by *taking active steps to reduce demand in peak periods and to increase demand when there is excess capacity*, respectively.

Two more approaches both involve *inventorying demand until capacity becomes available*. You can accomplish this either by *introducing a reservations system* that promises customers access to capacity at specified times, or by *creating formalized queuing systems* (or by a combination of the two).

In Table 16-1, I've linked these five approaches to the three basic situations of insufficient capacity relative to demand, sufficient capacity, and excess capacity, and added a brief strategic commentary. Many service businesses face all three situations at different points in the cycle of demand, and so should consider using at least two of the interventionist options we have described.

A variety of tools can be used to influence the level of demand for a service. Pricing is perhaps the best known, but changes in the product, modifying the time and place of delivery, and communication efforts all play a role.

Pricing Strategies

For price to be effective as a demand management tool, you need to have some sense of price elasticity for the service in question (i.e., how the volume of customer demand for service responds to increases or decreases in the price per unit). Different types of customers often have different levels of price sensitivity. For instance, a business traveler will usually pay more to travel by air than a vacationer will. Many firms recognize the existence of different demand curves for different segments by establishing distinct

Table 16-1. Alternative Demand Management Strategies for Different Capacity Situations

Approach used to manage demand	Capacity situation relative to demand		
	Insufficient capacity (excess demand)	Sufficient capacity* (satisfactory demand)	Excess capacity (insufficient demand)
Take no action	Unorganized queuing results. (May irritate customers and discourage future use.)	Capacity is fully utilized. (But is this the most profitable mix of business?)	Capacity is wasted. (Customers may have a disappointing experience for services such as theater.)
Reduce demand	Pricing higher will increase profits. Communication can be employed to encourage usage in other time slots. (Can this effort be focused on less profitable/desirable segments?)	Take no action (but see above).	Take no action (but see above).
Increase demand	Take no action, unless opportunities exist to stimulate (and give priority to) more profitable segments.	Take no action, unless opportunities exist to stimulate (and give priority to) more profitable segments.	Price lower selectively (try to avoid cannibalizing existing business; ensure that all relevant costs are covered). Use communications and variation in products/distribution (but recognize extra costs, if any, and make sure appropriate trade-offs are made between profitability and usage levels).
Inventory demand by reservation system	Consider priority system for most desirable segments. Make other customers shift (a) to outside peak period or (b) to future peak.	Try to ensure most profitable mix of business.	Clarify that space is available and that no reservations are needed.
Inventory demand by formalized queuing	Consider override for most desirable segments. Seek to keep waiting customers occupied and comfortable. Try to predict wait period accurately.	Try to avoid bottleneck delays.	Not applicable.

*"Sufficient capacity" may be defined as *maximum available capacity* or *optimum capacity*, depending on the situation.

classes of service, each priced at a level appropriate to that segment's behavior. In essence, each segment receives a variation of the basic product, with supplementary elements adding value to the core service in order to appeal to higher-paying customers. Top-of-the-line service by airlines offers travelers wider seats, more personalized service from flight attendants, and better food; in computer service bureaus, product enhancement takes the form of faster turnaround and more specialized analytical procedures and reports.

Changing the Product

Offering a different type of service is sometimes the only way to attract customers to a service facility when demand for the original service is seasonally based. Skiers won't buy lift tickets for a mountain that has no snow, no matter how low the price is. To encourage summer use of the lifts, the operator has to change the product by installing an alpine slide or by promoting the view from the summit restaurant and the hiking possibilities.

Solutions of a similar nature have been adopted by tax preparation firms that now offer bookkeeping and consulting services to small businesses in slack months, and by landscaping firms in snowy climates that seek snow-removal contracts in the winter when there's no demand for mowing lawns, planting shrubs, and pruning trees. These firms recognize that no amount of price discounting is likely to develop business out of season. However, resort areas such as Cape Cod may have good opportunities to build business during the uncrowded "shoulder seasons" of spring and fall (when some consider the Cape to be at its most appealing) by promoting different attractions and altering the mix and focus of services.

There can be variations in service mix even during the course of a 24-hour period. Restaurants provide a good example, marking the passage of the hours with changing menus and levels of service, dimming the lights, choosing different background music, rearranging the decor, changing employee uniforms, opening and closing the bar, and perhaps offering live entertainment at night. The goal could be to appeal to different needs within the same group of customers, to reach out to different customers, or to do both, according to the time of day.

Modifying the Timing and
Location of Delivery

Some firms respond to market needs by modifying the time and place of delivery. Theaters often offer matinees on weekends when people have leisure time throughout the day. During the summer in hot climates, banks may close for two hours at midday while people take a siesta, but remain open later in the evening when other commercial establishments are active.

Another strategy involves offering the service at a new location, or even bringing the service to customers rather than requiring them to visit fixed-site service locations. Traveling libraries and vans equipped with primary-care medical facilities are two examples that might be copied by other service businesses. For instance, a cleaning and repair firm that wishes to generate business during low-demand periods might offer free pickup and delivery of portable items at these times.

Service firms whose productive assets are mobile may follow the market when that, too, is mobile. Car rental firms often establish seasonal branch offices in resort communities, moving cars into the area for the use of visiting vacationers arriving by air.

Communication Efforts

Signage, advertising, and sales messages can remind prospective customers of peak periods and encourage them to use the service at off-peak times when it's less crowded, faster, or more comfortable. Examples include postal service requests to "mail early for Christmas," public transport messages urging noncommuters—such as shoppers or tourists—to avoid the crush conditions of the commute hours, and communications from industrial maintenance firms advising customers of periods when preventive work can be done quickly.

Changes in pricing, product features, and distribution must be communicated clearly, so that customers are fully aware of their options. Short-term promotions, combining both pricing and communication elements as well as other incentives, may provide attractive incentives to shift the timing of service usage.

Inventorying Demand Through Waiting and Reservations

What's a manager to do when the possibilities for shaping demand have been exhausted and supply and demand are still out of balance? Taking no action at all and leaving customers to sort things out is no recipe for service quality and customer satisfaction. Instead, product plus firms turn their search to strategies for ensuring order, predictability, and fairness in place of a random free-for-all. Service businesses can often inventory demand, either by asking customers to wait in line (queuing) or by offering them advance reservations.

Speed That Line, Cut That Wait: The Science of Queue Management

It's estimated that Americans spend 37 billion hours a year (an average of almost 150 hours per person) waiting in lines, "during which time they fret, fidget, [and] scowl," according to *The Washington Post*. Nobody likes to be kept waiting. It's boring, time-wasting, and sometimes physically uncomfortable. Yet waiting for service is an almost universal phenomenon: Virtually every organization faces the problem of waiting lines somewhere in its operation. People are kept waiting on the phone to make flight reservations, they line up with their supermarket carts to check out their grocery purchases, they wait for their bills after a restaurant meal, they stand in line to get into a theater. The root cause is sometimes to be found in one or more delays behind the scenes, where service personnel are themselves being kept waiting for a necessary action to occur somewhere else in the system. Flowcharts (see Chap. 10) and OTSU analysis (see Chap. 11) can help to pinpoint where problems might occur.

Physical and inanimate objects also wait for processing, of course: Letters pile up on an executive's desk, shoes sit on racks waiting to be repaired at the shoe repair store, checks wait to be cleared at a bank, an incoming phone call waits to be switched to a customer service rep. In each instance, a customer may be waiting for the outcome of that work—an answer to a letter, a pair of shoes ready to be picked up, a check credited to the customer's balance, or useful contact with the service rep.

Waiting lines—known to the British and to operations researchers as *queues*—occur whenever the number of arrivals at a facility exceeds the capacity of the system to process them. In a very real sense, queues are basically a symptom of unresolved capacity management problems.

> *Waiting lines are basically a symptom of unresolved capacity management problems.*

Analysis and modeling of queues is a well-established branch of operations management. MIT Professor Richard Larson traces queueing theory back to 1917, when a Danish telephone engineer was charged with determining how large the switching unit in a telephone system had to be to keep the number of busy signals within reason.

Queue management involves extensive data gathering: at what rate are customers (or things requiring service) arriving per unit of time, and how long does it take to serve each one? A typical operational strategy is to optimize use of labor and equipment by planning for average throughput. So long as customers (or things) continue to arrive at this same average rate, there will be no delays. However, fluctuations in arrivals (sometimes random, sometimes predictable) will lead to delays at times as the line backs up following a "clump" of arrivals.

To help American Airlines streamline its check-in service at Boston's Logan Airport, technicians from QED (Larson's consulting firm) installed pressure-sensitive rubber mats on the floor in front of the ticket counters. Pressure from each customer's foot upon approaching or leaving the counter recorded the exact time on an electronic device embedded in the mats. From these data, Larson was able to profile the waiting situation at American's counters, including average waiting times, how long each transaction took, how many customers waited longer than a given length of time (and at what hours on what days), and even how many bailed out of a long line. Analysis of these data, collected over a long time period, enabled American to plan its staffing levels to match more specifically the demand levels projected at different times.

Sometimes, increasing capacity is indeed the preferred solution, because it will help increase patronage, but there may be other alternatives to consider. Installing a reservations system is one; devising different queuing systems for different customers—such as express checkout lanes for small purchases—is another.

Not all queuing systems work on a first-come, first-served basis. Market segmentation is sometimes used to design queuing strategies that set different priorities for different types of customers. Allocation to separate queuing areas may be based on:

- *Importance of the customer*—a special area may be reserved for members of frequent user clubs.

- *Urgency of the job*—remember the decisions made by the triage nurse at the Beth Israel Emergency Unit? (See Chap. 10.)

- *Duration of service transaction*—with "express lanes" for shorter jobs.

- *Payment of a premium price*—separate check-ins for first-class and economy-class passengers.

A Systemic Approach to the Waiting Problem

Service delays are often caused by multiple factors, requiring multiple solutions. Leonard Berry and Linda Cooper describe the multipronged approach taken by one big bank to solve the problem. Facing increased competition from new financial service providers, the First National Bank of Chicago decided that it had to improve service to its customers. One element involved reducing the waiting lines for service in retail branches. The following threefold strategy was adopted:

1. *Improvements in the service operation.* An electronic queueing system not only routed customers to the next available station but also provided supervisors with on-line information to help match staffing to customer demand. Meantime, computer enhancements provided tellers with more information about their customers, enabling them to handle more requests without leaving their stations. And new cash machines for tellers saved them from selecting bills and counting them twice (yielding a time savings of 30 seconds for each cash withdrawal transaction).

2. *Changes in human resource strategies.* A revised job description for teller managers made them responsible for customer queueing times and for expediting transactions. Then an officer-of-the-day program equipped a designated officer with a beeper and made him or her responsible for assisting with complicated transactions. A new category of peak-time teller position was introduced, paying premium wages for 12–18 hours work a week. Regular full-time tellers were given cash incentives and recognition to reward improved productivity on predicted high-volume days. Finally, lunch breaks were reorganized to include half-hour lunch periods and catered lunches on busy days, as well as earlier opening of the bank cafeteria to serve peak-time tellers.

3. *Customer-oriented improvements to the delivery system.* Quick-drop desks were established on busy days to handle deposits and simple requests, in addition to new express teller stations reserved for deposits and check cashing. Lobby hours were expanded from 38 to 56 hours a week, including Sunday (First Chicago found that some of the "noon rush" has now been deflected to before-work and after-work periods). A customer brochure, *How to Lose Wait,* alerts customers to busy periods and suggests ways of avoiding delays.

Internal measures and customer surveys show that the improvements are reducing customer waiting times and increasing customer perceptions that First Chicago is "the best" bank in the region for minimal teller-line waits.

Psychological Considerations in Waiting

Operational approaches to queue management often focus purely on logistical issues without taking human ones into account. You shouldn't treat people who are waiting for service in the same way you might some inanimate object (although that doesn't stop many firms from doing so). For starters, we need to know how easily customers will balk and just walk away when they spot a lengthy line, and how long customers will wait for service before giving up. We also need to understand their feelings about waiting.

Psychological studies reveal that people often think they have waited longer for a service than they actually did. Overestimates can range as high as sevenfold. Citing the noted philosopher William James, who observed: "Boredom results from being attentive to the passage of time itself," David Maister has formulated seven principles about waiting time:

- Unoccupied time feels longer than occupied time.
- Preprocess waits feel longer than in-process waits.
- Anxiety makes waits seem longer.
- Uncertain waits are longer than known, finite waits.
- Unexplained waits are longer than explained waits.
- Unfair waits are longer than equitable waits.
- The more valuable the service, the longer people will wait.
- Solo waits feel longer than group waits.

The implications: When increasing capacity is simply not feasible, you should try to be creative and look for ways to make waiting more palatable for customers. The Bank of Boston found that installing an electronic news display didn't reduce the perceived time spent waiting for teller service, but it did lead to greater customer satisfaction. Restaurants solve the waiting problem by inviting dinner guests to have a drink in the bar until their table is ready (that approach makes money for the house as well as keeping the customer occupied).

Rental car firms sometimes speed the process by assigning agents to obtain information on customers' needs while they wait in line, so that service delivery (rather than information transfer) can begin as soon as they reach the head of the line. Theme park operators cleverly design their waiting areas to make the wait look shorter than it really is, find ways to give customers in line the impression of constant progress, and make time seem to pass more quickly by keeping customers amused or diverted while they wait.

Reservations

Ask someone what services come to mind when you talk about reservations and most likely they will cite airlines, hotels, restaurants, car rentals, and theater seats. Suggest synonyms such as "bookings" or "appointments" and they may add haircuts, visits to professionals ranging from doctors to consultants, vacation rentals, and service calls to fix anything from a balky refrigerator to a neurotic computer.

Reservations are supposed to guarantee that the service will be available when the customer wants it. Systems vary from a simple appointments book for a doctor's office, using handwritten entries, to a central, computerized databank for an airline's worldwide operations. When goods require servicing, their owners may not wish to be parted from them for long. Households with only one car, for example, or factories with a vital piece of equipment often cannot afford to be without such items for more than a day or two. So a reservations system may be necessary for service businesses in fields such as repair and maintenance. By requiring reservations for routine maintenance, management can keep time free for handling emergency jobs which, because they carry a premium price, generate a much higher margin.

Taking reservations serves to presell the service to customers, as well as helping the firm to balance capacity. In theory, it benefits customers by avoiding the need for queuing and guaranteeing service availability at a specific time. Demand can be deflected from a first-choice time to earlier or later times, from one class of service to another, and even from first-choice locations to alternative locations. However, problems arise when customers fail to show or when service firms overbook. Marketing strategies for dealing with these operational problems include requiring an advance fee for all reservations (not always feasible); canceling nonpaid reservations after a certain time; and providing compensation to victims of overbooking.

Yield Management

Service organizations often use percentage of capacity sold as a measure of operational efficiency: Transport services talk of the "load factor" achieved, hotels of their "occupancy rate," and hospitals of their "census." Similarly, professional firms can calculate what proportion of a partner's or an employee's time is classified as billable hours, and repair shops can look at utilization of both equipment and labor. By themselves, however, these percentage figures tell us little of the relative profitability of the business attracted, since high utilization rates may be obtained at the expense of heavy discounting—or even outright giveaways.

More and more, service firms are looking at their "yield"—that is, the average revenue received per unit of capacity. The aim is to maximize this yield in order to improve profitability. Strategies designed to achieve this goal are known collectively as yield management and are widely used in such capacity-constrained industries as passenger airlines, hotels, and car rentals. Sheryl Kimes emphasizes that formalized yield management programs, based on mathematical modeling, are of greatest value for service firms that find it expensive to modify their capacity but incur relatively low costs when they sell another unit of available capacity. Other characteristics that encourage use of such programs include fluctuating demand levels, ability to segment markets by extent of price sensitivity, and sale of services well in advance of usage.

Yield analysis forces managers to recognize the opportunity cost of accepting business from one customer or market segment when another might subsequently yield a higher rate. Consider the following problems facing sales managers for different types of capacity-constrained service organizations:

- Should a hotel accept an advance booking from a tour group of 200 room nights at $80 each when these same room nights might possibly be sold later at short notice to business travelers at the full posted rate of $140?

- Should a railroad with 30 empty freight cars at its disposal accept a request for a shipment worth $900 per car or hold the cars idle for another day in the hope of getting a priority shipment that would be twice as valuable?

- How many seats on a particular flight should an airline sell in advance to tour groups and passengers traveling at special excursion rates?

- Should an industrial maintenance shop reserve a certain proportion of productive capacity each day for emergency repair jobs that offer a high contribution margin and the potential to build long-term customer loyalty, or should it simply follow a strategy of making sure that there are sufficient jobs, mostly involving routine maintenance, to keep its employees fully occupied?

- Should a print shop process all jobs on a first-come, first-served basis, with a guaranteed delivery time for each job, or should it charge a premium rate for "rush" work and tell customers with "standard" jobs to expect some variability in completion dates?

Decisions on such problems deserve to be handled with a little more sophistication than just resorting to the "bird in the hand is worth two in the bush" formula. You need a way of figuring out the chances of getting better-value business if you wait. Good information (based on detailed record keeping of past usage), supported by current market intelligence and good marketing sense, is the key. The decision to accept or reject business

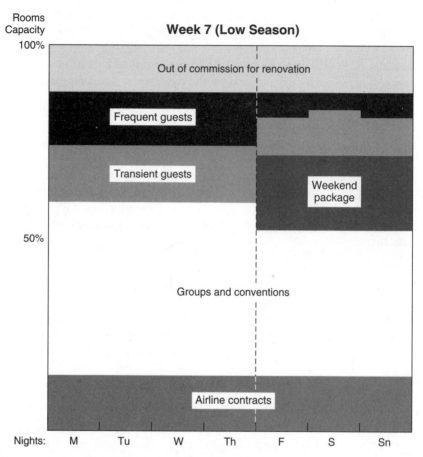

Figure 16-2. Setting hotel capacity allocation sales targets.

should represent a realistic estimate of the probabilities of obtaining higher-rated business, together with a recognition of the importance of maintaining established (and desirable) customer relationships.

There has to be a clear plan, based on analysis of past performance and current market data, that indicates how much capacity should be allocated on specific dates to different types of customers at certain prices. Based on this plan, "selective sell" targets can be assigned to advertising and sales personnel, reflecting allocation of available capacity among different market segments on specific future dates. The last thing you want the sales force to do is get price-sensitive market segments to buy capacity on dates when sales projections predict that there will be strong demand from customers

Week 36 (High Season)

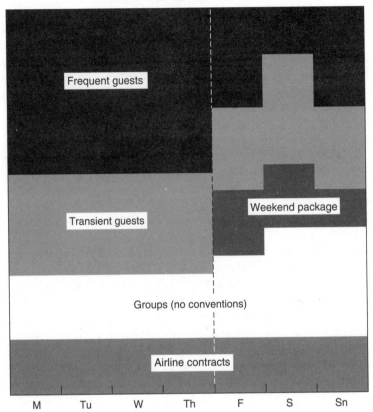

Figure 16-2. (*Continued*) Setting hotel capacity allocation sales targets.

willing to pay full price. Unfortunately, in some industries, the lowest-rated business often books the furthest ahead: tour groups, which pay much lower room rates than individual travelers, often ask airlines and hotels to block space more than a year in advance.

Figure 16-2 illustrates capacity allocation in a hotel setting, where demand from different types of customers varies not only by day of the week but also by season. These allocation decisions by segment, captured in reservation databases that are accessible worldwide, tell reservations personnel when to stop accepting reservations at certain prices, even though many rooms may still remain unbooked.

Charts similar to the one shown in Fig. 16-2 can be constructed for most capacity-constrained businesses. In some instances, capacity is measured in terms of seats for a given performance, seat miles, or room nights; in others it may be in terms of machine time, labor time, billable professional hours, vehicle miles, or storage volume—whichever is the scarce resource. Unless it's easy to divert business from one facility to a similar alternative, allocation planning decisions will have to be made at the level of geographic operating units. So each hotel, repair and maintenance center, or computer service bureau may need its own plan. On the other hand, transport vehicles represent a mobile capacity which can be allocated across whatever geographic area the vehicles are able to serve.

There's evidence that yield management programs can improve revenues significantly—many airlines report increases of 5 percent or more after starting such programs. But a word of warning is in order at this point. Yield management shouldn't necessarily mean short-term yield maximization at all cost. Strategies can easily become rigid, full of rules and regulations designed to prevent less price-sensitive segments from trading down to take advantage of lower-priced offers, penalties for canceled reservations, and cynical overbooking without thought for the consequences to disappointed customers who thought they had a firm reservation. To maintain goodwill and build relationships, you have to take the long-term perspective. So yield management programs should build in strategies for retaining valued customer relationships, even to the extent of not charging the maximum feasible amount on a given transaction (perceptions of price gouging do not build trust). There should also be thoughtfully planned contingencies for victims of overbooking, with recovery programs designed to maintain goodwill even under conditions of inherent disappointment.

Conclusion

The underlying theme of this chapter has really been *time*. Since many capacity-constrained organizations have heavy fixed costs, even modest improvements in capacity utilization over time can have a big impact on the bottom line. Similarly, changes in the mix of business to emphasize more profitable segments during periods of excess demand can also boost profits. Service-oriented firms that combine a strong marketing orientation with the information systems needed to develop effective demand management strategies at specific points in time will be well placed to achieve—or improve upon—success.

However, product plus organizations go one step further. In addition to managing demand over time, they also try to save time for their customers. Their strategies include reengineering processes to speed service and eliminate unnecessary delays, minimizing the burden and frustration of any remaining waits that would be too expensive to eliminate, and creating reservation systems that deliver what they promise: service at a guaranteed place and time. Demand and capacity management must be viewed from a service quality perspective if you want your customers to keep on coming back in the future.

When the data processing staff at
Pluperfect Insurance were asked to
simplify the billing format for
policyholders, they rose to the challenge.

17 Technology: Servant or Master?

*To an increasing degree, product plus performance depends on strategic
use of technology, especially the integration of computers and
telecommunications. Materials, methods, and information technology (IT)
collectively offer opportunities for faster delivery, better service
environments, enhanced information and other added-value service
elements, customer self-service, and improved productivity (often achieved
by leveraging employee performance). But remember that technology
exists to serve customers and employees, not the other way around. The
key to IT is to think holistically, so that each application creates a genuine
product plus, while also forming a coherent part of a broader network that
links the organization more closely to both customers and suppliers.*

George Gilder, senior fellow at the Hudson Institute and noted author, could scarcely contain his excitement as he began his testimony before a special "en banc" hearing of the Federal Communications Commission in Washington in 1990.

"You," he told the FCC commissioners, "are at the nerve center of one of the greatest transformations—perhaps *the* greatest transformation—in the history of technology. It's a technology of sand, and glass, and air." The sand, he explained poetically, represented the microchip, "a silicon sliver the size of your thumbnail and containing a logical pattern as complex as a street map of America, switching its traffic in trillionths of seconds." The technology of glass was that of fiber optics: "threads of glass as thin as a human hair, as long as Long Island, fed by lasers as small as a grain of salt and as bright as the sun." The contribution of the air would come in the form of a major enlargement in the use of the electromagnetic spectrum.

Although Gilder was waxing poetic, his presentation was no starry-eyed piece of science fiction, envisioning some distant future. Indeed, the marriage of telecommunications and computers that he described had already been consummated through networks ranging from international airline reservations systems to ATM systems in retail banking. But the offspring of this marriage, the baby which Gilder and others refer to as the "telecomputer," is only now starting to make its revolutionary presence felt.

Underlying this global revolution, which Gilder describes as a change that "leaves all previous technological history in its wake," are five key drivers:

- An enormous and sustained increase in computing power, paralleled by a rapid fall in the cost of this power

- Digitization of all types of information—from the analog waves of radio, television, and telephone calls to the images of movies and graphics—so that the information can be stored and manipulated in the binary language of computers

- A huge increase in the capacity of telecommunication links as new satellite and microwave linkages are installed and as fiber optic cable replaces conventional "twisted-pair" and coaxial cables

- A miniaturization of hardware and batteries that makes it possible to create a wide array of portable telecomputing devices

- Advances in software, digital switching technology, and network architecture that enable high-quality voice, picture, and data transmissions to move seamlessly between different types of terminals located all over the world

> *A change that "leaves all previous technological history in its wake."*
>
> **GEORGE GILDER**

In earlier chapters we saw some dramatic instances of how electronic technology is stimulating innovation in the service sector. Examples included Firstdirect, the all-telephone bank, and the COSMOS system created by Federal Express. The big issue for service managers is how to use technology in ways that create a genuine product plus: adding value to customers, tying the organization more closely to both customers and suppliers, leveraging employees' work and liberating them from truly mundane tasks, increasing productivity, and having a positive impact on the bottom line.

But a word of warning is in order: No technology is a magic elixir, guaranteeing successful results. In fact, rushing to adopt new technology without thinking through the implications for employees, customers, and the overall operating system can be a recipe for pain. Gregory Hackett has described investments in computers and communication technology as potentially "the service sector sinkhole," citing hundreds of billions of dollars spent on hardware and software with disappointing results.

On the other hand, as James Brian Quinn points out, these results don't tell us how much more "disappointing" they would have been for individual firms had they *not* made significant investments in technology, especially in infrastructure systems. "[T]he fate of the midsize financial service firms, airlines, and hospitals that failed to develop adequate technology infrastructures is instructive," he writes. "They disappeared as independent entities."

The Meaning of Technology

Every generation tends to use the word *technology* to describe, rather loosely, the practical application of cutting-edge tools and procedures. A key technology during the late eighteenth and early nineteenth centuries was the artificial channeling of water, harnessing it as a source of mechanical power wherever there was sufficient flow and vertical drop; a related technology involved channeling water as an inland transportation medium by digging networks of canals for use by horse-drawn barges. By the mid-nineteenth century, canals and watermills were giving way to the technology of water and coal-fired heat, which created steam-powered factories and rail transport. These, in turn, gave way to technologies based on oil derivatives and electromechanical power. Today, when people say, "Isn't technology wonderful?" they are probably referring to advances (or failures, depending on the tone of voice) in electronic technology. Tomorrow, technology may be synonymous with biotechnology and cold fusion. Or maybe not.

We have to be careful not to define technology too narrowly. Electronic technology is indeed affecting the service sector in numerous ways: ATMs for banking transactions, cellular telephones for people on the go, scanners at supermarket checkouts, electronic dispatching of couriers' vans, and on-line databases providing access to storehouses of knowledge for researchers or professionals. But there's more. A modern rail passenger car uses a wide variety of materials technology: metal composites for lightweight bodies, vandal-resistant plastics and artificial fibers for easy cleaning, and shatterproof insulating glass for good views without compromising climate control and safety. New manufacturing techniques and materials make possible not only high-technology, miniaturized hardware but mundane objects, too: energy-saving lighting to provide better security in shopping mall parking lots, and lightweight, corrosion-resistant plastic piping to transport natural gas to distant customers.

Of course, despite the modern marvels, many inventions remain very durable. We still benefit on a daily basis from technologies that have evolved only modestly from their nineteenth-century predecessors, from flush toilets to asphalt-surfaced highways, from electric railways to the coal-fired generating stations that still power some of them—and some of our computers, too.

Materials, Methods, and Information Technologies

"The holy trinity of technology" is how James Heskett, Earl Sasser, and Christopher Hart describe materials, methods, and information. *Materials technology*, they emphasize, is basic to the other two: Modern airliners are as dependent on strong, lightweight metals as computers are on silicon; new chemical compounds help janitors clean buildings faster and more effectively; while developments in glass make possible both laser printers and fiber-optic cables. And applications of plastics are everywhere.

Methods technology relates to the development of new machines, processes, and ways of working. It includes the design of the workplace and the service delivery environment, as well as the activities that take place within. Methods technology can be as simple as furnishing hotel bedrooms with box beds to simplify the cleaning task for housekeepers or installing beverage dispensers with automatic metering in a restaurant so that workers can perform other tasks while cups are filling. And it can be as complex as designing the working environment for a hospital emergency room, an all-telephone bank, or an automated warehouse. To be successful, methods technology must take into account necessary human involvement. "User-friendly" must be the watchword, requiring full and early participation in design from human resource and marketing specialists.

Information technology (IT) encompasses several key elements, beginning with the capture of data and its storage in memory systems ranging in size from the 200 bytes (equivalent to roughly three lines of typescript) of a credit card's magnetic stripe to the gigabytes in a large mainframe computer. IT is often identified with fancy hardware, but in fact software is the key to turning data into useful information (such as customer account profiles) or into the intelligence found in expert systems that tell users—or even machines—what decisions to make. Unfortunately, user-hostile equipment and software design combine with lack of user training and instructional manuals written in "techspeak" to turn users into hostages and servants of IT systems rather than their masters.

Increasingly, IT involves the architecture of network design and the use of both wired and wireless linkages to enable devices (and people) to communicate with each other. Computers, software, and telecommunications have become essential tools. But they still depend on data input from many different sources: fingers that touch screens, press keys, or manipulate pointing devices; voice-recognition systems; and machine-readable bar codes, magnetic stripes, optical text, or embedded microchips. Without the right data input, there's a risk of either an underutilized asset or GIGO (garbage in, garbage out).

The "gee-whiz" nature of IT innovations can be dangerously seductive. We need to ask how existing work patterns will need to change if the innovation is to fulfill its promise. Michael Hammer makes the point that companies often use technology simply to speed up existing processes. Instead of "embedding outdated processes in silicon and software," he argues, we should be using the power of technology to radically redesign business procedures and dramatically improve their performance. At the same time, we should never forget that glamorous high-tech may fail to achieve its full potential if management ignores necessary and complementary low-tech elements.

Glamorous high-tech may fail to achieve its full potential if management ignores necessary and complementary low-tech elements.

Consider my experience while checking out of a hotel. The receptionist quickly computed my bill on the monitor in front of her, transformed it into a paper copy on the adjacent printer, and asked me to sign the credit card slip; but then she walked off, papers in hand, to the far end of the long reception desk. There she remained several minutes, standing beside a couple of her colleagues. I began to fear that something horrible had happened to my credit line. Other customers behind me muttered restlessly. Finally, the receptionist returned. "You're all set!" she said. "What was the problem?" I asked. She gave me a tired smile. "Oh, we've only got one stapler on the desk, so I had to wait my turn to staple your bill and credit card slip together." For want of a low-tech, $3 stapler, was lost a sizable chunk of the potential gains in employee productivity and customer satisfaction to be derived from a computer system that probably cost ten thousand times as much! (Of course, assuming that a paper receipt is needed in the first place, a better solution would be to integrate bill and card receipt into a single document.)

Technology in the Service Sector

Where and how might technology offer leverage in your business? A starting point is to consider the core service. Then we'll move on to examine supplementary service elements.

What Type of Core Service?

The nature of the core service (discussed in Chap. 2) necessarily affects the type of technology needed to create it.

People-processing services place heavy emphasis on the materials technology of the physical facilities and supporting equipment from which customers receive service. Methods technologies are concerned with how employees, customers, and physical elements interact on site to create the desired service.

Many technologies are industry-specific. New airliners reflect the latest developments in aeronautical research and jet propulsion; maintaining and flying each specific model of aircraft requires special skills and carefully prescribed procedures. Hospitals are the beneficiaries of advances in both electronic diagnostic equipment and pharmaceutical research; methods of treatment and care giving are constantly evolving, too, requiring both human and technical skills that are often exercised in a team setting. Restaurants have improved their productivity by investing in new food technologies (such as pre-prepared meals and improved strains of vegetables) as well as in devices to simplify food preparation and cooking; however, methods vary widely, from a fast-food restaurant, where customers serve themselves in a highly industrialized setting, to full-service restaurants where the customer plays a much more passive role.

Possession-processing services also emphasize materials and methods technologies, since the core products tend to involve physical activities, ranging from transport to storage, from installation to cleaning, and from fueling to repair. But there's a key difference between people and "things." The physical shape of human beings has changed little in the last million years, so facilities must be designed to accommodate the customer rather than vice versa. However, the ease with which physical possessions can be serviced is intimately connected to their design: The first and best service that manufacturers and architects can give their customers is to design *serviceability* into physical goods and facilities.

> **The first and best service that manufacturers and architects can give their customers is to design serviceability into physical goods and facilities.**

This rule, of course, is broken all the time: We find equipment that is difficult to package and transport; machines that have to be totally disassembled by an expert to replace a simple part; electronic controls that only an 11-year-old video game specialist understands how to operate; and buildings whose surfaces seem to be deliberately designed to collect and retain dirt.

Information-based services are, predictably, driven primarily by advances in information technology. Advances in telecommunications, from cellular phones to satellite links to addressable cable TV, have opened up significant new possibilities for the information, news, entertainment, and education industries. Miniaturization of input, storage, and output devices— flat screens, tiny modems, portable faxes, cellular telephones, and pocketable hard disks holding the equivalent of over 10,000 pages of information—is dramatically extending the usefulness of information technology. Users are being liberated from the shackles of fixed site installations or the ball-and-chain of barely luggable equipment. Modern information-based services can dispense with the physical front stage almost completely. To an increasing degree, all the customers need is access to some form of input–output device—a voice telephone, a keypad, a display screen, a card reader—connected electronically to a remote backstage, which nowadays could be anywhere in the world.

Supplementary Services and Information Technology

What of the supplementary services that surround the core? Earlier (in Chap. 12), I grouped them into eight categories: information, consultation, order taking, hospitality, caretaking, exceptions, billing, and payment. Most petals on the "flower of service" are data-based or information-dependent, as shown in Fig. 17-1 (refer to Table 12-1 for details of individual service elements). As we revisit some of these petals, ask yourself how new uses of IT could leverage your employees or add value to the service your firm offers its customers.

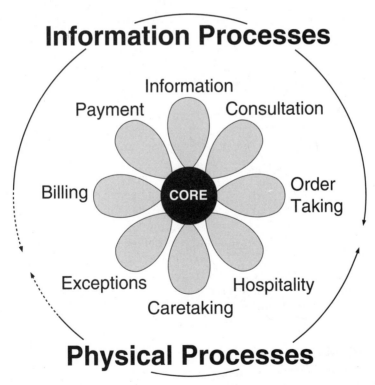

Figure 17-1. The "flower of service," showing petals that are data-based or information-dependent.

Information and Consultation

Customers need information about the goods and services that they buy and use, including confirmation of orders and documentation of account activity. New customers and prospects are especially hungry for both information and advice: They want to know what product will best meet their needs, where and when to get it, how much it costs, and how to use it. Traditional ways of providing the answers include employees (who are not always as knowledgeable as customers might like), printed notices, brochures, and instruction books. More recent possibilities include videotapes or software-driven tutorials, touch-screen video displays, computer-accessed bulletin boards, and menu-driven telephone recordings ("press 4 for today's schedule of events").

You can often turn your employees into instant experts by giving them easy access to relevant information. When a friend in Boston called Federal Express to request a pickup, the agent told him it was too late, but there was still time to deposit his package in a FedEx drop box; would he like street directions to the nearest one? When he said yes, she gave him easily understood instructions on how to find the box, including references to local landmarks. The customer was impressed, complimented her on the clear directions, and said "You really know Boston well, you must come from around here!" "No," she replied, "I work in the Chicago area and I've never even been to Massachusetts. I'm just reading this information off my computer screen."

The sheer size of a company like General Electric is enough to scare off even prospective business customers. To make itself more accessible and easier to do business with, the firm has created the GE Business Information Center (GEBIC) in Albany, New York. Backed up by an extensive database, 24 employees answer callers' questions about GE's technical, industrial, and commercial products (including services). About one-third of the 160,000 calls that GEBIC receives each year fall into the customer service category, including issues such as billing and complaints; another third turn out to concern products that have either been discontinued or are not made by GE; the balance come from callers needing more information about GE products or wanting to buy them. GEBIC puts these last customers in touch with one of GE's 3000 product experts or with a sales contact who can provide more detailed price and delivery information.

Order Taking

How can technology make it easier for customers to place orders and for suppliers to take them? The key lies in minimizing the time and effort required of both parties, while also ensuring completeness and accuracy. Automated telephone ordering is one route, with a computer-generated voice probing for item codes and number of units required, and the customer responding via the telephone keypad. But other methods are cleverer still.

McKesson, a San Francisco-based distributor of drugs, gives its druggist customers a laser scanner. One swipe of the scanner over the shelf label, bar-coded with the product's name and the customer's usual order quantity, and—zap!—the order is entered into the central computer at McKesson's warehouse. From there, it is transmitted wirelessly to an order filler in the warehouse, who wears a science-fiction-like device, comprising a two-way radio and computer on the forearm and a laser scanner strapped to the back of the hand. The order is displayed on the three-square-inch computer screen, telling the worker where the items are and laying out the most efficient route through the 22,000-item warehouse to get them. As *Fortune* described it:

> Dick Tracy would gasp with astonishment....As the employee chooses each item, he points a finger, like some lethal space invader, at the bar-coded shelf label beneath it, shooting a laser beam that scans the label and confirms that he has picked the right product. When the order is complete, his arm-borne computer radios the warehouse's main computer, updating inventory numbers and the bill. The result: a 70 percent reduction in order errors and a hefty rise in the productivity of order takers.

Restaurants have also been innovative. Pizza Hut has been testing an alternative to the traditional order pad. Instead, the waiter enters orders by number on a hand-held device the size of a large calculator and zaps it toward a small receiver in the ceiling, from where it's downloaded to the kitchen. Alternatively, there's Touch 2000, which lets customers at certain Arby's restaurants do the ordering themselves, pressing their selections on a touch-sensitive countertop menu. And finally, there's the fax menu that some take-out restaurants distribute to customers as an alternative to telephone ordering: fill it out, fax it in, and then drop by to collect your pizza.

Citibank has been using a take-out metaphor, too, with its advertising campaign, "Investments to go." Using automated consoles at any Citicard Banking Center in the New York metropolitan area, customers can buy, sell, or exchange shares of four money market funds, 24 hours a day, and obtain a printout displaying the current value of their investments.

Exceptions: Special Requests and Problem Solving

Special requests are particularly common in the travel and lodging industries, not least in response to medical and dietary needs. The basic challenge is to ensure that each request is passed on to those who will be responsible for fulfilling it.

> *Special requests are common in the travel and lodging industries. The basic challenge is to ensure that each request will be passed on to those responsible for fulfilling it.*

Reflecting its diverse mix of passengers, Singapore Airlines (SIA) offers a wide variety of special meal options, tailored to both health and religious needs. When, say, Mr. Mohammed Hassan makes his flight reservation and requests a Muslim vegetarian meal, the computer will print out a boarding card confirming this request and automatically download the request to catering. (If Mr. Hassan is a frequent flyer with SIA, his meal and seating preferences will be on permanent file, along with other relevant data, and he won't even need to ask.)

For flights that originate in Singapore, the food will be prepared by an SIA subsidiary, SATS Catering. The company's magnificent flight kitchens prepare over 25,000 meals daily, not only for SIA but also for dozens of other contracting airlines. The Swiss executive chef, resplendent in tall white hat, oversees a large staff of chefs and food workers, preparing everything from main courses and desserts to bread rolls and custom-made chocolates. (When I commented on how tasty some of the food appeared, compared to "normal" airline food, the chef told me that I was looking at a menu specially designed for first-class passengers on British Airways.)

It would be easy for a single request to get lost in such a busy setting; but the computer tracks orders for each flight, showing the number of passengers expected in each class and noting special requests. The tray bearing each special meal will be labeled with the passenger's name and seat number before being loaded, and the flight attendants will receive a seating list indicating which passengers are to receive which meals. So a flight attendant can quickly take the meal to seat 22A, say confidently, "Good afternoon, Mr. Hassan, here's the special meal you ordered," and let him see the tray label showing his name and request.

Technology speeds problem solving, too. USAA, a Texas-based firm specializing in insurance for military families and their dependents around the world, scans all documents electronically and stores them on optical disks. It now plans to digitize recordings of telephone calls reporting accidents and to store them with scans of photos and reports from lawyers, doctors, and appraisers concerning the same claim. The space required to store claim dossiers has already been reduced enormously (the company used to have a 39,000-square-foot warehouse), and the time wasted searching for missing dossiers—which were often on somebody's desk—has been eliminated.

Billing and Payment

Bills and account statements are important documents. Customers like them to be clear and informative, and itemized in ways that make plain how the total was computed. Unexplained, arcane symbols that have all the meaning of hieroglyphics on an Egyptian monument (and are decipherable only by the high priests of accounting and data processing) do not create a favorable impression. Nor does fuzzy printing or illegible handwriting. Enter the market researcher and the laser printer to the rescue. The researcher's job is to ask customers what they want in a specific financial statement. The laser printer, with its ability to switch fonts and typefaces, to box and to highlight, can produce statements that are not only more legible but also organize the information in more useful ways.

When Boston-based BayBank surveyed customers' preferences regarding bank statement formats, it found that people's opinions varied; so the bank ended up letting customers choose among three different formats with varying degrees of detail and emphasis. BayBank also offers customers a choice between getting back their canceled checks or, for a fee of $0.25 a month, subscribing to a service called CheckView, which provides image-processed pictures of all their checks, 18 to a page. (The technique was first adopted by American Express to reproduce charge card receipts.)

Merrill Lynch continues to enhance the way it documents information on its monthly CMA statements, which have to integrate data on investment activity (including purchases, sales, dividend and interest receipts, and investment value) with checking and Visa Gold Card activity. The first page of the monthly statement provides a series of boxed summaries, with comparative data for the previous month and year to date. At year-end, clients also receive an annual summary of checking and Gold Card activity, organized by expense category, both monthly and for the year. This information is valuable at tax time.

Corporate customers value well-presented information, too. American Express built its Corporate Card business by offering companies detailed documentation of the spending patterns of individual employees and departments on travel and entertainment.

Computing the Bill.   Busy customers hate to be kept waiting for a bill to be computed in a hotel, restaurant, or rental car lot. Marriott was the first hotel chain to offer customers the chance to preview their bills on the TV monitor in their rooms. Pizza Hut's experimental ordering devices not only tell the kitchen of your order, but also activate a printer to create an updated tab each time you place a new order. Want a coffee to finish off your meal? Punch, zap. A few minutes later, your coffee arrives, complete with a new bill for the complete meal (the server removes the old one at the same time).

Scanners in retail stores use technology to speed up the billing process at the checkout stations (but fears continue to be raised about overcharging). For retailers, the greatest benefit of scanners lies in the real-time collection of sales data for market research, inventory control, and even automated reordering of new stock to replace that which is being sold.

Although we're still a long way from the cashless society, use of debit cards involving electronic funds transfer at the point of sale (EFT-POS) is beginning to displace cash and checks in some instances. Meantime, wireless technology takes the checkout to the customer, rather than vice versa. At many rental car-return lots, attendants take details of your contract, fuel reading and mileage, and use a hand-held device to print out your bill on the spot. In France, a Dassault subsidiary has created "telepayment," using a portable wireless device to read charge cards and authorize card payments. Machines like these save time for customer and supplier alike, as well as reducing paperwork and minimizing the potential for errors that comes from manual transfer of data. That's a nice set of product pluses all around.

Control and Security.   A final aspect of billing and payment is making sure that people actually pay what is due. Technology can help here, too—not only by controlling access and validating card payments but also by helping to catch cheats. Cable TV subscribers are always shocked to see their screens go blank. But a few, when they turn in their control boxes for repair, get an even nastier shock: They are charged with cable piracy! Some cable companies shoot "electronic bullets" through their systems to blow out illegally installed chips that enable dishonest subscribers to steal signals for premium cable services without paying extra for them. Who knows where the Electronic Lone Ranger will pop up next?

Using Technology to Create a Product Plus

One reason why technology doesn't deliver the anticipated benefits to the bottom line is that it's often installed with only a single objective in mind, such as labor substitution or automated record keeping or appealing to a certain type of customer. Unfortunately, even if it achieves that objective, there may be negative consequences elsewhere in the organization. To achieve a product plus, technology investments should be planned to hit two or more birds with a single stone, without causing avoidable negative repercussions elsewhere.

Automated Systems for High-Volume Customers at Federal Express

To help customers manage their shipments more effectively and to draw them into a closer relationship with the company, Federal Express has created Powership, a family of automated shipping and invoicing systems. FedEx provides large customers—free of charge—with an electronic weighing scale, microcomputer terminal with modem, bar-code scanner, and laser printer. Powership rates packages with the right charges, automatically combining package weights by destination to provide volume discounts, and then prints out bar-coded address labels from the customer's own client database. Users can prepare daily invoices and internal analyses of shipping expenses by individual or product category; they can also trace their own packages through FedEx's COSMOS system. At day's end, they transmit their shipping data to FedEx. And at the end of each week, they send a computer tape containing the week's shipping data, plus payment for all charges incurred.

With Powership, FedEx has integrated most of its larger customers into its order entry, tracking, and invoicing systems. Customers not only bill themselves (saving FedEx from having to do so), but pay weekly. Most controllers would kill for such an arrangement! Customers gain from greater control, simplicity, and internal reporting. Better yet, they get free equipment for weighing, computing, and labeling. The more they use FedEx, the greater their volume discounts.

Telephone Account Management at BT

A decade ago, British Telecom (BT) was a stodgy government monopoly. Privatization, modernization, and new competition have changed the picture dramatically. Today, BT operates one of the world's most technologically advanced networks, boasting much higher service quality and a more customer-focused culture. It also uses technology to drive a sophisticated account management system that builds loyal relationships with customers even as it helps them take advantage of technological innovation.

BT wasn't always the customer's friend. "You are the most difficult people in the world to buy from," one business subscriber told Anna Thomson soon after she joined BT as a district marketing operations manager in

1985. From further analysis, she discovered that some 750,000 inquiries from customers of all types had not been followed up the previous year. Thomson saw that new developments in telecommunications could be very beneficial to small businesses. "The right telecom choices at the right time can enable such businesses to offer new services, cut operating costs, and steal a march on competitors," she declared. "But their owners don't have time to research this all alone, and so either miss opportunities altogether or make the wrong choices."

Recognizing that it wasn't cost-effective to call on small accounts with a field-based account rep, Thomson developed a telephone account management program, using BT's own medium, the telephone, as the key channel for sales and customer service contacts. Today most of BT's 650,000 small business accounts (loosely defined as those with between two and five lines) are assigned to a carefully trained telephone account manager (TAM).

"The job of TAMs," says Thomson (who has since moved on to global account management), "is to understand the business objectives and organization of their customers and to help them make the right decisions at the right time—so that we *and* they become increasingly successful." TAMs also stand ready at any time to help resolve problems. Adds Thomson's successor on the TAM program, Michael Tarte-Booth: "It's a partnership based on trust, which has to be earned through proven good advice over time." He points out that the value of an account to BT goes far beyond line rental and network usage fees, since it includes equipment sales, installation and maintenance charges, and the possibility of revenues from a wide range of added-value services, ranging from 800 numbers to electronic mailboxes. Over the years, those revenues can really mount up.

> *"The job...is to understand the business objectives and organization of...customers and to help them make the right decisions at the right time—so that we and they become increasingly successful."*
>
> ANNA THOMSON

The average TAM works with up to 1000 customers and makes about 25 calls a day, versus only four made by an account manager working in the field. Computer software leverages TAMs' skills, helping them to gather detailed information about each customer's business activities through a series of on-screen prompts. As it's gathered, this information is entered into the electronic file for that account, making each TAM an expert on every assigned account. This file is all the more vital for TAMs in that government regulation, designed to level the playing field for new competitors in Britain's telecommunication market, denies BT sales personnel access to BT's own customer billing records.

Customer research, market data, and BT revenue streams show that the TAM program has been very successful. Adds Tarte-Booth: "Customers like the cloak of invisibility provided by telephone contact. It gives them greater perceived control. Ultimately, they can drop the neutron bomb and hang up."

Making the Most of an ATM Network: The BayBank Experience

With assets of just under $10 billion, BayBank is not a very large bank by either American or European standards. In its home state of Massachusetts, however, where it controls around 30 percent of the retail market, its green-and-blue logo is ubiquitous. Many banks talk big about electronic technology, but BayBank has been among the leaders in deploying it as an integral component of strategy.

Although it's hard to imagine retail banking today without automated teller machines (ATMs), they were not exactly an overnight success (many people still resist using them). Today, 95 percent of BayBank cardholders use their ATM cards at least once a month, versus an American average of only 57 percent. That's partly because BayBank has done everything possible to make both staff and customers comfortable with the machines. In the late 1970s, customers were sent ATM cards and encouraged to use them through educational leaflets, personal demonstrations, and promotions. One popular summer promotion offered customers a coupon for a free ice cream from a local chain if they would visit a branch and let a customer service rep demonstrate how to use an ATM. As the number of active cardholders built, the marketing emphasis shifted to frequency of use. Another promotion entered customers in a Hawaiian holiday sweepstakes every time they used an ATM.

BayBank invested heavily in a large ATM network long before its competitors did. Looking back, a BayBank officer observed, "ATMs were originally seen as a way of reducing costs by getting machines to replace human tellers. But we noticed that customers responded to the convenience of an easy-to-use, all-hours delivery system, and we saw ATMs as a way to differentiate BayBank from its competitors on a marketing basis. We also found that the people who started to open accounts with us were just the type of customers that banks like to get—they were younger, better educated, and had significant earning potential."

To ensure reliability and reduce the risk of failure, BayBank invested millions of dollars in redundant systems. And 24-hour hot-line phones were installed at each ATM site, so that customers could always call an employee if they were having problems. One of BayBank's bywords is: "There's nothing less convenient than a convenience that doesn't work."

One of BayBank's bywords is: "There's nothing less convenient than a convenience that doesn't work."

The first ATMs were installed in bank branches, but soon BayBank was installing ATMs in many other easily accessible locations—in hospitals, shopping malls, airports, small storefronts, and freestanding kiosks. Robert P. Shay, a senior vice president of the bank, explains: "The conventional wisdom among many bankers is that remote ATMs are too expensive to justify. We view it differently. We've put ATMs in locations where a branch might not be justified but where people still want the convenience. 'Why not bring cash to the people?' we asked." By the time competing banks came to recognize the strategic importance of ATMs, BayBank had already preempted most of the best sites, including exclusive rights to Boston's Logan International Airport, where it collects a fee each time a customer of another bank uses one of its terminals.

Although all competitors now offer ATMs, BayBank's machines do more than anybody else's. Are they fancier machines? No, BayBank uses widely available Diebold models, but it has programmed them with smarter software so they can offer 10 banking-related services (as compared to only three for most competitors), plus sale of postage stamps. For instance, *Custom Cash* allows you to program your own preferred withdrawal amount, rather than having to key it in each time. Fee-based information services include *Check Update* (cost: $0.15), which allows customers to key in the number of a specific check to see if it has been received for payment yet; and *Account Update* (cost: $0.50), which offers a "ministatement," detailing the numbers, dates, and amounts of the last five checks received for payment, the three most recent card transactions, and latest deposit. Today, BayBank is testing state-of-the-art ATMs and banking consoles, offering color screens and an even broader array of services, but by using custom software, it continues to get far more out of its existing network than its competitors.

Kirin Beer: Tying in the Retail Network

Beer might seem like a low-tech industry if ever there was one. After all, brewing is an ancient technology, still undertaken at home in some countries (my father used to make his own). But more advanced technologies are increasingly present, too. In fact, new beers are "designed" in laboratories, while giant modern breweries are run by skilled production engineers.

In Japan, beer is a particularly competitive business. It's not that the Japanese are unusually heavy consumers of the beverage—on a per-capita basis, they drink less than half the American volume and one-third that of the average German, Dane, or New Zealander. But the Japanese beer market is totally dominated by just four big companies (Kirin, Asahi, Suntory, and Sapporo). A change of just one percentage point in overall market share can be worth 5 billion yen (about $50 million) in *marginal profits.*

Kirin Brewery is the top brewer in Japan and the fourth largest in the world, after Anheuser-Busch and Miller in the United States and Heineken of the Netherlands. Like many brewers, Kirin has also diversified into soft drinks, whisky, and other products. Facing intense competition, Kirin has innovated not only in new types of beer but also in new uses of information technology. In May 1985, Kirin became the first Japanese brewer to offer a line of computers to wholesalers and retailers throughout Japan. The custom-designed KN line—which offers cash register, inventory control, sales data, and invoicing—is part of the KIC (Kirin Intelligence and Communication) network.

Such a system obviously helps bind Kirin closer to its wholesalers, especially the more than 500 with whom it has exclusive agreements. But what about the 130,000 Japanese retailers, many of them small liquor stores, who sell all brands of beer and many other beverages? After all, a laser scanner will read the bar code on an Asahi, Sapporo, or Suntory product just as well as one of Kirin's. And that's the point, because the entire computer network is wired to Kirin headquarters, providing management with vital information for production and marketing planning, including immediate feedback on stock rotation and daily sales trends for all Kirin products and those of the competition, too. There's no need for Kirin to offer the KN line to every liquor retailer—just enough to represent a good market research sample.

Pursuing Desirable Outcomes

Electronic technology is, predictably, subject to hype. In his book, *Megamistakes: Forecasting and the Myth of Technological Change,* Steven Schnaars writes of what he calls a bias toward optimism. "Optimism," he says, "results from being enamored of technological wonder. It follows from focusing too intently on the underlying technology." The innovations most likely to succeed are those that offer clearly perceived value not only to the adopting organization, but also to those employees and customers who are expected to interact with them.

Your chances of employing any technology to best advantage depend on what desirable outcomes you intend to achieve with it. In the balance of this chapter, I'll lay out some priorities.

1. *Get the most out of existing hardware.* As the BayBank example shows, the same hardware can often be made to do much more simply by programming it with custom-designed software.

2. *Create relational databases.* Many service businesses have traditionally organized their data collection around activities or products, rather than around customer accounts. Investing in new software to generate account-based data (and sometimes in new hardware to access it on-line) yields powerful information for marketing and customer service. As a Discover Card executive emphasized: "Our customers expect us to have relational databases. If they call us, they not only expect us to know that they have a Discover Card, but [also] that they have a Discover Savers Account, a Discover CD, the travel program, the registry program, and so forth." He made that point in 1988. What do your customers expect of your organization today?

3. *Link service elements and processes.* Much of the power of information technology comes from the synergy created by linking information flows at each stage in the service delivery process, and then integrating the resulting transactional data with other information about the customer and the operation. For instance, we saw in Chap. 9 how information about each Federal Express package parallels its physical movements. Such linkages are often invisible to the outside observer—or even to competitors. Some of the most remarkable illustrations of linking discrete elements of IT (and other technologies) are to be found in the business integration centers created by Andersen Consulting. These exhibits, covering thousands of square feet of space, demonstrate a vision of how integrated technologies can be made to work together in contexts ranging from business logistics to supermarket operations to hospitals.

4. *Leverage employee skills.* No normal person could keep precise details of 1000 accounts in his or her head, but the computer makes each of BT's TAMs an expert on all 1000 of the accounts for which he or she is responsible. And if the TAM should be absent when a customer calls in, the data is still there with BT so that a colleague can pick up the ball without a fumble. Similarly, the order pickers who work in McKesson's warehouse are more accurate and waste less time, thanks to the intelligent terminals they wear on their arms. Expert systems have tremendous potential to leverage employees' performance and to allow them to take on greater responsibility.

5. *Create value by cutting time and hassle costs.* Technology has as much power to cut costs as it does to create benefits; better value can come from either direction. Pay particular attention to finding opportunities to improve value for your customers on supplementary service elements. Time-saving machines and methods appeal especially to customers with limited time budgets (who may be prepared to pay extra for them). Greater use of telecommunications for a host of service elements not only saves time, but also reduces the need for travel, with all its attendant mental, physical, and financial costs.

6. *Give customers more control.* Giving customers the option of self-service—as with ATMs or the FedEx Powership system—increases their flexibility and sense of control. And giving them better information on how they have used a service in the past often helps them decide how to make better use of it in the future. For instance, analysis of detailed travel and expense reports from (say) American Express may lead corporate travel departments to cut T&E budgets or to order high-living managers to use cheaper hotels, hire smaller rental cars, and find discount airline fares. Similarly, a logistics manager may zero in on Federal Express shipping expenses within specific departments, demanding that people send fewer packages by FedEx's premium next-morning delivery services and use the cheaper two-day service instead.

In the short run, such moves will cut Amex commissions and FedEx revenues. Aren't these two companies shooting themselves in the foot by enabling customers to obtain customized reports? The simple answer is that letting customers waste their money to boost your profits is not what partnership is all about. It violates the principle of looking out for your partner's best interest. Sooner or later, a competitor's sales rep will offer to analyze expenditures on T&E or express shipments (or whatever), and propose cost-cutting alternatives. Then good-bye, customer!

> *Letting customers waste their money to boost your profits is not what partnership is all about.*

---

7. *Inoculate customers against the competition.* Nothing, not even consistently good service, is guaranteed to tie a customer to your firm, especially if it's easy to switch to a competitor. So it helps to increase the cost of switching. Two technology-based barriers to switching are (1) a trusted adviser who knows a lot about you (or your company if it's a corporate

account), and (2) an electronic umbilical cord that links you to the supplier through the medium of specially provided hardware.

Short of database theft, it would be hard for a competing telephone company to duplicate the information that BT has gathered about its small business accounts, let alone the trust that comes from a proven track record of giving good service and sound advice. Both Kirin wholesalers and Federal Express shippers are tied to their respective suppliers by the systems that the latter have installed. Thinking rationally, neither would want to install duplicate equipment, operating side by side. Certainly, customers could always make a complete switch to another supplier at some point, but it would involve a lot of time and hassle.

Conclusion

Investments in technology (of all types) have often been couched in terms of cost displacement and productivity: Can we speed up operations? Can we eliminate part of the work force? Can we reengineer our work processes? Or they have focused on how to improve the firm's competitive posture by improving the appeal and performance of the core product and thus add value. Can we preempt the competition with a new product/delivery system? Alternatively, how quickly can we catch up with competitors who have already adopted a new technology? These may be sound questions for your organization, too, but as you think about this chapter, I'd like you to consider what technology can also do to improve value on the supplementary services that you offer.

Technology is a theme running through many of the chapters in this book. Since the next two chapters include global perspectives on service delivery, it's hardly surprising that innovative applications of telecommunications should receive special attention there.

18 24-365-Global: Service Anywhere, Anytime

As companies expand their marketing horizons from local to regional to global, customers increasingly expect to be able to obtain information, place orders, and resolve problems 24 hours a day, 365 days a year— wherever they may be. Travelers look for total availability of vital personal services, from banking to reservations. Customers who are responsible for equipment or facilities that are in continuous use tend to be particularly demanding: If something goes wrong, they want help right away. We see how Hewlett-Packard provides round-the-clock, round-the-world diagnostics and problem solving to its computer customers.

Once upon a time, if you wanted to get money from your bank account, you had to go down to your local branch during those few hours a week when they felt like being open for service (usually from 10 a.m. to 3 p.m., Mondays to Fridays). Traveling away from home and need money? Sorry, a request to draw funds from another branch of the same bank required special arrangements in advance. It was hard to believe it was your money and not theirs.

Today, with no more identification than a magnetically striped card (and knowledge of your personal identification number), you can withdraw funds from your account in local currency at any time from any bank in the world that offers 24-hour machines linked to the same global network as your own bank. Welcome to the world of 24-365-Global!

Driven by changes in technology, customer needs, and social mores, three interrelated developments are sweeping many parts of the world. One is seven-days-a-week service, a second is 24-hour service, and the third is global information networks, linked by various forms of telecommunications. When these three are put together, the result is service 24 hours a day, every day of the year, with information-related elements networked around the world. We've already looked at the emergence of modern global telecommunications. Now let's consider the forces that create round-the-clock service at the local level, and then let's examine how a computer company succeeds in offering its customers 24-hour service around the globe.

Extending the Hours and Days of Service

Some services have long been 24-hour operations, every day of the year. They include many services that respond to life- or property-threatening emergencies, such as fire, police, health, or repairs to vital equipment. Hospitals and first-class hotels provide 24-hour care or room service as a matter of course. Ships and long-distance trains don't stop for the night; they keep on going. Passenger aircraft have operated around the clock on intercontinental routes for decades. And telephone companies have long had operators available on a 24-hour basis.

But most retail and professional services historically tended to follow a traditional 9–5, five (or six) days a week routine. In large measure, this routine reflected social norms (and even legal requirements or union agreements) as to what were appropriate hours for people to work and enterprises to sell things. If you had a job, you either had to shop during your lunch hour—if the store itself didn't close for lunch—or on Saturdays. But the idea of Sunday opening was strongly discouraged in most Christian cultures and even proscribed by law, reflecting long tradition based on religious practice. Only services that emphasized entertainment and relaxation, such as movie theaters, bars, restaurants, and sporting facilities, geared their schedules toward weekends and evening hours when their customers had leisure time. And even here, there were often restrictions on hours of operation, especially on Sundays.

Reasons for Extended-Hour Operation

At least five factors are driving the move toward ever extended hours and seven-day operations. The trend has had its greatest influence in the United States and Canada, but it's spreading elsewhere.

> *Five factors are driving the move toward ever extended operating hours and seven-day operations.*

1. *Economic pressure from consumers.* The growing number of two-income families and single wage earners who live alone need time outside normal working hours to shop and use other services, since they have nobody to do it for them. Once one store or firm extends its hours to meet the needs of these market segments, competitors feel obliged to follow. Chains have often led the way in this respect.

2. *Changes in legislation.* A second factor has been the decline, lamented by some, of support for the view that Sunday should be legislated as a day of rest for one and all, regardless of religious affiliation. In a multicultural society, of course, it's a moot point which day should be designated as special—for observant Jews and Seventh Day Adventists, Saturday is the Sabbath; for Muslims, Friday is the holy day; and agnostics or atheists presumably don't care. There has been a gradual erosion of such legislation in Western nations in recent years, although it's still firmly in place in some countries and locations. Switzerland, for example, still closes down most retail activities on Sundays—except for the sale of bread, which people like to buy freshly baked on Sunday mornings.

3. *Economic incentives to improve asset utilization.* A great deal of capital is usually tied up in service facilities. The incremental cost of extending hours is often relatively modest (especially when part-timers can be hired without paying them either overtime or benefits); if extending hours reduces crowding and increases revenues, then it's economically attractive. There are costs involved in shutting down and reopening a facility like a

supermarket, yet climate control and some lighting must be left running all night, and security personnel must be paid to keep an eye on the place. Even if the number of extra customers served is minimal, there are both operational and marketing advantages to remaining open 24 hours.

4. *Availability of employees for "unsocial" hours.* Changing lifestyles and a desire for part-time employment have combined to create a growing labor pool of people who are willing to work evenings and nights. Some of these workers are students looking for part-time earnings outside their classroom hours; some are "moonlighting," holding a full-time job by day and earning additional income by night; some are parents juggling child-care responsibilities; others simply prefer to work at night and relax or sleep during the day; still others are glad to obtain any paid employment, regardless of the hours.

5. *Growth of automated self-service facilities.* Automated self-service equipment is increasingly reliable, and many facilities now accept card-based payments in addition to coins and banknotes. Installing unattended machines may be economically feasible in places that couldn't support a staffed facility. Unless a machine requires frequent servicing or is particularly vulnerable to vandalism, the incremental cost of going from limited hours to 24-hour operation is minimal. In fact, it may be much simpler to leave machines running all the time than to turn them on and off, especially if they are placed in widely scattered locations.

American retailing has led the way toward meeting customer needs for greater convenience, and other countries are now beginning to follow suit. A trend that began in earnest with early-morning to late-evening service in drugstores and so-called 7-11 convenience grocery stores has now extended to 24-hour service in a variety of retail outlets, from gas stations to restaurants to supermarkets.

Extended-Hours Customer Service

The customer's search for convenience has not been confined to the purchase of core products. People want easy access to supplementary services, too—especially information, reservations, and problem solving. Says an executive of Discover Card:

> There are a lot of two-income families. Our customers are busy with their personal lives, and they don't have a lot of time to handle their personal business. They expect us to be available to them when it's convenient for them—not when it's convenient for us; so they expect extended hours. And most of all, they expect one contact to solve their problem.

In many service industries, problem-solving needs were originally met by telephoning a specific store or facility during its regular operating hours. Led by airlines and hotel chains, separate customer service centers have evolved, reached by calling a single number regardless of the caller's location. Some of these centers are operated by the service provider, others are subcontracted to specialist intermediaries (hotel chains, for instance, often delegate the reservations function to independent contractors). Once a firm departs from locally staffed phones and installs a centralized system, most customers will be calling from hundreds or even thousands of miles away, rather than just making a local call. So, instead of forcing customers to pay the cost of a long-distance call, many firms have installed toll-free numbers; again, once one firm does so, competitors often feel obliged to follow the leader. North American companies have traditionally been more generous than European ones in this respect, but the latter are beginning to follow suit as the concept catches on. In most European countries, local calls are not free, so firms often offer a long-distance call for the price of a local one.

Providing extended-hours customer service is almost mandatory for any organization with a nationwide clientele in the United States and Canada, since each nation covers so many different time zones. If the switchboard closes at 5 p.m. Eastern time, for instance, customers on the West Coast are denied access to the number after 2 p.m. Pacific time. Even closing at 5 p.m. local time is inconvenient for people who want to call from home after dinner (if there's a mistake on your bank statement, for instance, you'll probably discover it when you read the mail at home in the evening).

When a North American business redefines its goal as offering continent-wide service from first thing in the morning Atlantic time (Puerto Rico, the Virgin Islands, and Nova Scotia) to mid-evening Alaska-Hawaii time, then managers don't need a fancy calculator to figure out that customer service lines will have to be open 18 hours a day. At this point, why not go to 24-hour operation and cater to people who work odd shifts themselves and get up very early or go to bed very late? It depends on your firm's priorities, the costs involved, and the value that customers place on total accessibility.

Emergencies don't just involve people. They involve vital equipment and processes, too.

When customers are dependent on a machine or a service 24 hours a day, downtime can be very disruptive. Emergencies don't just involve people. They involve vital equipment and processes, too. If a computer goes down, the consequences can range from personal inconvenience to shut-down of a major facility; if a transformer blows, electric power may be lost; if a furnace goes out, pipes may burst. Sometimes, these types of emergencies are handled by a duty person, reached by beeper or cellular phone, who drives to the site of the problem, makes a physical inspection, and undertakes whatever repairs are necessary. But using modern technology, engineers can sometimes fix problems involving high-tech equipment in another location without ever leaving their offices. And they can even do it from the opposite side of the world. *How* do they do it? Read on.

Worldwide Customer Support at Hewlett-Packard

Powerful computer systems—and the software to run them—are in use all over the world, from big-city banks to chemical plants near rural towns, and even in such exotic locations as remote mining sites in Australia, oil rigs above the Arctic Circle, airports on Pacific islands, hydroelectric projects in the Andes, and on ships sailing the seven seas. The applications to which they are put vary widely, but computers are only of use when they are up and running (or ready for service). System failures can have disastrous consequences.

Supporting the enormous installed base of equipment and software, as well as helping users to plan for future needs, is a big business, attracting both suppliers from worldwide vendors to local service firms. Ledgeway/Dataquest, a leading market research firm, projects that global revenues for customer support from information technology vendors will grow from $116.4 billion in 1992 to $195.5 billion in 1996. As a major supplier of computer hardware, the Hewlett-Packard Co. (HP) is also at the cutting edge of customer support—not only for its own products, but for customer networks incorporating other vendors' equipment as well. A key component in the total equation is HP's Worldwide Customer Support Operations (WCSO).

WCSO employs 16,000 people, operates some 32 Response Centers in the Americas, Asia, Europe, and Australia, and delivers a range of support services and tools beyond traditional hardware maintenance. Their services range from site design to systems integration and remote diagnostics. Unlike some competitors, who scatter responsibility for different customer-support activities among different divisions, HP unifies every program under the WCSO banner. Six R&D labs work constantly to improve existing services and use emerging technologies to create new forms of customer support. By providing total solutions that add value to the customer's information system, WCSO has built a healthy service business worth more than $4 billion in 1992 (some 25 percent of HP's total revenues), sufficient to put WCSO in the top quarter of the *Fortune* 500 if it were an independent business.

Key Design Issues in Telephone-Based Service Delivery

The calls received by HP's Response Centers cover a broad spectrum, ranging from simple questions—such as how to print a spreadsheet sideways—to problems involving complex networking technology that may take hours of engineering time to resolve. But although these centers are geared toward solving technical problems, HP argues that the systems it has developed could apply equally well to any business that utilizes information-intensive telephone transactions.

Whether you are designing systems for consumer affairs departments, catalog fulfillment operations, financial institutions, or a host of other applications, you will still have to address the same key issues:

- *Creation of an overall service delivery model.* The model (which describes how the system works) must meet two central customer requirements for good service: speed and quality.

- *Call management and administration.* The mechanics of answering, routing, and tracking calls may involve both telecommunications and database management; increasingly, the most powerful approaches link the two. Your procedures should ensure that the system works well for all parties.

- *Access to data and applications.* The information a firm needs to complete a transaction with a customer often resides in more than one database and runs on different hardware platforms. To deliver good service and simultaneously achieve operational efficiency (a fundamental of product plus service), your customer service reps will need instant, easy access to all relevant sources and applications.

- *Adapting to change.* Procedures and equipment do not exist in a vacuum. You have to make provision for integrating new systems with existing ones and accommodating future changes, including some that are not even commercially available yet. Unless systems are carefully planned in advance, installing even modest upgrades can be an awesome task. (Programmers joke that the reason God was able to create the world in only seven days was that He didn't have to deal with an installed base.)

The Path to Centralization

HP's worldwide network of Response Centers has evolved over the past 15 years from relatively simple origins. The first step was a formalized "Phone-In Consulting Service" (PICS), created in the late 1970s to relieve systems engineers in the field and help contain rising service and support costs. Initially, PICS customers simply called their local sales office when they encountered a problem. However, several drawbacks to this approach soon became apparent.

- *Variability in quality of response.* Since PICS calls were handled by systems engineers on a rotating basis, the quality of response varied according to the responding engineer's level of expertise in the caller's area of concern. This situation, which was likely to get worse as the volume and complexity of calls increased, was at variance with HP's goal of delivering a consistently high quality of service.

- *Inability to capture valuable data.* Each office had its own (usually manual) system for tracking call progress and resolution, making it hard to measure the efficiency and cost of the PICS system. Worse, there was no way to capture and archive problem/solution histories that HP engineers elsewhere could access later when other customers called with similar problems: The wheel had to be reinvented each time. Finally, there was no formal system for delivering customer feedback to HP engineering divisions, so that they might incorporate field experience into future product development work.

- *Inability to optimize use of available resources.* On any given day, engineers at some sales offices might be overloaded by calls, while colleagues in other offices had time on their hands. There was no realistic way to balance loads across different offices.

In 1984, HP established its North American Response Center, creating a centralized facility to handle all calls and remedy these problems. The strategy of using teams of engineers, who could pool their expertise to solve customer problems, led to dramatic improvements in the speed and quality of response. HP soon earned its first number-one ranking in independent surveys of customer satisfaction with service support—an accolade that has been bestowed many times since. Subsequently, HP extended the response center concept outside the United States, taking the first step toward creating a linked network of such centers, to operate seven days a week around the world.

HP's Service Delivery Model

What happens when you telephone an HP Response Center for assistance? The company takes a phased approach to each customer call. The first phase, logging the call at a response center, is carried out primarily by call coordinators, whose job involves: (1) validating that the caller is a legitimate HP customer; (2) determining the type of service contract purchased by this customer; (3) capturing a basic description of the problem; (4) obtaining a number for call-back and, rather than putting the person on hold, telling the customer to expect a prompt return call from an engineer. Customers can also log their own calls via a telephone keypad or electronic mail. The average call-back time is approximately 8 minutes for Priority One calls (urgent cases involving system interruption), and about 40 minutes for all others. HP's service contracts guarantee a response within 2 hours.

The second phase involves determining the best resource to solve the problem, based on the information received. Calls are then referred to the appropriate team for action in Phase Three. Engineers work to categorize the nature of the problem. Simple issues, typically involving personal computers, are handled on a first-in, first-out basis, with an average problem-resolution time of 20 minutes. More complex problems are handled by what HP calls the "classical method," in which an engineer attempts to resolve the problem using personal knowledge and database resources.

When engineers can't resolve the problem within a limited timeframe, they escalate the response by developing an action plan on how to proceed. This may involve a broader search for data, consultations with other experts, simulations of the problem on a diagnostic system, and other activities referred to collectively at HP as "background processing."

Call Management and Access to Data and Applications

Despite their importance, time spent on such administrative tasks as call tracking, documentation, and performance measurement tends to be regarded as a necessary evil by callers, engineers, and Response Center managers alike. So HP has designed administrative mechanisms to be as streamlined as possible.

One example of this streamlining involves use of a technology called Advanced Computerized Telephone. Using automatic number identification (ANI)—also known as "caller ID"—the caller's number is transmitted to the computer, which matches the number to an account in its database, and forwards the relevant customer identification screen to the call coordinator's workstation at the very same instant as the call itself. As one manager explained, "With ANI, we don't frustrate our customers by asking them a bunch of questions [about serial numbers, service contracts, etc.] they can't answer anyway. We get their records on the screen immediately and go straight to the problem." Other windows provide information about the customer's installation, service history, and previous call-in questions.

> *"With ANI, we don't frustrate our customers by asking them a bunch of questions they can't answer anyway. We get their records on the screen immediately and go straight to the problem."*

Jeff Landre, Americas Response Centers Manager for HP, sees the strategy of leveraging new technology—notably greater computing power and advanced telecommunications—as having dual goals: first, to create ever higher standards of service for customers; and second, to obtain a simultaneous increase in the productivity of HP's own operations.

Global Operations

HP now has 32 Response Centers around the world. They are all integrated into a network headed by four major centers: Bracknell, United Kingdom, Atlanta (Georgia) and Mountain View (California) in the United States, and Melbourne, Australia. Each local center is staffed during extended daytime hours, seven days a week, by between 12 and 200 engineers. The size of each center is a function of the volume of business in the local region. Problems that can't be resolved in a smaller center may be transferred to one of the major centers; which center actually receives the transfer may depend on the time of day at which the call is made. Because of time-zone differentials, at least one of the major centers is always in full operation at any time. The total staffing worldwide now exceeds 1500 support engineers, who collectively handle over 190,000 calls a month.

Workstations in all Response Centers are linked to a powerful database that stores years of HP product information. If you encounter a problem that has already been solved for another customer—even one on another continent—you should receive the solution almost immediately. HP also links its workstations to an extensive diagnostic center that contains one of almost every HP computer system ever made. One might almost describe it as a working museum.

> *HP links its workstations to an extensive diagnostic center that contains one of almost every HP computer system ever made.*

Until very recently, HP's approach to solving complex problems involved taking steps to duplicate the customer's system at the Response Center. In that way, an error in the customer's system could be replicated at the center; the engineer would then devise an appropriate solution and tell the customer how to replicate that solution back home. But now there has been a dramatic change in procedure. New advances in telecommunications, from satellite linkages to fiber-optic cables, allow transmission of vast amounts of data at great speed. As a result, in regions where the new telecom infrastructure is already in place, HP engineers are able to enter customers' systems directly from their own workstations and rapidly move gigabytes of data backwards and forwards between customer site and Response Center. Duplication is no longer necessary: The customer's system and the supplier's diagnostic and solution system are temporarily fused into a single entity. As a result, many problems can be fully resolved remotely, eliminating the need for costly on-site assistance.

HP's objective is to provide seamless service at any hour of the day or night. Consider, for instance, the customer in Washington, DC, who experiences a problem in a vital system at midnight. He calls an 800 number, which connects to HP's Atlanta Center, where a call coordinator takes the relevant information and promises a prompt call-back from an engineer. The coordinator then contacts Melbourne, where it is now mid-afternoon. Very soon, the Washington customer receives a call from an engineer responding to his problem; the line is so clear, she might be calling from down the street. If the customer is very observant, he might notice that she has an Australian accent.

HP has also been upgrading its language capabilities—human languages, that is—to provide even better levels of service. Let's say that the midnight call is made not in Washington but in Osaka, Japan, from where it goes to the Tokyo Response Center. A bilingual call coordinator then contacts Mountain View, where it's 4 p.m. Pacific time. A Japanese-speaking engineer, based in California, calls the customer back to obtain further information. Even if he can't solve the problem on the spot, he will at least be able to undertake some of the necessary data transfer and arrange for someone else to follow up later.

It's not always the customer who calls HP to report a problem. Sometimes, an engineer may initiate a call from the other side of the world to tell the customer that a problem has been spotted in the latter's system. Like other computer manufacturers, HP offers predictive support software that can be installed within a system to monitor the performance of disk and magnetic tape drives, system memory, peripherals, and networks. This software automatically reads and analyzes the system logs that record internal hardware events and errors, as well as monitoring line-error trends on the network. When these events or errors signal an emerging problem, the software automatically calls the Response Center, where engineers develop a diagnosis. It's as though the computer takes the initiative to call the clinic and say, "Doc, I'm not feeling so good!" Sometimes, the problem can be solved with a remote "fix"; but if on-site assistance is needed, the diagnosis will be forwarded to a locally based engineer responsible for that account.

Going Global

Hewlett-Packard's goals include providing global consistency in its level of customer service. Other firms with a global customer base, from banks to airlines to manufacturers of electric generating equipment, should be pondering strategies to achieve the same enviable level of service. One advantage of these global linkages is that 24-hour service can be offered without necessarily staffing each individual facility 24 hours a day.

Providing global service raises the question of whether to do it yourself, form a strategic alliance, or find a subcontractor. Information-based services involving voice and data communications can certainly be handled from a single global hub (as with Federal Express), but they must still be transmitted through an infrastructure of switches, cables, and perhaps satellites, with their accompanying need for uplinks and downlinks. If physical actions are involved in the process, such as removing money from ATMs or repairing and maintaining equipment, then the problem becomes more complex, especially if the number of potential service delivery sites is very large. Under those circumstances, working through agencies, distributors, or franchisees may be the only solution.

The marriage of computer technology to modern telecommunications offers the potential of bringing ever higher standards of customer service support to the global village that Marshall McLuhan envisaged over a quarter of a century ago. Linking workstations around the world to the storehouses of wisdom contained in specialized, centralized databases is the necessary technical step. But despite self-service and automated responses, most of these technological tools still remain no more than remarkable leverage for talented human problem solvers.

As companies move to operate more on a global basis, one of the challenges that they will increasingly face is serving customers who speak different languages. In the next chapter, we consider how product plus organizations can become more responsive to an increasingly multilingual society—not just in other countries, but at home as well.

Quadrilingual Swiss cow warns colleague of approaching train.

19 Parlez-Vous Français?

日本語を話しますか。

As societies become more multicultural, as people travel more, and as markets become international, doing business only in English may be seen by customers as a product minus. Solutions range from a multilingual staff to multilingual computers, from simultaneous translation to language-translating machines, and from universal signage to global phone numbers answered in various languages. Examples describe how Swiss banks offer ATMs that know which language customers prefer, how Euro Disney provides for visitors who speak many different tongues, and how you can telephone someone who doesn't speak English using AT&T's Language Line service.

Joseph Pulitzer, the famous nineteenth-century newspaper proprietor, is best remembered today for the Pulitzer prizes he founded. In his day, he was owner of the *New York World* and something of a megalomaniac. Not only did he believe that his paper should be "more powerful than the President," he even aspired to influence the inhabitants of other planets.

At one point, Pulitzer considered erecting an advertising sign for the *World* in New Jersey that would be large enough to be visible on Mars. He was dissuaded from this endeavor only when one of his assistants asked, "What language shall we put it in?"

As far as we know, Earth-bound businesses have yet to provide services to inhabitants of other planets. But more and more firms are finding themselves serving customers speaking different languages. This situation may arise from increased tourism and business travel (40 million foreign visitors come to America each year), expansion into new markets abroad, or trying to provide better service to linguistic minorities within domestic markets. For example, the 1990 Census found that there were 32 million people over the age of five who live in the United States but do not speak English at home. Almost 6 million of them were unable to speak English well, if at all.

So what language *should* we put it in? As societies become more multicultural, as people travel more, and as markets become global, doing business only in English may be seen by customers as a product minus. The more relevant question may be: What language does the customer prefer?

> *As societies become more multicultural, as people travel more, and as markets become global, doing business only in English may be seen as a product minus.*

Solutions to the language challenge range from employing multilingual staff to using multilingual computers, from providing simultaneous voice translation to using language-translation machines, and from displaying universal signage to offering global phone numbers answered in various languages.

The Divisive Power of Language

Sir Winston Churchill—whose mother was American—once described the United States and Britain as "two nations divided by a common language." He was referring, of course, to the subtle differences between the two countries in English usage (of which more later). Although differences in usage and accent within the same language sometimes lead to misunderstandings or raised eyebrows, they seldom cause hostility. In a multilingual context, however, the choice of which language to use offers all the hazards of entering a minefield without a map.

Culture has always been expressed through language, and modern concepts of national identity are increasingly centered on people's mother tongues. Uneasy lies the nation where two or more official languages are spoken, for one language is nearly always seen in the ascendancy at the expense of another—either because of differences in birth rates or because of broader cultural and economic variances. Let me offer some examples primarily from Western nations (while recognizing that similar problems exist everywhere in the world).

The Quebec Experience

In Canada, the division between anglophones and francophones long ago turned political. Studies in the 1960s showed that French, the language spoken by the great majority of *Québeçois*, was in decline. Many French-Canadians felt that their language and culture were under siege from English-speaking Canadians and American entertainment. They were also concerned that the dominance of English in business activities handicapped French-Canadian managers, and they worried that immigrants to Quebec from overseas were choosing to have their children educated in English-speaking public schools rather than French ones.

Deeply held cultural values often find expression in political action. Quebec nationalists argued that the solution to protecting French lay in the slogan, *Au Québec, tout en Francais* (in Quebec, everything in French), which was implemented by the Quebec National Assembly through the (in)famous Bill 101. This law not only enshrined French as the sole official language of the province but required all public and retail signage to be in French only, ordered companies to adopt appropriately French names, and limited publicly financed school education in English to children whose parents were both Quebec-born native English speakers (tough luck if your dad came from Vancouver—you had to go to a French-language school).

Enforcement, through what were dubbed the "language police," was viewed by anglophones as draconian. On the other hand, from the perspective of the large population that cared deeply about maintaining an historically important North American language, the policy has been a success: The first language of business in Quebec is now French, the percentage of Quebec residents who speak only English has fallen sharply, immigrants' children are becoming native French speakers, and Montreal now looks unequivocally like the world's second largest French-speaking city.

Dutch versus French in Belgium

In Belgium, part of the problem has been that the Flemings (who speak Dutch) have felt themselves under siege from the French language. The political solution here was to federate Belgium along linguistic lines into Flanders and Wallonia, each of which would be officially unilingual. Only the capital area of Brussels and a couple of towns along the linguistic border have been allowed to remain bilingual. This solution, while satisfactory to many, has also led to population shifts and some bitterness. Formerly bilingual institutions, such as the Catholic University of Louvain, have split themselves apart, with the Flemish section remaining in its ancestral home of Leuven and the French moving across the linguistic border into Wallonia to a new town aptly called Louvain-la-Neuve ("New Louvain").

A Belgian friend from Flanders, brought up from birth to speak both French and Flemish (and also speaking English and German), once created a scene in his country's consulate in San Francisco when he discovered that the consular official there could not converse with him in Flemish. My friend refused to speak French with the official. Stupid? No, as a Belgian citizen and a customer of the consulate, he had every right to be accommodated in his preferred tongue. Not all Belgians might have complained so vigorously and refused to speak in the other national language, but privately they might still have taken strong offense. The fact is, when cultural feelings run deep between different linguistic groups, even those who speak the other's tongue may prefer not to do so.

> *When cultural feelings run deep between different linguistic groups, even those who speak the other's tongue may prefer not to do so.*

The Swiss Experience

Some experts point to Switzerland—which has approximately the same land area and population as Massachusetts and New Hampshire combined—as a nation that long ago solved its linguistic differences with a cantonal system of government. The Swiss Confederation consists of 26 self-governing cantons and has four official national languages: German, French, Italian, and Romansch.

German is the mother tongue of 65 percent of all Swiss residents. The written language is virtually the same as standard "High German." But the spoken language is another matter altogether. People at all levels of Swiss society actually speak one of a variety of local Swiss-German dialects, known collectively as *Schwytzerdüsch*. Unfortunately, many visitors from Germany can't understand it, and the dialects are so localized that a resident of one Swiss-German canton may even have trouble understanding a visitor from another.

Eighteen percent of the Swiss population are native French speakers, and only a slight accent distinguishes them from residents of neighboring France. Italian is the mother tongue of 10 percent of the population, about half of them immigrants or migrant workers from Italy. And 1 percent, living near the Italian border in southeastern Switzerland, speak Romansch, which is said to be the closest living language to the Latin spoken by ordinary people in Roman days. The balance of the Swiss population are immigrants, who speak a wide variety of other languages.

Each canton's governmental powers include the right to establish its own official language. Most cantons are unilingual, and the language borders are quite sharply defined. National agencies, such as the Swiss Federal Railways, use the language of the canton in which they are operating, so the railroad stations have German signs and announcements in German-speaking areas, and so forth. Bilingual conductors and restaurant personnel serve passengers on trains that operate across language borders. One exception to unilingual signage involves safety notices: Signs warning people not to cross the tracks or to keep away from electrical wires appear in four languages—German, French, Italian, and English. Why English? The Federal Railways don't serve Romansch-speaking areas, but they do carry a great many foreign visitors.

Even Switzerland, however, has language problems. Several of the 26 cantons are officially bilingual (French and German), and the canton of Grisons is trilingual (German, Italian, and Romansch). There are continuing worries about dominance by another language (usually German). Young Swiss are required to learn at least one of the other national languages. In French-speaking cantons, most students learn High German and then find they can't converse with Swiss Germans, who prefer dialect and don't always like to speak either High German or French; sometimes, they solve the problem by speaking to each other in English. The small French-speaking minority in the overwhelmingly German canton of Bern wants to break away and join the canton of Jura, where French is the official tongue. Still, despite these problems, Switzerland offers some useful insights, which I share in this chapter.

More Language Hot Spots

There are many other linguistic hot spots around the world. In Spain, the regional government of Catalonia (whose capital is Barcelona) is actively promoting use of Catalan, a romance language which, like French and Spanish, has its principal roots in Latin.

Language is only one of the divisive forces contributing to the violent breakup of Yugoslavia. Five separate languages are spoken in the six former republics of the Yugoslav federation. Although the Serbs and the Croats share the same language—Serbo-Croat—the former write it in Cyrillic script (like Russian) while the latter use Roman script, and this visible difference has been exploited to the hilt.

In many former colonies, French or English has been retained as an official language alongside indigenous ones. In India, for example, the official national languages are Hindi and English (another 14 languages are recognized in the various Indian states). In some countries, however, there are movements to abandon the use of colonial tongues; Algeria, for example, recently abolished the official status of French.

The small island nation of Singapore, in contrast, has made something of a virtue of retaining English as one of its four official languages. Among a population composed of ethnic Chinese, Malays, and Tamils (originally from southern India), each of whom speak their own language, English serves as a *lingua franca*. Its official status has also proved to be a major commercial advantage for both business and tourism.

Strange as it may seem, the United States has no official language (an attempt by the Continental Congress in the late eighteenth century to declare German the official tongue was narrowly voted down). Some Americans worry that English is under siege from immigrant languages (notably Spanish) and want to prevent a Quebec-like situation from emerging by passing an amendment to the U.S. Constitution declaring English the official language. About one-third of all the states have adopted English as their official tongue, and some have gone so far as to outlaw use of other languages for many official purposes—even for human services that are particularly relevant to immigrant populations.

Language as a Product Plus

I hope I don't offend anyone with these stories. I tell them because most readers of this book are probably native English speakers, living in an English-language environment, and quite accustomed to having people of other tongues switch to English to converse with them.

You and I benefit from the fact that English is not only one of the most widely studied and spoken second languages, but has also become the *lingua franca* of international business in many parts of the world. In this context, it's all too easy for English-speaking businesspeople to forget how much others value their own mother tongues. These "others" may include their own customers, suppliers, and employees.

> *It's all too easy for English-speaking businesspeople to forget how much others value their own mother tongues. These "others" may include their own customers, suppliers, and employees.*

Product plus service means taking into account your stakeholders' native languages and their levels of proficiency in English, and then determining which language(s) they would prefer to use in various situations—both spoken and written. Obtaining and acting on this knowledge may well prove to be an important competitive advantage. One day, we may all be able to communicate through the medium of portable devices offering simultaneous translation of speech, but until technology progresses beyond its current limited (and stilted) text-translation capabilities, we'll have to look for other solutions.

Going Multilingual

Where does a company start in its efforts to be more user-friendly where languages are concerned? I think it's helpful to break down the use of foreign languages into five categories of communication, and then to examine each in turn:

- Signage
- Written communications (e.g., information, letters, users' manuals, instructions, brochures, questionnaires, printed advertising messages)
- One-way verbal communications (e.g., announcements, presentations, prerecorded messages, television advertising)
- Face-to-face conversations
- Telephone conversations

Solutions to providing service in multiple languages vary quite widely from one situation to another.

Signage

We were driving at about 7000 feet, heading for the top of the pass through the mountains. Rounding yet another bend in the road, we saw a vista point ahead of us. There was a big parking area, containing a half-dozen tour buses and several dozen cars. I pulled off and the family climbed out of the car to join the crowds admiring the magnificent view. There was a Eurobabble of chatter all around—French, German, Italian, and British-accented English.

The Alps or the Dolomites? No. The cars all bore California license plates with discreet rental car stickers. This vista point was high in the Sierra Nevada, looking across to Half Dome in Yosemite National Park. We wandered around enjoying the view and overhearing others' enthusiastic exclamations—*Wunderbar!*, *Jolly impressive, eh? C'est vraiment formidable! Che bello!* It was astonishing: My wife and children were the only American voices to be heard. Finally, a beat-up car from Kansas drew up and four young people got out to swell that small minority. (And before we left, another California car arrived; they may have been Americans, but I couldn't tell, for they were speaking Spanish.)

The National Park Service had done a nice job of the signage, with information about points of interest, how the exfoliating granite rock formations were created, and a warning about the risk of slipping on the smooth rock surfaces. But it was all in English except for one little sign. In English, Spanish, French, and German, visitors were asked not to feed the animals.

Our experience was perhaps a little unusual—a cheap dollar and deep discounts on Atlantic airfares were bringing European tourists to America in droves during the summer of 1992. But another indication of Yosemite's appeal to foreign-language visitors could be found at the visitor center in Tuolomne Meadows, a few miles farther up the road. In the bookstore, illustrated guides to the Yosemite area were for sale in seven languages, including Japanese.

Signs are everywhere—at airports, on highways, at banks and post offices, in retail stores of all kinds, at tourist sites, in hospitals. Almost any large service facility needs them to assist its customers and guide their behavior.

Many signs are quite brief. Some identify a particular facility ("Emergencies" or "Men's Shirts" or "Toilets"; some offer directions ("Public Beach 1/2 Mile" or "To Gates 16–30"); some tell you what to do ("School, 20 mph When Light Flashing" or "Have Passport Ready"); others, what *not* to do ("No Smoking" or "Do Not Enter"); some warn of danger ("Beware of the Dog" or "High Voltage: Keep Off"); others threaten unpleasant consequences if you do something naughty ("Violators Will Be Fined" or "Shoplifters Will Be Prosecuted").

Other signs are educational. They may identify historic sites or highlight points of interest. A very important type of sign explains to prospective customers how to use a particular service or piece of self-service equipment, from ticket-selling machines to public telephones.

In Europe, it's routine to see signs in several languages, especially in areas or facilities that are frequented by tourists and business travelers. America is beginning to catch on, but as the Yosemite example suggests, still has a way to go. If people don't understand the language in which a sign is written, they may get lost or into trouble. Alternatively, they may have difficulty using a service (or obtaining full value from it) because they don't understand the instructions.

One solution to the question, "What language shall we put it in?" is to use widely understood symbols rather than words, since symbols form an international language of their own. They range from international highway signs to the male and female pictograms identifying men's and women's toilets, and from the stylized wheelchair denoting handicapped facilities to the bold italic *i* used in Europe to signify an information center.

> *One solution to the question, "What language shall we put it in?" is to use widely understood symbols rather than words, since symbols form an international language of their own.*

The secret of successful symbol usage lies in clarity and familiarity; some symbols are self-explanatory, others need explanation. And it's not only foreigners who benefit from use of symbols: Well-designed pictograms may be easier to see in poor light, simpler to understand for those who have difficulty reading, and make a stronger impression than words on everyone. Which sign is more compelling and gets the point across faster, the one that reads "NO PARKING. VIOLATORS WILL BE TAGGED AND TOWED," or the one showing a P inside a slashed circle and a silhouette of a tow truck hauling away a car?

Other Written Communications

Some information is too detailed and complicated to put into symbols: It has to be written. Technology now provides an alternative to use of paper or notice boards. Consider this example from retail banking.

All automated teller machines (ATMs) require bank customers to undertake a series of steps to complete a transaction. At branches of Credit Suisse (and several other Swiss banks), the friendly, multilingual ATM is waiting to welcome customers. "GRUEZI" (a Swiss-German greeting) reads the screen, "BONJOUR, BUON GIORNO" (Good Day in French and Italian), "HELLO."

"PLEASE INSERT YOUR CARD" the ATM continues, in the same four languages. As the customer does so, an interesting thing happens. The machine switches to the customer's preferred choice of language for all further communication, up to the final "THANK YOU." How does it know? Simple. The relevant information is encoded on the card's magnetic stripe. When customers open an account with Credit Suisse, they are offered the chance to select one of four languages for use in ATMs and all computer-generated correspondence, including account statements. In addition, most forms, such as deposit slips, are printed in all four languages.

An alternative approach with electronic displays is to let the customer choose. At Heathrow Airport's Terminal 4, a touch-screen monitor offers a range of useful information to arriving passengers. The first step is to select one of 13 languages, each denoted by a flag. Americans, Australians, and Canadians must swallow hard and press the Union Jack, but in deference to other national susceptibilities, the screen alternates more than one flag each for Arabic and Chinese. Thereafter, the screen switches to your chosen language and provides detailed information on a variety of topics in response to touch-screen commands.

Many other creative possibilities exist for transmitting information to customers of several tongues. Package exteriors, instructional manuals, and survey questionnaires can be printed in several languages (Singapore Airlines uses five, including Japanese and Chinese, for in-flight questionnaires distributed to passengers). Computers can send information on command in any language the programmer desires; the great advantage of laser printers is that they can handle any script, from Chinese ideograms to the Devanagari script of Hindi.

But instructions translated from a primary source are only as good as the quality of the translation. I learned something interesting when I bought a Japanese VCR in Switzerland. The informational brochure came in 11 languages. "You speak English, don't you?" the salesman asked me in French. I nodded. "Good!" he continued (still in French). "I recommend you refer to the English instructions. That's the first translation made from the Japanese, and usually the best. All the other translations are derived from the English version."

One-Way Verbal Communications

If you have a smattering of another language and a pocket dictionary, you can often figure out the meaning of a piece of written information. But understanding the meaning of what somebody is saying in an announcement, presentation, or advertising message can be much more difficult, especially if he or she is talking quickly. Are there any alternatives to using an interpreter or having multilingual staff repeat the same remarks in several languages?

Technology can help solve the problem in various ways. On the intercity trains of the Swiss Federal Railways, standard announcements (such as "Ladies and Gentlemen, the train is arriving in Zurich...") are prerecorded and played to passengers at the appropriate time in three languages—the two most relevant official languages (depending on the train's route) and English. Many museums and historic sites offer rental cassette players in several languages to describe their exhibits; other machines will play a recorded message in the language of your choice when you push the relevant button (1 = English, 2 = Français, 3 = Español, 4 = 日本語 [Japanese] and so forth).

Video presentations can use subtitling, of course, but a better approach may be to offer two or more synchronized audio channels. Video has another advantage: It can portray sign language, such as Aslan, for the hard of hearing. Safety films on British Airways flights, for example, contain an inserted cameo of someone signing the spoken commentary.

Conversations

It's scary: You're traveling abroad and need assistance, but you know only a few words of the local language. You approach an official-looking person in a uniform and try to string a coherent sentence together. She doesn't get it. You try again and throw in a pantomime of sign language (it's not for nothing that I use the metaphor of service as theater). The good news this time is that she grasps your meaning. The bad news is that you cannot understand her reply. If you're fortunate, someone who speaks English overhears this painful dialogue and intervenes to save the day. If not, tough luck. The official shrugs and makes a "sorry, but..." grimace. You're left feeling helpless and perhaps somewhat humiliated.

Now reverse the situation: You're working in a position that brings you into contact with customers. Some fellow approaches you speaking hopelessly fractured English in a bizarre accent. All you can make out is the occasional word. He might have a Ph.D. for all you know, but he sounds like an idiot from a TV comedy show. You're busy. The phone is ringing and other customers are entering your office. How do you feel? How much time will you invest with this person before giving up with an apologetic smile and a "sorry, but..." grimace? You wish there was someone you could turn to, some way you could help, because it's the third time you've faced the problem this week.

There are certain jobs today which virtually demand a multilingual staff. These include any customer contact position that routinely serves either large numbers of international travelers or a resident non-English-speaking population. Some local businesses in the United States (notably small banks) have staked out profitable niche markets by serving immigrant populations in their own languages.

Does this mean that all front-stage staff have to speak two or more languages? Not necessarily. If service is provided by a team, then not everyone may need to be a language whiz; but within that team, there should be one or more employees on duty at any given time who can together handle the languages most commonly spoken by customers. On international flights, the cabin crew will usually include one or more flight attendants who speak the language of the destination or origin country (and perhaps several other tongues, too); these crew members can usually be identified by pins denoting which languages they speak.

What is an employee to do when foreign-language customers need assistance and nobody in the office can understand them? It could be an emergency. Sometimes, contingency planning can help. Do these customers have enough English to state the name of their native language? If not, showing them a display of flags may help establish their nationality. If other customers are present, a public request for help may yield a volunteer: "We have a gentleman here from Indonesia who needs assistance; is there anyone present who speaks his language and could interpret for us?" Another approach, when the array of requests for assistance is predictable, is to keep a supply of phrase cards or books in different languages. Customers can be asked to point to the relevant request in their own language (with the English translation beside it), and the staff member can respond by repeating the exercise the other way around.

Another approach is to use a telephone-based interpreter. Following the Vietnam War, nearly 65,000 refugees from Southeast Asia migrated to the area around San Jose, California. Language and cultural barriers were a problem for both new arrivals and local officials. So a San Jose police officer and an ex-Marine Corps interpreter devised a telephone-based interpretation service that put police officers in touch with a trained interpreter when they needed to converse with Vietnamese-speaking individuals. While providing this volunteer program, which worked extremely well, the two founders discovered that the San Jose area was also home to another 41 different language groups, all experiencing similar problems in communicating with police and other emergency service providers. This finding led them to create Communication and Language Line, Inc. (CALL) in 1984, with the goal of eliminating language as a barrier in any environment. Recognizing the potential of this service, AT&T acquired the company in 1989 and renamed it AT&T Language Line Services.

Telephone Conversations

If face-to-face conversations in another language are difficult, conversing by telephone is even worse if you're not fairly fluent in that language. Without a video screen, there's no chance of using facial expressions and hand gestures to convey meaning. And yet the telephone has become a vital business tool for delivering numerous supplementary services, from information to order taking to problem solving. What to do?

> *If face-to-face conversations in another language are difficult, conversing by telephone is even worse.*

Using multilingual staff is one approach that is widely used by international airlines, hotels, banks, and travel services. One step down is to train staff to recognize different languages, even if they do not speak them well, so that they may quickly transfer the call to a colleague who can assist the caller.

Another approach is to list different phone numbers for different languages. With increasing use of international toll-free numbers, I predict that more and more global firms will establish unilingual call centers in different countries, all linked to the company's main database. Customers and suppliers will be given specific numbers to call from anywhere in the world for their preferred language.

There are also good business opportunities for intermediary organizations to offer such services. Several international telecommunications firms are using their networks to link two callers who speak different languages with an interpreter in a third location through the medium of a conference call.

AT&T's Language Line services provide a good example. Users simply dial a toll-free number to "conference in" an interpreter on any call, whether local or international. It's a 24-hour, seven-day-a-week service employing highly trained interpreters who collectively speak more than 140 languages. The training includes familiarization with specialized terms that might be relevant to calls such as business discussions or medical emergencies. AT&T charges $3.50 a minute for the service, plus relevant long-distance rates, which can be charged to a credit card. Subscription service, at lower rates, is available to regular users, who include not only companies but also many local emergency service providers, such as police and hospitals.

If you need to place a call but don't speak the other party's language, you can request a Language Line interpreter before dialing. When the other party answers, the AT&T interpreter will introduce you and get the conversation started. A subscriber to this service who receives a call from someone speaking a different language can quickly conference in an interpreter. The Language Line operator can even help identify which language it is, if you're not sure.

Other services offered by Language Line include marketing research and operating a global telemarketing center on behalf of corporate customers. Multilingual agents can handle routine requests and inquiries, take orders, make sales calls, and qualify leads on behalf of the subscribing firm. Language Line also provides a wide array of written translation services. Other international telephone companies are beginning to offer similar services, but AT&T has maintained its lead.

Putting It All Together at Euro Disney

Euro Disney, located on almost 5000 acres of land some 20 miles east of Paris, is The Walt Disney Company's fourth and newest theme park. The complex, which was expected to attract 10 million visitors in its first year, opened in April 1992. For Disney officials, their new European venture represented even more of a challenge than their first foreign theme park, Tokyo Disneyland, which opened in Japan in 1983.

The French location had been selected over one in Spain because of its proximity to hundreds of millions of Europeans. It was a case of better access winning out over a better climate. Visitors were expected to come from all over Europe (and beyond). At any one time, there might be as many as 50,000 guests in the park. Unlike the California, Florida, or Tokyo park, no one nationality was expected to dominate at Euro Disney, so handling languages required careful planning.

The first decision—announced early in response to French concerns of "American cultural imperialism"—was that French would be the first official language at Euro Disney. However, almost all signage would be in both English and French (in addition to widespread use of international symbols), and knowledge of two or more languages would be an important criterion in hiring front-line employees (or "cast members," as Disney likes to call them).

Recruitment centers were set up not only in France, but also in London, Amsterdam, and Frankfurt. During the 1992 season, approximately two-thirds of those hired were French nationals; the balance comprised another 75 nationalities, principally British, Dutch, German, and Irish. Some knowledge of French is required of all employees; about 75 percent speak this language fluently, 75 percent speak English, roughly 25 percent speak Spanish, and 25 percent speak German.

Although Euro Disney retains the basic orientation of the other Disney theme parks, some adaptation has been made to European culture and languages. The popular "Pirates of the Caribbean" attraction, for instance, acknowledges that it wasn't only English-speaking pirates who enjoyed themselves attacking shipping and coastal ports in a jolly frenzy of looting, burning, and drinking, but also their equally colorful French and Dutch counterparts. So pirate songs are played in three languages. Similarly, "Sleeping Beauty's Castle" recognizes the European origins of the popular fairy story and is known instead as *Le Château de la Belle au Bois Dormant*. But "Main Street, USA" remains just that—it would hardly do to call it *Rue Principale, États-Unis*.

Many attractions and rides need little explanation, but guests can replace the French commentary in the "Visionarium" (a 360-degree film theater) by using audio receivers that offer a choice of English, Spanish, German, and Italian.

The reservations center caters to people of many tongues, with special phone lines for each of 12 different languages. The main information center in the park, "City Hall," is staffed by cast members who speak a broad cross section of languages. "But what if a guest speaks a language that nobody can understand?" I asked a Euro Disney official. "What happens if there's a medical emergency?" Special procedures, he told me, have been instituted at the park's medical center to handle such a possibility. With over 70 nationalities represented among its employees, there's a good chance that there's a cast member somewhere on site who can converse with that guest (or a companion). Euro Disney has noted the language capabilities of all employees, can access them by computer (who do we have on duty who speaks Turkish?), and can page them immediately by beeper or walkie-talkie. That's service!

> *Euro Disney has noted the language capabilities of all employees, can access them by computer (who do we have on duty who speaks Turkish?), and can page them immediately.*

Next Steps

If you're already serving customers in several languages, now may be a good time to review your practices and procedures. However, if the idea of working in another language is new to you, but you're interested in building market share among customers whose first language is not English, now is a good time to start thinking about how to proceed.

Several tools from this book may be helpful in beginning your analysis. One is flowcharting (see Chap. 10), which helps to identify all the contact points that a customer has with your organization when purchasing and using a particular product (remember that different flowcharts may be needed for different types of customers and products). Flowcharts also help identify backstage interactions between employees and suppliers where use of other languages may be helpful. The other analytical tool is the "flower of service" model (see Chap. 12), which categorizes all the supplementary service elements that are either included with, or might be added to, the core product.

As you create and review the flowcharts, ask yourself what information customers need at each point, and in what form communications might take place. Consider possible OTSUs (see Chap. 11), and ask yourself what might go wrong from the standpoint of miscommunication or failures to understand. Think, too, about possible exceptions and problems, and how customers can communicate their requests for special needs.

Then review the petals of the flower of service. Ask yourself what extra value might be created by offering customers additional languages for any specific supplementary service. How many customers would value such a facility? Would it create a product plus that competitors might find difficult to duplicate in the near term?

Conducting a Language Audit: Evaluating Existing Communications

If you're convinced that expanded language capabilities might create a competitive advantage for your firm (or remove a competitive disadvantage), then I recommend that you conduct a language audit to evaluate your current communication activities. At a minimum, this should address seven key questions.

1. *Is a unilingual approach turning off new prospects?* Think carefully about how new prospects first learn about your company and its services. Is it through advertising, brochures, signage, press stories, or word-of-mouth recommendations? If these are only in English, you (and they) may be missing out.

2. *What signage, written information, and electronic displays of information (if any) are currently available in other languages (and which languages are they?)* Answering this question requires that you undertake an inventory of information for all goods and services offered by your firm and

at all sites that it serves directly. If distributors or agents have prepared their own materials to describe your products, include these items, too.

3. *How good is the quality of each item of information in a foreign language?* Once the items have been identified, you're in a position to evaluate their quality against two criteria: their visual appearance and their content. Consistency of appearance—design, printing, paper or videoscreen format—may or may not be of great importance to your company, but ask yourself whether you would wish customers to see (say) handsome materials in English and (say) tacky-looking typewritten photocopies on cheap paper in their own language.

The second evaluation will require help from people who are native speakers of each of the languages in which your materials appear and who are also fluent in English. If an item has been translated from English, ask them how faithful it is to the original. Is it grammatically accurate? Does it read well, or does it sound stilted and clumsy? Are the idioms up to date and relevant to the population that will be reading it? If the item has been created specifically for a non-English-speaking population, you may wish to review an English translation to ensure that it portrays your company and its products in suitable fashion (no outrageous performance claims, for example).

4. *How easily understood by someone who is not a native English speaker are your English-language materials?* This evaluation might usefully apply to employee materials as well as to items intended for customers. Are your materials densely written, using long words and complicated sentence construction? If so, someone with limited command of English may find these items difficult to understand (in fact, even well-educated native English speakers may be turned off by technical jargon and lots of legalese).

5. *If you use symbols in signage or written materials, are they widely recognized and understood?* You can test this out through market research, asking customers and prospects, or seeking expert opinion. If the findings are negative, you will either need to redesign the symbols for greater clarity, choose new ones, or provide a key (in whatever languages are relevant) explaining their meaning.

6. *In what languages are personnel who answer incoming telephone calls to your organization able to respond?* This question needs to be asked in all offices that customers might call, at home and abroad. If they lack the necessary language capability, you will either have to hire and train new people with the necessary skills, upgrade existing employees' language skills, employ a telephone-based interpreter service, or create international call centers accessed by a toll-free number.

7. *Do you know what language skills each employee in your organization possesses?* You might be surprised at the result of this audit. Some people

are immigrants (or children of immigrants), some have lived abroad, and others have studied languages intensively. Be specific in your questioning—ask about level of capability separately for reading, writing, and speaking the language. Someone who can read a language well may not be able to speak it, and someone who speaks it fluently may have trouble writing a letter with grammatical accuracy. Ask about ability to speak dialects, too. If you intend to use these skills, you may wish to have them tested by an expert. Self-reports are not always accurate, but people whose knowledge is "rusty" from lack of use may respond quickly to an intensive refresher course.

The findings of this audit may also be applied to helping employees with limited skills in English. Some firms not only make a point of helping immigrant employees to learn English but also encourage supervisors to learn other languages (most commonly Spanish in the United States) to help improve internal communications and training. Another form of reaching out is to publish newsletters in languages other than English. At Boston's Beth Israel Hospital, for example, the weekly employee newsletter is published in English, Spanish, and French.

Using Expert Help

Conversing in fractured French or hesitant Hindi may score you brownie points—it shows you care enough to make the effort—but even if your (or a colleague's) command of another tongue is good, don't prepare important corporate communications in that language without expert assistance—or at least expert review.

Although I'm fairly fluent in French, I wouldn't send an important commercial letter in French without getting someone else to review it for grammar, style, and idiom—after all, I'm not ashamed to submit my English prose to my editor at McGraw-Hill. And I wouldn't even attempt to prepare a promotional brochure or technical manual in French. Writing for people in their own language requires that you think about style as well as syntax. In particular, you need to ensure that your idioms and metaphors are not only up to date but also appropriate for the products you offer and the target segments you want to reach. As any international advertising agency will tell you, direct translations are not always advisable when creating promotional materials.

When people who are not fluently bilingual attempt to write ads, notices, or news stories, the results are often laughable, as you can see for yourself sometimes when traveling. Unless your form of service theater is *Comedy Playhouse*, would you want your firm's messages in another language to make people roll their eyes and giggle?

And Finally, a Word About English

Earlier, I quoted Churchill's comment about Britain and America being divided by a common language. British and American use of English *are* different. It starts with the spelling reforms introduced in the United States by Noah Webster (such as *color* instead of *colour* and many, many more), continues through important differences in the meanings of apparently similar words (*subway*) and expressions (*to table a resolution* means to bring it up for discussion in the United Kingdom, to postpone indefinitely in the United States), detours through some grammatical variations, takes in parallel development of different words to describe the same object or activity (e.g., *elevator* and *lift*), and ends with a rich tapestry of idiomatic expressions and metaphors.

You may need to revise American materials for British customers—or vice versa—and even for Australians, Canadians, Indians, and other English speakers, who have their own subtle variants of the language. If you must write a single piece for worldwide use, beware of using terms that do not travel well, and watch out for sporting metaphors like "sticky wicket" and "striking out." Also, clarify currencies (which dollar? which pound? there are several of both), and remember that, except for Britain (which is halfway to full metrication), the United States is alone in the English-speaking world in continuing to use customary measures of weight, distance, and volume.

There are other traps, too. Avoid language that might be viewed as sexist or that might offend ethnic or religious sensibilities. Note that even within a single country there may be regional or dialectical variations in the use of words. Avoid unnecessary jargon and the use of legalese. If you must use technical terms that not all customers or prospects may understand, then define and explain them. In recent years, banks and insurance companies in the English-speaking world have undertaken one of the most substantial translation efforts in world history: transforming their agreements, policies, and terms of business from gobbledygook into plain English. Has your organization done the same?

> *In recent years, banks and insurance companies have undertaken one of the most substantial translation efforts in world history: transforming their agreements, policies, and terms of business from gobbledygook into plain English.*

Most of these observations apply with equal force to verbal presentations and conversations. Employees whose job entails constant contact with customers by phone should be given training in effective telephone techniques, voice control, avoidance of slang, and clarity of pronunciation.

In the past, firms which operated national telephone call centers tried to avoid using operators who spoke with regional accents (in America, Midwesterners were said to have the most neutral accents). When Federal Express was first experimenting with national call centers for its express package service in 1977, it conducted a test market in Newark, New Jersey, where customers dialing a local number would be linked not to their local stations but to operators at the company's head office in Memphis, Tennessee.

FedEx planners prepared for the test with painstaking care. Worried lest Newark customers be taken aback by the Southern accents of Memphis personnel (a problem described in internal memos as the "Ken ah hep ya syndrome"), executives circulated exhaustive lists of New Jersey town and street names and drilled the operators in proper pronunciation. They even changed the greeting from "Can I help you?" to "May I assist you?" Surveys after the test showed customers responding very favorably to what they sensed as a new aura of professionalism. Two-thirds of those surveyed had not even noticed the Southern accents.

There are two little morals to that story, which have nothing to do with accents. One is that, when competitive advantage is at stake, exceptional managers leave nothing to chance: They are willing to invest in technology, training, testing, and research to build a truly product plus service. The second is that one of the strongest value-creating elements in service delivery is creating a sense among your customers that they are dealing with dedicated professionals.

And that's not a bad note on which to end this chapter. Carefully examining language usage throughout your organization is a key step in developing product plus service in today's world. Wherever possible, put it in the customer's preferred language. It's the professional thing to do.

"We did everything when I was CEO—zero-based budgeting, TQM, employee stock options, reengineering....But no sooner had I introduced empowerment when the staff got the board to fire me!"

20 Sustaining the Human Side of the Enterprise

Despite advances in technology and self-service, many businesses still depend heavily on employees to serve customers directly or to work backstage in support of front-stage activities. This chapter provides some perspectives from organizations that are regarded as good places to work on how to recruit, manage, and motivate service employees, how to empower and enable them to use their own initiative, and how to help avoid burnout on the job. It also cites research findings on practices that lead to failure and those that lead to success for employees, customers, and the owners of service businesses.

All the technology in the world cannot disguise the fact that organizations mirror their people. The human side of the enterprise is what creates and sustains strategic vision, from the chief executive down to the most recently recruited customer contact employee.

According to Robert Levering and Milton Moskowitz, long-time researchers of the quality of work life, "most companies still offer dreadful work environments." The problem is that, all too often, such situations translate into dreadful service, with employees treating customers the way their managers treat them.

Old excuses—"you just can't find good people nowadays"—simply won't wash. A few years ago, experts in industrialized countries were worrying about the shortfall in skilled workers predicted for the future. Now the concern has shifted. Technological change, productivity improvements, and a shifting of jobs to lower-cost nations are leading to massive restructuring and "downsizing." How do we find work for all the talented employees who have been laid off?

Cycles of Failure and Success

As customers, most of our involvement with service employees is with low-level contact personnel, not managers. At the department store, you're served by sales clerks, not the chairman. Whom do you encounter at a fast-food restaurant? Not a vice president, that's for sure—more likely a teenage cashier. Call a professional firm, and you may have to go through a switchboard operator before you reach the busy man or woman you want to talk to (chances are, they're so busy that you'll have to leave a message with a secretary, anyway). When you visit your bank (if you still do), you probably deal with tellers, customer service reps, or loan officers most of the time. And you often have to be a VIP to get even a greeting from the general manager of a big hotel.

> *As customers, most of our involvement with service employees is with low-level contact personnel, not managers.*

Corporate customers may fare a little better in getting to deal with top brass, but the route to the executive offices still tends to be via parking lot attendants, security guards, receptionists, and executive assistants.

To the extent that our service experiences depend heavily on the performance of relatively junior front-stage personnel, it makes sense to think very carefully about how they are recruited, trained, and motivated. The reality is often discouraging—but not always.

The Cycle of Failure

In many service industries the search for productivity is on with a vengeance. One solution takes the form of simplifying work routines and hiring workers as cheaply as possible to perform repetitive work tasks that require little or no training. Leonard Schlesinger and James Heskett capture the potential implications of such a strategy in what they term the "cycle of failure." As depicted in Fig. 20-1, there are actually two concentric but interactive cycles: one involving failures with employees; the second, with customers. Both are enough to make you cry.

The employee cycle of failure begins with a narrow design of jobs to accommodate low skill levels, emphasis on rules rather than service, and use of technology to control quality. The design of fast-food kitchens has long been cited—both admiringly and despairingly—as an example of using technology to channel human behavior in a service setting (although, in fact, it's really a quasi-manufacturing operation). A strategy of low wages is accompanied by minimal effort on selection or training.

Consequences include bored employees who lack the ability to respond to customer problems, become dissatisfied, and develop a poor service attitude. Outcomes for the firm are low service quality and high employee turnover. Because of weak profit margins, the cycle repeats itself with hiring of more low-paid employees to work in this unrewarding atmosphere.

The customer cycle of failure begins with repeated emphasis on attracting new customers who, becoming dissatisfied with employee performance and the lack of continuity implicit in continually changing faces, fail to develop any loyalty to the supplier and turn over as rapidly as the staff, thus requiring an ongoing search for new customers to maintain sales volume. This churn of discontented customers is especially worrying in the light of what we now know about the greater profitability of a loyal customer base. For managers of conscience, the social implications of an enormous pool of "nomadic service employees moving from one low-paying employer to the next, experiencing a stream of personal failure with employers unwilling to invest in efforts to break the cycle" must surely be still more disturbing.

Even service organizations that are widely regarded as well managed continue to perpetuate the cycle. Schlesinger and Heskett report hearing a veritable litany of excuses and justifications:

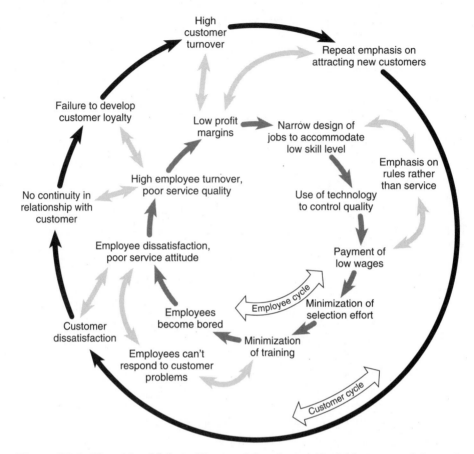

Figure 20-1. The cycle of failure. (*Reprinted from Leonard L. Schlesinger and James L. Heskett, "Breaking the Cycle of Failure in Services,"* Sloan Management Review, *Spring 1991, p. 18. Copyright 1991 by the Sloan Management Review Association. All rights reserved.*)

- "People just don't want to work today."
- "To get good people would cost too much and you can't pass on these cost increases to customers."
- "It's not worth training our front-line people when they leave you so quickly."
- "High turnover is simply an inevitable part of our business. You've got to learn to live with it."

What comes out of these comments most powerfully, I believe, is that too many managers make short-sighted assumptions about the financial implications of low-pay/high-turnover human resource strategies. Part of the problem, say Schlesinger and Heskett, is failure to measure all relevant costs. Left out of the equation are three key cost variables: the cost of constant recruiting, hiring, and training (which is as much a time cost for managers as a financial cost), the lower productivity of inexperienced new workers, and the costs of constantly attracting new customers (requiring extensive advertising and promotional discounts).

> *Too many managers make short-sighted assumptions about the financial implications of low-pay/high-turnover human resource strategies.*

Also ignored are two revenue variables: future revenue streams that might have continued for years but are lost when unhappy customers take their business elsewhere; and potential income from prospective customers who are turned off by negative word of mouth. Finally, Richard Whiteley adds two less easily quantifiable costs: disruptions to service while a job remains unfilled, and loss of the departing person's knowledge of the business (and its customers).

In a recessionary environment, employees may hold on to their jobs more tightly, but if they feel bored, powerless, and resentful about being exploited financially, they are unlikely to be highly productive or to provide good service.

The Cycle of Success

Some firms reject the assumptions underlying the cycle of failure. And they also take a longer-term view of financial performance. Schlesinger and Heskett cite service firms in a variety of industries that have prospered by investing in people to create a cycle of success (Fig. 20-2). Their examples come from banking (Wells Fargo and Fidelity Bank of Philadelphia), maintenance, food and janitorial services (ServiceMaster), and quick service restaurants (Au Bon Pain).

As with failure, success applies to both employees and customers. Broadened job designs are accompanied by training and empowerment practices that allow front-stage personnel to control quality. With more focused recruitment, more intensive training, and better wages, employees are likely to be happier in their work and to provide high-quality, customer-pleasing service. Regular customers also appreciate the continuity in service relationships resulting from lower turnover and so are more likely to

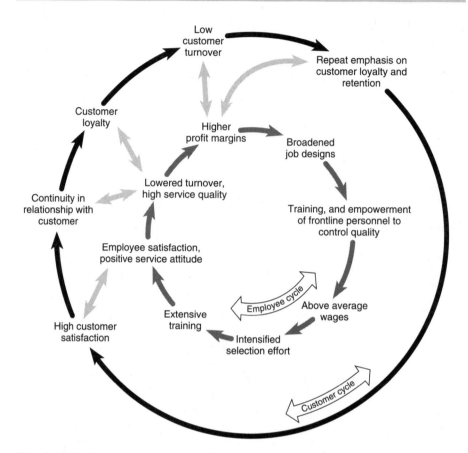

Figure 20-2. The cycle of success. (*Reprinted from Leonard L. Schlesinger and James L. Heskett, "Breaking the Cycle of Failure in Services,"* Sloan Management Review, Spring 1991, p. 20. Copyright 1991 by the Sloan Management Review Association. All rights reserved.)

remain loyal. Profit margins tend to be higher, and the organization is free to focus its marketing efforts on reinforcing customer loyalty. And remember: Customer retention strategies are usually much less costly to implement than strategies for attracting new customers.

Benjamin Schneider and other researchers have found strong correlations between employees' attitudes and perceptions of service quality among customers of the same organization. In a retail banking study, they found that customer intentions to switch to a competitor could be predicted, based on employee perceptions of the quality of service delivered. In short, frontstage employees are well aware of whether or not customers are getting the type of service needed to retain their business. The researchers also found that employee turnover probabilities were predictable, based on customer perceptions of service quality: Simply put, where customers reported high service quality, employees were less likely to leave. Another study found that higher levels of employee satisfaction were reflected not only in lower turnover but also in lower worker's compensation claims.

What Do Employees Want?

In 1991, the Gallup Poll surveyed working Americans about the importance of 16 characteristics of their work and how satisfied they were with each of these in their current jobs. Good health insurance and other benefits topped the list, being ranked as "very important" by 81 percent of respondents, followed by interesting work and job security, at 78 percent each, and then by opportunity to learn new skills (68 percent), having a week or more of vacation (66 percent), being able to work independently (64 percent), and recognition from coworkers (62 percent). Regular hours, having a job in which you can help others, and limiting job stress were rated very important by 58 percent. High income—whatever that may mean—was ranked eleventh at 56 percent, with flexible hours last at 49 percent.

More interesting, I think, are the differences between the percentage of respondents listing an item as very important and those saying they were satisfied with that item as it related to their own jobs. The highest gap, 54 percent, was found in health insurance and benefits (which is not entirely surprising in an American environment where so many workers lack adequate health coverage; a gap of this size would probably not be duplicated in countries that offer national health care and a better social safety net). Other large gaps are found in job security and high income (43 percent gap each), job stress (41 percent), recognition from coworkers (38 percent), interesting work and opportunity to learn new skills (37 percent each), and chances for promotion (a 33 percent gap).

When evaluating candidates for the second edition of their book, *The 100 Best Companies to Work for in America*, Robert Levering and Milton Moskowitz rated each firm on a five-point scale against six criteria:

- *Pay and Benefits* relative to other firms in that industry.

- *Opportunities* to learn new skills and to advance, with particular emphasis on training, promotion from within, and specific mechanisms for helping people to move up through the ranks.

- *Job security*, with an emphasis on "no-layoff" policies or, failing that, great sensitivity to employees during out placement.

- *Pride in their work and in the company*, including organization of work so that employees feel a direct connection with the firm's products and services, cite the positive social contribution of these products, and have good feelings about the company's role as a corporate citizen.

- *Openness and fairness*, as exemplified by accessibility of top executives, good two-way communications between employees and management, explicit grievance systems, and minimization of special perks for executives.

- *Camaraderie and friendliness*, including a sense of family, and enjoyment in working with other employees.

Against these criteria, Beth Israel Hospital, Federal Express, and Southwest Airlines were each ranked among the Top 10. If your own organization was not on the list of the "100 Best," how do you think employees would rate it against the six criteria above? And where do you think improvements would be most likely to lead to greater satisfaction with service among your customers?

Recruiting the Right People

There's no such thing as the perfect, universal employee. For starters, some jobs require prior qualifications, others offer employees the necessary training after they are hired. A nurse can apply for a job as a hotel receptionist, but the reverse is not true unless the applicant has nursing qualifications. Second, different positions—even within the same firm—are best filled by people with different styles and personalities. It helps to have an outgoing personality in many front-stage jobs that involve constantly meeting new customers; a shy, retiring person, by contrast, might be more comfortable working backstage and always dealing with the same people. Someone who loves to be physically on the go might do better as a restaurant server or courier than in a more sedentary job as a reservation agent or bank teller. Finally, as Levering and Moskowitz stress, "No company is perfect for everyone. This may be especially true in good places to work since these firms tend to have real character...their own culture. Companies with distinctive personalities tend to attract—and repel—certain types of individuals."

> *"No company is perfect for everyone....Companies with distinctive personalities tend to attract—and repel—certain types of individuals."*
>
> **ROBERT LEVERING AND MILTON MOSKOWITZ**

If a good personality match is important, even more so is a good fit between personal and corporate values. Says the Beth Israel Hospital's president, Dr. Mitchell T. Rabkin:

> One of the things that I look for when we're recruiting is whether people are willing to "join the village." We tend to get two kinds of response when recruiting physician-scientists at a fairly high level: those who show they appreciate the characteristics of our "village" and are willing to join it, and those who only talk about the resources he or she will require to do the job.
>
> Medicine is a very giving kind of profession. We want people who are going to be nurturing—it's tough to be sick, and when you are, you need some caring. There's a huge difference between looming large over the bed, looking at your watch, and saying "How ya doing today?" and sitting down nose to nose and asking how things have gone today. You may spend the same amount of time, but it's the difference between night and day.

The Recruitment Process at Southwest Airlines

"Work in a Place Where Elvis Has Been Spotted" reads the headline in the recruitment ad. Accompanying it is a picture of a grinning middle-aged man in a white Elvis suit, zipped open to the chest to show gold chains dangling from his neck. He's disco dancing on an airport concourse as startled travelers look on. Underneath the picture is printed the legend, "Herbert D. Kelleher, Chairman of the Board, President, and Chief Executive Officer, Southwest Airlines."

"...we're always looking for more fun-loving friendly people," continues the advertisement. "The qualifications? It helps to be outgoing, maybe a bit off-center. And be prepared to stay awhile. After all, we have the lowest employee turnover rate in the industry." And also the lowest level of passenger complaints to the U.S. Department of Transportation, plus the highest profits.

Ann Rhoades, vice president–people for Southwest Airlines, laughs as she looks at the framed copy of the 1990 advertisement hanging on the wall of her office. She says:

> We allow a great deal of flexibility at Southwest. We want our people to use their brains, their knowledge, and the wisdom they've acquired. We don't try to turn out cookie-cutter people: We hire them for their individual strengths.
>
> Recruitment ads like this are very appealing to the type of person we want, whereas they tend to turn off someone who feels it's ridiculous for

the chairman of the board to appear in public in an Elvis suit. That's great, as far as we're concerned, because people who want to work in a defined box won't be comfortable at Southwest Airlines.

With three aircraft painted as killer whales and a chief executive who appears in recruitment ads doing an Elvis act, Southwest Airlines is clearly not a very straitlaced organization. Certainly, it's serious about the things that really matter, such as safety, pleasing its passengers, making a profit, running an efficient operation, and taking good care of its people. But a sense of fun is never very far from the surface. In their book, Levering and Moskowitz noted not only how much fun employees seemed to have on the job, but also how hard everyone worked. "By some standards," they wrote, "Southwest has a workaholic culture."

As a company that has grown relentlessly, year after year, and sees ample opportunity for future growth ahead, Southwest can be somewhat confident about its no-layoff policy. At only 7.4 percent, the turnover rate among its 10,000-strong work force is very low. The company is 89 percent unionized, but the one area on which management will not negotiate is work rules. In sharp contrast to the "cycle of failure" approach to hiring, Southwest devotes enormous effort to recruiting, selecting, and training new employees, as well as to internal transfers and promotions. Although two-fifths of new staff members start in entry-level jobs paying only $6.05 an hour (in 1992), there's no shortage of applicants. However, the zany recruitment advertising and fun atmosphere that recruiters deliberately create for Southwest booths at job fairs does lead to some self-selection.

Any selection process begins not with the candidate but with the people responsible for recruiting. Before joining Southwest as VP–people, Ann Rhoades had worked in both the banking and car rental industries. Although her immediate past experience had been in human resources, she began her career in marketing, an orientation that strongly influences her approach today to managing the airline's People Department. "We purposely recruit from the marketing group," she declares. "Everyone we have hired for the People Department in the past three years has been hired from the marketing side. In order to continue the culture, we decided that we had to hire people who really, really thought about marketing to internal and external customers." (This definition can include individuals whose previous position ranged from director of advertising to flight attendant.)

Any selection process begins not with the candidate but with the people responsible for recruiting.

The People Department's marketing orientation includes internal research on job descriptions and selection criteria. "We ask our departments, 'What are you looking for?'" says Rhoades, "rather than telling them 'This is what we think you need.' After all, the experts in hiring ramp agents are ramp agents!" Southwest's recruitment process is also designed to help select candidates "who have the right attitude." Meaning? Basically, the airline wants to hire "people" people: "giving" people rather than "taking" ones; men and women who have a high degree of flexibility and initiative, and who also feel comfortable with a sense of humor and with themselves. Pilots are not hired solely on their technical qualifications; in fact, Southwest's hiring criteria tend to go against those found in other airlines. According to Rhoades:

> We don't want a hot-shot pilot who always feels he has to be in command. We want our pilots working as members of a team; ego gets in the way of that. Many airlines experience friction between pilots and mechanics. Here, we've succeeded in opening the lines of communication, so both sides make things easier for the other. It makes us better as a company.

Southwest's painstaking approach to interviewing continues to evolve in the light of experience; it's perhaps at its most innovative in the selection of flight attendants. A day-long visit to the company usually begins with applicants gathered in a group; recruiters watch how well they interact with each other (another chance for such observation will come at lunchtime). Since there are usually several job openings to be filled at once, it's possible that all (or none) of the applicants from any one group might be selected.

Then comes a series of personal interviews. Each candidate has three one-on-one "behavioral-type" interviews during the course of the day. Based on input from current employees and supervisors in a given job category, interviewers target eight to ten dimensions for each position. For a flight attendant, these might include a willingness to take initiative, compassion, flexibility, sensitivity to people, sincerity, a customer service orientation, and a predisposition to be a team player. The interviewers then create questions of a situational nature to examine these characteristics in each applicant.

The goal, as one interviewer explains, is to look at the applicant's past behaviors.

> A 20-year-old applicant for flight attendant won't have any previous experience in that job. So instead of asking: "What would you do if...?" which wouldn't be fair, we ask "What did you do when...?" The behavior is the issue, not the technical skills. So we ask about relevant experience at school, in part-time jobs, and with their families. Much the same is true for a mature woman returning to the workplace after bringing up a

family. Being a mother and housewife can often provide great experience
for working in a customer service position. By having them relive past
experiences—say, how they reacted to an emergency or a threatening
situation—we hear exactly what they did, we see the emotions, and so
it's not a textbook answer. More than just "what did you do?" we also
ask, "Why? What motivated you to do that?"

Adds another recruiter:

The ideal interview is a conversation. Our objective is to make candidates comfortable, so they'll open up to us more. They tend to be very
surprised that we don't ask the traditional job interview questions which
they've read about in some book called *Knock 'Em Dead Interviews!* the
first interview of the day tends to be a bit stiff, the second is more comfortable, and by the third they tell us a whole lot more. It's really hard to
fake it under those circumstances.

The three interviewers don't discuss candidates during the day but compare
notes afterwards, which reduces the risk of bias.

The People Department also invites participation in interviewing and
selection from supervisors and from the peers with whom successful candidates will be working. In this way, existing employees buy into the
recruitment process and feel a sense of responsibility for mentoring and
helping new recruits to succeed (rather than wondering, "who hired this
turkey?").

But perhaps the most unusual aspect of recruiting at Southwest is the
way in which the airline involves its customers in the selection process.
Frequent flyers are invited to participate in the initial interview process
and to tell prospective flight attendants what's important to them.

> **Southwest Airlines involves its customers in the selec-
> tion process. Frequent flyers tell prospective flight atten-
> dants what's important to them.**

The People Department admits to being slightly amazed at the enthusiasm with which customers have greeted this invitation. "When we started
this program," says Rhoades, "we wondered if these busy men and women
would want to take time out of their day to help us select flight attendants.
But they love the opportunity. We find they're very selective—usually
tougher than we are. They know what's important to them!"

Recruiting Service Workers for Technology-Based Jobs

It used to be thought that only manufacturing jobs could be exported. Today, however, technology allows both backstage and front-stage service jobs to be located around the world. American insurance companies, for instance, have recruited workers in Ireland to process claims; paperwork is flown in daily from the United States and digitized information transmitted from Ireland to mainframe computers on the other side of the Atlantic (because of the five-hour time difference, the Irish are using those mainframes at times when they would normally be underutilized).

Barbados, Jamaica, Singapore, India, and the Philippines are emerging as other potential English-speaking locations for telecommunicated services, not only for backstage work but also for such front-stage supplementary services as airline reservations and technical helplines. As we saw in the Hewlett-Packard example in Chap. 19, customers may be quite unaware of where the service person they are talking to is located. The key issue is that they deal with people who have the personal and technical skills—plus the enabling technological support—to provide high-quality service.

User-Friendly Software Creates Product Pluses All Around

Where productivity and customer service are concerned, innovations in hardware tend to capture more headlines than those in software. Yet many of the potential benefits of powerful computer systems can go unrealized if the software interface is not designed to be user-friendly.

Normally, it takes about three weeks to train a check-in agent for an international airline. Much of the training centers on correct use of the computer terminals employed to confirm (or make) reservations and assign seats. Perhaps you've wondered why some agents seem to be writing a novel as they clack away on their keyboards while you wait in line? Older reservations systems literally need to be programmed by the agents, who require a certain amount of technical skill to perform this task.

Recently, Singapore Airlines (SIA) was having trouble in recruiting and retaining check-in agents for its home base at Singapore's Changi Airport. With wages rising in this island nation, it was getting harder to recruit people with the necessary skills at the wages SIA was willing to offer. And once they were on the job, many agents found it rather unchallenging. The predictable result: relatively high turnover and constant repetition of the expensive recruitment and training process.

As part of a major program to update its departure control systems, SIA computer specialists worked to create new software for check-in procedures, featuring screen formats with pull-down windows, menu-driven commands, and other innovations on the video terminal displays—all designed to speed and simplify usage. The net result is that SIA has been able to lower the educational criteria for the check-in position. The job is now open to people who would not previously have qualified and who consider the work and the wages fairly attractive. Because the new system is so much easier to use, only one week's training is needed—a significant saving to SIA. Employee satisfaction with this job is up, and turnover is down. Finally, agents are able to process passengers faster, making the former more productive and the latter happier. How's that for product pluses all around?

Making better decisions is another area in which new software can help. *Expert systems* may affect both the skill levels required of employees for specific jobs and the level of performance achieved in those jobs. An expert system contains three elements: a knowledge base about a particular subject; an inference engine that mimics a human expert's reasoning in order to draw conclusions from facts and figures, solve problems, and answer questions; and a user interface that gathers information from—and gives it to—the person using the system. Like human experts, such systems can give customized advice and may accept and handle incomplete and uncertain data.

Expert systems can be used to leverage employees' skills to perform work that previously required higher qualifications, more extensive training, or simply years of experience. Some systems are designed to train novices by gradually enabling them to perform at higher levels. Rajendra Sisodia notes:

> Many expert systems capture and make available to all the scarce expertise of outstanding performers. American Express uses a well-known expert system called Authorizer's Assistant (originally called Laura's Brain, after a star authorizer), which contains the expertise of its best credit authorizers. It has improved the quality and speed of credit decisions dramatically, and contributed enormously to corporate profitability.

The Special Case of Employees Who Work by Phone

A growing number of customer contact employees work by telephone, never meeting customers face to face. As with other types of service work, these jobs can be very rewarding or they can place employees in what Barbara Garson has called "the electronic sweatshop." Recruiting people with the right skills and personalities, training them well, and giving them a decent working environment are some of the keys to success in this area.

BT, Firstdirect, Hewlett-Packard, and White Flower Farm are among numerous firms that are very dependent on recruiting and retaining employees who are good at telephone-based transactions with customers whom they never see. At BT, executives responsible for the telephone account management (TAM) operation described in Chap. 17 are highly selective in their recruitment efforts, seeking out bright, self-confident people who can be trained to listen carefully to the needs of business customers and use structured, probing questions to build a database of information on each account.

BT's initial recruitment interviews are conducted by phone, to see if candidates have the poise, maturity, and good speaking voice to project themselves well in a telephone-based job. Those who pass this screening go on to take written tests and are interviewed in person. The selection process concludes with psychometric scaling of each candidate.

> *BT's initial recruitment interviews are conducted by phone, to see if candidates have the poise, maturity, and good speaking voice to project themselves well in a telephone-based job.*

Successful candidates then go through intensive training. BT has built special training schools to create a consistent approach to customer care. Would-be account managers receive 13 weeks of training over a 12-month period, interspersed with live front-line experience back at their home bases. They must develop in-depth knowledge of all the services and customer-premises equipment that BT sells, as well as the skills needed to build relationships with customers and to understand their business needs. Modern telecommunications technology is bewildering, for so much is changing so rapidly. Customers need a trusted adviser to act as consultant and problem solver. And it is this role that BT's TAM program has succeeded in filling. Of course, for all the supporting technology, the program would fail without good people at the other end of the phone.

Empowerment of Employees and the Sociology of the Workplace

In recent years, the concept of empowering service workers has been advocated with almost religious fervor, often in the context of total quality management. From a humanistic standpoint, the notion of encouraging employ-ees to exercise initiative and discretion is an appealing one. Empowerment looks to the performer of the task to find solutions to service problems and to make appropriate decisions about customizing service delivery. It depends for its success on what is sometimes called *enablement*—giving workers the tools and resources they need to take on these new responsibil-ities.

Advocates claim that the empowerment approach is more likely to yield motivated employees and satisfied customers than the "production-line" alternative, in which management designs a relatively standardized system and expects workers to execute tasks within narrow guidelines. But is the choice between these two approaches really so obvious?

David Bowen and Edward Lawler suggest that different situations may require different solutions, declaring: "[B]oth the empowerment and pro-duction-line approaches have their advantages...and...each fits certain situ-ations. The key is to choose the management approach that best meets the needs of both employees and customers."

The payoffs from greater empowerment, they argue, must be set against increased costs for selection and training, higher labor costs, slower service as customer contact personnel devote more time to individual customers, and less consistency in service delivery. Bowen and Lawler also warn against being seduced into too great a focus on recovery, at the expense of service delivery reliability, noting that: "It is possible to confuse good ser-vice with inspiring stories about empowered employees excelling at the art of recovery."

"It is possible to confuse good service with inspiring stories about empowered employees excelling at the art of recovery."

DAVID BOWEN AND EDWARD LAWLER

Two Models of Organizational Design and Management

The production-line approach is based upon the well-established "control" model of organization design and management, with its clearly defined roles, top-down control systems, hierarchical pyramid structure, and assumption that management knows best.

Empowerment, by contrast, is based upon the "involvement" (or "com-mitment") model, which assumes that most employees can make good deci-sions—and produce good ideas for operating the business—if they are properly socialized, trained, and informed. It also assumes that employees can be internally motivated to perform effectively and that they are capable of self-control and self-direction. Although broad use of the term "empowerment" is relatively new, the underlying philosophy of employee involvement is not. For instance, the concept of participatory management known as the Scanlon Plan was created during the 1930s and subsequently adopted by a number of manufacturing firms. Its originator, Joseph Scanlon, was a steelworker and union leader who believed that within a given company, the employer, workers, and unions shared a common interest in its success.

In the control model, four key features are concentrated at the top of the organization:

1. Information about organizational performance (e.g., operating results and measures of competitive performance)

2. Rewards based on organizational performance (e.g., profit sharing and stock ownership)

3. Knowledge that enables employees to understand and contribute to organizational performance (e.g., problem-solving skills)

4. Power to make decisions that influence work procedures and organizational direction (e.g., through quality circles and self-managing teams)

In the involvement model, by contrast, these features are pushed down through the organization.

Levels of Employee Involvement

Bowen and Lawler argue that the empowerment and production-line approaches are at opposite ends of a spectrum that reflects increasing levels of employee involvement as "additional knowledge, information, power, and rewards are pushed down to the front line." Empowerment can take place at several levels.

- *Suggestion involvement* empowers employees to make recommendations through formalized programs, but their day-to-day work activities do not really change. McDonald's, often portrayed as an archetype of the production-line approach, listens closely to its front line; innovations ranging from Egg McMuffin to methods of wrapping burgers without leaving a thumbprint on the bun were invented by employees.

- *Job involvement* represents a dramatic opening up of job content. Jobs are redesigned to allow employees to use a wider array of skills. In complex service organizations such as airlines and hospitals, where individual employees cannot offer all facets of a service, job involvement is often accomplished through use of teams. To cope with the added demands accompanying this form of empowerment, employees require training and supervisors need to be reoriented from directing the group to facilitating its performance in supportive ways.

- *High involvement* gives even their lowest-level employees a sense of involvement in the total organization's performance. Information is shared. Employees develop skills in teamwork, problem solving, and business operations, and they participate in work-unit management decisions. There is profit sharing and employee ownership of stock in the business. As we saw in Chap. 9, Federal Express displays many such high-involvement elements, both front stage and backstage.

There's no such thing as a single best way to manage. Instead, say Bowen and Lawler, you should be evaluating the extent to which the following factors are present in your organization to determine how much empowerment is appropriate.

- Business strategy is based on competitive differentiation and on offering personalized, customized service.
- The approach to customers is based on extended relationships rather than on short-term transactions.
- The organization uses technologies that are complex and nonroutine in nature.
- The business environment is unpredictable, and surprises are to be expected.
- Existing managers are comfortable with letting employees work independently for the benefit of both the organization and its customers.
- Employees have a strong need to grow and deepen their skills in the work environment, are interested in working with others, and have good interpersonal and group process skills.

How would you rate your own organization on each of the factors above? And what strategic changes do you foresee in the future? Perhaps you believe that your firm needs to differentiate its goods and services more effectively from those of the competition, should increase customer value by offering more personalized service, and must focus on building extended relationships. Implementing such initiatives may require greater levels of empowerment for employees than presently exist.

However, Bowen and Lawler note that not all employees are necessarily eager to be empowered. Many employees do not seek personal growth within their jobs and would prefer to work to specific directions rather than having to use their own initiative.

Reworking the Sociology of the Workplace at Beth Israel Hospital

When people ask Beth Israel's president, Dr. Rabkin, "Do you still practice medicine?" he tells them:

> I was an internist and an endocrinologist. I still keep up with medicine, but what I practice is really psychiatry. In a sense, that's what management is: It deals with people, and with conflicts of goals, and with people's neuroticisms and strengths—each of which can either help or hinder them. And then there's the sociology of them all together. I think it's useful to look at it clinically, to the extent that you can, and think about the sociology of the workplace.

At Beth Israel (BI), managers are trying to rework the sociology of the workplace in ways that are appropriate to the complex environment of a caring hospital—rather than to introduce somebody else's formulation of "total quality management." As Laura Avakian, BI's vice president for human resources, points out, such a task cannot be accomplished through a quick fix. "You can't just tell employees: 'Congratulations, you're empowered!'" she declares. In fact, changing the sociology of the workplace is a slow process which takes years of constant effort. Moreover, it must reflect the culture and values of the institution itself.

In 1986, the BI began creating its own version of the Scanlon Plan, which it calls PREPARE/21 ("Prepare for the 21st Century"). The plan seeks to expand and deepen employee participation, improve quality, and find ways to cut costs. As a nonprofit, the hospital can't offer stock ownership, but employees do share 50 percent of all cost savings, referred to as "gains." The plan has been in full operation since October 1989.

PREPARE/21 includes formalized training, of course. However, much of management's task involves creating the right environment for employees. This, in turn, requires good measurement and communication systems. Says Rabkin:

> Deming [the quality pioneer] understood the importance of measuring in order to empower employees to know what was going on, thus allowing an employee to recognize before the boss that something was coming unstuck.

The BI has also focused on developing good internal communication systems, including an informal weekly newsletter that Dr. Rabkin writes himself. He remarks:

> Knowledge is empowering. When customers and visitors ask, the employees know what is going on and why. They feel they *are* the hospital, rather than answering "They don't tell me nothing!" If you don't tell

them, if they don't know, then distorted rumors start circulating. Worse yet, they feel excluded and not a true part of the hospital.

Employees, in general, are well motivated and want to do well. Furthermore, no one knows the job better than individual employees themselves. Therefore, if you create an environment in which they feel comfortable enough, knowledgeable enough, about the business to feel that they own the business in a sense, they will contribute—providing, of course, that their capacity to contribute is enhanced by a responsive upper structure of the organization.

Rabkin and Avakian are strong believers in the importance of enlightened managers who can coach employees in their use of quality tools and who can engage them in active problem solving. All Beth Israel supervisors participate in an intense 40-hour leadership development track.

One problem that top management has sought to address is that of uneven buy-in to PREPARE/21, particularly by physicians. However, these individuals are becoming more involved as they realize that the hospital's management is not assailing the quality of their care. Rabkin and Avakian note: "Physicians will buy in when we talk about improving quality of care through improving the quality of the *systems* by which they deliver care."

Although it may take time and effort to persuade existing employees to change their orientation and working habits, there's less of a problem with newcomers. In recruiting new employees, the hospital uses "value-based" interviewing, so that job applicants may be screened for participation and teamwork skills as well as for credentials.

Stress and Burnout

As the Gallup Poll indicated, a lot of employees are unhappy with the amount of stress in their jobs. We all know people who have burned out in a job. They have burned up the fuel that used to keep them going and are running on empty, mentally (and even physically) "out of gas." Sometimes, we're not surprised: Their jobs appear so burdensome, the pace so punishing, and their efforts so little appreciated; yet in other cases the jobs seem to be steady and not that demanding. But you may also know people who somehow remain fresh and happy in their jobs, year after year, despite the apparent pressures.

Burnout can be either an individual problem or a broad-based phenomenon in a dysfunctional company going through difficult times. Burned-out employees and managers are a problem in any organization, but especially in front-stage service positions, where customers may be quick to sense dispirited feelings or a lack of energy, focus, and caring. What can you do to prevent burnout, or cure it once it takes hold?

The insights of a physician-turned-chief executive are perhaps a good place to start. Says Dr. Rabkin:

> My view of burnout is that it has less to do with hard work and more to do with powerlessness. It can come from working hard and seeing things that are incongruous and inappropriate—and being utterly unable to do something about it. The first task in addressing and preventing burnout is to identify situations in which employees feel that way and to deal with those situations. You need to encourage people to voice their concerns and questions, their suggestions for change, and to give good answers.

"Burnout...can come from working hard and seeing things that are incongruous and inappropriate—and being utterly unable to do something about it."

MITCHELL T. RABKIN, M.D.

Rabkin's views highlight the need for a corporate-wide dialogue between management and employees, which may range from one-on-one discussions between employees and supervisors to formalized feedback mechanisms such as the Survey-Feedback-Action program at Federal Express.

Keeping People Challenged and Energized

Sometimes the problem of burnout is ascribed to people's staying too long in the same job. Southwest Airlines' Ann Rhoades believes that's an unwise generalization. "In every category, we have people who will probably be happy doing that job for the rest of their working lives and others who would like to move on. Actually, we still have 13 of the original 40 flight attendants who started with the airline in 1971!" Rhoades believes that providing ample opportunities to move internally within the company (subject to a one-year minimum in any position) is a way to keep people challenged and energized.

Having hands-on managers and supervisors who believe in MBWA ("management by wandering around") plays an important role in spotting employees who are unfulfilled in their present positions. Being short-tempered with customers (or other employees) is a common symptom, notes Rhoades, so supervisors encourage such employees to share their concerns and, where appropriate, to talk further with the People Department. "We want to keep good people within our company," she declares. "So we offer opportunities to move around and provide counseling and direction for people with career ambitions."

Like many strong service performers, Southwest has a commitment to promotion from within; 80 percent of movement within the company is internal. The airline offers a one-day course entitled, "Is Management for Me?" (which gives participants a good idea of what is entailed and helps reduce the risk of the Peter Principle: promoting people to their level of incompetence). Another course, "Career Directions," asks people to look into themselves and to figure out what their strengths and weaknesses are. "We need to invest time in helping employees develop better self-awareness," says Rhoades. She has found that a critical time for many front-stage employees comes after about five to six years in the job. Helping people to recognize what they like and dislike about a job and how these factors relate to their own situations may lead to a career change or development of more positive feelings about an existing job. "Many of our employees acquire a brand-new attitude after about seven years," declares Rhoades. "They realize: 'I'm OK' and they thrive."

Commenting on the positive changes they have seen in their years of studying employees and the workplace, Levering and Moskowitz include the rather surprising one of "more fun." They observe wisely that having more fun "is not inconsistent with operating a serious, profit-making business" and warn: "Watch out for companies where there is no sense of humor." After all, humor often provides a way of alleviating boredom and defusing—or even preempting—stress. Humor may also help to stimulate creativity and to build rapport with colleagues and customers.

> *"Fun is not inconsistent with operating a serious, profit-making business. Watch out for companies where there is no sense of humor."*
>
> **ROBERT LEVERING AND MILTON MOSKOWITZ**

Reducing the Risks of Emotional Stress

Burnout can also come from emotional stress on the job. Consider for a moment what it must be like to work in a hospital emergency unit (EU) as you listen to this young nurse, talking about a critically injured victim of a motor vehicle accident, who has been treated in the EU before being transferred to the intensive care unit—where he may or may not survive: "There are some [patients] that affect you more than others...like this person. You don't know his name, you don't know his family...but you just wonder if there is someone out there waiting for him to come home...As much as [the work] is task oriented, you can't take the human side out...You never get used to that part!"

With 15 years of experience as nurse-manager of the BI's emergency unit, Kathy Carr, R.N., has learned that there are ways to minimize the risk of emotional damage from such events:

> Burnout is not a word we use any more. The EU is one of the most stressful areas for a nurse to work in, but things change every minute. My staff leave here at the end of the worst day they could ever have and the next day it's totally different. That's a major factor.
>
> The set-up of the unit includes an acute [treatment] area, an intermediate area, and a triage position. We now offer our staff the opportunity to work in a different setting every day, depending on how they feel. When they come to work, they get to choose where they will work. The changeableness of the EU—and the ability to choose what you're going to do that day—both help.
>
> The third thing that helps [reduce stress] is that we emphasize opportunities to be involved in activities beyond direct patient care. It's very important to channel some of your hours at work into other professional activities. What made for burnout was no break from direct patient care, 40 hours a week, week in, week out. I saw a few years ago that staff who were interested and involved in unit projects complained less and were more satisfied with their work. Now, almost every nurse in the unit is involved in some work-related area of interest in the course of the week. There's a trauma committee, a victims of violence committee, a patient education group, quality assurance activities, and a group that's looking at peer review.

Leadership and Role Modeling

The need for leadership is not confined to chief executives or other top managers. Leadership traits are needed of everyone in a supervisory or managerial position. Federal Express believes this so strongly that it requires all employees interested in entering the ranks of first-line management to participate in its Leadership Evaluation and Awareness Process (LEAP).

LEAP's first step involves participation in an introductory, one-day class that familiarizes candidates with managerial responsibilities. About one candidate in five concludes at this point that "management is not for me." The next step is a three-to-six-month period during which the candidate's manager coaches him or her based on a series of leadership attributes identified by the company. A third step involves peer assessment by a number of the candidate's coworkers (selected by the manager). Finally, the candidate must present written and oral arguments regarding specific leadership scenarios to a group of managers trained in LEAP assessment; this panel compares its findings with those from the other sources above.

Federal Express continues its emphasis on leadership at every level through its "Survey Feedback Action" surveys, including the Leadership Index in which subordinates rate their managers along 10 dimensions (refer to Chap. 9, especially Table 9-1). Unfortunately, not every company is equally thorough in addressing the role of leadership among managers at all levels in the organization. In many firms, promotional decisions often appear totally haphazard or based on such criteria as duration of tenure in a previous position.

How One Chief Executive Sees His Role

While recognizing that leadership is needed at every level, the ultimate responsibility for shaping and maintaining the culture of the organization lies with its chief executive. To conclude this chapter, let's look at how Dr. Rabkin sees some of the key aspects of his job, in which he has long tenure.

> I've been President of Boston's Beth Israel Hospital for nearly 27 years now and have had a lot of time to begin learning the job. It evolves, of course, faster than my learning. My feeling about the role of chief executive officer is that of a role model and a source of information. I don't think that one can be so separate from a service organization that one's impact is made only in an intellectual way, or at a distance, and be effective.

What advice would Rabkin give to a newly appointed CEO who was moving to the organization from another company?

> Do a lot of listening without making any commitments. Listen to everybody, recognizing that you don't know the quality of the "facts " and "advice" that people are giving you. Try to examine as closely as you can—and as critically and as quickly as you can—the information system that will be telling you what is going on, so that you know what it is that you are measuring. Work hard to create an atmosphere where people are not afraid to speak their minds.
>
> You learn a lot from "management by wandering around," and you're also seen. When I visit another hospital and am given a tour by its CEO, I watch how that CEO interacts with other people, and what the body language is in each instance. It's very revealing. Even more, it's very important for role modeling. People learn to *do* as a result of the way they see you and others *behave.* An example from the Beth Israel that's now almost apocryphal—but is true—is the story of the bits of litter on the floor.

One of our trustees, the late Max Feldberg, head of the Zayre Corporation, asked me one time to take a walk around the hospital with him and inquired, "Why do you think there are so many pieces of paper scattered on the floor of this patient care unit?"

"Well, it's because people don't pick them up," I replied. He said, "Look, you're a scientist. We'll do an experiment. We'll walk down this floor and we'll pick up every other piece of paper. And then we'll go upstairs, there's another unit, same geography, statistically the same amount of paper, but we won't pick up anything."

So this 72-year-old man and I went picking up alternate bits of the litter on one floor and nothing on the other. When we came back 10 minutes later, virtually all the rest of the litter on the first floor had been removed and nothing, of course, had changed on the second.

And "Mr. Max" said to me, "You see, it's not because *people* don't pick them up, it's because *you* don't pick them up. If you're so fancy that you can't bend down and pick up a piece of paper, why should anybody else?"

I love that story of Dr. Rabkin's. It's a wonderful illustration of the power of role modeling. But role modeling is not just confined to chief executives. Every manager should be a role model to his or her peers and subordinates. All supervisors should be role models to those whose work they supervise. And experienced employees should be mentors and role models for new employees. The skills and behaviors that are taught in training sessions must be exemplified day-in and day-out on the job. Otherwise much of the effort put into careful recruitment will be wasted. And training will become just one more case of "Do as I say, not as I do."

21 The Strategic Route to Product Plus Management

Becoming and remaining a product plus organization cannot be accomplished through a series of tactical maneuvers. There has to be an overarching strategy. Although there's no sense in adopting strategic goals that are far beyond the reach of your firm's resources, don't set your sights too low, either: Be prepared to stretch your capabilities. Whatever your business, you'll need to think holistically. This means looking at the totality of customers' experiences and relationships through their eyes, understanding the full extent of service processes, and thinking systemically about the use of technology. Since product plus management involves creating value for customers, owners, employees, suppliers, and the broader community, particular attention will have to be directed toward integration of the marketing, operations, and human resource functions.

Selecting a Service Strategy

Straddling the Swiss–French border, about 80 miles east of Geneva, lies the international ski region known as Porte du Soleil (Gate of the Sun). It's made up of seven ski stations, two in Switzerland and five in France, which have banded together to consolidate trails, lifts, and ski tickets and thereby provide a wider choice of skiing possibilities. Their collaboration offers a nice example of the synergy that can result from a service partnership between potential competitors: in addition to stimulating demand, it also encourages more efficient use of the partners' lift and slope capacity. The region takes its name from a notch in the mountains through which the late afternoon sun sends a broad shaft of light into the Swiss valley below. As the sun settles toward the French horizon, the gate "shuts" and the beam is extinguished.

One day during my time in Switzerland, when I should probably have been working on this book, I decided to play hooky, hop a train, and go skiing at Porte du Soleil. Swiss Federal Railways also understands synergy: By selling discounted ski and rail packages, it promotes both its own services and those of ski stations served by train. From Lausanne, the train heads east along the shores of Lake Geneva, past Montreux and up the Rhone valley; viewed from the big picture windows, it's a wonderful ride. At the town of Aigle, I changed to a cog railway, a nineteenth-century technological breakthrough that revolutionized travel in the mountains.

Less than two hours after leaving Lausanne, the cog railway deposited me beside the cable station at Champéry. There I obtained a magnetically-encoded ski pass to insert into the turnstiles that control access to each lift. After a brief wait I was batched with another hundred-odd skiers into the giant cable car and whisked 2000 vertical feet toward the slopes.

Leaving the cable car station at the summit, I put on my skis and set off for Morzine in France, which I reached around lunchtime, following a series of ski descents down into the valleys and lift rides to the top of the next ridge above. After a sunny, outdoor lunch, priced in both Swiss and French francs, I skied the local trails and then took a lift up to the next ski resort, Avoriaz. This bizarre, artificial town, composed of tall apartment complexes whose wood-shingled exteriors are weathering to an ugly dark brown with age, is located above the treeline against a backdrop of rocky peaks. In the summer, to boost demand for accommodations when there are no skiers, the town hosts a horror movie festival. An inspired choice of venue, I thought to myself as I skied down the main street between its sinister, modernistic buildings.

After a couple more runs in France, it was time to head back to Switzerland. A chairlift up, a run downhill, another up, another down, one more chairlift and I stood on the frontier gazing into Switzerland toward

Les Dents du Midi, a dramatic, multisummitted mountain which looks like a row of particularly nasty teeth. A small notice advised that the border was patrolled and that people should carry identification, but no one was checking. My map showed red (intermediate) and black (expert) runs heading down toward Champéry. I decided to wait a moment, watching the other skiers, and then take the red.

Near me, a lad who looked to have a rather good opinion of himself was chatting with a group of young women. "Well, I'm off," he said to the girls in French. "See you at the bottom! *Ciao!*" And he pushed off across the gentle slope that lay between us and the beginning of the black piste, itself hidden from sight. Gathering speed, he shot over the edge; but as he disappeared, I heard a startled wail. "*Ooohh!*" he cried, "*Je vais mourir-r-r!*" (I'm going to die!).

His fear sounded genuine. Intrigued, I shuffled cautiously to the edge and looked down. There, between my ski tips, I could see a long and terrifying descent, with the added attraction of a little ice to increase the challenge on that particular day. (Later, I learned that this slope is one of the steepest in Europe.) There was a chalet far below me at the bottom of the slope, but of our young friend, no sign. Perhaps he made it down in one piece, perhaps not. In any case, I wasn't about to wait for the rescue helicopter (an important supplementary service for alpine skiers). Pushing myself carefully backwards, I headed off in search of something a little less scary, eventually making my way back to the base station, a couple of hours later, to conclude a memorable day.

Stretch and Leverage versus Fit

"Look before you leap" was surely the appropriate motto on this particular occasion. Thinking before acting is also sound practice when selecting a service strategy. As on the ski slopes, there are usually several alternative routes from which to choose. One "slope" may be just right for your company, while others may promise too little reward or appear too dangerous relative to your resources and skills. The terrain of business is constantly changing, and the economic weather is uncertain. Under such conditions it's easy to lose control, and a bad fall can put you out of business permanently. And yet, if you are realistic about your capabilities, plan ahead, and select slopes on which you know you can perform well, the rewards can be great.

As we saw from discussing quality management (Chap. 8), different strategies are appropriate for different companies, depending on their current level of performance: You don't send an organization with intermediate skills down an icy expert slope in competition with world-class competitors. Some of the players in your industry may be highly experienced and using the latest equipment: Do you really want to compete against them? On the other hand, even if your firm is still a relative novice in the field of service, do you want to remain that way? Gary Hamel and C. K. Prahalad warn companies against the temptation to scale down ambitions to match existing skills and resources. They claim that too often executives think of strategy as "fit" rather than "stretch" and "leverage."

> *Too often, executives think of strategy as "fit" rather than "stretch" and "leverage."*

I can relate this notion of "stretch" very well to my own skiing experience, especially in the company of people who are better at it than I ("Your dad doesn't like moguls much, does he?" remarked my nephew to his cousin as the two boys watched me struggle down a black slope that they had just zipped down with ease). Although I know I'll never be an expert skier, I do aspire to improve. Thanks to a combination of practice, mentoring, and better equipment, I'm still making progress.

Most companies, too, can upgrade their performance capabilities over time (and they have the added advantage of greater regenerative powers than the human body). Aspirations may be as important as immediate resources. Who would have anticipated a couple of decades ago, ask Hamel and Prahalad, that British Airways would triumph over Pan Am in the international airline market? "Only a dreamer," they declare, "could have predicted that [Pan Am] would be displaced by a competitor with far fewer resources—but far greater aspirations."

Given the right leadership, a firm's collective skills can be improved through training, selective hiring, creating strategic alliances, investing in new resources, and the learning that comes from exposure to increasingly challenging situations. But corporate performance represents more than just increasing the sum of all skills, it also reflects *leverage*—getting the most out of existing resources (and outsourcing those activities where the firm lacks the resources to excel). How well are your firm's available resources harnessed, integrated, and focused?

Expert skiers are in tip-top shape, physically very well coordinated (not my forte), and mentally focused on the task at hand. They are continually processing information, especially if the slope is an unfamiliar one—taking in the feel of the surface, how well their skis respond to each maneuver, the appearance of the next few yards of snow, and what the terrain looks like farther ahead, as well as keeping a watchful eye on how other skiers are performing. With practice, some of this activity becomes almost second nature, but it can never be taken for granted.

In all but one-person operations, leveraging personal skills requires that people work well together. Sporting metaphors of teamwork typically depict people working simultaneously, in close physical proximity. But teamwork may also imply working sequentially on different tasks in a service process. Team players may be working in the same facility (as in restaurant operations) or in geographically separated locations where informational networks offer conversational proximity (as in global financial services). Teamwork of a different nature is found among functional line managers working on planning and implementation of strategy.

Eliot Wadsworth II, owner of White Flower Farm, captured the psychological underpinnings of managerial teamwork when he described the "smart, experienced" people who filled the various specialized slots in his firm. His comments (from Chap. 13.) bear repeating: "We have a lot in common. We love what we're doing, we're all high energy, we like process and seasonality and plants. *We're metabolically in sync with one another*" [emphasis added]. With suitable adaptations to your own industry, can you say the same of the teams of which you are, yourself, a part?

Becoming and Remaining a Product Plus Organization

Some firms approach service tactically. Value for customers is improved by a short-term promotional price cut or provision of some service "extra" such as free drinks on a flight, a complimentary newspaper in a hotel, or gifts of coffee mugs and calendars for business customers. Training is ad hoc, with an emphasis on one-shot programs that don't seem to relate to each other. Meanwhile, investments in information technology are approached as a series of independent purchases and installations: a new laser printer here, a software upgrade there, new electronic cash registers here, a new PBX for the phone system there.

Strategy should drive tactics, not the other way around. Any one of these activities could represent a useful building block in a carefully prepared strategy, designed to take the firm another step along a chosen route that will enhance relevant competencies to compete in selected markets. But for this to happen, actions must be coordinated, take place in appropriate sequence, and be mutually reinforcing. They should also be designed to have a lasting effect. In looking to competitive advantage, product plus management is concerned with sustainable performance, not short-term gain.

Organizing Around Customer Processes

The strategic challenge of product plus management is to think holistically about service: about processes (which is why I emphasize flowcharting); about packaging core products with an array of supplementary service elements (hence the flower of service); about interlinked operational and delivery systems that combine both front-stage and backstage elements; about customer, supplier, distributor, and investor relationships as opposed to just transactions; about employee involvement instead of just job descriptions; and about organizations and alliances rather than functions and divisions.

> *The strategic challenge of product plus management is to think holistically about service.*

In this book, I've emphasized how important it is to understand the processes involved in delivering different types of core products (see especially Chap. 2). This understanding is vital when customers themselves are an integral part of a process, since any attempt to improve or reengineer that process will necessarily affect them. Customers are not mindless objects; unfortunately, user-hostile systems often treat them as though they were. When processes are redesigned without consulting customers, when no information is provided to explain a change, and when no assistance is offered to help customers adapt their behavior, then they may refuse to cooperate or head for the exits.

Many firms are unaware of the customer's overall experience—either because their organization is highly compartmentalized or because they have contracted out key process elements to intermediaries. James Brian Quinn advocates that firms should focus on their core intellectual and service competencies and outsource other activities. But he recognizes that, for all its advantages, outsourcing is not without risk. Quinn notes that "Loss of critical skills or developing the wrong skills for the future is perhaps the most often mentioned concern."

We need to draw a distinction between contracting out backstage processes and outsourcing front-stage activities. The latter strategy risks more than loss of consistency and lack of control. Even worse, it implies loss of knowledge about the customer's total experience and missed opportunities to learn how certain petals of the flower of service are evolving. It would be ironic if improvements in productivity and operational expertise came at the expense of a loss of customer focus and perspective. I believe that a firm's decisions on whether or not to outsource front-stage service elements should center on the quality and value of services provided to customers and the firm's own ability to remain close to its customers. The best alliances in outsourcing are those where both parties educate each other, share information, and work to provide customers with seamless service. Anything less is like grafting dandelion petals on a rose.

The Service Mosaic

Customers see a firm's activities in a very different way than do the people who work in the business. As we saw in Chap. 7, customers experience service much as an audience does a play. They are exposed only to what takes place "front stage"; under normal circumstances, they never go backstage. Sometimes—especially in possession-processing and information-based services—all that customers see is the tip of the operational iceberg. Jan Carlzon, chief executive of SAS, coined the phrase "moments of truth" to dramatize the importance of each interaction between the firm and its customers.

Other things that influence customer perceptions can come from off-stage contacts, ranging from random exposure to the firm's buildings and vehicles to chance encounters with uniformed service personnel; customers can also be strongly influenced by word-of-mouth comments from friends and acquaintances. In Chap. 1, we saw that such messages can sometimes be powerfully negative. (Like Southwest Airlines, you have to hope that unkind stories are directed against your competitors, not your own business!)

One of the most overused and ill-defined words in marketing is "image." I like to think of it as the sum total of everything that a customer knows about your organization. In some graphic media, images are composed of a series of small applications: the little tiles that make up a large mosaic, the small dabs of paint used by the neo-impressionists (a technique known as pointillism), the stitches of colored thread that create embroidery, or the thousands of dots comprised in a screen-printed photograph.

In Fig. 21-1 (which is derived from concepts introduced in Chap. 7, "Service as an Art Form"), I've used the analogy of a mosaic to depict how customers build up images of service businesses and their designated intermediaries. The tiles comprise a wide array of elements: facilities, equipment, service people, bills, other customers, advertisements—you name it. New customers will, of course, have a much less complete picture, but their little gray cells will still try to puzzle out the image and make sense of it (unfortunately, it's easy to misperceive reality under such circumstances).

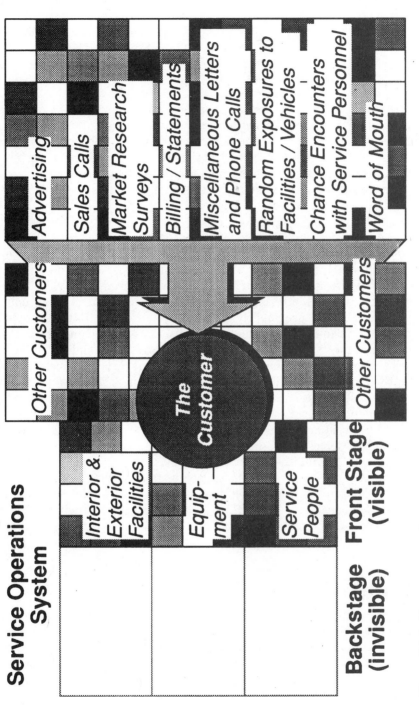

Service Operations System

Service Delivery System

Other Contact Points

- Advertising
- Sales Calls
- Market Research Surveys
- Billing / Statements
- Miscellaneous Letters and Phone Calls
- Random Exposures to Facilities / Vehicles
- Chance Encounters with Service Personnel
- Word of Mouth

Other Customers

The Customer

Other Customers

Interior & Exterior Facilities

Equip-ment

Service People

Front Stage (visible)

Backstage (invisible)

Figure 21-1. The service mosaic.

Creating a mosaic requires the artist to think carefully about how he or she wants the completed image to appear. Usually, detailed sketches are drawn in advance, and tiles are then matched to the colors in these sketches. Each tile must be carefully selected and positioned in order to contribute to the desired, overall impression.

How has your company approached the design of its own service mosaic(s)? Do you even know how customers see you? Does the sum of the impressions that your customers receive result in a "buzzing, blooming confusion" in their minds? Or do all the tiles fit nicely together, each contributing to the overall image in a harmonious and pleasing manner?

Service firms face a challenge in that their products are often intangible. So attention must be drawn instead to the front-stage delivery system. An outward impression of harmony can be created by corporate design, applying a distinctive logo and color scheme to such elements as vehicles, retail signage, building interiors and exteriors, office letterhead, and employee uniforms. Federal Express's vans, aircraft, offices, and drop-off boxes are instantly recognizable by their striking purple, red, and white colors and the rather unusual lettering used for the company's name (their employees are smartly, but more soberly, dressed in dark blue). BayBank appears to be a bigger bank than it really is because its eye-catching green and blue signage draws attention to its branches and freestanding ATM kiosks. Major car rental companies are easily identified by a single color—whom do you think of if I say "yellow" or "red"? However, while good packaging is a positive asset, it doesn't help much if the "contents" are no good.

Although I've used the mosaic in Fig. 21-1 to emphasize the perspective of external customers, there's no reason why you can't use the same basic approach to depict the views of internal customers, too. What's it like to be an employee playing the role of an internal customer in one or other of your various internal supply chains? In each instance, where is the "stage," who are the "actors," and how well does the "play" meet the needs of specific internal audience members? How new employees see their work environment may be particularly revealing, because their impressions are still fresh.

Creating Value

Just as "quality" was the buzzword of the late 1980s and early 1990s, so "value" is becoming the new watchword. It's often the supplementary services that enable customers to draw full value from a core product. This has important competitive implications. As Sandra Vandermerwe puts it: "The market power is in the services, because the value is in the results."

Discussions of value are usually presented from the perspective of trading off benefits against price. In this book—notably in Chap. 5—I've argued that you need to go farther.

1. *Include all benefit-creating activities.* The benefits that customers derive from dealing with your company need to be viewed from the perspective of "all actions and reactions" that they see themselves purchasing. In other words, the core product plus all the supplementary services (refer to Chaps. 3 and 12).

2. *Consider all costs incurred by customers.* In factoring the cost side of the equation into strategy, you have to consider more than just the monetary price you're going to charge customers. Instead, you've got to determine the totality of costs that they incur in buying and using the goods and services that you offer. You may not be stealing your customers' money, but are you stealing their time and their physical and mental energy? If research shows that the answer to any facet of this question is "yes," then creating better value may lie—at least in part—in reducing these other costs.

Any strategy aimed at reducing your customers' costs must include looking at opportunities to save them time. You should also consider how to reduce the physical effort involved in purchasing and using your products. Similarly, you'll need to think about minimizing the psychic costs—unwelcome mental effort and even stress—experienced by your customers in dealing with your products, your company and your designated intermediaries. Finally, you must try to reduce exposure to discomforting sensory experiences: Excessive noise and vibrations; unpleasant sights, smells, and tastes; or uncomfortable temperatures, humidity, drafts, and other tactile sensations. You ignore these nonfinancial costs at your peril.

3. *Consider how to improve value in other relationships.* There's more to creating a product plus organization than simply working on strategies to improve value for customers. You have to ask continually how to inject more value into the relationships that your firm also has with its employees, intermediaries, suppliers, owners, and the broader community. Even if it isn't possible to improve value simultaneously on all fronts, each action taken to increase value in one area must also be evaluated relative to its long-term implications for the others.

You have to ask continually how to inject more value into the relationships that your firm has with its employees, intermediaries, suppliers, owners, and the broader community.

The Service Management Trinity

In a service-driven company or nonprofit institution, three management functions play a central role in creating value: marketing, operations, and human resources. The customer should always be their primary focus—after all, serving customers is the reason that the firm is in business, but improving productivity and nurturing employees cannot be neglected.

Many firms now recognize what a few have always known: that nurturing the skills and motivation of their people can create a major source of competitive advantage—not least when there is a high degree of contact between employees and customers. It's probably harder to duplicate these human assets than any other corporate resource.

To the extent that employees understand and support the goals of your organization, have the skills needed to succeed in performing their jobs, work well together in teams, recognize the importance of ensuring customer satisfaction, and have the authority and self-confidence to use their own initiative in problem solving, the marketing and operational functions should actually be much easier to manage.

A growing number of progressive firms have upended the traditional organizational pyramid, in which a hierarchy of managers tells workers what to do. In the new, inverted pyramid, customers are on top, served by front-stage employees who are, in turn, supported and served by managers. However, changing traditional organizational perspectives doesn't come easily to managers who have been comfortable with established approaches. The problem is that managers sometimes become obsessed with their own function, forgetting that all functions must pull together to create a product plus organization.

Achieving the necessary coordination and synergy requires that you establish clear imperatives for each function. Each imperative should relate to customers and define how the function in question contributes to the overall mission. Figure 21-2 captures the spirit of both integration and customer focus. Of course, you'll need to create imperatives that are specific to your own business, but we can express the three imperatives generically as follows:

The Marketing Imperative. Your firm will target specific types of customers whom it is well equipped to serve, and then create ongoing relationships with them by delivering a carefully defined product package of "all actions and reactions" that they perceive they are purchasing. Customers will recognize this package as being one of consistent quality that delivers solutions to their needs and offers superior value to competing alternatives.

The Operations Imperative. To create and deliver the specified service package to targeted customers, your firm will select those operational tech-

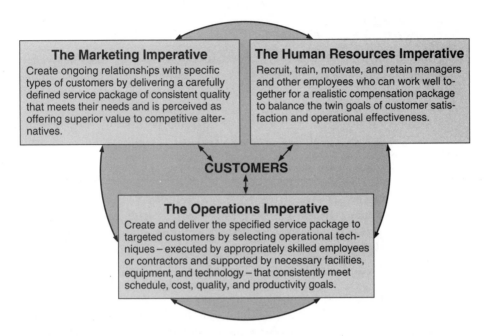

Figure 21-2. Integrating three functional imperatives.

niques that allow it to consistently meet customer-driven cost, schedule, and quality goals, and also enable the business to enhance its margins through continuing improvements in productivity. The chosen operational methods will be ones that match the skill levels of your employees or contractors. Your firm will have the resources not only to support these operations with the necessary facilities, equipment, and technology, but also to avoid negative impacts on employees and the broader community.

The Human Resources Imperative.   Your firm will recruit, train, and motivate managers, supervisors, and employees who can work well together for a realistic compensation package to balance the twin goals of customer satisfaction and operational effectiveness. They will want to stay with your firm because they value their working environment, appreciate the opportunities that it presents, and take pride in the goods and services that they help to produce.

Part of the challenge of service management is to ensure that each of these three functional imperatives is compatible with the others and that all are mutually reinforcing.

Giving Managers a
Multifunctional Perspective

As firms become more customer- and market-driven, the need for cross-functional coordination increases. But so, too, do the risks of conflict among marketing, operations, and human resource managers. Top management's task is to harness the energy of managers who have been used to working in different departments, rather than letting those energies be dissipated in internal disputes or permitting one department to dominate (and thereby frustrate) the others.

> *Top management's task is to harness the energy of managers who have been used to working in different departments, rather than letting those energies be dissipated in internal disputes.*

There are a variety of ways in which your firm can build new bridges to link the functions more closely (or expand and strengthen existing links). These approaches include:

- *Transferring managers* across functional areas.

- *Creating cross-functional teams*, ranging from strategic task forces to quality action teams.

- *Cross-training employees* to perform a broader variety of tasks.

- *Creating brand management organizations* to plan and coordinate the design and delivery of all front-stage elements for a particular product (examples include the brand management teams that British Airways creates to plan and monitor each of its different classes of service or the executive operating committees that manage individual hotel units in many chains).

- *Delegating authority to individual units*, transforming them from cost centers into profit centers, and empowering managers and employees to take greater responsibility for both revenue-generating activities and spending decisions, including hiring and salaries. As a result of this process, people who were formerly operations managers find themselves transformed into general managers.

- *Instituting gain-sharing programs* that allow employees to share in improved profits (or in cost savings achieved at a nonprofit organization). The most significant form of sharing in the fortunes of the business comes through employee stock-ownership programs (ESOPs), especially when participation is broadly based and employees own a substantial share of the equity.

Functional managers who fight for turf, territorial disputes between geographic units, and divisions that see nothing wrong in maximizing their own performance at the expense of others are unhealthy signs. Such compartmentalization is totally at odds with the compatible goals and strategic synergy inherent in product plus management.

The Change-Oriented Organization

Change is part of the culture in an innovative organization, facilitating the ongoing search to do things in new and better ways. It's easiest to create and nurture such a culture in a relatively new organization that began life with the intent of doing things differently, owes its ongoing success to continuing that philosophy, and actively encourages employees to use their initiative. More difficult is changing the orientation of an established organization that has been performing reasonably well, doesn't face any immediate threat to its existence, and subscribes to the "if it ain't broke, don't fix it" philosophy.

Change as Part of the Culture

Southwest Airlines, Federal Express, Hewlett-Packard, and BayBank exemplify companies that continually evolve in anticipation of changing environments. Although the corporate cultures of these four organizations are in many respects very different, each shares a willingness to accept change and embrace new opportunities.

Southwest has always been an innovator, delighting in taking an often contrarian approach to operations, marketing, and human resource management. Continued entry into new geographic markets presents an ongoing series of new challenges. So, too, does the task of holding on to—and increasing—its share of existing markets. Helping the company to remain fresh and responsive to change is the open and flexible culture of its people, sometimes manifested in a refusal to take themselves too seriously.

FedEx, too, has been an innovator from birth. It's driven by a desire to grow and excel in the very competitive market that its chairman, Fred Smith, originally created, and also by its intent to shape and exploit the use of technology in global logistics. It's a company that has always sought to stretch its people by exposing them to new challenges, including those associated with quality improvement, as described in Chap. 9.

Innovation and high technology would seem to go hand in hand. But in a world where major computer manufacturers have been going through wrenching changes, Hewlett-Packard has been more nimble than most. It has been reinventing its own organization as it seeks to anticipate technological change and global competition, while continually developing new products and services for its customers.

BayBank, by contrast, lacks the innovative origins of the other three companies. Twenty years ago it was just a holding company for a loose grouping of nine stodgy little banks. Under the leadership of its longtime chairman, William Crozier, it has taken advantage of changing bank regulations, evolving customer needs, and rapid technological advances to forge a unified banking organization that welcomes change and capitalizes on it.

Rabkin's Theory of Institutional Rust

At Beth Israel Hospital, its president, Dr. Rabkin, uses a physical metaphor, which he calls "institutional rust," to describe processes that have ceased to be optimal. "Institutions," he argues, "are like steel beams—they tend to rust. What was once smooth and shiny and nice tends to become rusty."

"Institutions are like steel beams—they tend to rust. What was once smooth and shiny and nice tends to become rusty."

MITCHELL T. RABKIN, M.D.

There are two main reasons, he suggests:

First, the external world changes. For example, our system for inpatient admitting was geared to patients who would arrive at 1:00 p.m. on, say, Monday in advance of an operation scheduled for the following day. They were in no rush. Then, pressure from third-party payers to minimize overnight stays led us to have the patient arriving early on Tuesday for surgery that same morning. The world had changed completely from the perspective of our admitting system...[which] had "rusted" as far as same-day surgical admissions were concerned.

Changes in competitive activity, technology, and customer needs are among the other environmental factors that could cause such rusting. Rabkin continues:

> Second, there's a natural deterioration of messages over time. It's a bit like the child's game of whispering in the next person's ear around the table. One day, for instance, I was in the EU, chatting with a house officer [physician] who was treating a patient with asthma. He was giving her medication through an intravenous drip. I looked at the formula for the medication and asked him, "Why are you using this particular cocktail?" "Oh," he replied, "that's hospital policy." Since I was certain that there was no such policy, I decided to investigate.
>
> What had happened went something like this. A few months earlier, Resident [physician] A says to Intern B, who is observing her treat a patient: "This is what I use for asthma." On the next month's rotation, Intern B says to new Resident C: "This is what Dr. A uses for asthma." The following month, Resident C says to Intern D, "This is what we use for asthma." And finally, within another month, Intern D is telling Resident E, "It's hospital policy to use this medication."
>
> As a result of conversations like these, well-intentioned but unofficial standards keep cropping up. It's a particular problem in a place like this, which isn't burdened by an inhuman policy manual where you must look up the policy for everything you do. We prefer to rely on people's intelligence and judgment and limit written policies to overall, more general issues. One always has to be aware of the growth of institutional rust and to be clear about what is being done and why it is being done.

What these comments imply is the need for continued reviews of institutional processes to search for those telltale signs of rust. It's curious how many service organizations have elaborate procedures to monitor equipment for any sign of problems and for performing preventive maintenance, and yet they fail to monitor service processes in similar fashion.

Many service organizations have elaborate procedures to monitor equipment for any sign of problems, yet they fail to monitor service processes in similar fashion.

Culturally, it can be difficult to challenge an established process that seems to be working. However, investigation will often reveal that performance would be improved if the process were revamped or even replaced altogether. The question then becomes, do we scour off the rust or do we scrap the beams altogether and build a new structure? In an environment of change, the latter route is often to be preferred. In a related analogy,

Michael Hammer, an expert on reengineering, argues against what he calls "paving the cow paths."

Remaking an Obsolete Culture

Somewhere, there's a giant junkyard for defunct organizations that either failed to adapt to changing times or grossly overestimated their capabilities. Many once-famous manufacturers can be found there, but lately it has been filling up with service firms. Recent arrivals include several well-known airlines and an almost unbelievable number of American banks and financial institutions.

Government corporations and firms in regulated industries were formerly protected from the risk of going to this junkyard. Job security and lack of concern about the market created a civil service culture in which putting oneself out for the customer and worrying about competition (if there was any) were not accorded high priority. Privatization and/or sweeping revisions in regulatory policy dramatically changed the environment of corporations such as BT and British Airways (just as court-ordered divestiture changed it for AT&T). Their success in remaking themselves shows that major cultural change programs, combined with massive reorganizations, can transform even the stodgiest of companies into innovative, market-driven firms. However, such programs may require years of repeated effort before they bear fruit.

Firstdirect offers an example of a new culture developing alongside—rather than within—that of a very traditional parent (Midland Bank). Given sufficient independence, Firstdirect's management has been free to create a culture that supports its new, telephone-based approach to retail banking. If this new culture is shown to be a powerful factor in marketplace success, then we may see it transfuse to the parent.

The Strategic Role of Information Technology

The impact of information technology (IT) has come up again and again in this book. Although I've cited a number of companies that have gained competitive advantage from information technology—including Federal Express, BayBank, Firstdirect, and McKesson—no single investment is likely to confer sustainable advantage for long. John Cecil and Michael Goldstein note two key reasons why IT by itself fails to deliver a sustainable competitive edge.

First, except for proprietary application systems, most technologies are freely available from vendors to all companies in an industry. Second, many advantages derived from applications expertise are soon ironed out as laggards turn to consultants to help them catch up and then contrive to hire away from competitors those employees who possess the necessary expertise.

The key question for any senior manager is whether IT is simply a tool or whether it's an integral part of strategy. Companies that view it in the latter way are more likely to gain enduring strategic advantages as opposed to quickly copied tactical advantages. Among other things, a strategic perspective leads to creation of interlinked systems rather than independent applications. Paul Cragg and Paul Finlay note that management of IT linkages can provide competitive advantage simply because rivals cannot easily see them.

> *The key question for any senior manager is whether IT is simply a tool or whether it's an integral part of strategy.*

Technology Transfer

Depending on their cultures and past experiences, some organizations are more comfortable than others with installation of new technology. Consider the views of Federal Express's former chief information officer, Dr. Ron Ponder. Speaking in 1990, Ponder observed that FedEx had a sharply different view of technology from most companies.

> Technology transfer—or being able to absorb new technology—is a cultural thing that we've built in here. One of the keys to our success is that we constantly embrace new technology. For most companies, that's very painful and they don't like it. It's painful to leave what works and is cheap for new, expensive, unknown approaches. So they don't do it. At Federal, we would rather get an innovation a year earlier and develop back-up systems to counter a relatively high failure rate than to wait until the failure rate—and the price—have been reduced to more "acceptable" levels. Most folks prefer to wait until a technology matures.
>
> You can view technology as a wave in the ocean, washing in debris. Most people concentrate on the debris that floats in. "Oh, isn't this neat!" they'll say of some device. "Where can I use it?" And that's where I think they mess up. I view technology as the wave itself, not the individual things that are brought to shore. We knew what we wanted to do 10 years ago, but the technology wasn't there. So we were waiting on the wave, and constantly prodding manufacturers to create what we needed as that wave rolled in.

This approach to technology not only gives Federal Express a first-mover advantage, it extends the duration of that advantage, since the company is willing to use innovations long before they have reached the level of reliability required by more risk-averse competitors. It also ensures that new hardware and software is customized to FedEx's own needs, rather than making compromises designed to please a broader market of adopters. Finally, the cultural acceptance of technological change within the company means that new applications can be adopted with greater speed and less disruption.

A Final Word About Strategy

I'd like to conclude with a fable that contains an important moral for strategists. It concerns an owl, a hippopotamus, and a butterfly, who all lived in the jungle. As the hippo was bathing happily in the mud one day, a butterfly came flying toward him and settled on his nose. The hippo looked wonderingly at the lovely creature, which soon spread its wings and fluttered off. In those few, brief moments, the hippo's heart was smitten. The butterfly reappeared at regular intervals, and each time it did, the hippo's heart gave a great bound. He would chase it playfully, his heart yearning for a meaningful relationship, but the butterfly always flew away again.

Discouraged by his lack of progress, the hippo decided to seek advice from the jungle consultant, the wise old owl. Finding the hollow tree where the owl lived, the hippo banged on the trunk and woke up the owl, who opened one eye and looked out sleepily. "Owl," said the hippopotamus, "I've got a problem and I need your advice." "Tell me what's up," responded the owl.

"I'm in love with a butterfly," said the hippo, "but I'm not making any progress with my suit. What should I do?" The owl opened both eyes wide in surprise. "I'll need to think about this for a moment," he said, and shut both eyes tight. Finally, the owl opened his eyes again. "It's obvious what you should do," he began, "Yes?" responded the hippo eagerly. "Yes—perfectly obvious. You must turn yourself into a butterfly! That will solve your problem!" And with this pronouncement, the owl disappeared back inside his tree hole.

The hippo was thrilled, and went gamboling off toward his pool in search of the butterfly. But halfway there, he stopped. He realized there was something missing in the owl's advice. So back to the hollow tree he went, and banged once more on its trunk. The owl looked out crossly. "Oh, it's you again!" he said irritably. "Yes," said the hippo. "You left something out!" "Rubbish!" countered the owl, my advice is always complete." "Not this time," responded the hippo. "You didn't tell me how to turn myself into a butterfly!"

At this remark, the owl looked very cross indeed. "Listen, fella!" he declared. "I just deal with strategy here. I don't get involved with implementation!"

Management is the art of the feasible. Sometimes you get lucky, but don't plan on miracles. Becoming and remaining a product plus organization can't be achieved with a wave of a magic wand. It will take time and hard work. Although there's no sense in adopting strategic goals that are far beyond the reach of your resources, don't set your sights too low, either: Be prepared to stretch your firm's ambitions—and its capabilities.

Notes

Chapter 1

Page

2   Christopher H. Lovelock, "Southwest Airlines (A)," and "(B)," (Harvard Business School Publishing Division, Boston, MA, 1975), cases 9-575-060 and 9-575-061.

5   The "cockroach" remark is attributed to Philip Baggeley of Standard and Poor's Corp., quoted in "Striking Gold in the California Skies," *Business Week*, March 30, 1992, p. 58. Additional information for this chapter was obtained from interviews and correspondence with Rollin King (a director of Southwest Airlines Co.), Dallas, 1992–1993.

Chapter 2

Page

11   The schematic presented in Fig. 2-1 and the text discussion is an extension of part of Chap. 2 of my book, *Services Marketing*, 2d ed. (Prentice Hall, Englewood Cliffs, NJ, 1991), pp. 26–27. The balance of that chapter contains a variety of other ways of classifying service businesses.

19   Interview in January 1993 with Richard C. Munn, senior vice president of Dataquest, and founder and former president of the Ledgeway Group, a firm acquired by Dataquest. (Munn is now president of Munn and Company, Lexington, MA.)

Chapter 3

Page

22   Information on Federal Express is derived from my own extended research into this company, from 1976 on.

24   The notion of core and supplementary services was first articulated by Eric Langeard and Pierre Eiglier in an article published in *Revue Française de Gestion*, March–April 1977, pp. 72–84.

25   Theodore Levitt, *Marketing for Business Growth* (McGraw-Hill, New York, 1974), p. 47. For another viewpoint, see Sandra Vandermerwe, *From Tin Soldiers to Russian Dolls: Creating Added Value Through Services* (Butterworth-Heinemann, Oxford, England, 1993), pp. 30–41.

27   *PC Magazine*, May 24, 1992.

Chapter 4

Page

34   Quoted in Patrick Ryan, "Get Rid of the People and the System Runs Fine," *Smithsonian*, September 1977, p. 140.

36   L. Therrien, "McRisky," *Business Week*, October 21, 1991, pp. 114–117.

37   Quoted in E. Langeard, J. E. G. Bateson, C. H. Lovelock, and P. Eiglier, *Services Marketing: New Insights from Consumers and Managers* (Marketing Science Institute, Cambridge, MA, 1981), p. 89.

37   The discussion of these seven operational concerns is adapted from Christopher H. Lovelock, "Managing Interactions between Operations and Marketing and Their Impact on Consumers," in D. A. Bowen, R. B. Chase, T. G. Cummings, and Associates, *Service Management Effectiveness* (Jossey-Bass, San Francisco, 1989), pp. 343–368.

40   Theodore Levitt, "Production Line Approach to Service," *Harvard Business Review*, vol. 40, November–December 1972, pp. 41–52.

41   For further insights into possibilities for customization, see Stanley M. Davis, *Future Perfect* (Addison-Wesley, Reading, MA, 1987) and B. Joseph Pine II, *Mass Customization: The New Frontier in Business Competition* (Harvard Business School Press, Boston, 1993).

42   "How American Express Measures Quality of Its Customer Service," *AMA Forum*, vol. 71, March 1982, pp. 29–31.

44   Interview with Human Resources Department personnel, British Airways, London, June 1992.

Chapter 5

Page

51   Milind M. Lele with Jagdish N. Sheth, *The Customer Is Key* (John
      Wiley, New York, 1987); Hal F. Rosenbluth and Diane McFerrin
      Peters, *The Customer Comes Second* (William Morrow, New York,
      1992); Tom Peters, *Liberation Management* (Alfred A. Knopf, New
      York, 1992).

55   Frederick F. Reichheld and W. Earl Sasser, "Zero Defections:
      Quality Comes to Services," *Harvard Business Review*,
      September–October 1990, pp. 105–111.

56   Leonard A. Schlesinger and James L. Heskett, "Breaking the Cycle
      of Failure in Services," *Sloan Management Review*, Spring 1991, pp.
      17–28.

56   Frederick F. Reichheld, "Loyalty-Based Management," *Harvard
      Business Review*, March–April 1993, pp. 300–309.

57   Valarie A. Zeithaml, "Consumer Perceptions of Price, Quality, and
      Value: A Means–End Model and Synthesis of Evidence," *Journal of
      Marketing*, vol. 52, July 1988, pp. 2–21.

59   Theodore Levitt, *Marketing for Business Growth* (McGraw-Hill,
      New York, 1974), p. 8; Levitt attributes the quote to Leo McGivena.

61   See E. Langeard, J. E. G. Bateson, C. H. Lovelock, and P. Eiglier,
      Services Marketing: New Insights from Consumers and Managers
      (Marketing Science Institute, Cambridge, MA, 1981), pp. 27–29.

62   Jerry Della Femina, *From Those Wonderful Folks Who Gave You
      Pearl Harbor: Front Line Dispatches from the Advertising War*
      (Simon & Schuster, New York, 1970).

64   K. Labich, "How Dick Ferris Blew It," *Fortune*, vol. 116, June 1987,
      pp. 42–44; J. E. Ellis and C. Hawkins, "The Unraveling of an Idea:
      How Dick Ferris' Grand Plan for Allegis collapsed," *Business Week*,
      June 22, 1987, pp. 42–43.

64   For details of this study and its methodology, see Jerry Wind, Paul
      E. Green, Douglas Shifflet, and Marsha Scarbrough, "Courtyard by
      Marriott: Designing a Hotel Facility with Consumer-Based
      Marketing Models," *Interfaces*, vol. 19, January–February 1989, pp.
      25–47.

Chapter 6

Page

68   Details of the proposed Flair chain are based on information in the case, Flair, Inc. (Harvard Business School Publishing Division, Boston, 1976), case 9-676-094.

71   Information on Firstdirect is based on interviews with company management in London, June 1992, and Leeds, November 1992, augmented by corporate publications and updated to September 1993.

77   "How Does Your Bank Rate?" *Which?*, November 1992, pp. 6–13.

78   Information on Southwest Airlines is based on interviews with company management, Dallas, October 1992, augmented by annual reports for 1990 and 1991, plus telephone interviews and correspondence with Rollin King (a director of the company), 1992–1993.

Chapter 7

Page

87   The application of theater-based metaphors to analyze and describe human behavior is termed "dramaturgy" in sociological research. For an academic review of its application to services, see Stephen J. Grove, Raymond P. Fisk, and Mary Jo Bitner, "Dramatizing the Service Experience," in *Advances in Service Marketing and Management*, vol. 1 (Jai Press, Greenwich, CT, 1992), pp. 91–121.

91   Mary Jo Bitner, "Servicescapes: The Impact of Physical Surroundings on Customers and Employees," *Journal of Marketing*, vol. 56, April 1992, pp. 57–71.

Chapter 8

Page

98   Gilbert Fuchsberg, "Quality Programs Show Shoddy Results," *The Wall Street Journal*, May 14, 1992, p. B1; "The Cost of Quality: Faced with Hard Times, Business Sours on 'Total Quality Management,'" *Newsweek*, September 7, 1992, pp. 48–49; *International*

Quality Study (Ernst & Young and American Quality Foundation, New York, 1992). Note that the quote is taken from the interim report; the final report was published in November 1992.

98   David A. Garvin, *Managing Quality* (The Free Press, New York, 1988), pp. 40–48.

99   Ibid., pp. 49–60.

100   Valarie A. Zeithaml, A. Parasuraman, and Leonard L. Berry, *Delivering Quality Service* (The Free Press, New York, 1990), pp. 15–26.

101   This section is distilled from Garvin, *Managing Quality*, chaps. 1, 2, and 10. Detailed references for all authorities cited will be found in this book.

105   Philip B. Crosby, *Quality Is Free* (New American Library, New York, 1979). The quotation is from Crosby, *Quality without Tears* (McGraw-Hill, New York, 1984), p. 76. Thomas J. Peters and Robert H. Waterman, Jr., *In Search of Excellence* (Harper & Row, New York, 1982). Garvin, *Managing Quality*.

106   Stephen Koepp, "Pul-eeze! Will Somebody Help Me?" *Time*, February 2, 1987, pp. 28–34.

107   This section benefited from discussions with Rob Evans, David Garvin, David Maister, and Diane Schmalensee, 1993.

110   Christian Grönroos, *Service Management and Marketing* (Lexington Books/D.C. Heath & Co., Lexington, MA, 1990), chap. 2, pp. 25–48.

111   The satisfaction formula was probably first articulated at the Harvard Business School in the 1970s; some people present it as "Satisfaction equals Perceptions minus Expectations," but I prefer my version since the former gives a satisfaction value of zero when perceptions and expectations are perfectly matched!

111   Zeithaml et al., *Delivering Quality Service*, pp. 23–33, 175–205.

114   Christopher W. L. Hart, "The Power of Unconditional Service Guarantees," *Harvard Business Review*, July–August 1988, pp. 54–62.

115   Ernst & Young, *International Quality Study*.

Chapter 9

Page

119   Information in this chapter is based primarily on research for my

case, "Federal Express: Quality Improvement Program" (IMD, Lausanne, Switzerland, 1990), case GM-456. Copyright © 1990 by the International Institute for Management Development (IMD), Lausanne, Switzerland. IMD retains all rights. Not to be reproduced or used without permission directly from IMD, Lausanne, Switzerland; an interview with Thomas J. Oliver, Paris, May 1992; and updates from company officials, 1993. An additional source was *Blueprints for Service Quality: The Federal Express Approach* (American Management Association, New York, 1991).

Chapter 10

Page

145   Ron Zemke with Dick Schaaf, *The Service Edge: 101 Companies That Profit from Customer Care* (New American Library, New York, 1989), pp. 149–152. Robert Levering and Milton Moskowitz, *The 101 Best Companies to Work for in America* (Currency Doubleday, New York, 1993), pp. 50–54, 505.

146   Interview with Mitchell T. Rabkin, M.D., president, Beth Israel Hospital, September 1988.

147   Interview with Kathy Carr, R.N., nurse manager, and other hospital management personnel, January 1993.

153   This portion of the chapter benefited from discussions with Michael Epelman. For a detailed discussion of service blueprinting, see G. Lynn Shostack, "Designing Services That Deliver," *Harvard Business Review*, January–February 1984, pp. 133–139; G. Lynn Shostack and Jane A. Kingman-Brundage, "How to Design a Service," in C. A. Congram and M. L. Friedman (eds.), *The AMA Handbook of Marketing for the Service Industries* (AMACOM, New York, 1991), pp. 243–261. For an alternative approach, see Sandra Vandermerwe, "Jumping into the Customer's Activity Cycle," chap. 6 of her book *From Tin Soldiers to Russian Dolls* (Butterworth-Heinemann, Oxford, England, 1993), pp. 48–71.

158   Interview with Mitchell T. Rabkin, M.D., January 1993.

159   David Marca and Clement McGowan, *SADT: Structured Analysis and Design Techniques* (McGraw-Hill, New York, 1988).

Chapter 11

Page

161 David Maister, now president of Maister Associates in Boston, coined the term OTSU while teaching courses in management of service operations at Harvard.

175 For a more detailed discussion of using flowcharts to evaluate alternative service configurations, see G. Lynn Shostack, "Service Positioning through Structural Change," *Journal of Marketing,* January 1987, pp. 34–43.

Chapter 13

Page

191 This chapter is based on a January 1993 interview with Eliot Wadsworth II, proprietor of White Flower Farm, supplemented by information from *White Flower Farm: The Garden Book,* Fall 1992 and Spring 1993, and my own involvement with the company and its products as a customer over several years.

Chapter 14

Page

207 Technical Assistance Research Programs Institute (TARP), *Consumer Complaint Handling in America; An Update Study, Part II* (TARP and U.S. Office of Consumer Affairs, Washington, DC, April 1986), pp. 34–41. This report includes a review of earlier foreign studies.

209 TARP, *Consumer Complaint Handling,* p. 81 (both Parts I and II of the TARP study provide many detailed examples of good procedures); Leonard L. Berry and A. Parasuraman, *Marketing Services: Competing through Quality* (The Free Press, New York, 1991), p. 35.

212 Information supplied by Southwest Airlines, 1992; Sandra Vandermerwe and Christopher H. Lovelock, "Singapore Airlines:

Using Technology for Service Excellence," (IMD, Lausanne, Switzerland, 1991), case M408.

213 TARP, *Consumer Complaint Handling*, pp. 51–67.

213 This policy was publicized in Thomas J. Peters and Robert H. Waterman, Jr., *In Search of Excellence* (Harper & Row, New York, 1982), p. 159.

214 Interview with J. W. Marriott, Jr., CEO, Marriott Corporation, Boston, May 1984.

215 Based on a presentation by the late D. Daryl Wyckoff, Philadelphia, June 1984; an abbreviated version appears in his article, "New Tools for Achieving Service Quality," *Cornell Restaurant and Hotel Administration Quarterly*, November 1984.

221 Frederick F. Reichheld and W. Earl Sasser, Jr., "Zero Defections: Quality Comes to Services," *Harvard Business Review*, September–October 1990, pp. 105–111. Telephone interview with Mr. Reichheld, Boston, March 1993.

Chapter 15

Page

231 Abbie Hoffman, *Steal This Book!* (Grove Press, San Francisco, 1972).

234 Interview with Audy Donelson, station manager, Southwest Airlines, Dallas-Love Field, October 1992. Interview with human resources, Firstdirect, London, June 1992.

234 Based on "Happy New Year!" by M. Auch and J. Haywood-Farmer, Western Business School, London, Ont., case 9-87-D007, 1987, plus a telephone interview with Professor Haywood-Farmer, August 1993.

Chapter 16

Page

240 Portions of this chapter are based on "Strategies for Managing Capacity-Constrained Service Organizations," in my book, *Managing Services: Marketing, Operations, and Human Resources*, 2d ed. (Prentice Hall, Englewood Cliffs, NJ, 1992), pp. 154–168.

245   Dori Jones Yang and Andrea Rothman, "Reinventing Boeing," *Business Week*, March 1, 1993, pp. 60–67.

247   Christopher H. Lovelock, "The 911 Emergency Number in New York," (Harvard Business School Publishing Division, Boston, 1975), case 9-576-259, based, in part, on a story in *The New York Times*.

252   Malcolm Galdwell, "The Bottom Line for Lots of Time Spent in America," *The Washington Post* (syndicated article, February 1993).

252   Richard Saltus, "Lines Lines Lines Lines...The Experts Are Trying to Ease the Wait," *The Boston Globe*, October 5, 1992, pp. 39, 42.

254   Leonard L. Berry and Linda R. Cooper, "Competing with Time-Saving Service," *Business*, vol. 40, no. 2, 1990, pp. 3–7.

255   David H. Maister, "The Psychology of Waiting Lines," in J. A. Czepiel, M. R. Solomon, and C. F. Surprenant, *The Service Encounter* (Lexington Books/D.C. Heath, Lexington, MA, 1985), pp. 113–123.

257   Sheryl E. Kimes, "Yield Management: A Tool for Capacity-Constrained Service Firms," *Journal of Operations Management*, vol. 8, October 1989, pp. 348–363.

260   Ibid.

Chapter 17

Page

263   George Gilder's comments come from a videotape of his testimony before the Federal Communications Commission's en banc hearing, 1990. For more detail, see his article, "Into the Telecosm," *Harvard Business Review*, March–April 1991, pp. 150–161.

264   Gregory P. Hackett, "Investment in Technology—The Service Sector Sinkhole?" *Sloan Management Review*, Winter 1990, pp. 97–103.

264   James Brian Quinn, *Intelligent Enterprise* (The Free Press, New York, 1992), p. 361.

265   James L. Heskett, W. Earl Sasser, Jr., and Christopher W. L. Hart, *Service Breakthroughs* (The Free Press, New York, 1990), p. 181.

266   Michael Hammer, "Reengineering Work: Don't Automate, Obliterate," *Harvard Business Review*, July–August 1990, p. 104.

271   Information on McKesson comes from Myron Magnet, "Who's Winning the Information Revolution?" *Fortune*, November 30, 1992,

pp. 78–82. I have observed the Pizza Hut system in operation at their restaurant in Lausanne, Switzerland.

272 Information on Singapore Airlines based on my own research in Singapore, June 1991; see also the case, "Singapore Airlines: Using Technology for Service Excellence," by Sandra Vandermerwe and Christopher Lovelock (IMD, Lausanne, Switzerland, 1991), case M408.

272 Information on USAA from Myron Magnet, "Who's Winning the Information Revolution?"

274 Susan Caminiti, "What the Scanner Knows about You," *Fortune*, December 3, 1990, pp. 51–52; Doug Bartholomew, "The Price Is Wrong," *Information Week*, September 14, 1992, pp. 26–36.

274 "'Electronic Bullets' that Blow Away Illegal Cable Boxes," *Business Week*, July 1, 1991, p. 51.

275 Based on information in Christopher Lovelock, "Federal Express: Quality Improvement Program" (IMD, Lausanne, Switzerland, 1990), case GM-456.

275 Based on information in Martin Bless and Christopher Lovelock, "BT: Telephone Account Management" (IMD, Lausanne, Switzerland, 1992), case M413.

277 Interviews with Robert P. Shay, Senior Vice President, BayBank, May 1990, January 1993.

278 Based on information in Dominique Turpin, Christopher Lovelock, and Joyce Miller, "Kirin Brewery Co.: The Dry Beer War" (IMD, Lausanne, Switzerland, 1991), case M394.

279 Steven P. Schnaars, *Megamistakes: Forecasting and the Myth of Rapid Technological Change* (The Free Press, New York, 1989), p. 47.

280 Interview with a vice president of Discover Card, Chicago, September 1988.

280 Andersen Consulting has developed a number of business integration centers, including Logistics 2000 in Atlanta, Hospital of the Future in Dallas, and SuperStore 2000 in Chicago.

Chapter 18

Page

286 Interview with a vice president of Discover Card, Chicago, September 1988.

288   *Critical Success Factors for the 90s* (Dataquest/Ledgeway, Framingham, MA, 1992), p. 2.

289   This section is based on an information supplied by Hewlett-Packard Co. and a telephone interview with Jeff Landre, Americas Response Centers Manager, Mountain View, CA, January 1993.

Chapter 19

Page

296   "Language Spoken at Home and Ability to Speak English for United States, Regions and States: 1990." Report 1990-CPH-L-133. Washington, D.C.: U.S. Department of Commerce, Bureau of the Census, 1993.

297   These examples are based on my own experience living and traveling in the countries concerned. Piet Vanden Abeele was helpful in clarifying the Belgian situation.

306   Information from AT&T Language Line, Monterey, CA, January, 1993.

307   Ibid.

308   Telephone interview with Jacques-Henri Eyraud, Communication, Euro Disney SCA, Noisy le Grand, France, May 1992.

313   For a fascinating discussion of the subtleties in English-language usage in different English-speaking countries, see Robert McCrum et al., *The Story of English,* revised edition (Viking Penguin, New York, 1993).

314   Christopher H. Lovelock, "Federal Express: Customer Service Department" (Harvard Business School Publishing Division, Boston, 1980), case 9-581-017.

Chapter 20

Page

316   Robert Levering and Milton Moskowitz, *The 100 Best Companies to Work for in America* (Currency/Doubleday, New York, 1993), p. xi.

317   Leonard L. Schlesinger and James L. Heskett, "Breaking the Cycle of Failure in Services," *Sloan Management Review*, Spring 1991, pp. 17–28.

319   Richard C. Whiteley, *The Customer Driven Company* (Addison-Wesley, Reading, MA, 1991), p. 110.

320   Schneider reviews his own and other researchers' work in Benjamin Schneider, "Service Quality and Profits: Can You Have Your Cake and Eat It, Too?" *Human Resource Planning*, vol. 14, no. 2, 1991, pp. 151–157.

321   The Gallup Poll, Princeton, NJ, 1991. Reprinted in Christopher Caggiano, "What Do Workers Want?" *Inc.*, November 1992, pp. 101–102.

321   Robert Levering and Milton Moskowitz, *The 100 Best Companies to Work for in America* (Currency/Doubleday, New York, 1993), pp. xvii–xviii.

322   Levering and Moskowitz, *The 100 Best Companies to Work for in America*, p. xvii.

323   Interview with Mitchell T. Rabkin, M.D., president, Beth Israel Hospital, Boston, January 1993.

323   Interview with Ann Rhoades, vice president–people, and other managers, Southwest Airlines, Dallas, October 1992.

327   Interviews at Singapore Airlines, Singapore, June 1991.

328   Rajendra S. Sisodia, "Expert Marketing with Expert Systems," *Marketing Management*, Spring 1992, pp. 32–47.

328   Barbara Garson, *The Electronic Sweatshop: How Computers Are Transforming the Office of the Future into the Factory of the Past* (Simon & Schuster, New York, 1988). See especially Chap. 2, "With Reservations," pp. 40–70.

329   Based on information in Martin Bless and Christopher Lovelock, "BT: Telephone Account Management" (IMD, Lausanne, Switzerland, 1900), case M413.

330   David E. Bowen and Edward E. Lawler III, "The Empowerment of
to   Service Workers: What, Why, How, and When," *Sloan Management*
332   *Review*, Spring 1992, pp. 31–39.

333   Interview with Mitchell T. Rabkin, M.D., Beth Israel Hospital, January 1993.

333   Interview with Laura Avakian, vice president—human resources, Beth Israel Hospital, January 1993.

334   Mitchell T. Rabkin and Laura Avakian, "Participatory Management

at Boston's Beth Israel Hospital," *Academic Medicine*, vol. 67, May 1992, pp. 289–294.

335   Interview with Mitchell T. Rabkin, M.D., Beth Israel Hospital, January 1993.

335   Interview with Ann Rhoades, Southwest Airlines, October 1992.

336   Levering and Moskowitz, *The 100 Best Companies to Work for in America*, p. xiii.

336   The nurse's comments come from a WGBH film of the Beth Israel Emergency Unit, 1989.

337   Kathy Carr, R.N., Beth Israel Hospital, January 1993.

337   The information on LEAP comes from *Blueprinting for Service Quality: The Federal Express Approach* (American Management Association, New York, 1991), pp. 22–26.

338   Mitchell T. Rabkin, M.D., Beth Israel Hospital, January 1993.

Chapter 21

Page

343   Gary Hamel and C. K. Pralahad, "Strategy as Stretch and Leverage," *Harvard Business Review*, March–April 1993, pp. 75–84.

344   Interview with Eliot Wadsworth II, proprietor, White Flower Farm, Boston, January 1993.

345   James Brian Quinn, *Intelligent Enterprise* (The Free Press, New York, 1992), p. 75.

346   Jan Carlzon, *Moments of Truth* (Ballinger, New York, 1987).

348   Sandra Vandermerwe, *From Tin Soldiers to Russian Dolls* (Butterworth-Heinemann, Oxford, England, 1993), p. 24.

352   See Torin Douglas, "The Power of Branding" and "The Seven British Airways Brands," reprinted in C. H. Lovelock, *Services Marketing*, 2d ed. (Prentice Hall, Englewood Cliffs, NJ, 1991), pp. 273–281.

354   Interview with Mitchell T. Rabkin, M.D., president, Beth Israel Hospital, Boston, January 1993.

356   Michael Hammer, "Reengineering Work: Don't Automate, Obliterate," *Harvard Business Review*, July–August 1990, p. 104.

See also Michael Hammer and James Champy, *Reengineering the Corporation* (HarperCollins, New York, 1993).

356 John Cecil and Michael Goldstein, "Sustaining Competitive Advantage from IT," *The McKinsey Quarterly*, 1990, no. 4.

357 Paul B. Cragg and Paul N. Finlay, "IT: Running Fast and Standing Still?" *Information and Management*, vol. 21 (1991), pp. 193–200.

357 Quoted in Christopher H. Lovelock, "Federal Express: Quality Improvement Program" (IMD, Lausanne, Switzerland, 1990), case GM-456.

Index

Note: The *f.* after a page number refers to a figure; the *t.* refers to a table.

About the Author

Christopher Lovelock is a management educator and consultant who is widely recognized for his pioneering work on managing services. He has more than 20 years of experience in working with service-oriented organizations across a wide array of industries. Born in Great Britain, he offers a distinctively international perspective, having lived and worked in both Europe and North America. Earlier a professor at the Harvard Business School for more than a decade, he has also taught at MIT, Stanford, the Theseus Institute in France, and the International Institute for Management Development (IMD) in Switzerland. Dr. Lovelock is author or coauthor of 10 books on service management, one of which has been translated into Japanese. He lives in New England.